NUMBER 34

THE ENGLISH
EXPERIENCE

ITS RECORD IN EARLY PRINTED BOOKS
PUBLISHED IN FACSIMILE

GEORGE CARLETON

JURISDICTION REGALL, EPISCOPALL, PAPALL

LONDON 1610

DA CAPO PRESS
THEATRVM ORBIS TERRARVM LTD.
AMSTERDAM 1968 NEW YORK

The publishers acknowledge their gratitude
to the Trustees of the Bodleian Library, Oxford,
for their permission to reproduce
the Library's copy.

S.T.C.No.4637
Collation: ¶⁴,A-Z⁴,Aa-Qq⁴.

Published in 1968 by
Theatrum Orbis Terrarum Ltd.,
O.Z. Voorburgwal 85, Amsterdam
&
Da Capo Press
- a division of Plenum Publishing Corporation -
227 West 17th Street, New York. 10011
Library of Congress Catalog Card Number:
68-54625
Printed in The Netherlands

IVRISDICTION

{ REGALL,
  EPISCOPALL,
  PAPALL. }

WHEREIN IS DECLARED

HOW THE POPE HATH INTRVDED

Vpon the Iurisdiction of Temporall Princes, and
of the Church. The intrusion is discouered, and the
peculiar and distinct Iurisdiction to
each properly belonging,
recouered.

written by GEORGE CARLETON.

IOHN 18. 36.

¶ *My kingdome is not of this world: if my kingdome were of this world, my*
seruants would surely fight.

LONDINI
Impensis *Iohannis Norton.* 1610.

THE CONTENTS OF THE SEVERAL
Chapters of this Booke.

TO THE MOST RE
VEREND FATHER IN GOD,
MY VERY GOOD LORD, THE
Lord Archbiſhop of Canterbvrie, his
Grace, Metropolitan and Primate of al England,
and one of his Maieſties moſt Honourable Priuie Counſell.
(*.*)

Ob the man of God, (moſt Reuerend Father in God) entring into the meditation of the care, labor, danger and deliuerance that we find in this preſent life, compareth it for danger to a warfare; Iob.7.1.
for care and trauell to the dayes of an hireling: which eſtate as euery member of the Church fin= deth in this life, ſo the ſame is much more apparant in the whole Church, which for the time of her war- fare here, as ſhe is, ſo is called, militant. As this aſ-

¶ 2　　　　　　　*ſured*

sured and expected warfare from the beginning hath kept the Church in continuall exercise and watch against many and strong aduersaries: so toward the end of this warfare, that is toward the end of this world, the aduersaries growing more skilfull, more bold and desperate then before, the warfare must of necessitie bee made more daungerous. The greatnesse of which daunger may draw the gouernours of the Church to a more sensible apprehension of their duties, who according to the daunger of the Church, cannot but vnderstand that their care, industry, vigilancy, and courage must be increased for the preseruation of the peace, and good of the Church of God which they gouern: so that the malice, industrie and desperate attempts of the aduersaries, are to them so many prouocations stirring thē vp more carefully to watch.

Which care hath singularly appeared in your Grace, who as a Generall in this warfare haue giuen no rest to your selfe, but by preuenting the purposes of the enemies by espying their secrets, by answering their present incounters, by incouraging inferiours, haue declared your carefull seruice in this warfare setting the battel in order and incouraging euery souldier in his proper standing, and place: vnder this conduct haue I vndertaken this peece of seruice for the opening the truth of Iurisdiction

*Ction of late so much oppugned, defaced, and con-
founded by the aduersaries. Wherein as I can not
promise any worth of my seruice, so I shall bee able
with a good conscience to challenge the reward of
faithfull and sincere dealing.*

*The question I confesse, requireth a man as skil-
ful in distinguishing this confused masse of Iurisdiction, which they now haue cast vpon the Pope, as
Archimedes was in examining the gouldsmithes
fraude, who hauing receiued a certaine Weight of
gould of* Hiero *King of Sicily to make a goulden* Vitruuius lib. 9.
cap. 3.
*crowne which he would offer to his Gods; stoale a-
way much of the gold, and put siluer in the place
thereof, rendring to* Hiero *his true weight againe.
To examine this fraud without melting of the
crowne, was a worke to exercise the great wit of
Archimedes himselfe: such is this masse of Iurisdiction, wherin fraudulent workmen (as they who
confound gold, siluer, coper, and brasse together)
haue taken the Iurisdiction of the Church, and of
kings; and mingling both together, adding much
of their owne drosse thereto, haue made it as a de-
ceiptfull crowne to offer to their great God, to set it
vpon his head. To distinguish this confused masse,
& to giue to each his own right, was a thing wherin I foũd the greater difficulty, because none of late
yeeres hath troden this path before me, whose foot-*

¶ 3 *steppes*

steppes might haue directed me. For the question of the Supremacy is handled learnedly & worthily by others, who though they haue giuen some light to this question of Iurisdiction, yet they doe it but in some passages, not handling the question fully and purposely, but by occasion sometimes falling into some parts thereof. Wherefore I thought it would be a necessary seruice to the Church, if this thing might be truely brought to knowledge, and the fraudulent confusion of this crowne of Iurisdiction standing vpon the proud head of the Pope examined & distinguished, the siluer seuered from the gold, and the drosse from both.

As Iurisdiction lay thus confounded by those false workemen of Rome, so at the first triall of it, when it was examined by vnskilfull and deceitfull triars, who set the rules of their triall not from the truth but from ambition and adulation, they taking vpon them to be triars of truth, made things as bad or farre worse by their handling then they were before: and so wrapped this question in newe difficulties. For when Henrie the eight tooke this title of supreme head of the Church of England, though the sounder and more iudicious part of the Church then vnderstood the words of that title so, as no offence might iustly rise by it : yet they that were suddenly brought from their olde opinion of
Poperie,

perie, *not to the loue of the truth, but to the obser-*
uance of the Kings religion; retained a groſſe and
impure ſenſe of thoſe words, as moſt cōmonly by ſuch
is retained to this day. For when Stephen Gardi-
ner *Biſhop of Wincheſter was at* Ratisbon *in Ger-*
manie vpon the Kings affaires, he there taking oc- Caluin in A-mos 7.
caſion to declare the meaning of that title, ſupreme
head of the Church giuen to king Henrie *the eight*
taught that the King had ſuch a power, that hee
might appoint and preſcribe new ordinances of the
Church, euen matters concerning faith and do-
ctrine, and aboliſh old : as namely that the King
might forbid the marriage of Prieſts, and might
take away the vſe of the cup in the Sacrament of
the Lords ſupper, and in ſuch things might appoint
what he liſt. This manner of declaring the Kings
Juriſdiction, did ſo much offend the reformed Caluin in A-mos 7.13. Præfat.in Centur.7.
Churches, that Caluin *& the writers of the Cen-*
turies doe much complaine thereof, and worthily,
For the Biſhop of Wincheſter ſought not like a cu-
rious triar of mettals to ſeuere the gold from the
ſiluer, and droſſe from both : but as hee found this
maſſie crown of Iuriſdiction vpon the Popes head,
ſo he tooke it with gold, ſiluer, coper, droſſe and all :
and ſet it vpon the Kings head. So that the thing
which procured ſo much offence, was not the title,
but the Biſhops falſe and erronious declaration of
that title. If

If any obiect against me: what then? will you take vpon you to handle this thing, better then such a learned and prudent Prelate? I answer, the Bishop wanted neither wit nor learning for the opening of this point, but onely a loue to the truth: which loue when I shall bring to this question, I finde my selfe therby so supported, that neither the perfections of other men, nor mine owne imperfections can daūt me so much, as to cause me to giue ouer the defence of the truth. True it is, that a more skilfull Archimedes might haue beene set on this worke, to distinguish the things that haue lien so long confounded in this question; or the common helpe of many might haue beene combined, wherin our aduersaries are now growen wiser in their generation then the children of light. And though it seeme, to be true, that an euill cause hath more need of helpes: yet there is no reason that they who haue the handling of a good cause, should in confidence of the cause neglect any helpe, that possibly they may attain vnto. Albeit we must confesse that the arme of God hath wonderfully declared it selfe by weak meanes against great.

For if a man should looke vpon the meanes on both sides with an eye of flesh, he would thinke as 2.Sam.6.7. Vzziah did, When the Arke was shaken, that the Church could not possibly stand vp by so weake meanes.

meanes: For on the one side the Pope sheweth himselfe with the riches of Saint Peters great and
potent patrimony, with the helpe of so many great
Princes, with the councell and policie of his Cardinals, with the armies of his Canonists, Priests secular and regular, but especially in these later years,
of his Iesuites, who glorying so much of their learning, and filling the world with their vaunts, being supported by wealth and policie, abounding
with all worldly meanes that their hearts can desire, incouraged by preferments, march like armed
troupes entring a battell: On the other side a company of poore men, Luther, Bucer, Zuinglius,
Oicolampadius, Martyr, Caluin and such like,
vtterly contemned of the Iesuites, bringing no o-
ther furniture with them, sauing a good conscience,
learning, and a loue to the trueth, seeme to make a
poore shew without force, without glory. If Gods
truth were to be vpholden by humane meanes, or if
the seruants of the truth were drawne to speake in
the Church, as Lawyers are for their fees at the
barre: then what hope could wee baue to stand a-
gainst the Iesuites the Popes Lawyers, who by inuincible clamours, facing and obstinacy, make not
truth, but victory the end they aime at.

    But as there is great oddes in the meanes on the
one side, so there appeareth no lesse difference in the

successe on the other side; For by these weake and
contemned means the world is subdued vnto Christ,
deliuered from the bondage of superstition, wisdome
is iustified of her owne children, and the truth tri-
umpheth in the sincerity and godlinesse of weake
meanes, against the malice, policy and strength of
her prepotent aduersaries.

Which successe compared with the meanes on
both sides, doth manifest the arme of God to be in
the cause, that groweth so much against the expectation of the world and meanes. For what other power could make so weake meanes preuaile so much,
against so great policy and strength, but the same
power (though not in the same measure) which by a
company of poore Fishermen (despised in the world)
subdued the whole world vnto the obedience of
Christ? As this successe and blessing by the presence
of God, hath beene hitherto apparant in this cause:
so the Jesuites take order that the same successe and
blessing may continually hereafter follow our cause,
vntill it hath rooted out all the aduersaries that
make opposition against it : for what greater
strength or aduantage can bee giuen to our cause,
then the wickednesse of our aduersaries doth giue?
How often doth Moses declare to the Church of
Israell, that the fauour of God was so much declared towards them, not for their owne righteousnes,
but

but for the wickednes of their aduersaries? So that if we should stand still and looke on, and holde our selues in patience, our aduersaries will worke the meanes, by their owne strange cruelties in their Inquisitions, by their prophane and vncleane conuersation, by their grosse Idolatry, by their horrible treasons and conspiracies against the liues of Princes, by their diuelish deuises for subuersion of whole States at one blow, by their hypocrisie, falshood and æquiuocations, and by that most admirable and exquisit villany that euer was inuented, in deprauing, corrupting, altering and chaunging all auncient writers: by these, and the like practises of wickednes, they themselues will worke the meanes of our successe, and of their owne destruction. And if the Prince of this world, and his first begotten had not blinded their eyes, and their hearts, they could not choose but see, and acknowledge the experience of Gods fauour and protection mightily declared from heauen vpon our cause our Prince and State; and of late much increased and made apparant to all the world by their owne wicked practises.

Then the difference being so great in the meanes and in the successe, so great also betweene our conuersation and theirs, must needes declare a great difference betweene our hopes and theirs, our Religion and theirs: they haue raised the Princes and

are

armies of the world against vs, when they pretended peace: wee neuer vsed deceit or wrong against
them: they haue by barbarous deuises attempted to
procure our vtter subuersion, we desire hartily their
conuersion to God: they curse, reuile, and baspheme
vs, wee pray for them: this difference may shew,
where truth and Religion is; and might if they entred into the serious consideration of things, drawe
them to ceafe from all wicked attempts, to follow
and embrace one trueth, and to worshippe one God
with vs.

But if there be no remedy, but that Princes and
States must be oppugned by a perpetuall league of
Conspiracy from Rome: if nothing can satisfie them
but the blood of Kings, then what remaineth but
that the Princes of Christendome prepare themselues to that great battel, which S. Iohn saith shal
be fought in the plain of the earth against Gog and
Magog. When God shall raise the spirits of princes to that worke, he will open the way and giue the
successe: for fire shall come downe from God, out of
heauen, and deuoure the enemies. Vnto which seruice there is nothing so effectuall to animate the
princes of Christendome, as is this new and strange
claime of the popes Iurisdiction ouer princes: which
thing because it is so much pursued by the Popes and
their flatterers, and onely by them, as the great
marke

Apoc.20.8.9.

marke whereunto they addresse all their attempts;
and the very summe of all their Religion: therfore
I haue endeuoured to open the whole, to distinguish
the parts, and to set this question in such a light as I
could, if not to satisfie all, yet at least to giue an occasion to the iudicious. I was desirous to leaue no
part vntouched, that all might come to a triall, and
am ready also withall, to bring my selfe to the triall,
willing to learne and to amend any error, after that
it shall be manifested by the truth to bee an errour:
for which cause, I submit all to the iudicious and
godly censure of the Church.

My care was also after my seruice to God, to
performe herein a true seruice to his Maiesty, by o-
pening the Iurisdiction of Kings: which I haue
done, not as they vse to doe who serue the Pope, re-
specting no other rules of that seruice, then his pleasure and their adulation, but I haue disputed the
Kings right with a good conscience, from the rules
of Gods word, knowing that the noble disposition of
his Maiesty will admit of no seruice, whereby God
or the truth is preiudiced. All which as I commend
to your Graces fauour and protection, to whom God
hath committed the care of his Church here, so with
my hearty prayers, I commend your Grace to the fauour and protection of God; who inrich your heart

with

with his plentifull graces, that as for your proper comfort and direction, you may enioy them, so you may vse them to the glory of God, and the comfort of his Church through Iesus Christ.

Your Graces to be commanded in all duety,

GEORGE CARLETON.

An Admonition to the Reader.

IT may be thought *strange*, *that so many are found to write in this contradicting age, one contrary to another: the trueth cannot bee on both sides, and therefore there is a great fault on the one side : the Reader that is desirous to trie where the fault is, may be intreated to marke with aduised obseruation some things, wherein our aduersaries wanting eyther knowledge or sincerity, haue broken all the rules of right writing, to deceiue such as cannot iudge(of which sort the greatest part consisteth). I do therefore intreate the Readers, especially such as reade my booke with a purpose to answer it ; to consider these things, wherin we challenge our aduersaries for euill dealing, in this particular Controuersie: First, In setting downe our opinion, they make it not that which we hold, but another thing ; and then make large discourses in vaine : they should vnderstand our cause as we deliuer it : for we deuise not their opinion, but take it out of their owne bookes, especially from the Popes Canons: Secondly, When they would refute vs, they bring their owne Canon law, which was deuised in preiudice of the freedome of Princes, and is our aduersarie, and therefore cannot be our Iudge: Thirdly, When they produce the testimonies of auncient fathers the abuse, for which we challenge them, is, that they will not vnderstand the question : for the fathers write for the spirituall Iurisdiction of the Church aboue Princes ; which thing we neuer denied. But against the coactiue Iurisdiction of Princes in matters Ecclesiasticall : which thing we hold, the Fathers neuer wrote, but they are for it. If these things were faithfully obserued(as they are all peruerted in

this

this cause by one that termeth him the Catholicke Diuine)
and if the truth were sought with conscience, and not preiu-
dice maintained with resolution, men would neuer presume
so much vpon the simplicity of the Readers, nor in the confi-
dence of their wit and learning, would they suffer themselues
to be set to the maintenance of any cause whatsoeuer. Let me
farther intreate him that would answere me, to enter into
this short and serious meditation with himselfe, thus: Ei-
ther my purpose is to serue God for the truth, and then I may
looke for a blessing vpon my labours; or else to serue man
though against the truth, and then I may looke for a curse
vpon my selfe and my labours: let this Meditation rule thy
pen and heart: I aske no more.   Last of all, let me intreate
thee of curtesie, to amend the faults escaped in printing, with
thy pen, thus.

P.2.Lin.10.Or some others, superfluous.P.13.l.2.as, superfluous.p.1 4.l
29.for more read meer.p.22.l.28.the superfluous.p.30.l.15 for teached.r.
touched.p.52.marg. r. שׁבעא‎ p.73.l.28 r against the infringers of the
priuiledges of the Sea Apostolick.p.85.l.19.therto superfluous.p.105.l.8.
r.M.Luther.p.107.l.2.r.M.Luther.p.108.l.16.r.M.Bucer.p 108.l.20. r.M.
Antonius Flam.p.109.l.10.r.M.Chemnicius .p.211.l.11. for opportunely
r.opportunity.p.229.l.31.for great r.greatest.p.234 l.15.for Frederic r.Lo-
douic.p.134.l.22.for Rhenes r. Rense.p.234. l.27.for Rhenes r. Rense.p.
250 l.28.r.adhærentium,& adhærere volentium.p.262.l.21. for ver r. viri.
p.272.l.18.for chusing r.choosen.p.272.l.22.for to.r.in.p.279.l.30.no super-
fluous.p.294.l.16.for cultus r.cultu.

OF THE IVRISDIC
TION OF Princes, IN
Causes and ouer Persons
Ecclesiasticall.

CHAP. I.

The state of the Question.

He lawfull authoritie and Iurisdiction of Kings in matters Ecclesiasticall, is now and hath beene, for some ages heeretofore much impugned by such, who by vsurpation hauing incroached vpon the right of Kings, seeke by all subtill and colourable deuises to maintaine that by skill and some shew of learning, which they haue gotten by fraud. All this mischiefe proceedeth from the Bishop of Rome, who vsurping powre, and taking to himselfe that honour whereunto God hath not called him, hath brought all authoritie Ecclesiasticall and Ciuill into great confusion; by vsurping the right both of the Church and of States. Now our de-

B   sire

fire being to open the truth, and to declare the lawfull right of
Princes and power of the Church : it feemeth needfull firſt to
fet downe what power is giuen to the Pope by them that flatter him : fo fhall the right of the King and of the Church better
appeare.

2 They yeeld to the Pope a fulneſſe of power as they teanne
it, from whence all Spirituall Iurifdiction muſt proceed to o-
thers ; fome adde alfo Temporall : of Spirituall Iurifdiction

De Rom. Ponti- *Bellarmine* faith[all Bifhops receiue Iurifdiction from the Pope]
fic.lib.4.cap.24 The like fome of them or fome others teach alfo of Temporall
power : the difference which they obferue is, that Spirituall
power is deriued from the Pope to all Bifhops : but Temporall
power is giuen to execute fome feruice. *Auguſtinus Triumphus*
of Ancona, who wrote about three hundreth yeeres agoe, at
the commaundement of *Iohn* 22. Pope, fet foorth of late by the
authoritie and priuiledge of *Gregorie* 13. did long before the
Iefuits difpute this queſtion of the Popes Soueraigne authoritie
ouer Princes: fince which time the Friars haue clofely followed

Lib.de poteſt.Ec- his footſteps. His aſſertion is, *Omnis poteſtas imperatorum &*
clef.q.1.Art.1. *regum eſt fubdelegata reſpectu poteſtatis Papæ.* And againe in the
fame place, *Omnis poteſtas facularis eſt reſtringenda, amplianda,*
executioni mandanda ad imperium Papæ. Thefe and the like pofitions are now refolutely and ſtiffely maintained by the Iefuits
and others of that faction.

3. This agreeth well with the Canon lawes, which are the
fundamentall lawes of the court of Rome. For thus they fay:

Clement.lib.2. *Nos tam ex fuperioritate quam ad imperium non eſt dubium nos*
de fenten & re. *habere &c.* That is, [we afwell by that foueraignetie and right
iudic.Can.2. which without all doubt we haue to the Empire, as alfo by that
power whereby we fucceed the Emperour in the vacancie of
the Empire, and no leſſe alfo by the fulneſſe of that power
which Chriſt the King of kings, and Lord of lords hath in the
perfon of Saint *Peter* graunted to vs though vnworthy : declare
all fuch fentences and proceſſes (made by *Henry* 7.)void and of

Extrau. Com. none effect] Thus faith *Clement* 5. Pope againſt *Henrie* 7.Em-
lib.1.de maior. perour. To the fame purpofe faith *Boniface* 8. Pope, in a Con-
& obed.c.vnam ſtitution of his. *Oportet gladium eſſe fub gladio, &c.* That is[one
fanctam. fword

sword must be vnder another sword, and the Temporall authoritie must be subiected to the Spirituall authoritie : for when
the Apostle saith:there is no power but of God, and the powers
that are, are ordained of God. They could not be ordinated,
vnlesse one sword were vnder another: and a little after. Thus
of the Church and of the power Ecclesiasticall is verified the
prophecie of *Ieremie*, behold I haue set thee ouer nations, and
kingdomes to plucke vp and to root out, and to destroy and to *Ierem*.1.10.
throw downe, and to build and to plant. And againe, we declare, we say, we define, we pronounce ; that it is necessarie to
saluation to beleeue that euery humane creature is subiect to .
the Pope of Rome.] These be the lawes of the court of Rome Answere to
which some of late haue so much adored as to call them Catho- the fift part of
like Diuinitie, and which for truth and certaintie, and for au- Reports.
thoritie ouer their consciences, they hold comparable euen
with the holy Scriptures.

4. By all which wee collect the doctrine of the court of
Rome or the Popes faction to be, that the Pope hath all power
Spirituall and Temporall aboue all other whatsoeuer. This I
call the opinion of the Court of Rome, or the Popes faction,
because we finde the most learned of the Church of Rome to
hold the contrary. For concerning spirituall power, the best
learned of the Church of Rome, yea and whole councels maintaine the Spiritual power of the Church, to be aboue the Pope;
as hereafter we shall declare. And for this Temporall power
aboue Kings and Emperours, claimed by the Popes in their
Canon Lawe, maintained by their flatterers : it seemeth so
straunge, so new and absurd, that they who maintaine it, are
not as yet agreed vpon the state of the question. For some hold
that the Pope hath this power directly ouer Princes, as the Canonists, to whom some of the Shoole-men may be added as
Triumphus, and some of late called *Congregationis Oratory*, as
Cardinall *Baronius, Bozius*, and such. Others denying this direct power, hold that the Pope hath the same power but indirectly, as depending vpon his Spirituall power ; of this opinion
is Cardinall *Bellarmine,* and others : these both hold the same
conclusion, but differ in the manner of holding it. Others there

be who are in some sort content to allowe the Popes Father-hood in spirituall matters, in case he would not prooue incor-rigible, but vtterly denie this power ouer princes, both direct and indirect : of this opinion was *Guil. Occham, Marsilius Pa-tauinus* and other learned men of the Church of Rome. And of late *Guil. Berclaius* a French Lawyer, hath with great lear-ning refuted both the former opinions, of the Popes power di-rect and indirect against *Bozius* and *Bellarmine*, and yet this man professeth himselfe to be resolued to liue and die a Papist : so that on the one side stand all the reformed Churches, and many of the best learned of the Church of Rome : I may say all the Church of old and of late. On the other side standeth the Pope with his faction, that is, his flatterers : and this I call (with some of former ages) the Court of Rome : this is the o-pinion of our aduersaries.

5. Our positiue sentence against this standeth in two parts, as the Pope hath incroached on two sides, both vpon the right of Kings, and of the Church. Concerning the Kings right, we hold *that in externall coactiue Iurisdiction the* King hath su-preame authoritie in all causes and ouer all persons Ecclesiasti-call aswell as Ciuill. This is that which hath bene published by diuerse writings and ordinances, which by publike authoritie haue beene enacted and published ; declaring that the King within his Dominions hath this soueraigne authoritie, and that heerein there is no forraine power aboue the King. The autho-rity of the Church hath beene in like sort vsurped by the Pope, by drawing to himselfe a supposed title of the head of the vni-uersall Church : by deuising a straunge authority in the fulnesse of power, by claiming a newe and straunge priuiledge of his not erring iudgement, and making himselfe the onely iudge of controuersies of faith. This power in iudging and determi-ning of controuersies of faith and religion, being partly in the Church, partly in the Scriptures, the Pope hath wrested from both ; first extolling the Church aboue the Scriptures, and then setting himselfe aboue the Church. Then, that the limits of each power may be truely knowne, we giue all spiri-tuall power to the Church, all externall coactiue iurisdiction to the

Iniunctions An.
1559 and Anno
1562.

the King : when each of these shall haue taken vp his owne
right, there will not be so much left to the Pope, as these great
flatterers the Iesuits seeke to heape vpon him. Our purpose is
first, to dispute the right which Kings haue in coactiue power
ouer all persons and in all causes euen Ecclesiasticall within his
dominions : by persons ecclesiasticall wee vnderstand Archbishops, Bishops, Deans, Rectors, and all other set in calling and
place Ecclesiasticall : by causes Ecclesiasticall wee vnderstand
causes Ecclesiasticall *of externall coactiue Iurisdiction.*

6. From this consideration of persons and causes, arise two
great questions. First, concerning the exemption of all causes
Ecclesiasticall, from the Kings Iurisdiction : secondly, concerning the exemption of Ecclesiasticall persons from temporall
audience and iudicature. For the better vnderstanding hereof, we may proceede by some distinctions:for when our aduersaries teach that the Pope is the head of the Church : and we,
that the King is the supreame gouernor of the Church, though
in some sound of wordes, these things seeme not much to differ : yet in truth there is great difference betweene their meaning and ours. For they calling the Pope the head, to distinguish him from Christ, whom the Apostle calleth the head of
the Church, say that the Pope is the ministeriall head : which *Ephes.1.22.*
deuise was first brought in by the Schoolemen : for among the
auncients it was not knowne, but all that speake of the head
of the Church before, acknowledge none but Christ. Concerning this deuise of the ministeriall head, we say with the ancient Fathers that the Catholike Church is but one, and hath
one head, Christ Iesus : because to one bodie there can bee
but one head, from whom grace is infused to the whole body.
This Catholike Church is as that head is, both perfectly known
to God, not to man : this then is but one in all times and places. But the visible Churches or particular, are many at many times, in many places : and therefore must haue heads or
gouernours, aunswerable to themselues : for many Churches,
many gouernours, These are either Spirituall gouernours or
Temporall. The spirituall gouernment of the Church is committed to spirituall gouernours, as first from Christ to his

twelue:

twelue Apoſtles, of whom none was aboue the reſt in this ſpirituall gouernment or kingdome of Chriſt, as the Lord doth often expreſly declare to them: from them to Biſhops and Pa-
ſtors, their ſucceſſors. Temporall gouernours are ſuch, as haue
the cuſtody of externall coactiue Iuriſdiction, both in Temporall and Eccleſiaſticall cauſes : for the power of the Church,
with all her ſpirituall Iuriſdiction, neuer reached to coaction.
This was by God firſt giuen to Magiſtrates, and neuer reuoked, in all times practiſed, but when the Church and Kings
were oppreſſed by the great power of Antichriſt. When wee
call the King the ſupreame gouernour of the Church, our
meaning is, that hee is appointed by God to be a Father and
preſeruer of religion, a keeper of Eccleſiaſticall diſcipline, and
as the Prophet *Iſaiah* calleth him, a nourcing father of the
Church; he is the ſoueraigne in all affaires of coactiue Iuriſdiction. Likewiſe this word Church, is not taken in the ſame ſenſe
by them and vs ; for our aduerſaries ſaying, that the Pope is the
head of the Church : vnderſtand thereby the Catholike
Church ſpread ouer the whole world, but we vnderſtand a particular Church, yeelding the King to bee gouernour next and
immediatly vnder God of his own dominions, and conſequently of perſons and cauſes within his owne dominions : ſo that
there is much difference betweene their meaning and ours.
Then we muſt come to ſuch an iſſue, wherein without equiuo-
cating the queſtion betweene vs is ſet ; for wee ſhall otherwiſe
run into that fault which is ſo rife, with the Popes Clarks, that
Bellarmine himſelfe confeſſeth it. *Notandum eſt* (ſaith he) *multos ex noſtris tempus terere, dum probant quod Caluinus & cæteri
hæretici concedunt.* This is moſt common among them to bee
large in diſputing that, which is not in queſtion betweene vs,
and it is a ſigne of ſome ingenuitie to confeſſe it : but neither
doth himſelfe for all his confeſſion auoid it ; neither doe they
that write ſince, and depend vpon his learning, ſhunne it after
ſo faire warning ; neither in truth can a falſe cauſe be maintained, in ſo many bookes and large volumes as now they ſet out,
vnleſſe they tooke this libertie to themſelues, to be large in diſputing things which are not in queſtion. The queſtion then is
concer-

Matth.18.1.
Marc.9.34.
Luke.9.46.

Iſai.49.32.

De eccleſ.mili-
tant.lib.3.ca.13

concerning the lawfull authoritie of Kings in their owne dominions, touching this part of Iurisdiction which is called Ecclesiasticall coactiue Iurisdiction.

7. For better proceeding, let the distinction be remembred, which is vsually receiued of Ecclesiasticall power : for all power Ecclesiasticall is commonly deuided into power of order, and of Iurisdiction. The power of order, by all writers that I could see, euen of the Church of Rome, is vnderstood to be immediatly from Christ, giuen to all Bishops and Priests alike by their consecration : wherein the Pope hath no priuiledge aboue other. Thus teach *Bonauenture in 4.sent.d.17.q 1. August Triumphus lib.de potest.ecclef.qu.1.ar.1. Ioh.Gerson li.de potest.ecclef. consid.1. Cardinal.Cusanus lib.de cathol.concord.2.cap.13.Cardinal.Contarenus tract. de ecclef. potest. pontifici s Bellarm. lib. 4. de Rom. Pont. cap. 22.* This then being the common confession of all, that the Pope hath no more power herein, then any other Bishop or Pastor, we moue no contradiction in this. As they confesse that in this power the Pope hath no præeminence, but that it is giuen from Christ to all Bishops and pastors equally : so wee confesse that in this power the prince hath no part, and that Bishops and pastors haue this power onely from the diuine ordinance, and not from earthly princes : then our question is onely, of the power of Iurisdiction.

8. This power of Iurisdiction is diuersly vnderstood by the writers of the Church of Rome. *Augustinus Triumphus* doth deliuer it thus. [The power of Iurisdiction is Temporall or Spirituall ; and this power considered in generall is threefold ; immediate, deriued, or giuen to execute some seruice : the power of Iurisdiction immediate of all things Spirituall and Temporall, is onely in the Pope. The power of Iurisdiction deriued is in Bishops, to them deriued from the Pope : the power of Temporall Iurisdiction giuen to execute some seruice for the helpe of the Church is in Emperours, Kings, and secular princes : this power is not immediat from God, but is giuen first to the Pope, and so to Kings for the vse of the Church, and helpe of Pope and Prelates]. I haue deliuered this in the very words of *Triumphus*, whom in this thing others followe :

De potest.ecclef. qu.1. art.1

though

though of late some of the finer Iesuits, who hold the same, are growen more cunning in the manner of deliuering it. *Bellarmine* loath to leaue the opinion, and ashamed so grossely to propose it, deuiseth a mollification of it thus. *Asserimus Pontificem vt pontificem, etsi non habeat vllam meré temporalem potestatem: tamen habere in ordine ad spirituale bonum summam potestatem disponendi de temporalibus rebus omnium Christianorum.* That is, [We auer that the Pope, albeit he hath not any power merely Temporall as Pope, yet hath power supreame in respect of Spirituall good, to dispose of all the Temporalties of all Christians. And in the next Chapter concludeth, that the Pope hath authoritie to depose hereticall kings and princes ; and answereth to an obiection, which I will set downe in his own words. *Quod si Christiani non deposuerunt olim Neronem, Diocletianum, Iulianum, Valentem & similes, ia fuerat quia deerant vires temporales Christianis.* That is, [If Christians of old deposed not *Nero, Diocletian, Iulian, Valens*, and the like, this was because Christians then wanted Temporall forces]. They will shortly without blushing tell vs, that Iesus Christ also submitted himselfe to the heathen Emperours, and to their deputies, because he wanted power to resist them : for this they may say with some sophisticall shew of reason, aswell as that which they doe say. Then his opinion is, that the Pope as Pope hath not any Temporall power, but yet the Pope and onely the Pope hath Temporall power aboue all Kings and Emperours. This is one of the greatest points wherein the Pope hath incroached vpon the right of Kings.

9. Besides this Temporall Iurisdiction, there is another part of Iurisdiction called spirituall : which the writers of the Church of Rome deuide into internall, and externall ; internall they referre to the Sacraments onely, *Gerson de potest. ecclesi. consid. 1. Bellar. de Rom. pont. lib. 4. cap. 22.* Bellarmine in the place last cited, disputing of Iurisdiction, saith, [there is a triple power in the Bishop of Rome : first of order, secondly of internall Iurisdiction, thirdly of externall Iurisdiction : the first is referred to the Sacraments, the second to inward gouernment which is in the court of conscience ; the third to that externall gouern-

Lib. 5. de Rom. pont. cap. 6.

gouernment which is practised in externall courts : and confesseth that of the first and second, there is no question betweene
vs, but onely of the third : *De prima & secunda non est questio,
sed solum de tertia*; saith he. Then of this wee are agreed, that
the question betweene vs and them, is onely of Iurisdiction in
the third sense, and therein especially *of Iurisdiction coactiue in
externall courts* : binding and compelling by force of law, and
other externall mulcts and punishments, beside excommunication : as for Spirituall Iurisdiction of the Church, standing in
examinations of controuersies of faith, iudging of heresies, deposing of heretickes ; excommunication of notorious and
stubborne offenders, ordination of Priests and Deacons, institution and collation of benefices and spirituall cures, &c. This
we reserue intire to the Church, which Princes cannot giue or
take from the Church. This power hath bene practised by the
Church, without coactiue Iurisdiction : other then of excommunication. But when the matters handled in the Ecclesiasticall consistorie, are not matters of faith and religion, but of a ciuill nature, which yet are called Ecclesiasticall, as being giuen
by Princes, and appointed to be within the cognisance of that
consistorie ; and when the censures are not spirituall, but carnall, compulsiue, coactiue : here appeareth the power of the
ciuill magistrate. This power we yeeld to the magistrate, and
here is the question, whether the magistrate hath right to this
power, or Iurisdiction, which is thus described by the Roma-
nists. Externall Iurisdiction Ecclesiasticall, is a power coactiue
giuen to gouerne Christian people in contentious courts: this is
the principal question which we haue here to search. Our English flatterers of the Pope that write now, and of late haue written, vndertake to prooue that this Iurisdiction is first and principally in the Pope, and from him deriued to Bishops, and that
Kings haue not this power at all, or any part of it, vnlesse by
commission from the Pope : our assertion is contrary, that this
power of Ecclesiasticall Iurisdiction externall and coactiue be-
longs to Kings only, & not to Ecclesiasticall persons, but as they
haue commission from their Princes. And because we would
not be mistaken in the question, we will set down the words of

*Lib.4.cap.22.
de Rom. Pont.*

What is the
Iurisdiction in
question.

C   the

De potest.Eccle.
consid.4.

the best of that side, for better euidence and assurance, who take the question thus, and not otherwise. *Iohn Gerson* saith, *Potestas Ecclesiastica Iurisdictionis in foro exteriori, est potestas Ecclesiastica* coactiua, *qua valet exerceri in alterum etiam inuitum.* *Bellarmine* speaking of the same power, saith it is, *ad regendum populum Christianum in foro exteriori.*

10. Then this is the thing which wee are to prooue, that Ecclesiasticall coactiue power, by force of lawe and corporall punishments, by which Christian people are to be gouerned in externall and contentious courts, is a power which of right belongeth to Christian Princes. Concerning the power of orders, and institutions, of excommunication and deposition, and of internall Iurisdiction in the court of Conscience, & in administration of Sacraments, & absolution by power of the keyes; this we giue not to Princes: but Princes, as they are preseruers of Religion, and nurcing fathers of the Church, are to see that Bishops and all inferiour ministers performe their faithfull duties in their seuerall places, and if they be found faulty to punish them; because that belongeth to external Iurisdiction coactiue. Thus much may suffice for the state of the question. For the manner of handling, I purpose to search the right of Kinges; first in the law of nature, secondly in the written law giuen by *Moses,* continued vntill the comming of our Lord Iesus Christ: thirdly to declare the confirmation of the same right by Christ and his Apostles, and the Church succeeding, vntill that time that the Pope drew a newe estate and Iurisdiction to himselfe. After which time I purpose to obserue how the Pope hath incroached, first vpon the Bishops, then vpon the right of kings, and last vpon the right of the Church and generall Councels. By all which will appeare, how late, how new and strange that Iurisdiction is, which the flatterers of the court of Rome now yeeld to the Pope.

CHAP.

CHAP. II.

Kings in the time of the Law of nature, had all power
Ecclefiaſticall,both of order and Iuriſdiction.

N the Law of nature we haue not many examples of Kings,that gouerned a people where the
Church of God was planted : there is onely
mention of *Melchiſedecke* King of Salem , of
him it is ſaid, *Gen.*14. *Melchiſedecke* King of *Gen.*14.19.
Salem was a prieſt of the high God.In his perſon theſe two offices, the kingdom & the prieſthood were ioyned; both which
offices followed the prerogatiue of the birthright : for that this
Melchiſedeck was *Sem*,is the receiued opinion of many inter-
pretours : wherein is ſome difference. Some take *Sem* to be the
eldeſt ſonne of *Noah* , but others from a probable collation of
Scriptures hold him to be the ſecond ſonne : but whether hee
were eldeſt or not , it is apparant , and out of doubt by that
bleſſing,*Gen.*9. that he had the birthright : for *Canaan* is made *Gen.*9.26,27.
his ſeruant,which is the auncient ſtile and euidence of the birthright,as is expreſſed in the birthright of *Iacob* ; & *Iaphet* is per- *Gen.*27.29.
ſwaded to dwell in the tents of *Sem*. Whereas therefore hee
hath that honor aboue both his brethren, the birthright is euidently confirmed vnto him,*Canaan* being made his ſeruant,and
Iaphet being directed to repaire to his tents : for as then the
Church was in tents. *Sem* hauing the birthright confirmed by
his fathers bleſſing,as *Iacob* had by the bleſſing of *Iſaack* afterward,hath conſequently all thoſe priuiledges confirmed to him
which followe the birthright. The priuiledges which in the
time of the law of nature followed the birthright, were theſe ;
The gouernement or principalitie, the Prieſthood,and a portion anſwerable to maintaine both theſe dignities : the two former were principall prerogatiues, the third followed as an ad-
herent to them ; a double portion anſwerable to a double dignitie. The princedome and double portion are generally acknowledged to belong to the birthright : but the prieſthood is

C 2　　　　　　not

not so much manifested, and would therefore somewhat more
be opened. I will here briefly collect the reasons, which proue
the priesthood to belong to the birthright, as wel as the princedome and double portion.

2. First from reason it is deduced thus, It cannot by reason
be imagined, but that God hauing a purpose to call a Church
out of this world, did set vp the gouernment and meanes wherby the Church might be instituted in the true knowledge and
worship of God : therefore this gouernment and those meanes
were set vp in the law of nature, in those principalities which
then stood. The first principalitie that was set vp to rule many
families, was a kingdome; as the first simply was in the gouernment of a family : for before there could be a common-wealth,
there must be a citie, or the collection of many families into the
lawfull right of one societie; and before there could be a citie,
there must bee particular houses and families : so that the first
gouernment that was in the world among men, was the gouernment of a family : now in the gouerment of a family, it is
absurd to thinke, and impossible to prooue, that the power of
gouernment was in the multitude. This I obserue the rather,
because some of the Popes flatterers of late, as others also to o-
pen a wide gappe to rebellions, haue written that the power of gouernment by the law of nature is in the multitude : but
euery man of reason carrieth thus much light and vnderstanding about him, as to iudge of this thing without errour. Because no man can conceiue in the first beginning any other gouernment of a family, then by one whom God and nature
made *Patrem familias*, the father of the familie. Now come
from the gouerment of one familie, to the gouernment of diuers; when many families were gathered together, the first gouernment that was erected among them, was that with which
they were first and best acquainted : for as in families, so in the
collection of diuerse families, one was in gouerment, as the father of the family was in his famiile. And what is a King by nature, but the father of a great family? and what is the father
of a familie by nature, but a little King? and therefore the first
gouernement of states by the lawe of nature, was by Kings.

Thefe

These principalities were first erected for the good of Gods Church; to minister as nourcing fathers to the Church. Thus were Kings erected, not onely by their authoritie to see that Gods seruice were established, but by the law of nature to performe that seruice in their owne persons. And therefore as *Adam* had this care first, so it is testified of *Seth* (to whom the birthright pertained after *Cain* was reiected) that in his time men began to call vpon the name of the Lord, which declareth that he established the true worship of God in his dayes.

Gen.4.26.

3. Another reason may be drawen from this blessing which *Noah* gaue to *Sem*, [blessed be the Lord God of *Sem*, and let *Canaan* bee his seruant: God perswade *Iaphet* that hee may dwell in the tents of *Sem*, and let *Canaan* be his seruant.] In which words three priuiledges of *Sem* are manifested. First that God is called the Lord God of *Sem*, Secondly that *Canaan* shal be his seruant: Thirdly that *Iaphet* shall repaire to his tents. The first and last are confirmations of the priesthood, the second a proofe of the primogeniture: then the priesthood is annexed to the birthright. Another reason is from the example of *Melchisedeck*, who was both King and Priest. In which example we consider that by the law of nature, before there was a positiue law to distinguish and separate these offices, both did naturally concurre in one person: for in this we vnderstand the ordinary course held in the law of nature. If wicked Kings neglected this godly order, it was because they were wicked, and had shaked off the feare of God, and as much as in them was, extinguished the light of nature. Another reason may be drawen from the testimony of *Moses*, who witnesseth that the Lord tooke the Leuites to minister in place of the first borne. [I haue taken the Leuites from among the children of Israel. And the Leuits shall be mine, because all the first borne are mine.] Vpon which wordes *Lyra* reporting the receiued iudgements of the best interpretors saith. *Ante legē datam ad primogenitos pertinebat offerre sacrificia:* and a little after, *Leuitæ succeſſerunt loco eorum:* and againe to the same purpose, *Cultus diuinus ante legem datam pertinebat, ad primogenitos Iſrael:* and againe, *Sacerdotium fuit annexum primogenituræ vſq, ad legem datam per Moſen.*

Gen.9.26.27.

Num.3.12. & 8.6.

Lyra in Num.3. 12.

In Num.8.16:

In Gen.14.

C 3   4. By

4. By all which thus much appeareth ; that by the law of nature, the first borne stood in the ministerie & seruice of God, to preach the knowledge of God to others, and to execute his ordinances and sacrifices. And as the first borne in families were thus to instruct and informe the whole familie, so the first borne in a nationall principalitie or kingdome were bound not onely to commaund as ciuill magistrates, but to execute the holy ordinances of God as the chiefe Priests of that nation , as is euident by these reasons, and by the example of *Melchisedeck.* The same light may appeare though much darkened, in the ancient gouernment of the heathen , for euen heathen Kings are witnessed in old times, to haue bene Priests of such gods as they serued : which auncient combining of these two offices in one person, came from the ancient practise in the time of the lawe of nature, and from the light of nature which was receiued among the heathen.

Plato in politic.
Arist.3. de re-
pub.Cic.2.de di-
uinat.Clem.
Alex.str.8.

5. But here a question may be moued, If Kings by the law of nature were Priests, and the lawe of nature stand alwayes in force, not abrogated : why then are not Kings now Priests? For aunswere, first we say, that it was altered by a positiue lawe of God, as hereafter we shall declare : and therefore the same authoritie that instituted this thing , hath also altered it. But it may be replied , that the positiue law of God which hath altered this thing, was partly ceremoniall, partly iudiciall: for these two dignities of the princedome and priesthood, which vnder the law of nature were combined in one person, were diuided vnder the law of *Moses,* and distinctly set in two persons. *Moses* keeping the ciuill gouernment, and *Aaron* the Priesthood. The gouernment of *Moses* and his successours being more ciuill, The Priesthood of *Aaron* & his successors ceremoniall; it followeth that this ancient ordinance of the law of nature was altered by such positiue lawes of God, which were either ciuill or ceremoniall : and consequently that this alteration taketh not away the auncient right.

6. If I might therefore in a matter of this nature declare my poore opinion, leauing the censure hereof to the learned that are able to iudge : I take it, that as it is not simply vnlawfull
that

that a King may be a Priest, and neuerthelesse keepe his kingdome : so I suppose this thing cannot be done without not only a lawfull, but also an ordinarie calling from God, and from *Heb.5.4.*
the Church:[For no man taketh this honour to himselfe, but he
that was called thereto, as was *Aaron.*] And this cannot bee
done without an ordinary calling:for when Kings were Priests,
and the first borne sacrificers,as in the law of nature ; then they
had an ordinary calling therto:for that was then the ordinance
of God,&ordinarie in the Church, which now is not. But if a
man were first a Priest, and afterward aduanced to a kingdome
by some Temporal right:in this case it were assuredly vnlawfull
for him to shake off his holy estate,and betake himselfe wholly
and only to his Temporall gouerment, as some Cardinals haue
done. Then by the law of nature the King had both the power of order and Iurisdiction/: and howsoeuer this is altered by a
positiue ordinance of God, yet all is not taken away : there remaineth still that part of Iurisdiction, so farre as it standeth in
power coactiue,in respect wherof the common law of this land *10.H.7.18.*
saith,the King is *persona mixta,* becaufe he hath both Ecclesiasticall and Temporall Iurisdiction.

7. This example of *Melchisedeck* both King and Priest,
hath much lifted vp the Pope and his flatterers : for of this
they take especiall hold,and thinke hereby to prooue the Pope
to be King of the Church,becaufe *Melchisedeck* was both King
and Priest. But to this we aunfwere, *Melchisedeck* had both
these honours by a lawfull and ordinarie calling, but so hath
not the Pope: for his Priesthood,we graunt he had once thereto a lawfull calling, both by locall and doctrinall succession :
which doctrinall succession *Irenaus* calleth *successionem princi-*
palem : Tertullian, doctrina cōfanguinitatē cum Apostolica Ecclesia: *Jren.li.4.ca.43.*
but now haue they forsaken that principall succession,and haue *Tertul. prescript.*
nothing left to glory in, but bare personall and locall successi-
on. Then to the office of a Bishop, the Pope may shew some
colour,though the colour be now worne thredbare: but to the
princely office which he claimeth ouer the Church,he can shew
neither calling nor colour: so that the example of *Melchisedeck,*
which the Popes parasites drawe with such violence to him,

doth

doth helpe him nothing, but rather helpeth the cause of Christian Kings against him : for it is certaine that Kings were Priests
by an ordinary calling before these two offices were distinguished ; but it can neuer be prooued that Priests were Kings by
such an ordinary calling, after that these two offices were set in
distinct persons. If any man suppose that we haue stretched the
example of *Melchisedeck* too farre , because he was a type of
Christ : I aumswere, this is nothing against my purpose , that
Melchisedeck was a type of Christ. For many men in their ordinary standing and executing ordinary functions , did also
beare some type extraordinarie : thus did *Moses, Ioshua, Dauid,
Solomon,* and others. I speake of *Melchisedeck,* as I finde him
in his ordinary place, a King, and a Priest.

     8. By all which we conclude, that vnder the law of Nature
Kings were in the beginning inuested with all power Ecclesiasticall both of orders and Iurisdiction : and therefore these
things are not incompatible by nature. All this time which lasted about the space of two thousand and fiue hundred yeeres,
Kings had Ecclesiasticall Iurisdiction without question. And
therefore this Iurisdiction of Princes, which we haue vndertaken to examine, is found aunswerable to the first gouernment
of the world, vntill the time of the law giuen by *Moses.*

CHAP. III.

*All externall Iurisdiction coactiue , was a right be-
longing to Kings vnder the Law.*

Ow let vs search what Iurisdiction in matters
Ecclesiasticall was found due, and acknowledged to belong to the Kings right all that
time vnder the Law. Then we find by an especiall commaundement of God : these two offices of King and Priest were distinguished, and
set in two seuerall persons : the one in *Moses,* the other in *Aaron*

ron. And the tribe of *Leui* was taken to the seruice of God, *Num*.3.12.
in stead of the first borne by an expresse commaundement : and & 8.6.
the first borne which in number exceeded the number of the
Leuites, were redeemed by fiue shekels a man : for the number *Num*.3.
of the first borne was taken 22273. the number of the Leuites
22000.so that the number of the first borne exceeded the number of the Leuites by 273. These were redeemed, and after that
redemption, the first borne of other tribes were discharged
from the attendance of the seruice of God,& the Leuites tooke
vp their place. Now the Kings office and the Priests being thus
distinguished, we must consider what things did properly belong to each office.

2. First we find that *Moses,* who had the place of a King in
gouernement, as he is also called a King; doth consecrate *Aa-* *Gen*.36,31.
ron the Priest. *Moses* is commaunded to consecrate him and *Deut*.33.5.
his son's *Exod.*28,and performeth it, *Leuit.*8.therefore it is repeated, *Num.*3. These are the names of the sonnes of *Aaron* *Num*.3.3.
the anointed Priests, whom *Moses* did consecrate to minister
in the Priests office. Heere then appeareth some Iurisdiction
of *Moses* ouer *Aaron.* But this I meane not to vrge, for it may
bee thought extraordinairly to belong to *Moses* as Gods
Apostle or Ambassadour and lawgiuer vnto *Israel* : for in such
great chaunges,as was from the law of Nature to the written
law, somewhat must bee admitted extraordinary : and this I
could be well content to vnderstand so : though many doubts
arise for the princes right, against the Priests. For first it may
be obiected, seeing there was a Prince and a Priest set vp distinct one from the other,why should the Prince consecrate the
Priest, and not the Priest the Prince ? But here we finde that
Aaron doth not consecrate *Moses* to be Prince,but *Moses* doth
consecrate *Aaron* to be Priest. Another doubt may be moued,
why *Moses* should consecrate not onely *Aaron*, but his sonnes
also. For though we should admit the consecration of *Aaron*
to be done by *Moses* of necessitie, as a thing extraordinary at
the first beginning of this Priesthood : yet this necessitie appeareth not so much in *Aarons* sonnes : for they might haue beene
consecrated by *Aaron*,after that himselfe had bene once conse-

D crated

crated by *Moses*. And yet we find that the confecration of *Aaron*, and his fonnes, is done altogether by *Moses*. Thefe things though they make faire fhew for the Princes Iurifdiction Ecclefiafticall ouer Priefts, yet wee purpofe not to ftand vpon them.

3. But when the Prieft was once confecrated and ordained, and all things fully perfected concerning his function, and two feuerall and diftinct functions fet vp: then will appeare without faile in *Moses* & his fucceffors the right of Princes, in *Aaron* & his fucceffors the right of Priefts. After all things thus perfected, we finde that all the lawes which in truth proceeded originally from God, were eftablished by the authoritie of *Moses* : and this we finde true, not onely in Iudiciall and Ciuill Lawes, which were to rule that ftate ; but euen in ceremoniall and Morall Lawes which were to rule the Church. There is not fo much as one ceremoniall law eftablished by the authoritie of *Aaron*, but in all the name and authoritie of *Moses* is expreffed: only we finde concerning *Aaron*, that if any doubt in the lawes ceremoniall did arife, for the interpretation of thofe lawes and of fuch doubts, the high Prieft muft fit as iudge. For the people are charged in matters that are hard, to confult with the Prieft and ciuill iudge, *Deut.* 17. 8. &c. Which the learned interpreters vnderftand thus : that if the caufe be mixt, partly Ciuill, partly Ceremoniall, or doubtfull ; that then both the Ciuill Magiftrate and the Prieft muft iointly determine it : but if the people haue diftinct caufes, fome Ciuill, other Ceremoniall, the Ciuill Magiftrate muft iudge the caufes Ciuill, and the Prieft muft iudge the caufes Ceremoniall : from the confideration of which place we may drawe certaine inferences.

4. Firft, all Lawes euen Ceremoniall, that is, Lawes whereunto Spirituall or Canon Lawes are anfwerable, are eftablished by the authoritie of the Ciuill Magiftrate. This taketh away all authoritie of the Popes Canon law, in all Chriftian kingdomes, where it is not eftablished by the authoritie of Kings in their kingdomes. For it is againft all reafon, and rules ; whether we looke vpon the light of nature, or vpon the Scriptures , or the lawfull practife of authoritie fince the Scriptures were written,

that

that any Lawes should be imposed vpon a Prince against or
without his consent: as the Popes haue indeuoured to impose
the Canon Lawes vpon Princes. And this appeareth in the
practise of Christian Magistrates, so long as lawfull authoritie
stood up without confusion in the world. But heere we consider the fountaine of that practise, which was from Gods Law:
wherein we see all Lawes confirmed and established by the authoritie of the Ciuill Magistrate. And if it could bee prooued,
that in some Lawes Ceremoniall the authoritie of *Aaron* was
requisite, yet this helpeth them nothing that plead for the
Popes Canons. For these men would impose these Canons vpon Princes without their consent:but in all these Lawes of *Moses,*(wherein is a perfect patterne for all law-makers) they cannot shew one Law, though neuer so nearely concerning the
Church, which is established without the authoritie of *Moses*
the Ciuill Magistrate. If they obiect,these things were all done
by an especiall commaundement of God, I aunswere this doth
more establish the authoritie of Princes, and confirme our purpose : for let them aunswere, why God would haue all these
things established by the Ciuill Magistrate, and not by the
Priest? This then maketh a greater and clearer confirmation
of the Princes right. Then the Church may interpret Scripture, determine controuersies of faith, but cannot establish a
Law: the reason is, because for the establishing of Lawes, coactiue power is requisite,which is in the Ciuil Magistrate,& not
in the Church. And therefore the Canon Lawes can haue no
force of lawes,but as they are receiued and established by Princes in their seuerall kingdomes. For neither can the law haue
the force of a law without coactiue power, neither hath the
Pope any coactiue power in the kingdomes of other Princes;
but onely in such places where himselfe is a Temporall Prince.

5. Secondly we obserue that the high Priest is appointed by
God a iudge for interpretation of those lawes that concerne
the Church,in questions of conscience,in causes mixt,or doubtfull. This might moderate the humours of some, who in loue
to innouation would leaue no place of iudicature to Ecclesiasticall persons :for these things are insert into *Moses* lawe, ta-

ken

ken from the law of Nature, and not as things Ceremoniall: which thing is apparant from the end, vfe, and neceffitie thereof: for the things which had a neceffary vfe before the written law, and muft haue a neceffary vfe after the abrogation of that law, muft be acknowledged to be taken from a perpetuall law: becaufe there muft be a perpetuall rule for a perpetuall neceffity. This then being perpetuall and neceffary (matters of queftion, and of Ecclefiafticall audience ftill arifing) the hearing and iudging of fuch things, belong to fuch as are moft skilfull in thofe affaires. And hence is the iudicature of fuch things affigned to the Prieft: which right of Ecclefiafticall iudgements and courts, ftandeth no leffe now due to them in the time of grace, then it was under the law: becaufe this office in iudgeing, hearing, and determining, is not heere giuen to Priefts as a thing Ceremoniall, but as I haue declared, deriued from the law of Nature, as a perpetuall feruice for a perpetuall vfe.

6. Thirdly we confider that the lawes Ecclefiaftical are eftablifhed by the authoritie of the Ciuill Magiftrate, but for interpretation of them the Prieft is appointed to iudge. Hence rifeth the ground of Iurifdiction both Temporall and Spirituall: wee confider Iurifdiction here as our queftion importeth, authority coactiue in externall iudicature in the execution of lawes. The fountaine of this authoritie is in him principally, by whofe authoritie the law is eftablifhed, and without whofe authoritie it is not. The execution of this authoritie is in them that are appointed iudges. And heerein there is no difference betweene Temporall and Ecclefiafticall authoritie, I fpeake not nowe of Spirituall gouernment by the lawes of God, executed within the court of Confcience, but of Ecclefiafticall gouernment in the execution of lawes Ecclefiafticall, wherin there is vfe of coactiue power. Thefe two things being in themfelues, and in nature fo diftinct, if this one diftinction might be remembred, it is ynough to aunfwere all the confufed collections of that Catholike Diuine, who wrote of late againft the fift part of Reports of the Lord *Cooke*. For all that hee writeth there, refting vpon no other ground, then vpon the confounding of Spirituall

all and Ecclesiasticall power, is answered in one word, by this one poore distinction betweene these two powers. Now the distinction is apparant : because in Spirituall gouernment there is no coactiue power : but in Ecclesiasticall iudicature there is coactiue power : which maketh an euident and famous difference in Iurisdiction : because this is most certaine, that all that Iurisdiction wherin coactiue power is vsed, is from the Ciuill Magistrate. Then if these two gouerments, I meane Ecclesiasticall and Temporal, be directed by coactiue power, there is no difference in the point of Iurisdiction betweene Temporall and Ecclesiasticall authoritie. For the King and only the King is to appoint iudges in matters Temporall and Ecclesiasticall, the King hath no more authoritie in reuersing the iudgement of the one, then of the other, being true, iust, and lawfull. So that the Kings Iurisdiction standeth not in a power to diffanull true and righteous iudgemens, but in a power supereminent, by which he is charged : First, to confirme lawes Ecclesiasticall and Temporall, Secondly, to place Iudges for both causes, Thirdly, to see that those iudges of both sortes iudge iustly according to right and equity, Fourthly, to punish them if they shall be found to giue vniust and corrupt sentences, Fiftly, and last of all, his Iurisdiction appeareth in appellations.

7. But heere a question will be moued, whether a man may appeale from an Ecclesiasticall iudge to the Prince. For that one may appeale from a Temporall iudge, I suppose it is not doubted, at least I see no reason why it should be doubted. But in a cause Ecclesiasticall and from a iudge Ecclesiasticall to appeale to the Temporall Magistrate, of this some Romish Doctors doubt. This doubt which the Canonists haue made, may be increased by that place, *Deut.*17.10.[Thou shalt not decline from that thing which they shall shew thee, neither to the right hand nor to the left. And that man that will do presumptuously, not hearkning to the Priest that standeth before the Lord thy God to minister there, or vnto the iudge that man shall die.]It might seeme to be collected hence, that there is no appellation from the Priest, no though hee should iudge as some Rabbins expound the words. I will declare their exposition because it

*Deut.*17.12.

D 3   sauoureth

sauoureth much like the expositions of some Papists, where the text saith, thou shalt not decline to the right hand, nor to the left, they expound it; that if the Priest shall say thy right hand is thy left, or thy left is thy right : this sentence thou must receiue and therein rest.

Verse 11.

8, But this is a fond assertion, not only without reason, but against the expresse words of the Scripture : for it is said, according to the law which shall teach thee, and according to the iudgement which they shall tell thee, thou shalt doe. Where we finde two rules for these two kindes of Iudges, the Priest and the iudge : the sentence of the Priest, must be according to the written lawe : the sentence of the other according to the truth of iustice and iudgement. If a man be able to shew that he is wronged, he may vndoubtedly appeale to a Superiour : now a man may be able to shew that he is wronged, if hee can shew that the Priest declineth from the law of God, which is appointed his rule, or the Temporall iudge from iustice. And therefore if there be a Superiour in the land, he may appeale : but if there be no Superiour, he is without remedie ; as when *Holy* was both Priest and iudge : from him at that time there could be no appellation. but where the forme of a kingdome is established, where one King is set vp in lawfull authoritie, by whose power iudges Spirituall and Temporall are placed in his dominions : heere appeareth a fountaine of Iurisdiction, deriued as it were into two inferiour riuers: and from these inferior powers appellation may be brought, if they shall not in their sentences, keepe their rules prescribed to them, the lawe and iustice : for the appellation being grounded vpon the lawe of Nature, to moderate the peruersitie and partialitie of iudges, it were an absurd thing to denie this in causes Ecclesiasticall, vnlesse a man would suppose that persons Ecclesiasticall may not be corrupt in their iudgements. Now if we shall once graunt appellations, then assuredly wee confirme the Iurisdiction of Princes in all matters wherein appellation may bee made to them. And because Iurisdiction is assuredly proued by appellation, we will for the farther manifestation of the truth, seeke to cleere this point : the rather because our aduersaries tell vs

consi-

confidently, that in matters Ecclesiasticall, all appellation belongeth to the Pope. The Popes say so; and they beleeue them: we hold that appellation in causes Ecclesiasticall is to bee directed to the King, who is by God set ouer the persons appellant.

9. In the Old Testament we haue fewe examples, or none, that I remember, of any that appealed from any inferior iudge Ecclesiasticall to the Soueraigne : but in the New Testament there is one example sufficient to confirme the truth. S. *Paul* Act. 25. & 23. Being accused for causes Ecclesiasticall, appealed from the high Priest to *Cesar*. Therfore it is lawfull in matters Ecclesiasticall to appeale from iudges Ecclesiasticall to the Ciuill Magistrate. The consequence resteth vpon this, that Saint *Paul* heerein did nothing but that which he might doe iustly and lawfully : which thing I suppose the greatest enemie of Saint *Pauls* Doctrine, will not denie : for he came vp to Ierusalem with this profession and purpose. [I am ready not to bee bound onely, Act.21.13. but euen to die for the name of the Lord Iesus. Neither durst he for sauing of his life, giue a scandall to the Gospell.] The antecedent consisteth of these two parts, First that the matters for which Saint *Paul* was accused, were matters Ecclesiasticall : Secondly, that therein he appealed from the high Priest : both are witnessed by the expresse words of the Scripture. For *Festus* saith, [They brought no crime against him, but had certaine questions against him of their owne superstition, and of one Ie- Act. 25.18 19. sus which was dead, whom *Paul* affirmed to be aliue.] These questions be out of doubt Ecclesiasticall, euen in the iudgement of our aduersaries : that he appealed from the high Priest, reskuing himselfe from his iudgement, it is euident by the words in the twentie three Chapter, where the Apostle speaketh to the high Priest, as to his iudge. [Thou sittest to iudge me accor- Act. 23.3. ding to the law.] And when he was reskued from the Priests by *Lysias*, and sent to *Felix*, and left by him to *Festus* : he neuer thinketh of appealing from any of these ciuill gouernours. But when *Festus* asked him, if he will goe to Ierusalem, and there be iudged of these things, then *Paul* vtterly refusing the high-Priest appealed to *Cesar* : by which it followeth that in matters Act.25.10.

Ecclesi-

Ecclesiasticall, a man may appeale from iudges Ecclesiasticall to the Soueraigne Prince. Whereupon this vndoubtedly followeth, that there resteth Soueraigne Iurisdiction in the Prince. And therfore the Popes & their flatterers vnderstanding well, that Supreame Iurisdiction could neuer bee prooued to rest in the Popes, vnlesse first Appellation should be made to them, wrought by all subtilty, as hereafter we shall declare (by right or wrong they neither cared nor spared) to cause Appellations to be made to them: which thing when once they had obtained, that in all causes Ecclesiasticall Appellation might be made to the Popes: then and not before, this opinion was resolued, that Supreame Ecclesiasticall Iurisdiction was in the Popes. And therefore we prouing that Supreame and last Appellation doth by the law of God, belong to none but to the Soueraigne Prince; conclude vndoubtedly that Supreame Iurisdiction belongeth to him onely.

10. Heere a question may be mooued, whether Saint *Paul* did well and orderly when he appealed to *Cæsar*, and whether *Cæsar* was made iudge of these questions, which were Doctrines. We aunswere, Saint *Paul* had no meaning to make *Cæsar* iudge of any point of faith. But whereas hee was persecuted by the high Priests, who sought his life; in this matter of coactiue power Saint *Paul* giueth Iurisdiction to *Cæsar*. There is also a difference betweene that power which heathen Princes haue, and that which Christian Princes haue: for heathen Princes haue all power coactiue whatsoeuer the cause be: and without this helpe the Church could neuer deale in matters of this nature. Christian Princes besides this coactiue power, haue also, as appeareth in the gouernment of Israel, externall discipline in matters Ecclesiasticall.

11. Thus we haue declared the distinct right of the King and the Priest, after that they were distinguished by the written law of God: we haue prooued that the Soueraigne Iurisdiction coactiue resteth in the Prince by a right which God hath giuen, and therefore may not be taken away by man. It followeth to consider, how this right hath beene accordingly exercised by the godly Kings of Israel. *Iosua* commanded the people

ple

ple to be circumcised, and not Eleazerus, the cause was Ecclesiasticall, but to command in such causes declareth iurisdiction. *David* reduceth the Arke, he appointeth Priests, Leuites, Singers, Porters to serue at the Tabernacle: he assigneth Officers of the sonnes of *Aaron*. All which being matters Ecclesiasticall, the Prince as hauing soueraigne authority in both causes ordaineth. *Solomon* buildeth the Temple, and consecrateth it. *Asa* remoueth Idols, and dedicated the Altar of God that was before the porch of the Lord. *Iehosaphat* abolisheth Idolatry, cutteth downe the groues, sendeth Priests and Leuites, to teach in Townes and Cities: Setteth vp Iudges both ciuill and Ecclesiasticall, and commandeth both to iudge according to godlinesse, truth, and Iustice. Because in the words of *Iehosaphat*, these things are distinctly deliuered, we will obserue the whole place. The wordes are these, And hee set iudges in the land throughout all the strong Cities of Iuda, Citie by Citie. And said to the Iudges, take heed what you doe, for you execute not the iudgement of man, but of the Lord, and he will be with you in the cause and iudgement. Wherefore now let the feare of the Lord be vpon you, take heed and doe it, for there is no iniquitie with the Lord our God, neither respect of persons nor receiuing of reward.

Moreouer in Ierusalem did *Iehosaphat* set of the Leuites and of the Priests, and of the chiefe of the families in Israel, for the iudgement and cause of the Lord, and they returned to Ierusalem. And he charged them saying, thus shall you doe, in the feare of the Lord, with a perfect heart: And in euery cause that shall come to you of your brethren, that dwell in your Cities, betweene blood and blood, betweene Law and precept, Statutes and iudgements: you shall iudge them, and admonish them, that they trespasse not against the Lord, that wrath come not vpon you and vpon your brethren. And behold *Amariah* the high Preist, shall be the chiefe ouer you in all matters of the Lord.

12. From which words, we collect thus much, concerning the Kings Iurisdiction, and the things wherein it consisteth. First the King appointeth and placeth both Temporall and

Margin references:
2.Sam.6.
1.Paral.16.
1.Paral.24.
2.Paral.6.
2.Paral.15.
2.Chron.19.5
6.
7.
8.
9.
10.
11.

E   Ecclesi-

clefiafticall Iudges, and commandeth and chargeth them fo placed, to execute their functions faithfully, we inferre vpon this
command in both alike, that hee hath Iurifdiction ouer both
caufes. But here let me remember a trifling obiection, which
fome of our aduerfaries haue deuifed of late, they would diftinguifh betweene command and Iurifdiction : For they deny not
but that all fortes of perfons are vnder the Kings commaund
and gouernment : whom he may command, each to doe their
Office, and yet they ytterly deny the Kings Iurifdiction : and
tell vs that command and Iurifdiction muft not be hudled vp
together. Now let vs confider what hudling is in this, when the
Kings command and his Iurifdiction are fet as things depending and cohæring one to the other. When we fay the King
may command, we meane plainely as we fpeake, that the King
hath from God lawfull authoritie to command, and to punifh
them that breake his command : This is the common vnderftanding of the Kings command, But thefe Romifh fophifters
when they fay the King may command, do not vnderftand, neither will they acknowledge at any hand, that the King hath
lawfull authoritie from God, to punifh the breach of his command: for they vtterly deny that the King hath any authoritie to
punifh a Clarke, though he fhould breake his commandement.
And call you this a command? The King may command and
goo without, as the faying is. This is the deuils fophiftry, taken
vp by men hardned againft fhame, content to ftoupe downe to
gather vp the meaneft and bafeft fhifts to dazell the fimple.
The Iefuites refolue of this, as of a truth moft foundly concluded in their fchooles : That the King may not punifh Ecclefiafticall perfons: that the Kings Court may not heare , examine
and iudge them, though they fhould commit murders, adulte-
ries, robberies, or what other wickednefle foeuer. And yet
they tell vs, that the King may command them. Now to fay
one thing, and yet to let the world fee, that they are refolued
in the contrary : this fauoreth ftrongly of the fpirit of illufion,
whom reafon, learning, honeftie and all faileth, yet well fare a
bold and hardned face, which neuer faileth this generation.

13. The truth is, if the King haue not lawfull authority to
punifh

Anfwere to
the firft part
of reports, c. 9.

punish,he hath not lawfull authoritie to command , and punish he cannot vnlesse he hath authority to judge, or cause iudgement to be done; so that they who take away from the King power to iudge persons Ecclesiasticall, take from him power to punish, and consequently power to command : but the Doctrine of the Papists this day, (as shall hereafter appeare in his due place)taketh from the king power to iudge per sons Ecclesiastical,therefore, they rob him of power to punish, and to cōmaund;for nothing can more strongly take away the Kings command,then to deny him power to punish and to iudge. And yet they are not ashamed to tell vs,that they deny not the kings cōmand,but his Iurisdiction.Then to leaue these men with their absurd and perplexed contradictions: where the King may command,he may iudge and punish the breach of that command, and therefore his Iurisdiction appeareth in his lawfull authority and command. Then by this charge and commaund of *Iehosaphat*,is declared his Iurisdiction in these causes,wherein he hath this authority to command :for otherwise the Kings command is but as the word of a priuat man,or of a child,if he haue not power to iudge and punish.

14. Moreouer wheras *Iehosaphat* commandeth the Priests and Leuites to iudge betweene blood and blood, Law and precepts, statutes and iudgements: In things that concerned questions of blood, as when blood was shed by casualtie, in which case the party offending,had remedy by sanctuary, and the high Priest was the immediat iudge;as also in matters concerning lawes, precepts, statutes, iudgements, that is ordinances,ceremoniall or morall: In these things stood the Ecclesiasticall Iurisdiction which then was practised in the Church, for to take that distinction which we must often remember in this question,it is confessed that all Ecclesiasticall power is either of order or Iurisdiction. In both which the King hath a part,but differently : In the power of orders, the Kings part and office,was to see that things of that nature were orderly done,and the breach thereof punished, but himselfe was not to execute any thing,wherunto the Priests were apointed, by the power of their orders,as to offer incense,&c. Wherefore

Vzziah

2.Chron.26.

Vzziah was ſmitten with leproſie for medling with that part of the Prieſts office. Now Iuriſdiction is diuided into power internall, which as often wee haue ſaid, belongeth not to the King; and power externall: which power externall when it is coactiue, is nothing but that which wee call the Kings Iuriſdiction, though it be in matters Eccleſiaſtical. And this Iuriſdiction is here teſtified to be in *Iehoſaphat*, and from him deriued to all, to all iudges vnder him, both Temporall and Eccleſiaſticall. For as he commaunded the Temporall iudges, ſo in like ſort he commaunded the Eccleſiaſticall. And as the Eccleſiaſticall iudges might replie (if they had bene ſuch as now theſe are of the Romane Clergie) that Eccleſiaſticall iudgements were holy and the cauſe of God, and not of the King: ſo doth the King witneſſe of Temporall iudgements, for ſpeaking to Temporall iudges, he ſaith: you execute not the iudgements of man, but of the Lord. Then Temporall iudgements are the Lords cauſe aſwell as Eccleſiaſticall, and herein they differ not.

15. Now this Iuriſdiction which is in coactiue power wee prooue to be in the King, and onely in the King. (I ſpeake according to the forme of the ſtate of Iſrael in thoſe dayes wherof we now ſpeake, aunſwerable to which is the Soueraigne magiſtrate in any other ſtate.) This right I ſay, we prooue to bee onely in the King, and from him deriued to other iudges both Temporall and Spirituall, by theſe reaſons: firſt the King, and onely the King commaundeth both iudges to doe their duties in their ſeuerall places, and hath lawfull power to puniſh them if they doe otherwiſe: therfore the Kings Iuriſdiction coactiue is ouer both ſorts alike. The antecedent hath two parts, the firſt drawen from the expreſſe words of the Scripture in this text: the ſecond followeth by a neceſſitie. For the commaund of a King is ridiculous, and no commaund vnleſſe he haue authoritie to puniſh. The conſequence followeth by the very definition of Iuriſdiction, which will prooue the ſecond part of the antecedent. For this Iuriſdiction for which we plead, is defined by the moſt learned of the Church of Rome, authority coactiue. If it be authoritie, it may command; if coactiue it may puniſh: then it followeth, that where *Iehoſaphat* had firſt authoritie

1.

thoritie

thoritie to commaund and laſt to puniſh, that queſtionleſſe hee had this Soueraigne Iuriſdiction.

16. If againſt this any obiect, that the King may command in matters of orders, of preaching the Word, adminiſtring the Sacraments, &c. In all theſe things the King may lawfully command the parties to doe their duties, and may puniſh them if they doe otherwiſe : and yet no man will put the Kings Iuriſdiction in theſe matters of orders, Preaching, Sacraments, &c. For aunſwere, let me intreat the reader with attention to conſider theſe three things : Firſt to commaund, ſecondly to execute ; thirdly to puniſh. Iuriſdiction ſtandeth wholly in the firſt and laſt, and nothing at all in the ſecond : that is, in authoritie and not in action. So that though the King ſhould execute a thing which belongeth to his office, yet in the execution therof, his Iuriſdiction ſhould not appeare, howſoeuer his wiſedome, knowledge, and actiue vertues might appeare therein : for Iuriſdiction is in the authoritie of commaunding, and power of puniſhing, and ſupereminence that riſeth from both. And therefore in the preaching of the Word, adminiſtration of Sacraments, the King hath no part ; becauſe therein Iuriſdiction ſtandeth not : theſe things being matters of execution not of commaund : but the authoritie to commaund theſe things, by making or vrging lawes for them : and to puniſh the tranſgreſſion by corporall puniſhments ; this becauſe it includeth coactiue power, is in the Soueraigne Magiſtrate onely. If the Magiſtrate ſhould either neglect his dutie, as the heathen did ; or commaund falſe doctrines to be preached, as the Arian Emperours did : in this caſe the Church hath warrant to maintaine the truth, but without tumults and rebellion, and rather in patience to looſe their liues then to forgo any part of the truth.

17. Another reaſon to prooue this Soueraigne authoritie coactiue to be only in the King, and from him reſpectiuely deriued to both ſorts of iudges, may thus bee drawen. For the iudges Temporall, there is not ſo much queſtion made : all the doubt is of iudges Eccleſiaſticall, the chiefe of which iudges Eccleſiaſticall in the Church of Iſrael, was the high Prieſt. Then this Iuriſdiction whereof we ſpeake muſt be confeſſed to haue

2.

beene

been principally and originally, either in the king or in the high
Priest: but in the high Priest it was not, Therefore in the King
it muſt be. That it was not in the high Prieſt, we proue by theſe
reaſons. The high Prieſt is commaunded, corrected, puniſhed
and depoſed by the King, and not the King by the Prieſt: therefore the Soueraigne Iuriſdiction is not in the high Prieſt, but in
the King. Againe, the high Prieſts did neuer practiſe coactiue
authoritie, vnleſſe when they were Soueraigne Magiſtrates, as
ſometimes the high Prieſts in Iſrael were, but as high Prieſts
they had no ſuch power : for the cauſes betweene blood and
blood, which were of their cogniſance, are by the interpreters
vnderſtood ſuch caſes, wherein a man was killed by chaunce,
without the purpoſe, or againſt the will of the offender : in
which caſe the high Prieſt might graunt him the priuiledge of
ſanctuary : and ſo deliuer him from the auenger of blood : but
he had no power coactiue to inflict death, or ſuch puniſhments
at his pleaſure : which trueth was ſo conſtantly receiued and
preſerued in the Church afterward, that euen in the greateſt
power & higheſt ruffe of Poperie, the Church of Rome did not
take this full coactiue power, but onely proceeded to degrada-
tion, and then to deliuer men vp to the ſecular powers: which
was a ſecret confeſſion that they had no right to this power
coactiue, though they had vſurped many parts thereof.

18. A third reaſon to prooue this authoritie to bee in the
Ciuill Magiſtrate, is as I teached before, confirmed by the right
of Appellations. For in matters of coactiue Iuriſdiction, a man
might appeale from the high Prieſt to the King, as Saint *Paul*
did to *Cæſar :* which was vtterly vnlawfull for him to doe, vnleſſe he might as lawfully haue appealed to a King, if that ſtate
of Iſrael had then beene ruled by a King, as at other times it
was. For that right which Saint *Paul* giueth to *Nero*, to heare
Appellations, he would vndoubtedly yeeld to *Dauid*, or *Ezekias*, or any other godly King in his owne Dominions. Wherefore it followeth, that either Saint *Paul* muſt be condemned for
yeelding an vnlawful power to Emperors : or Kings muſt haue
the ſame priuiledge : which thing being admitted in matters
Eccleſiaſticall, doth inuincibly prooue the Kings Iuriſdiction
in

in such matters.   The same thing is also confirmed from those 4.
words of the Apostle, he is the minister of God : and, he bea- Rom.13.4.
reth the sword. If the Magistrate be the minister of God ; then
he hath full authoritie and Iurisdiction from God, whose minister and vicegerent he is : if he beare the sword, hee hath all
power coactiue : for coactiue power doth alwayes follow the
sword, which God hath giuen to the Ciuill Magistrate to beare.
Therefore *Ioh. Chrysostom* saith, *Regi corpora commissa sunt, sa-*
cerdoti anima, rex maculas corporum remittit, sacerdos maculas
peccatorum : ille cogit, hic exhortatur: ille habet arma sensibilia, hic
arma spiritualia. Hom.4. de verb. Esa. vide dom. Then the true
difference betweene the Magistrate and the Priest, concerning
this point, is ; *Ille cogit, hic exhortatur :* so that coactiue power
is left wholy to the Magistrate. *Ambrose* likewise speaking of the authoritie of the Church, and of Bishops, saith :
Coactus repugnare non noui, arma enim nostra preces sunt & la-
chryma. orat. in Auxent. where he declareth the difference betweene these two powers, leauing nothing to the Church, but
preces & lachrymas, wherin there is no coaction. In which sense
Thomas Aquinas saith : *vindicta qua fit authoritate publica pote-*
statis, secundum sententiam iudicis, pertinet ad iusticiam commu-
tatiuam. 2.2. qu. 8. art 1. Therefore vindicatiue power or coaction belonges not to the Church, but the Magistrate that ex-
erciseth commutatiue iustice.

19. In regard of which high power Princes are called Gods, I Psal. 82.
haue said you are Gods. And because an aduersarie of late hath Mat. Tortus Pa-
told vs, that this name is giuen aswell to Ecclesiasticall gouer- piensis.
nours as to Kings : we reply, that it cannot be shewed that this
name is giuen to Ecclesiasticall gouernours, but either where
such gouernours haue receiued authoritie from the Ciuill Magistrate, or where themselues are the chiefe Magistrates : so
that it is a name giuen in respect of Soueraigne power. For to
manifest the Soueraigne eminency of the Prince, compare the
Prince and Priest together, and by this comparison wee shall
euidently know the truth: for we find the Prince called a God,
not onely in respect of the people, but in respect of the Priest
also. Where the Lord himselfe speaketh to *Moses* of *Aaron*
                                                            com-

Exod. 4. 16.

comparing their power and offices together, he saith thus : [He shall be thy spokesman vnto the people, and he shall be as thy mouth, and thou shalt be to him in stead of God.] In this comparing of these two great offices, *Moses* is the directour; *Aaron* the interpretour and preacher. Where the Prince or Soueraign Magistrate is called a God, not onely in respect of the people, as in diuers other Scriptures : but in respect of the Priest, thou shalt be to him, euen to *Aaron*, as a God. We find then that the Prince is called a God in respect of the Priest, but we can neuer find that the Priest is called a God in respect of the Prince. This declareth a Soueraigne authoritie of the Prince in matters of God, and of Gods true Religion. For he who by his office is to establish true Religion in his dominions, doth heerein represent a liuely ex mple, both of the goodnesse and power of God : and therefore Magistrates are called Gods, as being Gods Vicegerents for establishing of true Religion.

Moses Legislator & interpres Dei.

20. And this our Sauiour Christ confirmeth, for whereas *Psal.* 82. They are called Gods, I haue said you are Gods; Our Lord expoundeth that place, declaring in what sense they are so called. For he saith: [If he called them Gods, vnto whom the word of God was giuen, and the Scripture cannot be broken, &c.] Then the Magistrates who are here called Gods, are such to whom the word of God is giuen. For further declaration of the truth, let this question be demaunded : to whom is the word of God principally giuen? to whose Soueraigne custodie is the word of God committed? The words of our Sauiour Christ containe an aunswere, to the Ciuill Magistrate. For it is certaine that all that Psalme whence Christ taketh those words, is wholly and intirely vnderstood of the Ciuill Magistrates, and not of Priests or Ecclesiasticall gouernours. Why then? and is not the word of God giuen to Ecclesiasticall gouernours aswell as to Kings? Yes verily, but diuersly : for to Ecclesiasticall gouernours the knowledge of the word is giuen to publish by preaching. [For the Priests lippes shall preserue knowledge, and they shall seeke the law at his mouth; for hee is the messenger of the Lord of hostes.] Then if the question be asked, to whom is the word giuen by the way of knowledge

Ioh. 10. 35.

Malach. 2. 7.

to

to preach and publish it? The answere is, to the Priest: but
Christ speaketh not here of that manner of giuing the word,
but he toucheth that Commission which is giuen to Magistrates. For to Magistrates it is not giuen by way of especiall
knowledge to preach it; but by way of an especiall commission, to keepe it, to establih it by authoritie, to command obedience vnto it, and to punish the violatours of it. This is the
authority of a Christian Prince, for he hath called them Gods
to whom the word was giuen: Whom hath hee called Gods?
Ciuill Princes: for of such, onely of such, that Psalme speaketh.
Why are they called Gods? Becauſe they are Gods vicegerents by their authority to establish Gods wo d. Therefore
they are acknowledged to bee *custodes vtriuſ ue tabula*, for
which cause it was an ancient ceremony in the Church of Israˉ
el, that at the Kings Coronation the Booke of God should be
giuen into the hand of the King, as we read in t e Coronation   *2.Reg.11. 12.*
of *Ioaſh*: Which thing is confirmed by a comm undemant in
the Law, why was this thing ſo ſolemnly comm nded? ſo reli-   *Deut.17.18.*
giouſly preached? but to ſhew that God hath committed the
care of Religion principally to the King, that b/ the vtmoſt of
his power and authority, it might be established in his Dominions.

21. This doth proue that *Moſes* was a Prince and not a
Priest, and *Aaron* a Priest but not a Prince: becauſe *Moſes* is
called *Aarons* God, but *Aaron* is not called *Moſes* his God, but
his mouth. Which thing though it bee ſo euident, as that it
ſeemeth to be the vndertaking of an idle and vn-neceſſary diſcourſe to proue it: yet becauſe many bookes are of late filled
with this conceit, that *Moſes* was a Prieſt, which thing is taken
as an eſpeciall ground to build vp the Popes temporall Monar-
chie: Let vs in a few wordes refute this fancy. *Franciſcus Bozius* who vndertaketh to proue this, taketh a foundation ſo ruinous and fallacious, that it is no maruell if his whole building
be anſwerable, for he concludeth that *Moſes* was a Prieſt properly ſo called becauſe, *Pſal.99*. it is written, *Moſes* and *Aaron*
among his Prieſts, and *Samuel* among ſuch as call vppon his
name. The anſwere is eaſie and vulgarly knowne, for *Coha-*

nim

Psalm. 99.6.

So 2. Sam. 20.
26. Where
Tharg.hath a
Prince, or
mighty.

nim (which word is there vsed) signifieth both Priests and Ciuill gouernors. It is vsed for Ciuill gouernors which stand in some honourable place. *2. Sam. 8.18.* where the sonnes of *Dauid* are called כהבים which cannot be translated Priests, as the Latin vulgar hath it. Though this word כהן somtimes be takē, for a Priest, yet it is certaine that *Dauids* sonnes were not Priests, but chiefe rulers about the King, as it is expounded *1. Chron.18.17.* Then we answere that no proofe can bee drawne from this word כהן to proue *Moses* a Priest, because the word is ambiguous, applyed both to Priests and to Ciuill gouernours. And therefore the word is fitly applied to *Moses* and *Aaron*, comprising both their Offices in one short word. But that *Moses* was no Priest, we prooue thus. If he were a Priest, it must be either before that *Aaron* and his successors were assumed to that Office, or after. Before the law assumed *Aaron* and his sonnes to be Priests *Moses* could not bee Priest, because the Priesthood was annexed to the birth-right. But *Moses* was not the first borne of *Amram*, but *Aaron* was the

Num. 33. 39.

eldest, for we read *Num. 33. Aaron* was one hundred twentie three yeares old when he died. But *Moses* out liuing *Aaron* was

Deut. 34. 7.

but one hundred twenty yeares old when he dyed. *Deut. 34.* Therefore *Aaron* was questionlesse the elder brother. If any obiect that the birth-right was sometimes taken from the eldest by an especiall appointment of God, as appeareth in *Sem* and *Iacob*; I answere, this cannot help in this point, for *Aaron* was so farre from loosing this priuiledge of his birth-right, by any appointment of God, that he had the Priesthood famously confirmed to him and to his posterity. So that neither by the law of nature, nor by any precept of God, can *Aaron* be said to loose any priuiledge that belonged to the Priesthood. Then before the institution of the Leuiticall Priesthood, *Moses* could not be Priest. After the institution thereof, the Priesthood was so appropriated to *Aarons* house, that none could be Priests but *Aaron* and his sonnes onely. Therefore it was not possible that *Moses* could be a Priest at all, either before the consecration of *Aaron*, or after.

    22 Another reason may be drawn from those places, which
declare

declare that *Iosua* was appointed by God to succeede *Moses*, and to gouerne as he did. In all which places it appeareth, that *Iosua* succeeded *Moses* in his place and function, and was that in Ifrael, in his time, which *Moses* was before him. But it is certaine that *Iosua* was no Prieft: therfore as certaine that *Moses* was no Prieft. For *Iosua* was the full and entire succeffour of *Moses*. The fame appeareth by the whole courfe of *Moses* his gouernment. Who commandeth as a Prince, is obeyed as a Prince, both by the Priefts and people. By which command in matters temporall and ecclefiafticall: if they suppofe that a Priefthood is proued: by the fame reafon all the Kings of Ifrael may as well be concluded to haue been Priefts. For they commaunded in all fuch thinges as *Moses* did. Some obiect that *Moses* facrificed, *Exod.*24. But this obiection is friuolous. For the words of the Scripture are againft it. It is exprefly faid, that *Moses* fent young men to facrifice: thefe were the firft borne of the 12 Tribes. For this was before the inftitution of the Leuiticall Priefthood. If any obiect that *Moses* did something which might feeme to belong to the office of a Prieft: I anfwer, fo did the Kings of Ifraell fome things which might feeme to belong to the office of a Prieft. For *Iofias*, when all the people were gathered together, read in their eares all the words of the booke of the couenant. Which thing might feeme to belong to the Priefts office. So true is that principle of our common Law, founded vpon the profound principles of diuinitie and good gouernment: *Rex eft perfona mixta*; becaufe he hath both temporall and ecclefiafticall iurifdiction.

23 And thus haue wee declared the Kings right vnder the Law; from the precept of the Law, & practife of godly Kings. Thus did *Ezekiah*, thus did *Iofiah*, and others: and in fo doing, they vfurped no vnlawfull power, but ftood faithfull in the execution of that lawfull right, which GOD committed to them. From this commiffion they may not turne either to the right hand, or to the left. For as it was a great finne in *Vzziah* on the one fide, to vfurpe the Priefts office: fo fhould it be a great finne on the other fide, for a King to neglect any part of a Kings office. From all which, wee collect the power of a Prince in

Num.27.17.18
Deut.31.14.
Iof.1.17.

Exod.24.5.

2.Reg.23.2.

1463773

2.Chron.26.

matters

matters ecclesiasticall to stand in these things. He is to establish
all ecclesiasticall Lawes, for which no power is sufficient without his.   Neither is it reason that they should establish Lawes,
in whom there is no power to defend and maintaine the Maie-
stie of those Lawes so made. He is to punish all transgressours
of those Lawes, hee is to appoint ecclesiasticall Ministers their
places, to be Iudges in matters of ecclesiasticall Lawes : and if
they offend, to punish them, hee may place and displace according to their merits : So *Salomon* displaced *Abiathar*, & made
Zadock high Priest in his roome. But because of late, suborned
Mat. Tortus speaking of this example, saith, that *Salomon* did
displace the high Priest as he was a Prophet; not as hee was a
King : let vs by the way open the vanity of this shift. The fault
that *Abiathar* had committed was worthy of death, as *Salomon*
saith : [Thou art worthy of death.] But yet hee shewed him
mercy, because hee had borne the Arke of the Lord before his
Father *Dauid*; and had suffered in all things wherein *Dauid*
was afflicted. So that the thing which *Salomon* did to *Abiathar*,
he did as iudge of life and death. To be a Iudge of life & death,
was not the office of a Prophet, but of the King : therefore
Salomon did it not as a Prophet, but as a King. Againe, the
Prophets office was extraordinary, but this thing is so far from
an extraordinary example, that wee see rather that *Salomon*
doth mitigate the ordinary punishment of that crime which
Abiathar had committed. Moreouer, to punish or to release
the punishment of treason, belongeth not to the office of a
Prophet, but of the King : but *Salomon* in this action punishing
the treason of *Abiathar*, releaseth some part of it. All which
proue the distorted shift of *Tortus*, to be so vaine and shamelesse, that the blushing Hat of a Cardinall, is not broad enough
to couer the shame. In these things, and in supreame appellation, standeth Ecclesiasticall iurisdiction, which by diuine right
was placed in these Kings, and by them practised.

1. Reg 2.26.

CHAP.

CHAP. IIII.

Externall Coactiue Iurisdiction was not left by Christ to his
Church, nor practised by the Church all that while, that
the Church was without Christian Magistrates : where-
in is declared the Iurisdiction of the Church, and of Bi-
shops, that the power of excommunication proceeded not
to Coaction.

Ow let vs make search in the Church of Christians, wherein we will consider first the state
of the Church, after it was called by Christ and
his Apostles, and gouerned by the Fathers for
the space of the first three hundred yeeres : in
all which time no Christian was the Soueraigne
Magistrate. In this time it will be to good purpose to search
the Iurisdiction of the Church, for this is the time wherein it
will most cleerely appeare. And Christ that appointeth all times
& states for his Church, appointed that all this time she should
be without Princes for her nourcing Fathers : that by wanting
it so long, we might vnderstand the greatnesse of this blessing.
But when the Church of Rome grew insolent by abusing this
blessing, taking the right of Princes from them, and thereby re-
mouing the ancient bounds of the Ordinances which God had
set of old, then it was not to bee marueiled, that such iudgements followed of blindnesse and ignorance among the people, of confusion and contempt vpon Princes and Kings: which
iudgements haue beene so famously apparant in the sight of
the world. But let vs proceed to the examination of the
Churches Iurisdiction, for if we consider what Iurisdiction
Iesus Christ left to his Church, it will consequently appeare
what Iurisdiction is in Ciuill Princes : for all that Christ gaue
not to his Church, remaineth with Princes.

2. The places from which they would prooue Iurisdiction,
are these : *Mat.*18. [Whatsoeuer you shall binde on earth, $^{Mat.18.18.}$

F 3   shall

shall be bound in heauen.] And, [whosoeuers sinnes you retaine, shall be retained.] Now these places make no proofe of
this Iurisdiction which is in question. For all Popish writers
that I could see vpon this question, acknowledg these Scripturs
not to be meant of externall Iurisdiction coactiue, which is our
question, but of the inward power of remitting of sinnes, practised within the court of conscience by the power of Gods spirit, and declared by the Priest, and ordinarily practised in excommunication, or otherwise. The greater condemnation de-
serueth that Catholike Diuine, who to disprooue the Iurisdiction of Princes, and to proue the Popes pretended Iurisdiction bringeth these places of Scripture which speake of neither.
Other places they cite, as that : [Thou art *Peter*, and vpon this
rocke will I build my Church : and I will giue to thee the keyes
of the kingdome of heauen.] And, [*Simon* louest thou mee?
feede my Lambes, &c.] These and such like places they bring
to proue the Popes Iurisdiction. All of this sort are throughly
handled with exact iudgement and learning, in that worthy
conference written by Doctor *Raynolds* of blessed memory :
which booke as a gantlet of one of the worthies of our Church
hath lien long betweene vs, and the host of the Philistims :
and none of our aduersaries hath had the courage to take it vp
and to aunswere it.

Answere to the
fift part of Re-
ports.

*Mat.*16.18.

*Ioh.*20.15.

3. It is sufficient for vs to pleade, that none of the auncient
Fathers did euer expound these Scriptures thus ; or did euer
dreame of such senses, as they haue found of late out of their
owne decretall Epistles. It is sufficient that some of their owne
best learned writers, yea some of their most learned Popes, before they were Popes; haue with such learning and iudgement
refuted their new deuised expositions of these Scriptures, as
that from themselues and out of their owne mouthes, God hath
drawen testimonies to ouerthrow these carnall and absurd expositions of Scriptures. *Iohn Gerson* saith, that these texts thus
by the Popes flatterers applied to prooue his Iurisdiction, are
vnderstood by them : *Grossé & non secundum regulam Euangelicam.* And *Æneas Siluius*, hath with great life and learning o-
uerthrowen these grosse and corrupt expositions : of whom we
shall

*Serm. pro viagio
regis Rom. di-
rec.*1.
*Lib. de gestis
Basil. consil.*

shall speake hereafter in due place, where it will fully appeare
that thefe expofitions of Scripture are by the learned, free, and
iudicious men of that fide, acknowledged to bee inuented by
flatterers, as the fame Pope *Pius* the fecond, witneffeth : to
be new and ftraunge, and to be vrged by miferable and wretched foules, which will not vnderftand that thefe challenges of
their Iurifdiction, are nothing but either the words of the
Popes themfelues; that would inlarge their fringes without
meafure:or of their flatterers who being blinded by ambition,
and caried with the winde of vaineglory, doe flatter the Popes
in hope of reward. Though now thofe flatterers haue gotten
the vpper hand in the Councell of Trent; and haue vfurped the
name of the Church, who before were alwayes efteemed a bafe
company, ftanding for the Popes Iurifdiction againft the graue
and learned men of that Church.

4. Then for the places of Scripture which they bring for
this Iurifdiction, we fay with their owne beft learned men, that
they are (in that fenfe wherein they vfe them) new deuifes
drawen of late by ftrange and abfurd contortions into this new
flattering fenfe, by the Popes flatterers, againft the auncient
expofitions of the Fathers and Doctors of the Church. Concerning the Iurifdiction which Chrift left to his Church, let all
the Scriptures be fearched, and there will nothing be found of
externall Iurifdiction confifting in power coactiue : but all that
Chrift left was partly, yea principally, inward and fpirituall
power, partly externall for eftablifhing doctrines of faith and
good order in the Church, by Councels, determinations, iudicature, fpirituall cenfures, excommunication : depofing and
difpatching of the difobedient, fo farre as the Church could
proceede without coactiue power. For by this fpirituall power without coaction, the Church was called, faith was planted,
diuils were fubdued, the nations were taken out of the power
of darkeneffe, the world was reduced to the obedience of
Chrift; by this power the Church was gouerned for three hundred yeeres together without any coactiue Iurifdiction. But
what coactiue power may worke in the Church without this,
we haue a lamentable experience in the prefent court of Rome,

falling

falling away from the truth, and from the comfort of the spirit, and therefore from the true vse of the power of the spirit of God : when the Popes being destitute of this power of the spirit, tooke vpon them power aboue the Ciuill Magistrate, practising wholly coactiue power which they called Spirituall, when they had forsaken the power of the spirit and reiected it from them.

5. The Iurisdiction which the Apostles practised was partly from the commission of Christ, spirituall : partly from the law of Nature, and from the example of that gouernment which was established in the Church of the Iewes. The things which belonged to Apostolicall Iurisdiction, either concerned the gouernment of the ministery, or of the whole Church. Touching the gouernment of the ministery, these things belonged to the Apostles so long as they liued, and afterward to Bishops their successours. First a power to ordaine ministers, Thus did *Paul* and *Barnabas* when they called Churches through Lycaonia, Pisidia, and Pamphylia : [They ordained Elders in euery Church.] Elders, that is, Pastors, Preachers to preserue the Doctrine continually which the Apostles had once planted. And this charge to ordaine Elders or Priests, did the Apostles leaue also to them that succeeded in the gouernment of the Church. This commission Saint *Paul* gaue to *Titus.* [For this cause I left thee in Crete, that thou shouldest continue to redresse the things that remaine, and ordaine Elders in euery city, as I appointed thee:] which ordaining signifieth also institution in the place or cure they ministred in.

6. The Apostles had also in themselues, and left to their successours, power and Iurisdiction to command those Pastors which thus they had ordained, to preach the truth without mixture of false doctrines. This power as Saint *Paul* had in himselfe, so he left the same to *Timothie*, and consequently to others. [As I besought thee to abide still in *Ephesus*, when I departed to *Macedonia*, so doe, that thou maist command some that they teach no other doctrine.] These were the principall parts of Iurisdiction which the Apostles left to their successors, to continue in the Church for euer. For the end and vse

1.

*Act.*14.23.

Titus 1.5.

2.

*1.Tim.*1.3.

vfe of this gouernment is perpetuall, as to ordaine Preachers, and to fee that they fo ordained, fhould teach the truth without herefie. It followeth certainely, that fuch gouernours as the Apoftles themfelues ordained in the Church for thefe perpetuall vfes, are to remaine perpetuall gouernours in the Chutch. Thus was the gouernement of Bifhops placed by the Apoftles, to ftand and continue till the end of the world, becaufe the Apoftles placed fuch for the ordination of minifters, and the preferuation of true Doctrines. For they who aunfwere that thefe offices and places wherin the Apoftles placed *Timothie* and *Titus*, were either extraordinarie, or to indure for a fhort time, do not confider the end and vfe of thefe places: which end and vfe is neither extraordinary nor temporary, but ordinary and perpetuall. For minifters muft be ordained, & commanded to prefcrue the truth without herefie, as long as the Church ftandeth. Then the neceffitie and vfe of the ends, will prooue the like neceffitie and vfe of thefe gouernours, which by the Apoftles were placed for thefe endes.

7. Another part of this Iurifdiction, and depending vpon the laft, was that which the Apoftle leaueth in commiffion to *Titus*, ἐπισομίζειν, to ftoppe their mouthes. For which caufe the Angell of the Church of Thyatira is reproued by Chrift, becaufe he fuffered a falfe Prophetefse to teach, and to decciue the people, and to make them commit fornication, and to eate meat facrificed to idols. If *Titus* be commaunded to put fome to filence, and the other reproued for fuffering a falfe teacher to teach; then the gouernours of the Church haue authoritie and Iurifdiction in thefe things : but how farre it is extended, we fhall confider hereafter. But becaufe it may be queftioned whether ἐπισομίζειν be to filence minifters, or to conuince them by argument. To this wee aunfwere, that albeit wee denie not conuiction by reafon to be alfo included in the word, yet there is a further meaning of iudiciall proceeding by authoritie heere vnderftood; which thing will appeare by conference of this and other places. For Saint *Paul* hauing firft declared that he left *Titus* at Crete to ordaine Elders, defcribeth what manner of men they muft be that are fo to be ordained. For a Bifhop

*Tit.*1.11.
*Apoc.*2.20.

*Tit.*1.5.

7.

G

10. shop must be vnreproueable, &c. Then he declareth that many
be otherwise: for there are many disobedient and vaine talkers,
and deceiuers, &c. If the question be demaunded, what shall
be done to these deceiuers? the wordes immediatly following

11. containe an aunswere: whose mouthes must be stopped. So
that the sense of these words is the same with that which hee

1.Tim.1.3. saith to *Timothie*, charging him; to command some that they
teach no other Doctrine. Then the word containeth not only
conuiction by argument, but Iurisdiction also. For conuiction by argument onely would not haue serued to suppresse the
false Prophetesse of Thyatyra. And if a minister be accused of
heresie, or such like, he was to be iudged by such as were set in
chiefe authoritie in the Clergie. For that there was a consistory and iudiciall proceedings set vp, it is euident; and no lesse e-
uident that the Bishop was iudge. [Against an Elder (saith S.

1.Tim.5.19. *Paul* to *Timothie*) receiue none accusation, but vnder two or
three witnesses.] Now he that is appointed to heare accusati-
ons, to receiue the testimonies of witnesses, is placed in a place
of iudgement with Iurisdiction: and therefore hath authoritie
not onely to conuince by argument, but also to proceed iudicially against false teachers, and to put them to silence.

8. Thus farre was Iurisdiction practised ouer ministers, the

4. things which follow touched the whole Church. Another
part of Iurisdiction practised by the Apostles, touching the
Church in generall; was to call Councels for the determination of such controuersies, as were raised vp by them that troubled the doctrines of the truth, and peace of the Church. Such

Acts 15.6. was the Councell gathered by the Apostles, *Act*.15. Consisting
of Apostles and Elders, that is, of persons Ecclesiasticall, wher-

7. in sentence proceeded after good deliberation and great disc-
tation. This is the greatest power or Iurisdiction of the Church:
because the whole or many chiefe parts together, is greater
then any one part.

9. Further concerning the extension of this Iurisdiction, it cannot be denied but that there is a power in the Church, not only internall, but also of externall Iurisdiction: of internall power there is no question made. Externall Iurisdiction being vnderstood

derstood all that is practised in externall Courts or consistories,
is either definitiue, or mulctatiue. Authority definitiue in matters of faith and religion, belongeth to the Church. Mulctatiue power may be vnderstood, either as it is referred to spirituall censures, or as it is with coaction; as it standeth in spirituall
censures, it is the right of the Church, and was practised by
the Church, when the Church was without a Christian Magistrate, and since. But coactiue Iurisdiction was neuer practised
by the Church, when the Church was without Christian Magistrates: but was alwayes vnderstoode to belong to the ciuill
Magistrate, whether he were Christian or heathen. We denie
not but that the Apostles did sometimes take vengeance vpon
the disobedient, but that was not by the materiall sword (in the
power whereof we place coaction) but by the spirituall sword,
which alwayes shewed it selfe in their Ministery, sometimes in
an extraordinary manner, as in the striking of *Ananias* and *Sa-* | *Acts.5.*
phira with present death: in the striking of *Elimas* the Sorcerer
with blindnesse, and such like. These were signes of extraordinary power, but wee seeke heere the ordinary Iurisdiction of
the Apostles, which they left to their successours.

10 Vpon these grounds ioyned with the assured knowledge
of the History of those times, the auncient Fathers deliuer it as
a truth neuer questioned, nor doubted, that in the gouernment
of the Church, the Bishops are the vndoubted successours of the | *Lib.5.*
Apostles. *Irenæus* speaking of heretikes, saith: *Omnes hi poste-*
riores sunt episcopis, quibus apostoli tradiderunt ecclesias. If Bishops were before any heretikes, they were questionlesse in the
Apostles time, and by the Apostles instituted, because some he-
retikes were euen in the Apostles time. *Irenæus* saith also: *Ha-* | *Lib.3. cap.3.*
bemus annumerare eos, qui ab Apostolis instituti sunt episcopi in Ec-
clesiis. And a little after: *Quibus etiam ipsas Ecclesias commit-*
tebant. And againe in the same place: *Quos & successores reli-*
querunt, suum ipsorum locum magisterij tradentes. Cyprian saith, | *Cyprian. Epist.*
Potestas peccatorum remittendorum Apostolis data est, & Eccle- | *75.*
siis, quas illi à Christo missi constituerunt, et episcopis qui eis ordina-
tione vicaria successerunt. The same hee hath also *Epist.* 69. | *Epist. ad Eua-*
Hierome saith, *Potentia diuitiarum & paupertatis humilitas vel* | *grium.*

G 2   *subli-*

sublimiorem vel inferiorem Episcopum non facit. Caterum omnes Apostolorum successores sunt. It were hard to kicke against all these pricks. Against so euident grounds of Scripture, so expresse testimonies of Fathers, to deuise a new gouernment of the Church. Leauing the auncient and knowne gouernment, which hath the testimonie of those that liued in the first age, and heard and sawe those that were endued with miraculous gifts : (as *Irenæus* testifieth of himselfe, that hee heard those which spake by the spirit in all languages, and sawe them who often raised the dead to life againe.) Leauing, I say, the testimonie of these, whose name and authority is so reuerend in the Church, and striuing for a gouernment which came but of late to the knowledge of men; seemeth to proceede from affections too much blinded with the loue of innouation.

11 But though this be true, that Bishops in the gouernment of the Church succeede the Apostles, yet we are cautelously to distinguish betweene the things, wherein they succeede the Apostles : and those things which since the Apostles times haue beene added to their gouernment by godly Princes. For the preseruation of true doctrine in the Church, the Bishops are the great watch-men. Herein they are authorized by God. If Princes withstand them in these things, they haue warrant not to obey Princes, because with these things Christ hath put them in trust. Therefore S. *Paul* saith not, that it is the Kings office, but the Bishops, to commaund that they teach no other doctrine. Vpon which ground S. *Ambrose* was bolde to withstand *Valentinian* Emperour. For *Ambrose,* as the watch-man of the Church of Millaine, would not suffer *Auxentius* an Arian Bishop, to haue any place to teach in his Diocesse. *Auxentius* complained to the Emperour, as the contention grew thus betweene them, the one like a vigilant watch-man, seeking to remoue all dangers from his flocke, the other like a Wolfe seeking to spoile : at the earnest entreaty of *Auxentius* the Emperour, willed that the cause betweene these two might be heard in the *Ecclesiasticall consistorie,* and that the Emperour might sit as Iudge in the cause. This thing *Ambrose* vtterly denied : and of this hee writeth thus to the Emperour. *Quando audisti clemen-*

Lib. 5.
Lib. 2. ca. 57.

1. Tim. 1. 3.

Ambrose lib. 4.
Epist. 32.

Idem ibid.

clemẽtissime imperator, in causa fidei, Laicos de Episcopo iudicasse?
And againe : *Si vel Scripturarum seriem diuinarum, vel cætera
tempora retractemus, quis est qui abnuat in causa fidei, in causa
inquam fidei Episcopos, solere de imperatoribus Christianis, non imperatores de Episcopo iudicare?* And in another place : *Volens Orat. in Auxent.
nunquam ius deseram, coactus repugnare non noui; arma enim nostra preces sunt & lachryma.* This example of *Ambrose* his courage, is worthily commended by all posterity, wherein this
worthy man seemeth to direct a true rule of obedience. For
Iustina the Emperours mother, seeing she could not draw *Ambrose* to fauour the Arians, purposed to put him from the gouernment of the Church. Which thing would haue beene effected, if he had not refused to appeare in *the Court*, where the
Emperour was to sit as Iudge. There appeared in him courage,
godlinesse, and exact obedience, all truly tempered. He denieth the Emperour to be a sufficient Iudge in a cause of faith and
religion. *In causa fidei, in causa inquam fidei.* For this hee re-
peateth precisely, desirous to be rightly vnderstood : he would
rather die then admit such an example as to betray the trueth,
and that commission and charge wherein G O D had set him.
And yet if the Emperour would by force doe any thing, he denieth that there is any power in him, or in the Church to resist
by force. The faith and right of the Church, was not, in his
iudgement, to be maintained by force and armes, but by prayers and teares. Thus resolute is this godly man in the cause of
faith against the Emperour : but in other causes he claimeth no
priuiledge, no immunities, and therefore in the same place hee
saith : *Si tributum petit imperator non negamus, agri Ecclesiæ tributum soluunt. Athanasius ad solitar. vitam agentes* ; speaking to
Constans the Emperour, saith : Let religious Bishops perswade
the Emperor, that he corrupt not the Church, nor mingle the
Romane Empire with Ecclesiasticall constitutions. And *Hilla- Lib. ad Constan-
tium August.
rie* writing to *Constantius*, saith to the same purpose : *Prouideat
& decernat clementia tua, &c.* Let your clemency prouide and
establish, that all Iudges to whom the care of publike businesse
belongeth, may abstaine from religious constitutions. Thus
did the auncient Bishops gouerne the Church, not suffering

any

any King or Emperour, to meddle with the determinations of matters of faith: For of such matters are these testimonies to be vnderstood, and onely of such. In like manner *Chrysostome* resisted *Gaina* generall of the forces of Arcadius Emperour. Who would haue had a Church within Constantinople for himselfe and the Arians. The Emperour was willing to gratifie him, or not willing to displease him for his greatnesse; but *Iohn Chrysostome* did vtterly denie it, as a thing vnlawfull. Thus by the warrant of Scriptures and examples of Fathers we giue to *Cæsar* all coactiue power which is due to him : but spirituall gouernment we giue not to him: this is that gouernment which is reserued to Bishops, as the Apostles successours. After which example *Gregorie* the first writeth thus, *Serenissimi domini animum non ignoro, quod se in causis sacerdotalibus miscere non soleat.* Gregorie calleth those causes with which the Emperours medled not, *causas sacerdotales :* meaning therby the same which *Ambrose* calleth causes of faith.

Theodoret.lib.5. cap.32.

Lib.3.epist.20.

12. Besides this Spirituall gouernment which is peculiar to Bishops, there is also another part of gouernment giuen to Bishops; which commeth from Princes, which *Constantine* first gaue, as hereafter we shall declare. Of this *Chrysostome* saith : *Iam vero pars illa,quam Episcopum tractare in iudicys conuenit,infinita odia , infinitas offensiones parit ; quæ ipsa præterquam quod negotijs quamplurimis plena est, tam multas etiam difficultates affert, quam multas ne forenses quidem iudices sustinent :* and much more to the same purpose. *Augustine* complaineth that he was too much troubled with these matters of iudicature. And *Synesius* professeth that he can not attend both businesses. *Antiquum tempus* (saith he) *tulit eosdem & sacerdotes & iudices, etenim Ægypty, Hebræorumq; gens multum temporis à sacerdotibus gubernata est;* and a little after, *Non condemno Episcopos qui versantur in negotiis, &c. Si qui vero sunt,qui à rerum diuersarum aggressione non læduntur,illis forsitan possunt simul & sacerdotio fungi , & ciuitatibus præesse.*

De sacerdotio lib.3.

August.epist.9.

Synes.epist.57.

In all these parts of Episcopal Iurisdiction,which either by Apostolicall right or institution, or by the fauour of Princes,haue beene giuen to them : the Pope hath intruded like a Foxe,and main-

maintaineth his intrusion like a Lion. For as Christ left an equa-
litie and paritie among his Apostles, often affirming and con-
firming that one of them should not be greater then another;
and yet the Apostles were in gouernement aboue other Ministers : and that by the institution of Christ himselfe : For the
Lord after that he had chosen his twelue Apostles, did chuse also seuentie Disciples [and sent them two and two before him
into euery citie where he himselfe should come] saith S. *Luke* ;
then Christ himselfe is the authour of this order in the Church:
which the Church hath since that time euer held, the Bishops
succeeding the Apostles, as the inferiour Pastors succeeded the
seuentie Disciples: So the Apostles after them left the like equa-
lity among Bishops, that one of them should not bee aboue a-
nother; and yet Bishops in gouernment aboue other Ministers:
for Iurisdiction was neuer in the multitude, but in gouernours :
the Bishops thē being the gouernors after the Apostles, the like
Iurisdictiō was in all. As *Cypr.* saith, *Episcopatus vnus est cuius à
singulis pars in solidum tenetur.* And *Hierom* saith, *Vbicunq, fuerit Episcopus siue Romæ, siue Eugabij, &c, eiusdem meriti, eiusdem est & sacerdotij.* Which power in Bishops the Pope hath
by surreption drawen to himselfe, and now out of his fulnesse
imparteth to Bishops at his pleasure ; as if hee were the fountaine of Iurisdiction.

13. As thus he hath drawen their auncient right from Bishops : so hath he drawen from Temporall Princes that which
of auncient right was theirs : we shall better vnderstand what
he hath taken from Temporall Princes, if we consider the true
limits betweene the power of Princes, and the power of the
Church. We say therefore that the Iurisdiction of the Church
was neuer extended to coactiue power : because God hath giuen all coactiue power to the Ciuill Magistrate, to whom hee
hath committed the sword. And as coactiue power belongeth
not to the Church, so neither dooth it belong to the power
of the Church, to erect or establish, to disfanull or dissolue
this coactiue power, as the Pope pretendeth to doe by excommunication, deposing Kings and freeing their subiects from
their faith and allegeance. This dissolution of coactiue power
cannot.

*Mat.*18.1.
Marc 9.34.
*Luc.*9.46.

Luke 10.1.

*Cypr.lib. de vni-
tat.Eccle.
Hiero.ad Eua-
grium tom.2.*

cannot belong to the Church, becaufe this is both Temporall and coactiue: the power of the Church being Spirituall, cannot bee called either Temporall or coactiue. Now that the power exercifed by the Pope in excommunication is, Temporall and coactiue, is the graunt of *Bellarmine* : for hee faith that the

Lib.5.cap.7. de Rom.Pont

Church of old did not depofe *Nero, Diocletian, Iulian, Valens, &c. Quia deerant vires temporales* : then he graunteth that in this prefent practife of the Popes, there are *vires temporales* : what is this, but temporall coaction? The Church in old time had all that power which Chrift committed to his Church, but then, by the confeffion of *Bellarmine* ; the Church had no coactiue power : therefore this coactiue power which the Pope vfeth by Temporall force in depofing of Kings, was not by Chrift graunted to his Church, And if we fhould yeeld Temporall coaction to the Church, what power is left to the Magiftrate? Thus we fee the auncient hedge is plucked vp, and the bounds are chaunged, which of old ftood betweene thefe two powers Ciuill and Spirituall.

   14. Againft this difordering of the auncient bounds wee

Iohn 18.36.

haue the words of our Sauiour Chrift. [My kingdome is not of this world, if my kingdome were of this world, my feruaunts would furely fight, that I fhould not bee deliuered, &c. But becaufe when thefe wordes are vrged againft our aduerfaries, they looke afcant vpon them, as if they touched them not : Let vs confider how the kingdome of the Pope, and his pretended Iurifdiction in depofing of Kings, is vtterly ouerthrowen by thefe words, which declare the power properly belonging to Chrifts kingdome, that is to his Church. Chrift aunfwereth heere to *Pilats* queftion, *Verfe* 33. [Art thou the King of the Iewes?] By which queftion it appeareth there was fome fufpition and feares, that Chrift pretending for a kingdome, might confpire againft the ftate, and worke the trouble and diffolution of the gouernment eftablifhed. For as *Herod* when he heard that Iefus was borne the King of the Iewes, was troubled and all Ierufalem with him;

Mat. 2. 3.

and entred into fuch feares and fufpition, that mooued him to kill all the young children from two yeeres old and vnder : fo

the

the high Priefts fuggefted the fame fufpitions to *Pilate.* From
this ground rifeth this queftion of *Pilate*, Art thou the King of
the Iewes? To this he aunfwereth, my kingdome is not of this
world. From which aunfwere applied to fuch a queftion, thefe
pofitions iffue : It is againft the nature of the kingdome of
Chrift to worke any trouble to the kingdomes of the world.
And, that kingdome which worketh trouble to the kingdomes
of this world, is not the kingdome of Chrift. Chrifts kingdome which is not of this world, is his Church, which is in this
world, but not of this world, as himfelfe faith, [If you were of
this world, the world would loue her owne , but becaufe
you are not of this world, but I haue taken you out of this
world, therefore this world hateth you.] Then we reafon thus :
The gouernment of Chrifts Church breedeth no trouble, much
leffe diffolution to the ftates of this world : but the gouernement of the court of Rome, (now commonly called, the
Church of Rome) breedeth trouble and diffolution to the ftates
of this world : therefore the gouernment of that court, is contrary to the gouernment of Chrifts Church : the affumption is a
confeffed truth too well knowen, that the gouernment of the
Popes court or Church, breedeth trouble and diffolution to
States by excommunications. The propofition is prooued by
the aunfwere of Chrift to *Pilats* feares : my kingdome is not of
this world : whereby hee fatisfieth *Pilate* that he needed not
feare any trouble, or diffolution of eftablifhed authoritie by
him, for this was *Pilats* feare. So that if wee admit that Chrift
did aunfwere to the purpofe, and that *Pilats* feares and fufpitions were remooued by his aunfwere, it muft be confeffed that
by that aunfwere the State was fecured, that Chrifts gouernement would not raife any trouble to it, or procure the diffolution thereof. And it muft be well obferued, that Chrift thus
fecuring the prefent State, doth not fpeake of his owne perfon
onely, but vndertaketh for all that belong to him, and his kingdome. Therefore he faith not, I am not : or, my perfon is not
of this world : but, my kingdome is not of this world. Then
as hee fecureth this State from any trouble that they might
feare from his perfon, fo he fecureth all States of the world, du-

Ioh. 15.19.

H   ring

ring the time of this world, from all troubles that they might feare from his members, and from his kingdome which is his Church. Wherby it followeth by strong euidence of reason that they who put States in feare of troubles, or work the dissolutiõ of Ciuill gouernment (as the Pope doth by excommunication) are not the members of Christ, nor belonging to his kingdom.

15. This is further declared in the same place, by the words following. [If my kingdome were of this world, then would my seruants surely fight that I should not be deliuered to thee.] In which words wee finde that Christes seruants may not fight, not stirre vp tumults, vproares and warres, for the maintaining of their kingdome. Therefore that Kingdome for which they raise so much warre, is not the kingdome of Christ, not Christs Church : nor they that raise vp such warres, Christs seruaunts. Christ forbiddeth his seruaunts to fight for him, and his kingdome : the Pope commandeth his seruants to fight for him and his kingdome. Can you haue two kingdomes more opposite? two Kings more contrary?

16. This doctrine that the Church may not stirre vp any vproares or warres against the Magistrate, hath beene alwayes maintained by the auncient Fathers. For we finde that in the greatest persecutions, the auncient Bishops taught Christians alwayes to liue in peace, and to pray for the Emperours and gouernours, though they were persecutors, according to the commaundement of Christ; [Loue your enemies : and pray for them that persecute you.] *Iustin Martyr* saith, [We pray that you (speaking of the Emperour) may be found to haue a good and sound mind with your imperiall power.] *Plinie* writing to *Traian* of the auncient manner of Christians, saith they assembled to worship Christ, and bound themseluer in a Bond, not to set vppon any wicked practise, *Sed ne furta, ne latrocinia, ne adulteria committerent, ne fidem fallerent.* Contrary to which practise the Pope by his excommunication, deposing of Princes, and discharging subiects from their oath and Allegeance, bindeth men to raise warres and tumults, to breake and violate their faith, and to commit many disorders. *Tertullian* saith *Oramus pro Imperatoribus &c:* That is, [We pray for Emperours,

Iohn.18.36.

Mat.5.44.
Iust.apol.2.

Plin. epist.li.10.

Tertul.apo'.
cap.39.

rours,for their deputies,for powers,for the State of this world, for the quiet and peaceable gouernment of things.] Contrarie to which the Popes raise warres,make the gouernment of States tumultuous, and take away peace from the earth. *Optatus* saith, [For good cause doth *Paul* teach, that we must obey Kings and powers ; yea though an Emperour were such an one as liued after the manner of the Gentiles.] *Augustine* saith,[we are not to yeeld this power to any but onely to God, the power I say to giue kingdomes &c. Who giueth earthly kingdomes both to godly and vngodly.] And in another place hee prooueth,that euill Kings and Tyrants are to be obeyed,wherof he giueth a reason : because saith hee [Men consist of two parts, a bodie and a soule, as long as wee are in this life, and neede the helpes of this life,we must by that part which belongeth to this life,be subiect to the powers of this world : but by that part whereby we beleeue in God, we owe no subiection to man, but onely to God.] *Ambrose* saith, If the Emperour should commaund any thing vnlawfull: hee would not obey, neither durst he resist by force, but onely beare with patience: *Arma enim nostra sunt preces & lachryma.* *Gregorie* the first was so farre from this tumultuous disposition of his successours,that hee held himselfe bound to obey the Emperour in the promulgation of that law,which he thought the Emperour should not haue made. *Ego quidem iussioni tua subiectus* (saith he to the Emperour *Maurice*) *eandem legem par diuersas terrarum partos transmitti feci,& quia lex ipsa omnipotenti deo minime concordat, ecce per suggestionis mea paginam serenissimis dominus nunciaui: vtrobiq; ergo qua debui exsolui, quia & Imperatori obedientiam prabui, & pro deo quod sensi minime tacui.* So farre were these auncient Fathers from the newe and strange practises of disobedience and rebellion against Magistrates, which is nowe so stiffely taught,and vnmercifully executed by the Popes vassals vnder pretence of Religion.

17. But they tell vs, that the Pope vseth onely his spirituall censures : hee excommunicateth Kings for heresie or schisme, and thereby deposeth them, and dissolueth the obedience of Subiects. I answer; excommunication as it is a censure of Christs

Optat.lib.3.

De ciuit. dei lib. 5.cap.21.

Lib.de natur. boni aduers. Manich.cap.22. Expositio quarund.questionum ex epist.ad Rom. proposit.72.

Orat.in Auxent.

Lib.indist.11. cap.100.

H 2   Church,

Church, containeth no coactiue power, that is no such power as to depose Princes, or to dissolue the faith and alleageance of Subiects. Which thing is proued both by the vse of excommunication, and by the power of the Church. First, if we consider the vse of excommunication, we finde it was vsed in the Church of the Iewes, and from them taken by the Church of Christians. Then excommunication being found among the Iewes in his full vse and force, all the kindes thereof being distinctly obserued by the learned Iewes, namely by *Elias Leuita*, who obserueth out of the writings of the aunctient Rabbines, three diuers kindes of excommunication in vse in the Iewish Church: it followeth, that this censure of the Church can be no farther extended in the Church of Christians, then it was in the Church of Israel, where it was first instituted and established. But in the Church of Israel, it was neuer extended to deposing Kings, and destroying obedience of Subiects: therefore in the Church of Christians, it may not be extended to these practises. What can be denied heere? For neither can they denie, but that the censures of the Church should bee of greatest power there, where they were first instituted: neither can they denie, that excommunication was first instituted in that Church of the Iewes: neither can they shew vs, that any King of that Nation was at any time deposed for pretended heresie, or for knowne and professed idolatry: though the Kings there were often great idolaters: though the Priests were bolde and couragious in Gods cause: yet we neuer finde that any Priest did by excommunication depose the King, or destroy the bond of allegeance. This thing then being neither practised by the Iewes, where these censures were in first and chiefe force, nor by Christ and his Apostles, nor by the Fathers of the Primitiue Church, nor known in the Church for the space of almost a thousand yeares (as hereafter wee shall declare) wee haue great reason to conclude that excommunication, as it is an Ecclesiasticall censure, hath no power coactiue to alter any temporall authority, to depose Kings, to destroy and dissolue allegeance, or to trouble any lawful authority established in this world.

18 This will no lesse appeare, if wee consider the power
which

Elias, Thisbet. verbo שׁמתא

which the Church hath alwaies practised, for coactiue power was a thing which the Chnrch yeelded alwayes to the ciuill Magistrate. And if the Bishops of Rome did sometimes breake out beyond their bounds: yet were they in those ancient times alwayes repressed by the authority of the Church. For, that we may take a short suruay of the Iurisdiction of the Chureh, during the first three hundred yeres: so long as the Apostles liued, no man doubteth but that they ruled all, and that the greatest Iurisdiction of the Church was in them, if we speake of spirituall Iurisdiction. And if any one Apostle liued after the rest, there was more power acknowledged to be in him, then in any one that liued in the Church in his time. Now it is for an assured historicall truth recorded by *Eusebius*, and before him by *Irenaus* (whom the full consent of the auncients follow heerein) that S. *Iohn* liued after all the other Apostles were dead, & that he continued in the gouernment of the Church, vntill the times of Traian Emperour. In which time the Bishops of Rome after *Peter* are recorded to be these *Linus, Anacletus, Clemens, Euaristus, Alexander.* If the Bishop of Rome had then been the head of the Church, the chiefe Pastor, the Monarch, the fountaine of all Iurisdiction, as his flatterers now make him: it must be confessed that *Alexander* in his time, and *Euaristus* before him was S. *Iohns* head: and before him *Clemens*, and before him *Anaclet*, and before him *Linus*. Did these rule and gouerne S. *Iohn*, or S. *Iohn* them? shall we say that they had Iurisdiction ouer S. *Iohn*, or S. *Iohn* ouer them? If these Bishops each in his time had Iurisdiction ouer S. *Iohn*, then there was an authority in the Church aboue the authority of the Apostles. If they were gouerned by him, then the Bishop of Rome was not the head of the Church. There is no sober spirit that can doubt of these things: or can thinke that in those dayes any liued in the Church, who was not vnder the Iurisdiction of an Apostle.

19 After Saint *Iohns* death, who was liuing in the yeare of Christ 100. and after: in the Church of Rome, were *Sixtus, Telesphorus, Hyginus, Pius, Anicetus, Soter, Eleutherius, Victor.* These gouerned the Church of Rome in succession, by the space of one hundred yeares together. In which times they seemed

willing

willing to put to their helping hands,to aduance the Church of
Rome. For Sathan hauing a purpofe thence to raife Antichrift,
began betime to worke, and to abufe thofe good men,as it was
not hard for him to beguile better men then they were,though
we admit them to be good men,and holy Martyres. Then were
they drawne into a loue to aduance their feate and Iurifdiction, yet fo, as neither in them is proued pernicious, neither was
it thought by the Church to be very dangerous, feeing they
yeelded and fubmitted themfelues in the end to the graue and
godly aduife of the Church.

    20 The things wherein the Bifhops of Rome fought firft to
aduance their power, was by *impofing ceremonies* vpon other
Churches. Thus did *Anicet* contend for the celebration of Eafter: but was quieted by *Polycarp*; who for the peace of the

*Eufeb.lib. 5. ca.
24.*

Church, made a iourney to Rome, and pacified *Anicetus*. And
was fo much honoured of *Anicetus*, that there he practifed the
function of a Bifhop, as *Eufebius* reporteth, taking the ftorie
from *Irenaeus*. Thus was peace and loue then maintained on all
fides, whileft the Bifhops of Rome were content to be ruled by
others.

    21 .A little after, *Victor* grewe more violent in the fame
quarrell, and excommunicated the Eafterne Churches, which
did not obferue Eafter after the maner of the Church of Rome.

Eufeb.ibid.

But *Victor* was refifted, and fharply reproued by *Polycrates* Bifhop of *Ephefus*, and the reft of the Eafterne Bifhops, as alfo by
Irenaeus Bifhop of Lions in Fraunce. Thefe did freely reproue
Victor,for that he regarded not the peace of the Church : they
declare that in ceremonies there was great difference of olde,
and yet the Bifhops liued in loue and peace together : that the
differences in ceremonies, did not breake the confent in faith :
that thefe differences were before the time of *Victor*: and that
hee was therein to followe the examples of his aunciets, who
preferued loue and peace, and the doctrines of faith fincere,
with fome diuerfity in outward ceremonies. This was all that
the Bifhops of Rome attempted in thofe dayes: wherein there
appeareth no Iurifdiction ouer others, but rather the contrary.
For the godly Bifhops of Afia reproued them, and made them
fee

see and acknowledge their owne rashnesse, and caused them to desist: therefore the Church did not then acknowledge the Popes Iurisdiction.

22 Betweene *Victor* and *Syluester* the first, succeeded 18. Bishops of Rome, in the space of 100 yeares next. In which time there was no great attempt made for superiority or Iurisdiction: onely the Bishops of other Churches did honour the Bishop of Rome, following the Apostles rule [In giuing honor goe one before another.] Which honour if they could haue remembred as well to giue to others, as they did to receiue from others, there could haue risen no question of Iurisdiction : but that which began in loue and courtesie, was afterward drawne to Iurisdiction. We denie not but some of the auncients haue yeelded to S. *Peter* a Priority among the rest of the Apostles, because of his great zeale and loue to Christ and to his trueth, and for his excellent vertues : and to the Bishops of Rome wee finde likewise that the auncients yeelded great and honourable titles, but this was in respect of their vertue, learning, and integrity. For the auncients knewe no other rule of fauouring men, but vertue : he was in the Church most honourable, and accounted chiefe in succeeding the Apostles, whose life and conuersation was most Apostolicall. Wherefore as the auncients gaue this honour to the Bishops of Rome, for their godly liues, to call them the Apostles successours, so when they found other Bishops who in vertue excelled, they gaue these titles in as great honour to them, as euer was giuen to the Romane Bishop. For we finde these titles as much or more giuen to others, then wee can finde giuen to the Romane Bishops. *Basill* writing to S. *Ambrose*, saith of him, that he doth hold the sterne of that great and famous ship, the Church of God, and that God had placed him in the primary and chiefe seat of the Apostles. Of the Bishop of Rome, it is hard to finde in all antiquity a more honourable title, then this is of *Ambrose*. Now if S. *Ambrose* helde the sterne of that ship the Church of God, and if hee sate in the chiefe and highest seat of the Apostles : it must follow, that an inferiour seat was reserued for the Bishop of Rome, as long as *Ambrose* liued : and that hee was esteemed the

Rom. 12. 10.

Titles of honour giuen to other Bishops as much as to the Bishops of Rome.

Basil.Epist.55.

ἐπὶ τὴν προεδρίαν ἰῶν ἀποςόλων.

the chiefeſt in Apoſtolicall ſucceſſion, who came neereſt the A-
poſtolicall vertues : or that they were ⲧⲣόⲉⲇⲣⲟⲓ , preſidents a-
like in Chriſts Church. And throughout all the Epiſtles of *Ba-
ſil*, wee obſerue, that albeit hee wrote often to the Weſterne
Church, wee finde no ſuch honourable mention of the Biſhop
of Rome : but ſomewhat ſounding to the contrary. For in the
tenth Epiſtle, he noteth the pride and ambition, which then began to be eſpied in the Biſhops of Rome : complaining to *En-
ſebius* Biſhop of Samoſata, that the Church could haue no help

ⲡⲟῖⲁ βⲟήⲑⲉⲥⲁ
ἡⲙⲓ̃ⲩ ⲧῆς ⲇύⲧⲓ-
ⲕῆς ὀφⲣⲩⲟⲥ. ⁴

from the pride and ambition of the Weſt. Then concerning this
title, to be called the ſucceſſour of the Apoſtles, it was ſomtimes
giuen to the Biſhops of Rome, onely in regard of their vertue,
godlineſſe , and faith which once appeared in thoſe Biſhops.
And ſo it is giuen to *Ambroſe* and to other Biſhops. In this
ſenſe we vnderſtand thoſe titles giuen by *Sidonius Appollinaris*
Biſhop of Aruern, to diuers Biſhops in France in his time. For
writing to Pope *Lupus* (as he calleth him) a Biſhop in France,

Lib.6.Epiſt.1.

he teſtifieth that hee had liued 45 yeares in the ſea Apoſtolicall.
In ſede Apoſtolica nouem iam decurſa quinquennia. And againe

Lib.6.Epiſt.4.

to the ſame man he ſaith : *Pater officium quod incomparabiliter e-
minenti Apoſtolatui tuo ſine fine debetur, &c.* The ſame title he giueth alſo to *Fontellus*, another Biſhop in France , declaring that

Lib.7.Epiſt.4.

therein he greatly reioyced : *Quod Apoſtolatus veſtri patrocini-
um copioſiſſimum conferre vos comperi.* And writing to the ſame

Lib.6.Epiſt.7.

Fontellus: Ego quoq̃, (ſaith he) *ad Apoſtolatus tui noticiam accedo.*

    23. Then by this Title Apoſtolicall, no Iuriſdiction will riſe
to the Biſhops of Rome, ſeeing the ſame is giuen to others, as
well as to them. Neither was there then in the Biſhop of Rome
any power aboue others, neither in the whole Church was coactiue power found. To prooue this, *Euſebius* reporteth a Storie, which we wiſh to bee well obſerued , becauſe it maketh an
euident proofe of the Iuriſdiction of the Church , which thing

Euſeb.lib.7.cap.
23.24,25.&c.

wee ſeeke : The Storie is thus. *Paulus Samoſatenus* Biſhop of
Antioche, taught that Chriſt was a meere man. To repreſſe
this wicked hereſie, a Councell was gathered at Antioche. The
Church was then without the helpe of a Chriſtian Magiſtrate.
In chiefe accompt among them that liued in the Church at that
time

time,was *Dionysius* Bishop of Alexandria, a man for his great learning and godlinesse much renowned in the Church then, and alwayes since : he was so aged and weake at that time that he could not be present in the Councell,but by writing confirmed the truth against *Paulus* the Hereticke. Among them that were assembled there, was *Gregorius* Bishop of Cæsaria, who had the gift of working miracles : in which respect *Basil* maketh honourable mention of him in diuers places : *Dionysius* was then Bishop of Rome.The famous Bishops of the East had diuers meetings against *Paulus*;the last meeting was in the time of *Aurelianus* Emperour about the yeere of Christ, two hundred seuentie and fiue. At what time *Paulus* was fully refuted and repressed, especially by the labour,industry, and learning of *Malchion* : hee was condemned saith *Eusebius* of all the Churches of Christ which are vnder heauen. After the conuiction of this Heresie,the Councell wrote to *Dionysius* Bishop of Rome; and to *Maximus* Bishop of Alexandria, (for *Dionysius* died before this Councell ended, and *Maximus* succeeded him in Alexandria :) and to all the Church of Christ vnder heauen. The Epistle is extant in *Eusebius*, and was directed to these Bishops,that by them other Churches might haue knowledge of this thing.

Damnatur ab omnibus quæ sub cœlo sunt Ecclesiis Christi.Euseb. ibid.
Omni Ecclesiæ Catholicæ quæ sub Cœlo est.ibid.

24. After all this *Paulus Samosatenus* held the Church of Antioche,and gaue no place to *Domnus*, (whom the Councell excommunicating and deposing *Paulus*, had decreed should take his place.) The Bishops in this case were driuen to seeke the aide of the heathen Emperour *Aurelian*; at the suit of the Councell, the Emperour commaunded that the Church of Antioche should be deliuered to him,to whom the Church of Italie and the Bishop of Rome would write. By this it appeareth that the Church had no Iurisdiction coactiue : for when the Bishops of this Councell had proceeded as farre as they could, by Ecclesiasticall censures, (against all which censures *Paulus* held the Church by force)finding that without coactiue power *Paulus* could not be repressed,and finding no such power in themselues, they were forced to seeke the Emperours helpe,acknowledging thereby that all coactiue power rested in

I   the

the Emperor. Moreouer by this we obserue the beginning of that practise, which afterward drew the opinion of Iurisdiction after it. For the Bishop of Rome had no authoritie then ouer other Bishops, neither did he challenge any. And when some fewe of that Sea, did seeme to pretend some authoritie in matters of conformitie and ceremonies, as *Anicetus, Victor,* and some few other: they were quickly repressed by the Church, & were content to be ruled by the Church. But because the heathen and persecuting Emperours were content for the glory of Italy, to giue this honour to the Church there, and especially to the Bishop of Rome, that other Bishops should find fauour for his sake (as appeareth euidently by this Story, wherein it is recorded that the Bishops of that Councell had no meanes to helpe themselues but by the Emperour, and the Emperour not regarding the cause, onely to honour the Bishop of Rome, referred the matter to him), hence, as reason was, the Churches were compelled to make much of the Bishop of Rome, and to seeke his fauour, without which they sawe the heathen Emperours would not be drawen to doe them iustice.

Euseb.lib.7.
cap.4.5.

25. About this time, *Stephanus* Bishop of Rome threatned likewise to Excommunicate some Bishops for rebaptising of heretickes, but he was repressed by *Dionysius* Bishop of Alexandria. Some also that were excommunicate in *Africa,* came to Rome to seeke the fauour of *Cornelius* : who without examination of the cause, receiued them to the Communion. Of which thing *Cyprian* complaineth much : they saile to Rome

Cyprian.Epist.55

saith he, *cum merce mendaciorum.* Against this hee declareth, that it was ordained that neither the Bishop of Rome, nor any straunger should be iudge of the causes of their Church. And to *Cornelius* he writeth thus : *Quum statutum sit ab omnibus, &*

Ibid.

aquum sit pariter ac iustum, vt vniuscuiusq́ causa illic audiatur, vbi est crimen admissum, & singulis pastoribus portio gregis sit ascripta, quam regat vnusquisq́, & gubernet, &c. Oportet vtiq́, eos, quibus præsumus; non circumcursare, & episcóporum concordiam cohærentemsua subdola & fallaci temeritate collidere, sed agere illic causam vbi & accusatores habere, & testes sui criminis possunt. That is, [Seeing it is decreed by all, and it is a thing both equall
and

and iuſt, that euery mans cauſe ſhould be heard there, where the crime was committed, and a part of the flocke is appointed to each Paſtor, which each in ſeuerall muſt rule and guide, &c. Verily it behooueth that they whom we gouerne, ſhould not gad and run about to others, nor by their crafty and fallatious raſhneſſe breake in ſunder the coherent concord of Biſhops: but there ought they to plead their cauſe, where they may haue accuſers and witneſſes of their crime.]

26. Thus albeit the Biſhops of Rome did ſeeke ſome inlarging of their authoritie, ſometimes by giuing countenance and patronage to criminous and ſcandalous men, yet they were repreſſed and brought into order by the godly and learned Biſhops, that then liued in the Church: Who would not ſuffer the priuiledges of the Church to be loſt, or any title of Iuriſdiction to grow, where there was no right. Thus for the firſt three hundred yeeres the Church of Rome had no Iuriſdiction ouer other Churches: but the Biſhops there were reuerenced by other, partly for their wiſedome, learning and godlineſſe; partly becauſe the Emperours fauoured them aboue other: and becauſe they were Biſhops of the chiefe citie and ſeat of the Empire. For as they had ſome fauour aboue the reſt with heathen Emperours, ſo they found much more fauour from Chriſtian Emperours; which thing cauſed them to be regarded by other Biſhops, but no Iuriſdiction was as yet acknowledged.

I 2   CHAP.

C H A P. V.

Of the estate and Iurisdiction of the Church from the end of the first three hundred yeeres, vntill the yeere of Christ, sixe hundred. Wherein is declared that coactiue power was in the Christian Emperors : from whom the Church receiued some parts of coactiue. Iurisdiction. The Popes began to seeke Iurisdiction by forgerie.

Owe let vs consider the times that followed, when the Church had peace from persecution and found the fauour of Christian Emperours. In which time no Iurisdiction will be found in the Church of Rome, aboue other ; and all coactiue Iurisdiction was acknowledged without question, to bee in the Christian Emperours ; from whom the Church receiued some part thereof.

2, *Constantine* who did as much honour the Church, and was as much honoured of the Church, as euer any Christian Emperour : leauing therein an example, which standeth as yet alone without a match, did notwithstanding take all that to himselfe, which is now called Ecclesiasticall Iurisdiction coactiue, without any let, or contradiction, nay by the generall approbation of all that then liued. When *Cæcilianus* Bishop of Carthage was accused by *Donatus* and some other of that faction, for deliuering the holy Scriptures to the enemies of Religion to be burned : *Constantine* commaunded *Cæcilianus* to come to Rome, with a certaine number of Bishops which accused him, and other that might heare and vnderstand the cause. And commaunded the Bishop of Rome, then *Miltiades*, with certaine Bishops of Fraunce (to the number saith *Optatus* of nineteene) to heare and end the matter : the Bishops condemned *Donatus*, who appealed from the sentence : and albeit the Emperour was much offended at his appellation, yet hee could not choose but receiue it. In all this processe, the Emperours Soueraigne

Optatus lib. 1.

Euseb. li. 10. ca. 5

Soueraigne Iurisdiction appeared, the cause was a pretended crime of a Bishop : the Emperour appointeth iudges, and receiued the appellation : which things declared Iurisdiction.

3. Likewise after he had banished *Eusebius* Bishop of Nicomedia, and *Theognis* Bishop of Nice, he wrote an Epistle to the people of Nicomedia, declaring the iust causes of their banishment, and signifieth that his especiall pleasure and desire is, to haue Bishops, *castos, orthodoxos, humanos* : and shutting vp his speech, he saith : *Quoáſi quis audacter inconsultéq̄, ad memoriam pestium illarum exarserit, illius ſtatim audacia miniſtri dei, hoc eſt, mea exequutione coercebitur.* Where we see *Constantine* vseth coactiue Iurisdiction ouer Bishops, he punisheth them, he declareth the true ground of his Iurisdiction from the word of God, by which warrant he is placed the Miniſter of God. This is that coactiue Iurisdiction ouer Ecclesiasticall persons, which did alwayes belong to the Soueraigne Magistrate, and was neuer by God giuen to any other. *Theodoret. lib. 1. cap. 19.*

4. It was alwayes held by all sober writers of the Church of Rome, as hereafter shall be further declared, that in the Church there is no power aboue the power of a Councell. And yet this authoritie of a Councell, so much and so worthily reuerenced could not restraine *Constantine*, but he vpon good and iuſt causes brought the rash proceedings of some Councels to a newe examination. For when *Athanasius* was wronged by a Councell of Arians, he complained to *Constantine*. The Emperour sent for all the Bishops of that Councell, to render an accompt of their proceedings before him : which declareth that his Iurisdiction coactiue, was aboue the power coactiue of the Councell. For heere we consider onely Iurisdiction coactiue, and not the matter or subiect : for otherwise wee acknowledge, as before is declared, that the determinations of generall Councels, are matters of an higher truth and authoritie, then the Statutes or decrees of any Emperour. But wee speake heere of that Soueraigne Iurisdiction coactiue, which hath alwayes appeared in the power of the ciuill Magistrate, and wherein the Church had no more part, then that she receiued from the liberalitie of godly Emperours : for as Kings receiue *Socrat. lib. 1. cap. 33. 34.*

ceiue the knowledge of faith and Religion from the Church, and not the Church from Kings : so coactiue Iurisdiction the Church receiueth from Kings , and not Kings from the Church.

5. There was no Councell held in *Constantines* time, whether of Orthodoxe or heretikes , but either by the expresse commaundement, or licenfe of the Emperour. *Ruffinus* faith, he called the Councel of Nice at the requeft of the Bifhops: *Ex facerdotum fententia apud vrbem Nicaam concilium Epifcopale conuocat.* *Epiphanius* faith that Councell was obtained of the Emperour, at the fuit of *Alexander* Bifhop of Alexandria. So the Bifhops who then liued in the Church, held it to be of the Emperours right and Iurifdiction to call Councels. *Theodoret* rehearfeth a Dialogue betweene *Constans* the Emperour, and *Liberius* Bifhop of Rome, who afterward for feare and through weakeneffe, and irkfomneffe of his exile, was drawen to fubfcribe to *Arianifme,* as witneffeth *Hierom, Ruffinus, Platina,* and other: In that Dialogue thefe words are worth the noting. *Constans* willing *Liberius* to forfake the Communion with *Athanafius,* and to condemne him; *Liberius* his anfwere is, *Ecclefiastica indicia cum fumma iufticia obferuatione fieri debent : quare fi tua pietati placet, iudicium cogi impera, vbi fi damnandus* Athanafius *videatur, fententia in illum ordine modoq; Ecclefiastico feratur: nam fieri nequit vt condemnetur à nobis, de quo iudicium datum non fit.* That is, [Ecclefiasticall iudgements ought to proceed with exact obferuation of iuftice. Therefore if it pleafe your Godlineffe, command a Councell to be called, wherein if *Athanafius* feeme worthy to be condemned, let fentence paffe againft him in Ecclefiasticall order and manner. For it cannot be that by vs hee fhould bee condemned, feeing wee haue no authoritie to iudge him.] The Bifhop of Rome here confeffeth, firft, That *Iudicia Ecclefiastica,* Ecclefiasticall iudgements are to be appointed and eftablifhed by the Emperour; then he graunteth him Ecclefiasticall Iurifdiction, and granteth, that to call a Councell belongeth to his Iurifdiction. Secondly, the Emperour cannot make a man an hereticke, but this muft be done by a Councell or by the iudgement Ecclefiasticall.

This

This being a thing not of coactiue Iurisdiction, but of know-ledge in the word of God. Thirdly, the Bishop of Rome re-nounceth all right and authority of iudicature vpon *Athanasi-us*, therefore in those daies hee had no Iurisdiction ouer other Bishops.

6. This mixt Iurisdiction which now is practised by Bi-shops, began in the time of Constantine. So *Nicephorus* wit-nesseth : *Constantinus Clericos omnes constitutione lata immunes liberosq́, esse permisit; iudiciumq́, & iurisdictionem in eos Episcopis, si ciuilium iudicum cognitionem declinare vellent, mandauit, & quod Episcopi iudicassent, id robur & autoritatem sententiæ omnem ha-bere debere decreuit.* That is : [*Constantine* by an edict graun-ted the priuiledge of immunity to all Clerkes, and graunted to Bishops iudgement and Iurisdiction ouer Clerkes, in case they would decline from the courts of ciuill Iudges : and he decreed that whatsouer the Bishops iudged, that should stand in all strength and authority of a decree.] *Sozomen* declareth by what occasion it grew first : For some began then to appeale from ciuill iudgements to Ecclesiasticall, and some Bishops receiued the appellations : which thing being approued by *Constantine*, gaue great authority to this kind of Iurisdiction. *Episcopi* (saith he) *in causis ciuilibus sententias pronuntiarunt, si qui à iudicibus ci-uilibus ad eorum autoritatem appellassent. Quam rem propter ve-nerationem Episcoporum adeò approbauit Constantinus, vt ratas ha-beri, potioresq́, quàm aliorum iudicum sententias, nec minus quàm ab ipso imperatore essent pronunciata, per Magistratus & milites Magistratuum ministros ad effectum perduci lege edixerit.* That is : [Bishops pronounced sentence in ciuill causes, if any appea-led to them from ciuill Iudges. This thing for the reuerence of Bishops *Constantine* approued so much, that hee ordained by Law, that these iudgements should be ratified, and of greater authority then the sentences of other Iudges : yea, to be held of no lesse force, then if the Emperour himselfe had pronounced them, so to be executed by the Shriefs & their seruants.]

7 By which it appeareth, that these courts with this Iuris-diction were vnderstood then, no other then the Emperours courts. The Emperour graunteth this Iurisdiction, saith *Ni-cephorus.*

Lib.7.cap.46.

Sozom. lib. 1. ca.9. Tripartit. lib.1.cap.9.

cephorus, the Emperour ratifieth thefe iudgements, faith *Sozo-men*, the Emperour commaundeth that the fentence of the Bi-fhop fhould be euery where receiued, as if it proceeded out of his owne mouth. Which words are well to be obferued. For the Emperour commaundeth not, that the Bifhops fentence fhould be receiued as a diuine fentence, but only as an humane: not as proceeding from the mouth of God, but as proceeding from the mouth of the Emperour. Now if thefe Courts were then fo euidently proued to be the Emperours Courts, our ad-uerfaries may acknowledge their owne ignorance & folly, who make declamations and many idle difcourfes, without folid proofe, againft them that call Ecclefiafticall Courts the Kings Courts: as if this were a thing new, ftrange, and neuer heard of before thefe late yeares. Their error is that common Sophifme which filleth moft of their bookes, which *Ariftotle* calleth *Arift. Elench.* παρὰ τὶω σωίϑεσιν, compounding & confounding thofe things which we diftinguifh, and which are diftinct in nature. For in this word of Iurifdiction, they confound thefe two diftinct things, both that which is fpirituall Iurifdiction, yeelded by vs the right of the Church, and all that alfo which Princes haue giuen to Ecclefiafticall Courts: fuch as thefe priuiledges which *Conftantine* gaue to Bifhops Courts, and other Princes fince haue continued and enlarged. If thefe things be not diftingui-fhed, the truth can neuer appeare in this queftion: by this the Reader may vnderftand, who they are that hide and deface the truth by new varnifhing of olde rotten Sophifmes.

8 Then all coactiue Iurifdiction came into the Church from the authority of Princes; for as the power of the Church is in-ternall and fpirituall, fo externall and coactiue power was the right of Princes. To this purpofe *Eufebius* reporteth a fpeach of *Conftantine* at a banquet: calling himfelfe a Bifhop for things externall, as they were for matters internall. His words are *Eufeb. lib. 4. de* thefe: *Vos quidem eorum quæ intus funt in Ecclefia agenda, ego ve-* *vita Conftan-* *ro eorum quæ extra hanc funt, Epifcopus à Deo fum conftitutus.* And *tini.* whereas Iurifdiction is beft knowne by appellations, it hath been often feen that frō the Pope mēn haue appealed to a coun-cel, as hereafter we are to declare, but from a councel we find no appel-

appellation to the Pope, but to the Emperor for some personall wrong. *Athanasius* being vniustly condemned by the Synod of Tire appealed to *Constantine*, as *Socrates* witnesseth. In like sort *Flauianus* appealed to the Emperour, when the Synod of Capua had referred his cause to *Theophilus*, and the Bishops of Egypt. Yea, the heretiques themselues in those dayes knew no means to appeale from the Emperour. *Augustine* saith, that *Donatus* did still appeale to the Emperour, being condemned by the Bishops and by Synodes. And so religious were these auncient Bishops, in preseruing the Emperors Iurisdiction, and yet maintaining the truth without feare: that when they were oppressed by Arians, and by the power of an Arian Emperour, yet they would vse no other meanes, then these direct meanes. And therefore the Bishops hauing a purpose to condemne the Arians, craued a counsell of *Valens*, an Arian Emperor, who granted them a counsell at Lampsacum, wherein they condemned the Arian doctrine. So that without the Emperour they would not gather a counsell, though it were to conclude directly against the Emperours purposes. Thus doth *Socrates* report the calling of that councell: but *Sozomen* saith, it was not obtained of *Valens*, but of *Valentinian*.

    9. Besides these publique and generall Synods, there were also some more priuate and particular, in calling whereof the Bishops had power. The Bishop of the Diocesse vsed to call a Synod of his Clergy, but could proceed no farther. Prouinciall Synodes were called by Metropolitanes: but in a generall Synod of many Nations, the Emperour had alwayes the right of calling it: as a King hath the onely right of calling a Synod, of those Nations that are vnder his gouernment. For as the counsell of Nice was called by *Constantine*, so were all the counsels of these next three hundred yeares, called by the Emperours that gouerned at such times. *Theodosius* gathered the councell of Constantinople against the heresie of *Macedonius*, in the third yeare of his raigne, which was the yeare of Christ 383. saith *Prosper*. The councell of *Ephesus* against *Nestorius*, was gathered by the authority of *Theodosius* the younger: and the fourth generall councell at Chalcedon, by the authority of *Martianus*

Socrat. lib. 1.
cap. 23.
Ambros. Epist. ad
Theodos.

August. Epist.
162. et alibi.

Socrat. lib. 4.
cap 2.

Prosper in Chro
nicis.

K   and

and *Valentinianus* Emperours. *Leo* the firſt, was a great man in theſe afſaires, and hee is the fitteſt to certifie vs of the truth, a-gainſt whoſe witneſſe our aduerſaries haue no reaſon to except. This Pope then writing to the Emperour *Theodoſius*, ſaith: *Pi-etas veſtra apud Epheſum conſtituit Synodale concilium.* And af-terward declaring his obedience and conformity thereto, ſaith: *Meum ſtudium commodaui, vt Clementia veſtra ſtudijs pareatur.* And againe: *Ne autem piiſſimi Principis diſpoſitioni, noſtra videa-tur praeſentia defuiſſe, fratres meos miſi, &c.* he hath the ſame alſo, *Epiſt. 23. ad Theodoſium.* Againe, hee writeth to *Pulcheria*, to moue the Emperour to command a councell to be holden with-in Italy, declaring that he wrote to the Emperour to intreat the ſame: Which thing hee moueth alſo in other Epiſtles. And though he much deſired this, that the Emperour would haue beene intreated to hold a councell within Italy, yet could he not obtaine it, and therefore was ready to obey the Emperour, at-tending his pleaſure therein, who appointed it in another place.

10 Which thing we obſerue, the rather becauſe our aduer-ſaries of late haue yeelded this as a proper right to the Pope to call councels. *Catholici munus connocandi concilia generalia* (ſaith *Bellarmine*) *ad Romanum pontificem propriè pertinere volunt.* And when they are driuen by theſe open and euident teſtimo-nies, they ſhift it thus: as to ſay, another may doe it by the Popes conſent: but if the Pope neither appoint the place, nor no other by his commaundement or conſent, then it is no coun-cell, but a conciliable. Theſe bee vaine and friuolous ſhifts of Friars. For it is true, that the Popes conſent was to theſe aun-cient councels, but no otherwiſe then as the conſent of all other Biſhops. They conſented becauſe they could not chuſe, becauſe they were reſolued to be obedient: but they could not appoint either place or time. For *Leo* could not haue it where hee would, but it was where and when the Emperour appoin-ted.

11 Before the councell of Chalcedon, there is the Writ of the Emperours *Valentinian* and *Martian*, called *Sacra*: to call Biſhops to *Nicaa*. But another *Sacra* is ſent to reuoke that, and

to

Marginal notes:

Leo.Epiſt. 12.

Ibid.
Epiſt. 17.

Epiſt. 24.

Epiſt. 31.

Bellarm. de concil.cap.12.

Bellar. Ibid.

to call them to Chalcedon. So that all this while the Emperors rule, as those that haue Ecclesiasticall Iurisdiction. They call councels, they punish offenders of the Clergy, they establish Ecclesiasticall Courts, they are acknowledged the nourcing Fathers of Religion, the keepers and preseruers of both Tables, and of the discipline of the Church. And therefore *Leo* writing to *Constantinus* Emperour, who called the sixt Synod, saith thus : *Cognouimus quod sancta & vniuersalis maxima sexta Synodus, quæ per Dei gratiam imperiali decreto in regia vrbe congregata est, &c,* [Wee know that the holy and vniuersall great sixt Synod, which by the grace of God is called and gathered by the imperiall decree, in the imperiall City, &c.] And a little after : *Pietas vestra fructus misericordiæ, potestas custos disciplinæ.* [Your godlinesse is the fruit of Gods mercy, your power is the keeper of discipline.] And againe : *Nec enim minor regnantium cura est praua corrigere, quam de aduersarijs triumphare, quia ei nimirum potestatem suam seruiendo subijciunt, cuius munere imperare noscuntur, &c. Vnde diuinitus præordinata vestra Christianissima pietas, &c. Caput Ecclesiæ Dominum Iesum Christum veram pietatis regulam amplectendo, &c.* [For Gouernours ought to haue no lesse care to correct vngodly things, then to triumph ouer their aduersaries: for they submit their power to his seruice, by whose power they are knowne to rule, &c. Therefore your most Christian zeale preordained of God, &c. acknowledging our Lord Iesus Christ the true rule of godlinesse, to bee the head of the Church.] Wherein the Bishop of Rome doth acknowledge, first, that the generall councell is to be called onely by the authority of the Emperour, *imperiali decreto.* Secondly, that the Emperours power is such a power, as is *custos disciplinæ.* Hee speaketh here in an Ecclesiasticall cause, and of Ecclesiasticall affaires. Now that power which is *custos disciplinæ Ecclesiæ,* what is it, but Ecclesiasticall Iurisdiction ? This word Iurisdiction was not then worne in such vse as now it is, but we see the auncients vse words counteruailing it. The Bishop of Rome acknowledgeth Ecclesiasticall power and Iurisdiction to be in the Emperour, when hee yeeldeth him such a power as is preseruer of the discipline Ecclesiasticall. Thirdly, he confesseth that the care of

Leo Iunior. Act.18. Synodus sexta.

K 2　　　　　　　　　　the

the Church & Church-gouernment for eſtabliſhing the truth,
doth no leſſe belong to the office of a Prince, then to triumph
ouer his foes in warre. Fourthly, the Biſhop of Rome as then
acknowledgeth no other head of the Church, then Ieſus Chriſt
as appeareth by his words. To the ſame purpoſe Saint *Auguſtine* ſaith, *Diuinitus præcipi regibus, vt in regno ſuo bona iubeant, mala prohibeant, non ſolum quæ pertinent ad humanam ſocietatem, verum etiam quæ ad diuinam religionem. Contra Creſcentium li. 3. cap. 51.* That is, Kings are commaunded to eſtaliſh good things,
and prohibite euill in their Kingdomes, not onely in things belonging to Ciuill ſocietie, but in ſuch things alſo that belong to
diuine Religion. *Gregorie* the great following the footſteppes
of his Fathers, yeeldeth the ſame authoritie to the King: For
writing to *Theodoricus* King of France, he ſaith: *Iterata vos per*

Regiſt. ca. 273. *veſtram mercedem adhortatione pulſamus, vt congregari Synodum iubeatis.* This part of Iuriſdiction for calling of Councels,
is ſo fully confirmed to be the Emperours right by the Aunceants, that Cardinall *Cuſanus* (ſure no Lutheran) diſputing of

Cuſanus lib. de this priuiledge, concludeth from the confeſſed teſtimonies of
Cath. concor- the Aunceants, theſe two things: Firſt, That Emperours and
dantia 2. cap. 19 Kings by their office muſt call Councels, Secondly, that their
office is likewiſe by coactiue power, to ſee the things maintained and obſerued, which are defined in general Councels.

 12. Hitherto then haue we found the Soueraigne Iuriſdiction
alwayes in Chriſtian Magiſtrates, and neuer in the Biſhop of
Rome. How then commeth the Biſhop of Rome to this practiſe of Iuriſdiction, which now he claimeth? Let vs here conſider one Pageant of theirs, which will declare the firſt claime
and beginning of Iuriſdiction, which they haue ſo much increaſed ſince. The firſt attempt was to winne Iuriſdiction ouer Biſhops, the ſecond was to get the ſame power ouer Kings, and
by that meanes ouer all. Theſe we meane to open, with as
much breuitie as we can, and the matter will beare. Firſt then
to bring Biſhops of other Nations vnder their power, a ſhameleſſe deuiſe was plotted by the Biſhop of Rome, diſcried and
reiected by the auncient Fathers that then liued; but yet ſo
cloſely followed afterward by the Popes, that in the end it preuailed.

uailed. I will declare the storie as it is deliuered by their owne writers, who haue collected the tomes of the Councels.

13. The sixt Councell of Carthage was gathered in the yeere of our Lord foure hundred and twentie: against the here-sie of *Pelagius :* it lasted sixe yeeres and more. In it were gathe-red two hundred and seuenteene Bishops, among whom was that worthy Father Saint *Augustine,* and others of famous note, as *Prosper, Orosius,* and diuers other of great vertue and lear-ning. *Aurelius* Bishop of Carthage, Metropolitan of Affrica was chiefe. In the time of this Councell, three Bishops of Rome succeeding one another, mooued great contention and quarell with the Fathers 'of this Councell for Iurisdiction, which the Popes then began to claime, affirming that they had Iurisdicti-on ouer the Church of Affrica , which thing these Fathers of this Councell vtterly denied : the contention began vpon this occasion. *Prosper in Chre-nicis.*

14. *Apiarius* a Priest of the Church of Sicca , in Affrica, was for his infamous and scandalous life excommunicated not onely by *Vrbanus* Bishop of Sicca , but by a whole Synode of Bishops met together. This fellow thus censured in Affrica, fled to *Zozimus* Bishop of Rome, to him he complained of wrong that the Bishops of Affrica had done him, as he said. *Zo-zimus* without examination of the cause, vndertooke to main-taine him , and admitted him to the Communion. After this vnderstanding, that the Bishops of Affrica were gathered in their Synode, he sendeth to them *Faustinus* Bishop of Potentia, and with him two Priests, *Philip* and *Asellus.* Them hee char-geth to defend the cause of *Apiarius,* to cause the Synode of Af-frica to receiue him to their Communion, to excōmunicate *Vr-banus,* Bishop of Sicca, or else to call him to Rome, vnlesse hee will reforme, that is, vndoe all that he had done against *Apia-rius.* Further he commaundeth them, to draw the Councell to yeeld to the Iurisdiction of the Bishop of Rome , and to ac-knowledge it lawfull for any Bishop or Priest, to appeale from the sentence of their Metropolitan to Rome : he commaundeth them also to signifie, that he sent his Legate into Affrica, who might vnderstand the causes of appellants that were grieued. *concil. Affrican. cap. 101.*

To effect this thing the better, he chargeth them to declare, that the Nicen Councell hath giuen this Iurisdiction to the Bishops of Rome: for proofe hereof he deliuereth vnto them in writing a counterfeited Canon of the Nicen Councell.

15. *Faustinus* comming to Affrica with these instructions, and being admitted into the Councell, declared that he had from *Zozimus* a Commission which he called *Commonitorium*; and withall he declared the Iurisdiction of the Bishop of Rome, confirmed by a Canon of the Nicen Councell. *Aurelius* President of the Councel answered, let this Commission first be read which our brethren haue brought: hereupon *Daniel* the notary reade, and recited the Commission thus. [*Zozimus* Bishop of Rome, to our brother *Faustinus* Bishop, & to our sons, *Philip* & *Asellus* Priests: this businesse you know, you are to doe all things as if our presence were with you, nay becaufe it is with you: and the rather seeing you haue both our expresse command, and the words of the Canons, which for more full assurance we haue added to this Commission. For thus (most beloued brethren) it is decreed in the Councell of Nice concerning the appellation of Bishops.] (And then forsooth the forged Canon of the Councell of Nice followeth thus.)

Concil. Carthag. 6.

Placuit autem vt si Episcopus accusatus fuerit, & iudicauerint congregati Episcopi regionis ipsius, & de gradu suo deiecerint eum, & appellasse Episcopus videatur, & confugerit ad beatissimum Ecclesiæ Romanæ Episcopum, & voluerit audiri & iustum putauerit vt reuocetur examen, scribere his Episcopis dignetur, qui in finitima & propinqua prouincia sunt, vt ipsi diligentur omnia requirant, & iuxta fidē veritatis definiant. Quod si is qui rogat causam suam iterum audiri, deprecatione sua mouerit Episcopum Romanū, vt è Latere suo presbyterum mittat, erit in potestate Episcopi Romani, quid velit, & quid existimet: & si decreuerit mittendos esse qui presentes cum Episcopis iudicent, habentes authoritatem eius à quo destinati sunt, erit in suo arbitrio. Si vero crediderit sufficere Episcopos, vt negotio terminum imponant: faciet quod sapientissimo consilio suo iudicauerit. That is, [We thought good that if a Bishop be accused, and the Bishops of that Prouince haue giuen sentence, and deposed him; if this Bishop seeme to appeale and*

Concil. Carthag. 6. cap. 3.

flie

flie to the most blessed Bishop of Rome, and desire to be heard : if he thinke good to reuoke the sentence, it may please him to write to those Bishops which are in that Prouince, that they may diligently search the matter, and iudge it truely. But if he, that moueth his cause may be heard againe, shall by his petition intreat the Bishop of Rome to send a Legat from his side, it shall be in the power of the Bishop of Rome, to doe what hee thinketh best. And if he decree to send some, who with the Bishops of the Prouince may be present to iudge, hauing authoritie from him, from whom they are sent, it shall be in his pleasure. And if he thinke that the Bishops of that Prouince may suffice to end the businesse, let him doe whatsoeuer in his most wise Councell he iudgeth best.]

Before I proceed in this narration, let some things of note bee obserued : First, the Bishops of Rome were now growen from the honest and godly conuersation of their Auncestours, to admirable impudency that durst suborne a Canon of the Nicen Councell, and publish their owne shame, in the sight of the Church then, and leaue an eternall monument thereof to the world, for euer extant in publike Councels. Secondly, the ground of the Iurisdiction of the Bishop of Rome, is forgerie, famously attempted, and famously conuicted at that present time. And yet this practise preuailed mightily afterward, this vnblessed deuise of forgerie, being attempted in a number of decretall Epistles, to drawe in this Iurisdiction, a practise wherof no learned Papists can speake or thinke without blushing, and yet such is their miserable captiuitie, that they are willing to make vse of that falshood, whereof they cannot thinke without a secret confession of forgerie. Thirdly, the ingenuous reader cannot but see, and vnderstand the vanitie of the Popes flatterers, who striuing now for this Iurisdiction, would blasphemously draw it from Scriptures, such as thou art *Peter*, &c. And feede my Sheepe, &c. These Scriptures were first drawn by the forged decretall Epistles to proue the Popes Iurisdiction, and are now commonly drawen to the same purpose: but when *Zozimus*, *Boniface*, and *Caelestinus* began first to contend for Iurisdiction, they claimed it not frō Scriptures: this deuise

uise was not then found out, but they laid all the cause vpon a forged Canon of the Councell of Nice. So that this is but a late knauerie of the Popes flatterers, to countenance their newe found Iurisdiction by Scriptures.

16. When this Canon was recited by the notarie, the Fathers of the Councell were much offended and troubled at the absurditie thereof : there were then present some of the best learned Diuines then liuing in the world, they knew well there was no such Canon, they neuer read it in any copies of the Nicen Councell, they neuer heard of this thing before : they resolued therefore not onely to denie the Canon, but to refute the falshood of the Pope so famously, that it might be knowen to all the world, and that the Church afterward might take warning of the Romane ambition : therefore they aunswered for the present, thus : that this Canon was not to bee found in their bookes. And for a more full and sufficient examination of this matter, they would send for the autentike copies of the Nicen Councell, before they could graunt the Popes request. To this purpose they writ a letter to *Zozimus*, which was presented to *Boniface* his successour, and is extant in the Tomes of the Councels.

Concil. Affrican.
cap.101.

17. *Boniface* first receiuing these letters (for *Zozimus* was dead before they returned) pursueth the claime of Iurisdiction by corruption of the same Canon, and with obstinate and resolute peruersitie maintaineth the falshood begun by his Predecessour. In the meane time two copies autentike of the Nicen Canons were sent to the Fathers of the Councell of Carthage, one from *Cyrillus* Bishop of Alexandria : another from *Atticus* Bishop of Constantinople. These copies were read, but no such Canon could be found, as the Bishop of Rome had foisted in : the Fathers vnderstanding the fact, and hauing taken the Bishop of Rome in a flagrant crime, decreed that the true Canons of the Nicen Councell should be obserued, reiecting this suborned and supposititious Canon. This decree they sent to Pope *Boniface* : but Gods iudgements hastily following these corruptors, *Boniface* was dead before it came to Rome, and *Calestinus* next succeeding receiued it.

18. *Cale-*

18. *Cælestinus* as stiffe for this Iurisdiction as any of his predecessours, maintained the cause by the same meanes, resolued with shame ynough to stand for the adulterated Canon : which pertinacy after open conuiction, declareth that the pollicie of the Church of Rome began then to forsake religious courses, and to rest vpon falshood and forgery to obtaine their willes. And therfore it is not to be marueiled, if the truth of Religion afterward forsaked them. *Apiarius* gaue a new occasion to the Pope to worke vpon: for after that this man was receiued vnto the Communion by *Zozimus* and *Boniface*, he returned to the Trabacens, where for his foule and scandalous life he was excommunicated againe. To recouer this disgrace, he flieth to his onely refuge the Bishop of Rome then *Cælestinus*, who receiueth him, admitting him to the Communion; and directeth his Legats *Faustinus*, *Philippus*, *Asellus*, to Affrica, with a streight charge to draw the Councell to yeeld to the demaunds of his Predecessours : for want of other helpe, hee furnisheth them throughly with impudencie and inuict audacity: for what other vertues were left to maintaine such a cause ? The Legats cōming with this Commission, require of the Councell that *Apiarius* may be admitted to their Communion, and that they would be content to submit themselues to the Romane Iurisdiction. The Fathers of the Councell produce the autentike copies of the Nicen Canons, which they had procured from Alexandria and Constantinople : by which the Romane forgery was euidently conuinced. Here began a fresh contention, *Faustinus* resolued to execute his Commission to his vtmost power, exclaimeth against the Sea Apostolike, against the violatours of the Nicen Canons. The Councell protesteth that they will imbrace all true Canons, that they will yeeld to the Church of Rome all true priuiledges: onely in the lawfull, warrantable, and necessary defence of their owne freedome, and of the Churches freedome, they must stand, and therefore could not admit a forged claime without shew of truth. As they were in the heat of contention, the one side striuing to impose the yoke of their Iurisdiction vpon the Church; the other re-

L   solued

solued to stand close and faithfull for the freedome of the Church : behold of a suddaine *Apiarius* the firebrand of this contention, touched by the very finger of God, and drawen to giue God the glory, and so to end this contention ; falleth downe on his knees before them all, and confesseth all those crimes to be most true, which were obiected against him : and with humble supplication craueth pardon of the Councell. And so this Tragedy ended.

Concil. Affrica. cap.:05.

19. The Fathers of this Councell hauing this experience of the Popes corruption and dishonestie : write to *Cælestinus* to this purpose. They intreat him not to trouble the Church, by patronising such wicked men as *Apiarius:* that he would not accept of appellations, made by such scandalous and condemned men, who would seeke a refuge for their wickednesse at Rome: they declare that the Nicen Canons derogate nothing from the African Church : that the Fathers of the Nicen Councell sawe with great wisedome, that all suits were to be ended in the places where they began ; that the grace of the holy Ghost should not be wanting to any Prouince ; that if any bee offended hee may appeale to a Prouinciall, or to a generall Synode ; that transmaritim iudgments ought not to be admitted, where witnesses cannot be conueniently produced, either for sexe or age: that to send any Legats from the side of the Romane Bishop, is a thing found in no Synode established ; that the Canon of the Nicen Councell, by which the Popes claimed this Iurisdiction is not to be found in the autentike copies of that Councell, and therefore falsified. Last of all they admonish him, that hee and his successours must take good heede, *Ne fumosum typhum sæculi in Ecclesiam Christi, &c.* That is, that they induce nor the smoke of arrogancie to darken the Church of Christ, which Church doth bring the light of simplicitie and the bright day of humilitie to such as desire to see God. Thus write the Fathers of that Councell to Pope *Cælestinus* ; intimating by what meanes, that smoke did begin to rise to darken the Church which is prophesied in the Reuelation, which came out of the bottomlesse pitt like the smoke of a great furnace. Vpon these reasons they make a decree, to preuent his ambitious desires, by

Concil. African. cap.105.

Quæcun� nego- tia in suis locis vbi orta sunt, fi- nienda : nec gratiam spiritus S.vnicui�, Pro- uinciæ defutu- ram.

A:oc.9.2.

by which decree they forbid all appellations to Rome, or to a-
ny other place from Affrica : it is extant in the Affrican Councell, and this it is.

Item placuit vt presbyteri, Diaconi, vel cæteri inferiores Cleri-   Concil. Affrica
ci in caufis quas habuerint (fi de iudicys Epifcoporum fuorum quç-   cap. 92.
fti fuerint) vicini Epifcopi eos audiant. [Moreouer it was thought
good that Priefts, Deacons, or other inferiour Clarkes, if in
their caufes they complaine of the iudgements of their Bifhops, they fhall bee iudged by the next adioyning Bifhops,
&c.] And a little after, *Quod fi & ab ijs prouocandum putaue-*
rint, non prouocent nifi ad Affricana Concilia, vel ad primates Pro-
uinciarum fuarum. Ad tranfmarina autem qui putauerit appellan-
dum, à nullo inter Affricam in Communionem fufcipiatur. [And
if they appeale from them, they fhall not appeale but to the
Affrican Councels, or to the Primates of their Prouinces. Whofoeuer appealeth to outlandifh places, fhall be admitted to the
Communion by none within Affrica.

This was not fo much a new decree, as the maintaining of that
auncient decreed right, which *Cyprian* doth mention, teftifying
that it was decreed euen in his time by all the Bifhops of Affri-
ca, *Statutum eft ab omnibus :* that the caufe fhould bee there   Cyprian. Epif. 55
heard and examined, where the fault was committed. This
Canon which was thus eftablifhed in the Affrican Councell, is
for clearing of the truth, and preuenting of thefe ambitious
courfes, and claimes of Rome, repeated and confirmed alfo in
the Mileuitan Councell : where Saint *Auguftine* was alfo pre-   Concil. Mileuit.
fent. For it muft be obferued that the fixt Carthaginian, the fe-   cap. 22.
uenth Carthaginian, the Affrican, and Meleuitan Councels
were held all about this time by the fame men: fo great was the
care and diligence of the Fathers, that by many Councels
as it were by fo many lights, they might difpell the fmoake
of the darkeneffe, which they faw then rifing out of the Church
of Rome : which fmoake after thofe times quenched the light,
and couered the fight of the Church, as a mift couereth the
heauens.

20 Thus did thefe worthy Fathers difpell this fmoke for that
time, and reiect the yoake of the Popes Iurifdiction. In all this

businesse S. *Augustine* had an especiall hand and head. And as long as he liued, the Popes could neuer preuaile. But the Bishops of Rome hauing thus once cast off all regard of truth and modesty, were resolued to proceed on in this wretched course, and neuer gaue ouer, till at last they obtained their purpose. There is an Epistle of *Boniface* the second, written after these times, extant in the Tomes of councels, which whether it bee true, or counterfait (as much other stuffe is of this argument) we are to obserue something out of it, because it concerneth this question. This Epistle is intituled, *De reconciliatione Car-*

Epist.2. Bonif.2.
inter decreta
eiusdem.

thaginensis Ecclesiæ, written to *Eulalius* Bishop of Alexandria: he certifieth the Bishop of Alexandria of great ioy, for as much as the Church of Carthage is now returned, saith hee, *ad communionem nostram*: and receiueth all our mandates, which by our Legates wee send them. Hee signifieth that supplications must be made to G O D, that other Churches may likewise be brought home to the same obedience. That the Bishop of Alexandria must giue notice heereof to all the brethren about him, that they cease not to giue thanks for such benefites of the heauenly fauour. For, saith he; *Aurelius præfatæ Carthaginensis Ecclesiæ olim Episcopus, cum collegis suis instigante diabolo, superbire temporibus prædecessorum nostrorumBonifacij atq̃ Cælestini contra Romanam Ecclesiam cœpit,&c.* That is: *Aurelius* once Bishop of Carthage, began with his colleagues, by the instigation of the diuell, to wax proud against the Ro̅ mane Church, in the dayes of our predecessours *Boniface* and *Cælestinus*. But *Eulalius* at this time Bishop of Carthage, finding himselfe for the sins of *Aurelius*, cut off from the co̅ munion of the Church of Rome, hath humbled himselfe, and sought peace, and the communion of the Church of Rome by his subscription, and together with his colleagues hath by Apostolicall authority vtterly condemned all Scriptures and Writings, which by any wit haue beene framed against the priuiledges of the Church of Rome.

   21 Whether this Epistle be forged or not, it commeth all to one reckoning. For if it be forged, let the Bishop of Rome take the shame of the forgery. If it be the true writing of the Bish. of Rome, then he auoucheth that the holy & worthy ma̅ of God S.

Augu-

Auguftine, with *Aurelius*, and the reft of his colleagues were
ftirred vp by the inftigation of the diuell, to withftand this Romane Iurifdiction. We may the better beare the reproaches of
the Romifh Sinagogue, when they fharpen their tongues and
pennes againft the feruants of G O D in our times, feeing they
haue done as much againft the auncient godly Fathers. For
what can the late Popes fay more againft *M. Luther, Iohn
Caluin*, or any other of the worthies of the reformed Churches,
then this *Boniface* the fecord faith againft holy S. *Auguftine*,
that he with the reft of his company were ftirred and inftigated
by the diuell, to ftand againft the Iurifdiction of the Romifh
Church? Then when we denie their Iurifdiction, wee denie it
with the Fathers: when wee are therefore condemned by the
Pope and his Court, we are condemned with the auncient Fathers, with them we fuffer, with them we are reuiled, and condemned. The goodneffe of our caufe, the fellowfhip of the
auncient Saints, the warrant of the truth, is able to fupport vs
againft the impotent malice and fury of thefe men, that haue no
other caufe to be offended at vs; then their Fathers had againft
S. *Auguftine*, and the reft of the auncient and holy Fathers, who
haue refifted the Romifh Iurifdiction, and therein haue left a
worthy example to vs, to follow their foot-fteps. Thus we fee
the Popes Iurifdiction was firft attempted by forgery, and afterward by falfhood, and tyrannie effected.

22 Other Churches were afterward in time drawne to the
obedience of this Iurifdiction. The Churches of Rauenna, A-
quileia, and Millane, were long after this brought vnder the
fame yoake by Pope *Stephen* the third, faith *Sabellicus*. But
Platina faith, that *Millaine* was drawne to this obedience by
Stephen the ninth. If this be true, then *Millain* ftoode out till
the yeare of Chrift nine hundred and fourty. And thus the
quarrell for Iurifdiction was begun by *Zozimus*, maintained by
Boniface, and *Caleftinus*, but reiected by thefe Affrican Councels. The caufe was much helped by fome that fucceeded as
Leo, and others. Who though in fome things they were deceiued, and by the fleighty and fubtill worke of Sathan drawne
to doe it, vpon this fo much fancied Iurifdiction of Rome : Yet

*Epift. Stephani
3. apud Sabel-
licum.
Platin. Ste-
phano. 9.*

(as in charity we are to iudge) they were preferued by the mer-
cie of God, from that fhamelefle impudency of fome of their
predeceffours, and were content to leaue things as they found
them. And fo the Church of Rome ftoode vntill the time of
Gregorie the firft.

C H A P. VI.

Of the ftate and Iurifdiction of the Church, from the yeare of
Chrift 600. vntill the conqueft of England. Wherein is
declared how this Iurifdiction was firft refuted by the
Popes, and after obtained by the fucceeding Popes. How
the Popes refifted the Emperour, and furprifed the Empe-
rours Iurifdiction and lands, and how fome Emperours
recouer Iurifdiction againe.

Ow we enter into thofe fatall times of our captiuity: For wee confefle that our Fathers were
by a iuft iudgement of God brought into a captiuity farre greater then the Babilonian. Our
Kings, our Bifhops, our people, our Church,
and all were oppreffed. And they that led vs
captiues aske vs, where was our Church then ? Wee anfwere, in
captiuity. For though the greateft number then followed the
pleafures and delights of Babilon, yet among them the true Ifrael of God remained. And we are able, by the grace of God,
to proue a true Church to haue continued in the doctrines of
the trueth, vntill God fent in his wonderfull mercy, a deliuerance from this captiuity. But this belongeth to another queftion.

2 After thefe times the Iurifdiction of Princes and of the
Church, was oppreffed by the Pope. But before they came into that great oppreffion and captiuity, it pleafed God, for better teftification of his truth to all ages, and for the confufion of
this

this tyrannie gotten and maintained by forgerie; to cause one of the Popes to dispute this question with such zeale and courage, that it remaineth an euerlasting testimonie against this Iurisdiction, and against all his successours. For when *Iohn Bishop* of Constantinople would haue had this title of Oecumenicall Bishop confirmed to him, *Gregory* the first (questionlesse the best Pope that hath beene since his time) vseth such reasons against *Iohn*, as are sufficient to proue, that no Bishop hath right to that Iurisdiction which now the Popes claime, and that hee who vsurpeth that place aboue his brethren, is Antichrist. And if the iudgement of *Gregory*, be sufficient to determine this controuersie, it will follow that Antichrist hath beene raised vp in the Church of Rome presently after *Gregory*, and hath in the succession of those Bishops sit there euer since: because since the time of *Gregory*, they haue taken and claimed this title, and thereby so much increased in pride, ambition, and enormous practises against the Church, and against states, that he that compareth these times with the former, shall finde it another state, then it was in the time of *Gregory*.

3 And because the Pope now glorieth in this title of vniuersall Bishop, from which title he would draw a Iurisdiction ouer all Bishops, *Gregory* herein is peremptory, that whosoeuer taketh that title, robbeth Christ of his place and glory. For, saith he: *Sub vno capite omnes membra sunt Ecclesia, sancti ante legem,* *Lib.4.indict.13.* *sub lege, sancti sub gratia: et nemo se vnquam vniuersalem vocari Epist.82.* *voluit.* [All the Saints as members of the Church are vnder one head, the Saints before the Law, vnder the Law, and vnder grace: and no man would euer suffer himselfe to be called an vniuersall Bishop.] This was then the learning of the Church of Rome, that because Christ was the onely head of the vniuersall Church, therefore no man may be. For the deuise which after this the Friars brought in, of *caput ministeriale*, was then vnknowne. The reason of *Gregory* is well to be obserued: because euery man is a member of the vniuersall Church, no man can be both head and member of the same. And therefore hee vrgeth this thing often; as namely where he saith: *Vniuersa sibi Epist.36.lib.4.* *tentat ascribere, & omnia qua soli vni capiti coharent, videlicet* *Christo,*

Chriſto, per elationem Pompatici ſermonis, eiuſdem Chriſti ſibi ſtu-
det membra ſubiugare. That is : he ſeeketh to aſcribe all to himſelfe, and whoſoeuer as members are knit to one onely head,
that is Chriſt, he deuiſeth by the pride of this Pompaticall title
to ſubdue to himſelfe. Thus ſaith *Gregory* of him that ſought
this title of vniuerſall Biſhop. In many other places he proueth
the ſame : that Chriſt is the onely and ſole head of the Church,
and therefore no man can challenge this title of vniuerſall
Biſhoppe, *or head* of the vniuerſall Church. Whoſoeuer doth
it, muſt bee that Antichriſt that thruſteth Chriſt out of his
place. For it is well to bee obſerued, that the reaſons of *Gre-*
gorie againſt the claime of vniuerſall Biſhoppe, or head of
the vniuerſall Church, doe as well and truely refute all theſe
names of pride now chalenged by the Popes, as this which
then was chalenged by *Iohn* of Conſtantinople. For now theſe
titles are giuen to the Pope as his due ſtile : *Princeps Sacerdo-*
tum, Uicarius Chriſti, caput Eccleſiæ, fundamentum Eccle-
ſiæ, pater & doctor omnium fidelium, ſponſus Eccleſiæ, Epiſcopus
vniuerſalis. All theſe being titles of the like pride and pompe,
are alike condemned by *Gregory.* Of this title of vniuerſall Biſhop *Gregory* ſaith ſo much, as might iuſtly deterre all his ſuccef-
ſours from that or any of the like nature. For he calleth it : *Vo-*
cabulum profanum, vanum, nomen vanitatis, vocabulum peruer-
ſum, vocabulum elationis, ſceleſtum, ſuperſtitioſum, ſuperbum;
Thus in diuers places he ſetteth out that title, and farther ſaith
that it is : *Appellatio nefandi nominis, profani nominis ſuperbia, ap-*
pellatio friuoli nominis, vanitas ſtulti nominis, nomen Pompaticum.
By all which termes diſperſed in diuers parts of his workes, hee
hath declared his zeale againſt the pride of them that take ſuch
names vpon them, declaring that the blaſphemy of this name
was a proofe, that Antichriſt was riſing in the Church. For he
ſaith, that hee that taketh this name of vniuerſall Biſhop, is the
fore-runner of Antichriſt. For that Antichriſt muſt be Lord of
the Clergy, *Gregory* witneſſeth, ſaying, *Sacerdotum ei præpara-*
tur exercitus.

    4. Now ſeeing that from theſe names of pride, they would
proue the Popes Iuriſdiction: We anſwer, this proofe is founded

Bellar. de Rom.
Pont. lib.2. cap.
31.

ded vpon a rotten and ruinous ground-worke, seeing their auncient Popes haue vpon the same reasons grounded the proofe
of Antichrist. After the death of *Gregory, Sabinian* succeeded,
who sate but fiue moneths and nineteene dayes. And then came
Boniface the third, who obtained of the Emperour *Phocas*, that
title which *Gregory* had so condemned. Then and neuer before
was the Church of Rome made the head and Mistresse of all o-
ther Churches, and the Pope the chiefe Bishop of all Bishops.
This was done in the yeare of Christ sixe hundred and sixe. And
this *Boniface* is accounted the threescore and sixe Pope from
Peter, as *Caranza* noteth. Then we say, that whatsoeuer *Gre-*
gorie hath written against *Iohn* Bishop of Constantinople, all
standeth strong against *Boniface* the third, and all the Popes after
him. For he first obtained this Antichristian name, and all the
rest haue enioyed it, & much encreased both titles of pride and
power answerable to those titles.

5. But because *Bellarmine* would salue vp the wound that
Gregory hath giuen to all Popes after *Boniface*, let vs briefly
consider his shifts, and so proceede. First he saith, that by *Gre-*
gory his words the Pope should not be Antichrist, but onely *præ-*
cursor Antichristi, the fore-runner of Antichrist. *Nam præcur-*
sor, saith he, *non debet esse idem cum eo quem præcurrit, sed longe*
minor. Si ergo præcursor Antichristi est ille, qui se facit Episcopum
vniuersalem, ipse Antichristus verus non hoc se faciet, sed aliquid
maius. We answer: *Boniface* the third, who first obtained this
title in the Church of Rome, was the fore runner of Antichrist,
and began to his successours, but his successours encreased that
dominion which *Boniface* began: For they were not onely vniuersall Bishops, that is, Lords of Bishops, but they were also
Lords of Kings: that is, more then *Boniface* was: and therefore
wee yeeld, that the fore-runner is lesse then Antichrist in his
height, and yet we say, that *Gregory* his words stand both against
the one and the other, vnanswered by *Bellarmine.* Another testimony of *Gregory*, he would shift thus. *Pari ratione* (saith Bellarmine) *cum ait Gregorius: Sacerdotum ei præparatur exercitus:*
non vult dicere Sacerdotes vt Sacerdotes, ad exercitum Antichristi
pertinere, sic enim seipsum etiam in illo exercitu collocasset, sed Sa-

M   *cerdotes*

Bellar. de Rom.
Pont. lib.3. cap.
13.

Bellar. ibid.

cerdotes vt superbos Antichristo exercitum præparare. Graunting all true that *Bellarmine* saith, the wound is not cured which *Gregory* hath giuen to the proud Popes, and to their proud and luxurious Priests: these salues of *Bellarmine* are so farre from curing of the sore, that they make it much worse. Moreouer, *Bellarmine* sometimes would shift it thus, as if *Iohn* Bishop of Constantinople, when hee sought to be Oecumenicall Bishop, did not meane to be the chiefe of all Bishops, as the Pope is, but to be the onely Bishop, that there should be no other Bishop in the world but himselfe: so that he would inferre that the thing which *Boniface* obtained, was not the very thing which *Gregory* so lately before, and so hainously had condemned. Wee will therefore out of approued Histories briefly shew, that the honour which *Boniface* obtained, was no other thing, then that dishonorable title which *Iohn* Bishop of Constantinople sought to get, and which *Gregory* so much reproued & abhorred.

6   And certaine it is, that the thing which *Gregory* so sharply reproued, was that which *Iohn* sought. Now that *Boniface* obtained the same thing, they who write thereof, beare sufficient witnesse. *Paulus Diaconus* saith thus: *Hic (Phocas) rogante Papa Bonifacio, statuit sedem Romanæ Ecclesiæ, vt caput esset omnium Ecclesiarum, quia Ecclesia Constantinopolitana primam se omnium Ecclesiarum scribebat.* That is: [This man at the suit of *Boniface*, ordained that the sea of Rome should be head of all Churches, because the Church of Constantinople wrote her selfe the chiefe of all Churches.] Then by this testimony wee finde, that *Boniface* obtained no other thing of *Phocas*, then that which *Iohn* Bishop of Constantinople had sought before. *Abbas Vspergensis* saith. *Post Sabinianum Bonifacius eligitur ad Pontificatum: cuius rogatu Phocas constituit sedem Romanæ et Apostolicæ Ecclesiæ caput esse omnium Ecclesiarum, nam antea Constantinopolitana se scribebat primam omnium.* That is: [After *Sabinian Boniface* was chosen Pope, at whose suit *Phocas* ordained, that the sea of the Romane Apostolike Church should be the head of all Churches: for before this, the Church of Constantinople had writ her selfe the chiefe of all.] Then this thing was graunted by *Phocas*, at the suit of *Boniface*; and what was granted? no other thing

Paul. VVarnefrid. Phoca.

Vspergens. Chronic.

thing then *Iohn* of Constantinople had sought before. *Platina* witnesseth the same thing : *Bonifacius à Phoca imperatore obtinu-* *Platin. Bonifac.*3. *it, magna tamen contentione , vt sedes beati Petri Apostoli, quæ caput est omnium Ecclesiarum, ita & diceretur & haberetur ab omnibus : quem quidem locum Ecclesia Constantinopolitana sibi vendicare conabatur.* That is : [*Boniface* obtained of *Phocas*, but with great suit, that S. *Peters* sea which is the head of all Churches, so should be called and accounted of all : Which place the Church of Constantinople sought to take to her selfe.] Then this was gotten by the importunate suit of *Boniface*, and he obtained nothing, but that which *Iohn* Bishop of Constantinople had sought before. And thus the Writers that make any mention of this thing, witnesse without question, that *Boniface* by importune suit and great contention, obtained no other thing then that which the Bishop of Constantinople had so lately sought, and which *Gregory* the first Pope had so peremptorily condemned as a thing blasphemous, sacrilegious, preiudiciall to the gouernment of Christes Church, thrusting Christ downe, and raising Antichrist vp, and therfore vtterly vnlawfull for any Bishop to seeke or to hold. For that herein was included that principality ouer Bishops, which *Gregory* also so much condemned, no man maketh question. *Blondus* saith : *ad huius (Bonifacij) petitionem Phocas antistitem Rom. principem Episcoporum omnium dixit.* That is : [At the suit of *Boniface*, *Phocas* appointed the Bishop of Rome to be the Prince of all Bishops.] And *Nauclerus* *Vol.*2.*Generat.*21. saith : *Bonifacius insolentiam Patriarchæ Constantinopolitani οἰκουμένικον se appellantis , compescuit. Phocas enim Pontificis suasione, publica, ac ad vniuersum orbem dimissa sanctione, constituit, vt Rom.Ecclesiæ, Romanoq́; Pontifici omnes orbis Ecclesiæ obedirent.* That is : [*Boniface* repressed the insolence of the Patriark of Constantinople, calling himselfe Oecumenicall. For *Phocas* at the suit of the Pope, ordained by a publique decree, published ouer the world, that all that Churches in the world should obey the Church of Rome and the Bishop of Rome.] Then this matter is so euident the no shift can help it, no cloake can hide the shame : so that either *Gregories* workes should haue beene burned for Heresie, or this title of Oecumenicall Bishop, should not haue beene taken vp by the Popes.

· 7. And hence is the originall of the Popes Iurisdiction ouer all Bishops, he had once as much Iurisdiction ouer Bishops, as *Phocas* could giue him. But who gaue him Iurisdiction ouer Princes? That part of Iurisdiction was not then knowen in the world. But after this it crept in, the occasion thereof grewe thus. When the Empire was vtterly decayed in the West, and so weake in the East, as not able to keepe Italy in obedience; though for a time rather by the bare name and opinion of auncient gouernement, then by any present strength, they kept some commaund in Italie by their Exarches abiding at Rauenna : *Gregorie* the second Pope, espying this weaknesse, and watching for an opportunitie to take the Empire at such disaduantage : to driue the Emperour quite out of Italie, vsed the helpe of the Lumbards against him ; and preuailed so far that he gaue the Emperors army the ouerthrow in a pitched field: and slew *Paulus* the Exarch in battell. *Hac tempestate* (saith *Palmerius*)

In Chronic. an. 726,

inter Pontificem & imperatorem maxima discordia fuit : quam ob causam contra Pontificem in Italiam missi sunt primum Paulus Exarchus ; mox eo interempto in eius locum substituitur Eutychus : sub quo varie pugnatum est diuisa Italia. In quo bello Antipharium Longobardorum ducem, auxilia Pontifici prabuisse Constat. That is, [At this time a great discord rose betweene the Pope and the Emperour : for which cause first *Paul* the Exarch was sent to Italy, but he was slaine, and *Eutychus* sent in his place : vnder whom many battels were fought with variable fortune; Italy being diuided. In which warre it is well knowen, that *Antipharius* Duke of the Lombardes did aide the Pope against the Emperour.] *Nauclerus* declareth that one especiall occasion of this breach betweene *Leo* the Emperour, and *Gregorie* the second Pope, was, that *Leo* abolished images which were worshipped, and commanded the Pope to do so : wherat the Pope was so inraged that hee drewe all Italie from the obedience of

Naucler. Vol. 2. generat. 25.

the Emperour. *Tantamq, authoritatem tunc habuerunt Romani Pont. decreta* (saith *Naucler*) *vt Rauennates primi, exinde Venetia, populi atq, milites, aperta in Imperatorē Exarchumq, rebellionē pra se tulerint. Ac eo processit rebellio, vt depositis Exarchi magistra-*
tibus,

tibus. singula ciuitates, singula oppida proprios magistratus, quos duces apellabant, creare & præsicere curarent. [Such authority then had the Popes decrees, that first the Rauennates, after that the Venetians did raise an open rebellion against the Emperour and the Exarch. And this rebellion proceeded so farre, that euery city, and euery towne put downe the Exarches, and created proper Magistrates to themselues, whom they called Dukes.] Thus fell the gouernment of Italy into so many partes euery one catching what they could, as men vse to doe at a great shipwracke. And the Pope was carefull to prouide that his part should not be the least.

8. When thus the Pope had driuen the Emperour out of all Italie, and by that meanes had drawen Italie into as many Dominions in a manner, as there were great Cities ; the strongest began to pray vpon the weaker. Heere began the fire of emulation to kindle betweene the Pope and the Lumbards, for the Lumbards were the strongest part of Italie then, and the Popes part was the second : all other were weake in respect of these two ; and these two thereto agreeing well hitherto, so long as both conspired against the Empire : began now to fall at variance about the deuiding of the spoile. The Pope finding the Lumbards too strong for him, in this parting of the spoile of the Empire ; as before hee had vsed the strength of the Lumbards, to suppresse the Emperour : so now following the same arte, called *Pipin* the Constable of Fraunce into Italie, by whose power hee repressed the Lumbards : and compelled *Astulphus* their King to receiue conditions of peace. *Platina* saith, that *Gregorius* chiefe Secretary to the Emperor, did meet *Pipin* as he came into Italie, and intreated him that if he should ouercome the Lumbards, he would restore the Exarchate of Rauenna to the Emperour, to whom of right, said hee, it belonged, (All that poore right that then he sought to hold in Italie, detained as then by the Lumbards, but presently falling vnto the Popes share) and that he would not yeeld it to the Pope. The aunswere of *Pipin* was, he came into Italie to gratifie the Pope, and that he would helpe him as much as he could. That which after the victorie fell to the Popes part, and to Rome, was saith

Platina,

Platina, all that lieth betweene Padus and the Appennine, from
Placentia, to the Venetian standing waters ; and whatsoeuer is
contained betweene the riuer Isaurus and Appennine. *Paulus*
Æmylius saith, all that which before was called Flaminia,
wherein was Rauenna, was hereupon commaunded to bee called Romandiola. The match by negotiation betweene *Pipin*
and the Pope was made thus : that all that which was recouered from the Lumbards, being before parcell of the Empire,
should be adiudged to the Pope, and to Rome : and *Pipin* for
his seruice should bee made King of Fraunce by the Pope,
and *Chilperie* the lawfull King should be deposed. All this was
accordingly performed ; and *Pipin* was absolued from the Oath
of Allegeance, and so were all the Barons and people of France
absolued from the Oath of obedience : which before they
had taken to *Chilperie*, or as some call him *Hilderic*, their
King.

Vspergensis
Nauoler.

9. This Storie I haue briefly set downe, that the ground of
the Popes Iurifdiction may be the better obserued : for from
such straunge grounds, these Romane Catholikes draw the
Popes Iurifdiction, and the parts thereof, as a man of ordinary
reason would least suspect : so capricious are they now growen.
As for example, from this fact of Pope *Zacharie*, who absolued
subiects from the Oath of Allegeance to their true King ; who
would thinke that the Popes Iurisdiction could bee drawen ?
who would not rather iudge that the Popes arrogancy, pride,
vsurpation, oppression, corruption might by this be prooued ?
And yet *Augustinus Anconitanus* maketh this fact the onely
ground and proofe of his Iurisdiction: we looke for such a Iurisdiction as Christ left to his Church, we looke for proofes from
Scripture : but we find no other Iurisdiction prooued, then the
Iurisdiction of Antichrist, opposite to Chrifts Iurisdiction, and
ouer Princes : for proofes out of the word of God, we find no
other proofes, then such as are drawn from the Popes rebellion and conspiracie against the auncient Emperours, from their
vniust vsurpation, and oppression of lawfull Kings, from an impious power pretending authority to breake and violate oaths,
and faith, and Allegeance of subiects. And this manner of
                                                        proofe

proofe is held so strong, that nothing is more common among
them then thus to proue Iurisdiction. One of that ranke would
after the same maner proue this Iurisdictō by the Popes dispen-
sing against oathes and vowes. For, saith he, [*Edward* the Confessour had made a vowe to goe in person to Rome, but was
dispensed by Pope *Leo* the ninth, King *Iohn* sued to Pope *Innocentius* the third, to be dispensed with all for his oath ; which
he had made to the Barons of England. And *Henrie* the seuenth
procured from Pope *Iulius* the 2. that notorious dispensation
for Prince *Henrie* his sonne, to marry the Princesse *Katherine*
of Spaine, left by his brother *Arthur.* Hereupon hee inferreth
thus, these alone are sufficient to shew what opinion was held
from time to time by the Kings of England, concerning the
Popes Soueraigne Supreme Iurisdiction in spiritual matters belonging to conscience and directing of soules : thus farre the
Romane Catholike.]

An answere
of a Catholike
Diuine to the
fift part of re-
ports of Sir
Edward Cooke
p.123.

10. If this kinde of proofe please them to prooue the Popes
Soueraigne supreame authoritie, they may haue ynough thereof. For as Pope *Zacharie* dispensed with the oath of *Pipin*, and
all the French Barons, and subiects ; so doe the Popes since
practise this part of Iurisdiction with great seruency or rather
furie : they dispense with the oathes of subiects, they raise vp
rebellions against true, natural, and lawfull Kings, they aduance
vsurpers. This Iurisdiction wee graunt Popes haue practised
but with shame ynough, heere is the difference betweene them
and vs, betweene an euill cause and a good, betweene impudencie, and confidence in the truth: both they and we bring the
same examples, but to contrary ends : they bring these examples of the Popes practises, to prooue Iurisdiction : wee vrge
the same examples to shame the Pope with his Iurisdiction. Let
the indifferent and ingenuous reader iudge, whether applie
them to the true right and proper end. For let them aunswere
vs, if they can, whence the Popes haue authoritie to execute
such a Iurisdiction, as they haue neither from Christ, nor from
the Princes of this world ? For certaine it is that to dispense
with oathes, to stirre vp subiects against their naturall Princes ;
to mooue rebellions : is a power which the Pope hath not receiued

ceiued from Chrift, nor from the Princes of this world. From whence then hath he it, let them tell vs, who make it a part of his Iurifdiction.

11. After this, *Charles* the great, fonne to *Pipin*, was made Emperour by *Leo* the third Pope. At this time it appeareth, that the Iurifdiction which by the Emperour before this, was vfually practifed vpon the Bifhop of Rome, and other Bifhops began to be taken out of the hand of the Magiftrate. For when *Charles* hearing many complaints againft this *Leo*, concerning his life and conuerfation, called him to an examination in a great meeting of Bifhops, it was aunfwered by a great accla-mation: *Sedem Apoftolicam omnium Ecclefiarum caput, à nemine (laico præfertim) iudicari debere.* That is, [It is not meet that the Apoftolicke Sea, the head of all Churches fhould be iudged of any man, efpeciall a Lay-man.] This moued *Charles* to omit the matter: fo foone had they learned to turne this power againft the Emperor, which they had fome two hundred yeres before receiued from the Emperor. This Iurifdiction then by this time had receiued a great change; for in former times, as the inqui-fition of falfe doctrines belonged to the care of Bifhops, fo the examination of the life and manners of Bifhops: belonged al-wayes to the Magiftrate. So *Solomon* depofed *Abiathar.* So *Conftantine* banifhed diuers Bifhops, and reformed the Clergie. The godly Popes and Bifhops in former times yeelded this power to the Magiftrate, which God hath giuen him; knowing that euery foule is fubiect to them, euen Bifhops, euen Popes: yea, Apoftles themfelues. But now by the fall of the Empire, Papacy rifing, and a newe ftraunge image of the Empire, rifing vp in the Papacy, this Iurifdiction was then in hatching, which afterward was brought foorth by a monftrous birth.

12. My purpofe is, to note the occafions of alteration of Iu-rifdiction in the Church of Rome; and how the Popes hauing caft off the Iurifdiction of the Ciuill Magiftrate, did in time draw to themfelues a new forme of Iurifdiction; increafing the fame by degrees. For wheras at the beginning as we haue fhew-ed, the Bifhops of Rome with others, were vnder the coactiue Iurifdiction of the Ciuill Magiftrate: the abfence and fall of the Empire

Platin. Leone 3. Naucler. gener. 27.

Empire gaueopportunity to the Bifhops of Rome to raife thé-
felues. The firft beginning of their Iurifdiction, was by getting
appeales to be made to them: the enlarging & aduancing of it,
was by obtaining the title of *caput Ecclefia*, & vniuerfall B. The
Pope was not called *caput Ecclefia*, but the Church of Rome got
that title vnder *Phocas*, the Pope got it by his flatterers long after. And in the time of *Charles* the great, they had gotten in
one foote farther into this Iurifdiction; for then they began to
refufe the coactiue Iurifdiction of the ciuill Magiftrate. All this
while they were not come to the height and top of their Iurifdiction, to practife coactiue power ouer and againft the ciuill
Magiftrate, to depofe Princes, to raife vp rebellions, to abfolue
fubiects from their faith and alleageance, though fome of thefe
things were a new founding, yet they were not come to their
perfection till after this time: as we purpofe in order to declare.
And as we note their practifes, fo we muft no leffe haue an eye
to the men and meanes, which withftood them in thefe ambitious courfes.

13 Thefe attempts of Iurifdiction were then moft famoufly
withftood, when they were brought to their full hight. For after that the Popes had begun to ftretch their Iurifdiction to the
preiudice of Kings and Princes, then began the oppofition moft
to appeare, learned men being ftirred vp to write, and throughly to examine this queftion. Whereof my purpofe is to fpeake
farther in the laft Chapter of this Treatife. Here we will onely
note what refiftance it found at the beginning, before it was
growne vp to that hight, whereunto it came in time. Firft, wee
finde that both *Charles* the great himfelfe, and other Princes
and Bifhops, haue withftood the Bifhop of Rome heerein; and
feeking to giue euery one his right, haue giuen many parts of
that Iurifdiction, which now the Pope claimeth, to the ciuill
Magiftrate. For after that *Charles* had fubdued the Lumbards,
as his father *Pipin* had done before him: and befieging *Defide-
rius* King of the Lumbards, came to Rome from the fiege, to
know what hee fhould haue for his trauaife, for recouering S.
Peters Patrimonie, as the late Patrimonie of the Emperour fal-
ing to the Pope, then began to be called, (for the Pope had

promised to *Charles* for oppressing the Lumbards, and recouering this new Patrimonie, so much desired, so hotely pursu'd,
so dearely bought, that hee should be made Emperour of the
West, and the auncient authority and Iurisdiction of the Empire should be restored to him.) For the better effecting of these
affaires, *Charles* hauing sea a strong siege about Pauy, and taken
order with his Captaines for that seruice, left the siege & came
to Rome, bringing with him a great number of Bishops & Abbots, to holde a Synod with Pope *Hadrian*; and therein by all
their industry and knowledge, to finde out what were the true
and auncient priuiledges of the Empire, and what was the Emperours Iurisdiction confessed. Pope *Hadrian* receiued *Charles*
honourably, and at his pleasure called a councell. Wherein questionlesse some parts of the auncient Iurisdiction were restored
to *Charles*. For that Synod gaue him power to choose the Bishop of Rome, and in all Prouinces of his gouernment to inuest
all Archbishops, and Bishops. Thus much is acknowledged by
as many witnesses in a manner, as are Writers of the Story of
this time. But of late some haue quarrelled against this Story,
denying it to be true: which quarrell I purpose to handle and
discusse in the next Chapter, in his proper place. *Theodoricus de
Niem* writing of this councell, and of the end and purpose of
those that held it, saith, that this Synod was gathered purposely
to search out the auncient vses, lawes, and customes of the Empire and Church: that each power knowing their owne limits,
the one might not encroach vpon the other. *Celebrata est* (saith

Theodor. de
Niem.

he) *ab 153. viris religiosis, Episcopis & Abbatibus, &c. ab vniuersis regionibus et crasinibus almæ vrbis, à cuncto etiam Clero huius
sanctæ Rom. Ecclesiæ, exquirentibus vsus, leges, & mores eiusdem
Ecclesiæ et imperij.* That is: [It was celebrated by one hundred
and fifty three religious men, Bishops & Abbots, &c. by all the
regions and degrees of the City of Rome, by all the Clergy of
this holy Church of Rome, making search and inquisition for
the vses, lawes, and customes both of this Church and of the
Empire.] Then we see that *Charles* recouered some part of the
auncient Iurisdiction of the Empire. Which notwithstanding
since his time, the Popes by inuincible contentions, wrested

from

from the Emperours, chalenging it to be a part of their owne
Iuriſdiction, and charging the Emperours with Hereſie and
Schiſme for practiſing that right, which other Popes before
them, acknowledged to bee the auncient right of the Empire.

14 And becauſe to the Iuriſdiction of Princes it belonged
of olde, both to call councels and to confirme them, therefore
Charles did not omit this part of Iuriſdiction, though as the e-
uent declared, it was much againſt the Popes pleaſure. He called a Synod at Frankford, wherein was condemned the doctrine
of worſhipping of images, which doctrine the Pope had late before confirmed. The occaſion hereof grew thus. *Leo Iſaurus*
Emperour, being much offended that the Saracines had that
great and iuſt exception againſt Chriſtians, that they worſhip-
ped images: called a Synod at Conſtantinople, wherein the
worſhip of images was condemned, and the images burned. He | *Paulus Diacon.*
ſent alſo to the Biſhop of Rome, as then *Gregory* the ſecond,
commaunding him to doe the like, if he would haue his fauour,
ſaith *Paulus Diaconus. Gregory* the ſecond tooke this in ſuch indignation, that he rebelled againſt the Emperour, and raiſed all
Italy into a rebellion, by which meanes the Emperour loſt all
that then was left in Italy. *Gregory* the ſecond, in the middes of
theſe ſtirres died, and *Gregory* the third ſucceeded, who proſe-
cuting the purpoſe of his predeceſſour, called a Synod at Rome
in the yeare ſeuen hundred thirty three by *Sigebert:* ſeuen hun- | *Sigebert.*
dred thirty nine by *Palmerius.* In this Synod the doctrine of | *Palmerius.*
worſhipping images was confirmed; *Leo* the Emperor was excommunicated and depriued. Thus began the Pope to practiſe
a new Iuriſdiction, in depoſing Emperours. After this *Conſtan-*
tine ſirnamed, or rather nick-named, *Copronimus,* in the yeare of | *Sigebert.*
Chriſt, ſaith *Sigebert* ſeuen hundred fifty fiue, called a Synod at
Côſtantinople, wherein the worſhip of images was againe condemned. But another Synod was held at Rome by Pope *Ste-*
phen the third, in the yeare of Chriſt ſeuen hundred threeſcore
and eight, wherein the worſhipping of images was againe approued. Which was more famouſly confirmed in the yeare of
Chriſt ſeuen hundred foure ſcore and eight, by another *Conſtan-*
ſtine,

tine, and his mother *Irene,* who called the second Nycen Synod, wherein Imagerie preuailed much by the helpe of Pope *Hadrian.*

15. Vpon these stirres, *Charles* the great was moued to call a Synod at Franckford. Thither sent Pope *Hadrian* the acts of the second Nicen Synod, to be approued there, and to direct this Synod at Frankford, if they would take any direction from the Pope. But the Fathers of this Synode not regarding the Popes direction, tooke a meane course betweene the Greekes, who destroyed and defaced images, and the Church of Rome, which maintained the worship thereof. For they decreed that it was not impious to set vp images, but to giue any worship to them, this they held to be vtterly against Christian faith, and to be a thing receiued from the superstition of the Gentiles. This Synod was called and confirmed by *Charles* the great. Then belike the Pope had not gotten all Iurisdiction ouer Kings, which now he claimeth. For the Emperour called Synods : not the Pope. Neither as then had hee gotten Iurisdiction ouer all Bishops, because we see many Bishops were found in Germany, France, Aquitany, and England (for all these Nations *Charles* nameth in his letter to *Elepandus* Metropolitane of Tolet, as fauouring and maintaining the trueth against the worship of images) which resisted the Pope in this matter : so that his great and soueraigne Iurisdiction was not then established.

In Synodo Francford.

16. About this time that most worthy, most religious, and learned King *Alfred* raigned in England. *Aser Meneuensis* writing his life, entituleth him, *Omnium Britanniæ insulæ Christianorum rectorem.* Which title doth not much differ from that which is now in part giuen to the King : supreame Gouernour of all persons Ecclesiasticall. For whereas at this day the discipline of the Court of Rome, exempteth Clerkes from the Kings Courts, and consequently from the Kings gouernment, it appeareth that in King *Alfreds* time, this thing was vtterly vnknowne to the world : therefore this King is called and acknowledged to bee the Gouernour of all Christians within his dominions. Now because Bishops and Clerks were Christians, he was hereby questionlesse vnderstood the gouernour of Clerkes

Aser præfat. ad Alphredum.

as

aswell as of others. As then all forraine gouernement and
Iurisdiction was excluded by that title, so nowe there is
no other thing sought but in like sort to exclude all forraine power and Iurisdiction, whether the Popes or any other.
At this time when King *Alfred* liued and raigned, the sense,
iudgement, and vnderstanding of the world, was no other; but
that Kings were supreme gouernours of all persons and causes
Ecclesiasticall and Temporall within their owne Dominions.
I vnderstand gouernment here, as throughout this question I
haue often admonished, gouernment or power coactiue: for
this exemption of criminous Clarkes from their Kings Courts,
was a thing vnknowen in the world in those dayes. And therfore whereas it is commonly taken by our aduersaries (who vse
to begge such principles, as they cannot prooue) that the religion, sense, and iudgement of the world ranne wholly for the
Iurisdiction, which now is practised in the Court of Rome, this
wee vtterly denie. For we are able to shew when the sense,
iudgement, and religion of the Church, was against them, in
euery part of their pretended Iurisdiction. For first whereas the
Pope claimeth Iurisdiction ouer Bishops, this is one part of his
Iurisdiction, and is now the sense and iudgement of the Court
of Rome, but in the times of the sixt and seuenth Carthaginian
Councels, of the Affrican, and Mileuitan Synodes: at this time,
I say, and alwayes before, the religion, sense, and iudgement of
the whole world ran contrary. If any obiect, that these were
not generall Councels, but prouinciall: I aunswere, wee vrge
not their Canons onely, to rule the Pope, but their testimonies
to know the truth of those times and before. For they made an
exact and diligent search through all the famous Churches of
Christendome, for the Popes Iurisdiction ouer Bishops, and
hauing once so famously refuted that Iurisdiction, we take and
reuerence their testimonies, which will for euer be held honorable in the Church. Before these times, the religion, sense, and
iudgement of the world was not, that any Bishop or Clarke of
forraine Prouinces might appeale to Rome, which now is the
sense and iudgement of the Court of Rome. The Pope claimeth now this Iurisdiction likewise, to depose Princes, to dis-

solue:

solue and vndoe the obedience of subiects; this is now the sense
and iudgement of the Court of Rome : but before the time of
King *Pipin*, the sense and iudgement of the world ran alwayes
contrary. That the Pope is vniuersall Bishop ; and the Church
of Rome the head of other Churches, yea, the Pope the head
of the vniuersall Church, is now the sense and iudgement of
the Court of Rome : but this was not the sense, iudgement, and
religion of the Church of Rome before the time of *Gregorie* the
first, as the same *Gregorie* doth sufficiently witnesse. That criminous Clarkes should be exempted from the Courts of their
Kings, is now the practise and iudgement, sense and religion of
the Court of Rome ; but before the yeere one thousand, this
was not the sense and iudgement of the world. That the Pope
is aboue a generall Councell, is now the sense, and religion of
the present Court of Rome : but it was not the sense and religion of the Church of Rome before the time of the Councell of
Trent. In like sort of any part of their Iurisdiction whereof here
we speake, we are able to point to the time, when it was not
the sense, and iudgement of the Church of Rome.

17. About the time wherein *Alfred* raigned (who began his
raigne in the yeere of Christ eight hundred seuenty two, & died
in the yeere nine hundred.) The Popes hauing already intruded
vpon the Iurisdiction of Bishops and Archbishops, beganne to
make many desperate attempts vpon the Iurisdiction of
Kings also : but they were repressed where the Emperours had
any power to resist; and though they assumed Iurisdiction o-
uer Emperours, yet they brought not all to an effect. *Crantzi-*
us speaking of those times, saith : [The Emperour placed a Bishop in Monster: and maruaile not that a Bishop was appointed by the Emperour ; for this was the Custome of those times,
when Emperours had power to place and displace Popes : for
there was no free election of Chapters, as now : the Apostolicall confirmation was not then necessary, for whomsoeuer the
Prince did nominate, that man was to be consecrated a Bishop
by the next adioyning Bishops. Concerning this Iurisdiction
there was a long contention between the Papacie and the Empire, this was the Iurisdiction which the two *Henries*, the father

Metrop. Crantzij
lib. 2. cap. 29.

ther and the sonne ; which the two *Fredericks* likewise, the Grand-father and the Grand-child, sought long to defend and maintaine : but the sword of the Church preuailed, and forced the Emperours to relinquish their right to the Churches.] By this it may appeare, that before the yeere one thousand, the Popes entred into no great contention with the Germane Emperours concerning this Iurisdiction. But as the contentions betweene the two *Henries*, and the two *Fredericks*, and others, did fully open and reueale to the world the Popes purpose for Iurisdiction : so when it was once reuealed and fully knowen to the world ; it was denied and oppugned by the men of the best learning, that then liued in the Church of Rome : which thing we are more fully to declare hereafter.

CHAP. VII.

How the Papall Iurisdiction was aduanced from the time of the conquest and somewhat before, vntill the yeere of Christ, one thousand three hundred. The meanes raising that Iurisdiction is declared to be by Forgeries, Friars, Oathes, and the parts of the Iurisdiction, inuestitures, exemptions, lawes imposed, appellation, deposing of Kings, and absoluing their subiects from faith and Allegeance.

IN the time of *William* the Conquerer, about the seuenth yeere of his raigne, *Hildebrand* was chosen Pope, named *Gregorie* the seuenth. This man aduaunced the Popes Iurisdiction to an higher pitch, then euer it was before. Now all that power which was extorted from Princes by such violent practises as *Hildebrand* vsed, was afterward supposed to belong to the Popes Iurisdiction. And these late Iesuits make no doubt to tell vs, that all came from Christ, and his Apostles : and that it was a thing neuer heard, that Temporall Princes should

meddle

meddle in ſuch matters : and that the Religion, deuotion, ſenſe, and iudgement of all men ranne wholly for it. Wee are therefore to obſerue, how the Popes wreſted Iuriſdiction from temporall Princes. This thing will appeare better, if we take a ſuruay of theſe times, and of the meanes and parts of that Iuriſdiction, which wee finde chalenged by the Popes in theſe ages.

2. At this time the Popes began firſt of all to ſtriue for inueſtitures. Pope *Gregory* the ſeuenth began this contention with *Henry* the fourth Emperour : which was the occaſion of great warres and blood-ſhed through Chriſtendome, eſpecially in Germany. I will for the better vnderſtanding of theſe proceedings, with breuity and fidelity report, out of the ſtories of this time, in what ſtate the Church of Rome then ſtoode. In the time of *Henry* the third Emperour, the Court of Rome was peſtered with a ſort of men, infamous & prodigious : who taught Necromancy, practiſed poiſoning, ſet vp, as it were a ſchoole of vnlawfull Arts, abominable to God, and pernicious to men. One chiefe of this profeſſion was *Theophilactus*, which was afterward Pope *Benedictus* the eight, called *Benedictus* the ninth. This *Theophilact* was Maſter to *Hildebrand* in his Art Magick, who for his better furtherance in that knowledge, was alſo inſtructed by *Laurentius* the Malfilan Archbiſhop, and by *Iohn* the Archprieſt of S. *Iohn de porta latina.* This *Theophilact* gaue himſelfe wholly to the ſacrifices of deuils, with his complices and ſchollers, as he had beene iuſtructed by *Gerbertus*, which was Pope *Sylueſter* the ſecond. By theſe Maſters and meanes *Hildebrand* aſpiring to the Papacy, ioyned himſelfe in a ſtrict league with one *Brazutus*, who poiſoned ſixe Popes in the ſpace of thirteene yeres: their names mine Author ſetteth down in order thus. *Clemens* (this was *Clemens* the ſecond) *Damaſus* 2, *Leo* 9, *Victor* 2, *Stephanus* 10. *Benedictus* (this Pope eſcaped the poiſon, but was caſt out by force and cunning of *Hildebrand*) *Nicholaus* 2. Thus he practiſed to make way for himſelfe to the Papacy, by poiſoning all that ſtood in his way.

3. For redreſſing of theſe enormities *Henry* the third Emperour, was entreated by the religious ſort of Cardinalls, to
purge

Beno Cardinal. in vita & geſtis Hildebrand. Auent. lib.5. Annal.

Beno Cardinal.

purge the Church of this hellifh rabble, that thus peftered it.
The Emperor being drawne to feeke fome reformation of thefe
diforders, becaufe many Popes vfurped the Papacie at once, he
draue *Theophilact* to flight: *Gregory* the fixt, he fhut vp in prifon,
and after that exiled him : he caufed the Bifhop of Sabinum to
relinquifh the Papacie, and returne to his owne fea : and he fet
vp Pope *Clement.* *Hildebrand* was commaunded to goe into
banifhment with his Mafter *Gregory* the fixt. This *Gregory* dy-
ing in banifhment ; *Hildebrand* (as the fame Author faith:) *Per-
fidiæ fimul & pecuniæ cius hæres extitit.* That is : [Was heire both
of his perfidioufnefle, and of his money.] The Emperours patience, pitifull and too gentle nature is touched by the fame
Author : *Nimia pietate deceptus , nec Ecclefiæ Rom. nec fibi, nec
generi humano profpiciens, nouos Idolatras nimis laxè habuit.* That
is : [His gentle nature deceiued him, for he gaue too much li-
berty to thefe new Idolaters , neither prouiding well for the
Church of Rome, nor for himfelfe, nor for mankinde.] To
make fhort : *Hildebrand* attaining a releafe from banifhment,
came to Rome, and there falling to his olde practife, ftroue to
make *Brazutus* Pope, of whofe friendfhip he was affured ; their
mutuall familiarity being confirmed by many odious and blou-
die practifes. This is that *Brazutus*, by whofe meanes fixe
Popes were poifoned, as wee haue declared. But *Hildebrand*
perceiuing that the Emperour and the Cardinals were wholly
auerfed from a man fo infamous, and odious : fet vp *Alexander*
the fecond. Who perceiuing himfelfe fet vp againft the Emperours will, profeffed that hee would not keepe the place, without the licence and fauour of the Emperour. For this thing he
was well beaten and buffeted by *Hildebrand*, who ruled all, and
receiued the reuenewes in the time of *Alexander* : and after his
death, *Hildebrand* (faith the fame Author) was chofen Pope,
*eâdem horâ à militil us, fine affenfu cleri & populi : in cuius electio-
ne nullus Cardinalium fubfcripfit.* That is : [At the fame inftant
by Souldiers, without the affent of Clergy or people : none of
the Cardinals fubfcribed to his election.] *Nauclerus* declareth
an vngratious ftratagem of his, fuddenly practifed, to draw the
Cardinals to confent to his election. For when the Clergy and

O　　　　　　　people

*Naucler.2.gene-
ration 36.*
people were gathered together for the celebration of the fune-
rall of the former Pope, of a suddaine a cry was raised among
them, that S. *Peter* had chosen *Hildebrand* for Pope. That this
man may better be knowne, I will set downe the iudgement of
a Councell gathered at Brixia, consisting of a great number of
Bishops and Abbots, out of Italy, Germany, France. These Pre-
*Auentin.lib.5.
Naucler.2.gene-
ration.37.*
lates meeting in a publike Synod together, pronounce *Hildebrand* to be, *Falsus monachus, magus, diuinaculus, somniorum
prodigiorumq̄, coniector, male de religione Christiana sentiens. Pri-
mus omnium* (say they there) *Pontificatum maximum contra mo-
rem maiorum, inuitis omnibus bonis emit, &c. ius humanum diui-
numq̄, peruertit, falsa pro veris docet, sacrilegia, periuria, menda-
cia, homicidia, incendia, veluti benefacta indulget, collaudat, ad hæc
perpetranda classicum canit, &c. Suauis homo Sacerdotes qui vxo-
res habent legitimas, sacrificos esse pernegat, interim tamen scorta-
tores, adulteros, incestuosos aris admonet.* [A false Monk, a Ma-
gitian, a Witch, a South-sayer by dreames and ostents, one that
thought corruptly of Christian Religion: the first that bought
the papacie against the custom of his auncestours, against the
good will of all good men: he peruerteth all right humane and
diuine, teacheth falshood for trueth, he fauoreth and commen-
deth as things good and iust these things, sacriledges, periuries,
lies, murthers, burnirgs, he exhorteth and incourageth men to
these outrages; a sweet companion that denyeth preists that
haue lawfull wiues to say Seruice, but admitteth whoremon-
gers, adulterers, incestuous men to the Sacraments.] This is
the iudgement of a full Councell against his vnholinesse: as *A-
uentinus* and *Naucler* report.

    4. This is the man that began the contention for Iurisdicti-
on with the Emperour *Henrie* the fourth. *Tali dedicatore dam-*
Tertul.apol.ca.5
*nationis nostræ etiam gloriamur: qui enim scit illum, intelligere po-
test non nisi aliquid bonum grande ab* Hildebrando *damnatum.*
For of him wee may iustly vse the same words in the cause of
Princes, which *Tertullian* vseth of *Nero* in the cause of Christians. *Hildebrand* being made Pope began to moue many contentions with the Emperour, then being *Henrie* the fourth: one
speciall quarrell was for inuestitures. For whereas before that
               time

time the auncient cuſtome of the Empire was (ſaith *Naucler*) *Naucler. Vol. 2. gener. 36.*
that when a Biſhop was dead, the chapter vſed to ſend a ring
and the paſtorall ſtaffe to the Emperour, which the Emperour
deliuered to him whom he appointed Biſhop of that place: this
auncient priuiledge of the Empire *Hildebrand* would not indure, and therefore calling a Councell at Rome, of one hundred
and ten Biſhops, he curſed *Henrie* the Emperour : and all Biſhops that receiued inueſtiture at his hands, or any other Lay-
men. In this Councell he remooued married Prieſts from Diuine Seruice. But before he proceeded thus farre, he ſent firſt
to the Emperour, warning him to remooue all Symoniacall Biſhops from their places : the good Emperour either ſuppoſing
that this might proceed from an honeſt zeale, or willing to declare that in him there ſhould bee no want in reforming, did
accordingly thruſt out all ſuch as were ſuſpected of Symonie
from their Biſhoprikes : but behold, *Machiauell* ſet to Schoole.
Hildebrand hauing made all theſe Biſhops thus hatefull to the
Emperour, and hating him : preſently reſtored euery man to
his place againe; and to binde them ſure to himſelfe againſt the
Emperour, tooke an oath of them all, as mine author ſaith :
Quos regi infeſtos reddiderat, eos ſibi familiari amicitia reconcilia- *Beno. Cardin.*
bat ; & multis & magnis iuramentis ſibi fidos & obnoxios effici-
ens, præ alijs exaltabat. That is, [When he had once made them
to hate the Emperour, then he reconciled them to himſelfe in
familiaritie, and hauing made them ſo obnoxious to himſelfe,
bound them by many and great oathes, to be true to him; theſe
he preferred aboue all other.] Giuing the beſt preferments to
them.

5. Hauing thus by ſubtiltie ſpoiled the Emperour of his
friends, of a ſuddaine without any lawfull accuſation, without
Canonicall citation, without Iudiciall order; he thundreth out
an excommunication againſt him, depriueth him, abſolueth his
nobles and ſubiects from their oath of Allegeance. Whileſt he
denounced this ſtraunge ſentence, the Pue wherein he ſat, being made ſaith Cardinall *Beno* of new and ſtrong timber, of a
ſuddaine, brake in peeces. *Hildebrand* thus triumphing ouer the
Emperour, began to depoſe all ſuch Biſhops as had receiued
inueſtitures

inueftitures frō a Lay-hand:of this right of inueftitures we fhall
fpeake in fit place. Firft,let vs take a viewe and furucy of that
Iurifdiction which wee finde practifed in this age, and of the
meanes whereby the Pope attained thereto. If firft we confider the meanes which were vfed for the winning hereof, the
Iurifdiction will bee more apparant, and better knowen :
which Iurifdiction wee will alfo declare by the feuerall parts
and braunches thereof,fo farre as we are able to vnrippe them.

§ I.

Of the Forgeries whereby this Iurifdiction was firft challenged.

6. THe Popes and the Court of Rome, perceiuing well
how much it made for the aduancement to that Sea, if
they might be fecured for the right and title to this Iurifdiction
which they purpofed to challenge and practife : And vnderftanding that none would belceue that they had any right to it,
vnleffe they fhewed fome antiquity for it: finding alfo that they
wanted Scriptures, & the teftimonie of the ancient Church:be-
gan a moft defperate and vile practife, to forge antiquities, de-
uifing certaine writings,& fathering the fame vpon the ancient
Bifhops of Rome ; all was to make fome fhew and title to this
Iurifdiction, whereof they were fo much inamoured. In our
dayes there is leffe feare of daunger from thefe forged Epiftles, becaufe they haue bene throughly examined and refuted
by many learned men, as *Marfilius Patauinus, Laurentius
Valla, Antonin. Archiep. Florent. Nicholaus Cufanus, Æneas
Siluius, Hieronymus Paulus Catalanus, Raphaell Volateranus*:
all before Mafter *Luther*. In fo much as the learned Papifts are
afhamed of this ftuffe, and cannot denie the Forgery: but when
firft they were deuifed, (whether by *Anaftatius Bibliothecarius,*
as fome iudge, or by fome other trufty Champion of the Court
of Rome) they carried the world then into fuch an illufion,that
we may well iudge, it proceeded from the deepeneffe of Satan
in fubtiltie and falfhood, and was receiued with wonderfull
fimplicitie

simplicitie and ignorance of that age. For when the fatall time was come that Antichrist must send vp that smoak, wherwithall the truth was darkened : then fell such a iudgement vppon the world, that together with the darkening of Scriptures : learning, knowledge, and iudgement was decayed ; and they did with greedinesse beleeue lies and forgeries, who could not examine the truth. Then began they to publish new decretall Epistles, vnder the names of *Clement, Anaclet, Euaristus, Sixtus, Telesphorus, Higinus, Pius, Anicetus Soter, Eleutherius, Victor :* and many others. In whose names, certaine Epistles are framed to claime this Iurisdiction, but so absurd, the stile so vnfitted to the ages wherin these Bishops liued, that the learned Papists themselues blush at the forgerie. The argument of all these Epistles is in a manner one and the same, all plead for Iurisdiction : and if this question might be determined by these testimonies, then should they obtaine their Iurisdiction without controuersie. The things which are most of all handled and repeated therein ; are, the Primacie of the Pope, the power and authoritie of the Church of Rome ; exemption of Clarkes, and appellation to the Sea Apostolicke : these are the things handled and repeated ouer and ouer. The proofe for all, is set from, *Tu es Petrus & super hanc petram, &c.* And *pasce oues meas,* and *oraui pro te Petre :* and such like deprauations of holy Scriptures.

7. Heere is the true ground of their Iurisdiction, thus they got it by forgeries : and these forgeries in that age, (such was the ignorance thereof) were nothing suspected : other men, who detested such vile practises measured the mindes of Popes in charitie, by their owne : who would euer haue thought so basely of Popes, that they would haue entred into such dishonest practises ? Therefore this Iurisdiction was by many receiued, because they suspected no falshood, in such as should haue beene examples of vertue and godlinesse. But when the knowledge of good learning was raised againe, then began these Epistles to be examined, and were found such as they are. *Bellarmine* speaking of these Epistles, though glad he would be to maintain them if he knew how, yet dares not denie them to be forged. *Nec indubitatas esse affirmare audeam :* saith he. But if   *Lib.2.Cap.14. de Rom.Pont.*

you dare not auouch them to be vnforged : why then dare you auouch that Iurisdiction of the Pope, of which the world neuer tooke knowledge, before these Epistles had deuised proofes for it? And why dare you make vse of such forgeries? For *Bellarmine* confessing that he dare not iustifie them from suspition of forgerie : yet laboureth to take vse of them, as pretending that they are auncient : as though antiquitie in falshood could helpe? Or as if a robber and murtherer being taken in the manner and not able to iustifie his action, should plead that *Barrabas* was an auncient robber and murtherer ; and thinke to helpe himselfe by that plea. And because vpon this rotten foundation the Popes Iurisdiction is builded : let vs obserue some of the best and most substantiall proofes for Iurisdiction, out of these forged Epistles.

Anaclet.Epist.1. 8. *Anaclet* is made to say thus for the priuiledges of the Church, such priuiledges as exemption of Clarks, and such like as were introduced after the yere one thousand. *Priuilegia Ecclesiarum & sacerdotum, sancti Apostoli iussu saluatoris intemerata & inuiolata omnibus decreuerunt manere temporibus.* That is, [The priuiledges of Churches and of Priests, the holy Apostles decreed that they should remaine inuiolated for all times. For *Ibid.* Iurisdiction, he saith , *Quodsi difficiliores ortæ fuerint questiones, aut Episcoporum vel maiorum iudicia, aut maiores causæ fuerint, ad Apostolicam sedem si appellatum fuerit, referantur : quoniam Apostoli hoc statuerunt iussu saluatoris, vt maiores & difficiliores questiones semper ad sedem deferantur Apostolicam, super quam Christus vniuersam construxit Ecclesiam, dicente ipso Petro : tu es Petrus & super hanc Petram ædificabo Ecclesiam meam.* And a-*Anaclet.Epist.2.* gaine, *Summi sacerdotes, id est Episcopi, à Deo sunt iudicandi, non ab humanis aut praua vitæ hominibus lacerandi, sed potius ab omnibus fidelibus portandi.* This is often repeated that scandalous Clarkes must not be accused ; yea, though one of them should *Euarist.Epist.2.* liue most inordinately : *Licet sit inordinatus, quia pro meritis subditorum disponitur à Deo vita rectorum.* For proofe these Scrip-*Euseb.Epist.1.* tures are brought, *qui vos tangit, tangit pupillam oculi mei, & nolite tangere Christos meos , & in prophetis meis nolite malignari.* From this deepe Diuinity *Thomas Becket* resisted *Henrie* the second

cond, and would not suffer the King to execute iustice against
robbers, fellons, murtherers, practisers of Treason, if they were
Clargie men : he defended them by these Scriptures, as we shall
declare hereafter. This witch-craft came from Rome, and from
these forged Epistles. *Anaclet* saith again, *Hæc sacra sancta Ro-* *Anaclet.Epist.3.*
mana, & Apostolica Ecclesia , non ab Apostolis sed ab ipso domino
saluatore nostro primatum obtinuit, & eminentiam potestatis super
vniuersas Ecclesias : and to proue all, this is alleadged, *Tu es Pe-*
trus, &c. Another saith, *Si quis vestrum pulsatus fuerit in aliqua* *Sixtus.Epist.2.*
aduersitate, licenter hanc sanctam & Apostolicam appellet sedem,
& ad eam quasi ad caput suffuginm habeat. And another, *Iudi-* *Zepherin.Epist.1*
cia Episcoporum maioresq́, Ecclesiæ causæ, a sede Apostolica, non ab
alia (sicut Apostol: & sancti successores eorum statuerunt) cum alijs
Episcopis sunt terminandæ. And to proue that scandalous men of
the Clargie should not be punished or examined by Lay-men,
this reason is often repeated in diuers Epistles, that if since
the Apostles times that course had beene taken to punish
such, then few or none should now haue beene left aliue in the
Clargie : which is a secret confession that all the Clargie of the
Court of Rome were at this time of euill and scandalous life
and conuersation. *Marcellus* as writing to *Maxentius* the ty-
rant is produced to say thus : *Synodum absq́, huius sanctæ sedis* *Marcell.Epist.*
authoritate Episcoporum (quanquam quosdam Episcopos possitis
congregare) non potestis regulariter facere, neq́, vllum Episcopum
qui hanc appellauerit apostolicam sedem damnare, antequà hinc sen-
tentia definitiua procedat. These and such like are their grounds
of Iurisdiction, which need no refutation ; for absurdities carie
alwayes their owne bane in themselues : this is refutation y-
nough for such things to make those things well knowen.

9. These testimonies for Iurisdiction drawen from these
forged Epistles, may giue vs occasion to obserue. First, that the
Bishops of Rome haue long & greedily gaped after this Iurisdiction, & to obtain their purpose herein haue made no bones at
forgerie. As first they attempted that forgerie of a Canon of
the Nicen Councell in Saint *Augustines* time, but were then repressed : so the diuell to bring them to greater shame, mooued
them afterward to greater forgerie in deuising so many decretall

tall Epiftles, to eftablifh this Iurifdiction by this fhamelesse attempt, which by other direct meanes they could not doe. Se-
conly, fo greedily are they fet vpon this purpofe, as men blinded with affection, that they confider neither manner, nor matter, nor coherence: onely the impotent loue to this Iurifdiction
carrieth them through thicke and thin : as in many things may
be obferued. I obferue onely that which toucheth our queftion, for in thefe Epiftles this Iurifdictió of the Church of Rome,
and appellation to that Church is maintained as from the inftitution of Chrift himfelfe, out of thefe words : *Tu es Petrus, &c.*
Now thefe Epiftles muft be fuppofed to be written long before
Saint *Auguftines* time, when *Zozimus, Boniface,* and *Caleftinus,*
claimed the fame Iurifdiction by the forged Canon of the Nicen Councell : for before thofe times thefe Bifhops liued, who
are deuifed the authors of thefe Epiftles. If thefe Epiftles had
then beene extant, why did not the Popes claime their Iurifdiction by thefe teftimonies, which were fuppofed to be written
fo long before the Canons of the Nicen Councell ? What needed they to haue forged a Canon, if they had fo faire euidences to fhew ? And why did they claime it by a Canon of the
Councell, when they might haue laid their claime directly from
the commaundement of Chrift ?

10. But if thefe Epiftles were not then extant (as certainely
they were not) why fhould any credit bee giuen to things fo
manifeftly forged ? Why fhould any claime be made to Iurifdiction vpon fuch falfe grounds. Thirdly, we obferue alfo the
curfed obftinacie and affected blindneffe of the learned Papifts,
Bellarmine and fuch who know well that thefe Epiftles are forged, and confeffe it : knowing that this Iurifdiction of the
Pope was neuer claimed *iure diuino,* as from Chrifts owne inftitution, before thefe Epiftles by forgerie inuented that claime :
are fo bewitched in the feruice of the Pope, and in this queftion
of Iurifdiction, that againft learning, iudgement, confcience &
all, they hold this Iurifdiction to be *iure diuino,* in the groffeft
fort; & maintaine it no otherwife then thefe confeffed forgeries
haue taught them, by thofe deprauations, corruptions and de-
tortions of Scriptures, *Tu es Petrus,* and fuch like. An indifferent

rent man would thinke, that either they should not confesse these forgeries; or confessing them, they should hate and abhorre these grounds of Iurisdiction, which onely the forged Epistles haue deuised from Scripture. Fourthly, by this we may looke a little further into the deepenesse of Satan, and behold how the Popes Clarkes lie plunging for Iurisdiction.

11. For the Councell of Trent being awaked at the preaching of Master *Luther* and other, and finding that the corruptions which were brought into the doctrines of the Court of Rome could not bee mainteined by Scriptures, being directly repugnant thereto : deuised a very foule shift, to maintaine all by vnwritten traditions. And for this purpose enacted a Canon, that the traditions of the Church of Rome, must be honoured and imbraced with the like honour and reuerence, as the holy Scriptures are honoured. Therefore they deuise the word of God to be either written in Scriptures, or vnwritten in Traditions, which vnwritten Traditions they reuerence for Gods word, no lesse then the holy Scriptures themselues. And if you aske, how shall men trie true Traditions, they aunswere there is no better triall then the iudgement of the Church of Rome. *Ex testimonio huius solius Ecclesiæ sumi potest certum argumentum ad probandas Apostolicas Traditiones.* By these principles, if they might once haue them graunted, they thinke themselues able to conclude any thing, to delude the holy Scriptures, and to set vp prophane, and Barbarous forgeries in place of holy Scriptures. For if wee denie this pretended Iurisdiction, they will aunswere that it is grounded vpon the word of God: if we demaund, what word they haue for it? They tell vs : *Tu es Petrus,* &c. and such like. If wee say the sense and meaning of those Scriptures doe no way maintaine that Iurisdiction, the auncient Fathers neuer expounded them so : that that sense was neuer drawen from these Scriptures, before these forged decretall Epistles deuised it. To this they will say, they take that sense of Scriptures, which the Church of Rome taketh, and the Pope, who onely hath authoritie to giue the sense of Scriptures. The summe and conclusion of all, is this : the Traditions of the Church of Rome, are to be honoured and reuerenced

Concil.Trid.sess. 4.decret.1

Bellar.de verbo Dei non scrip. lib.4.cap.9.

uetenced with the fame honour as the holy Scripture: but thefe filthy, forged, and corrupt Epiftles containe the Traditions, yea, are the Traditions of the Church of Rome : therefore thefe filthy forgeries of corrupt men, are to be honoured, and reuerenced as the holy Scriptures.

12. Now though fome men vnlearned may be caried away with this vaine fhew of Traditions, yet wee fee not how their learned men can plead ignorance, or excufe, who know that thofe expofitions of thefe Scriptures, were firft forged in the decretall Epiftles : thefe be their Apoftolicall Traditions, thefe be matched with holy Scriptures. I appeale to the confcience of any Papift that either is, or would bee efteemed learned : whether thefe Epiftles be not forged, in his iudgement? And whether the ground of their Iurifdiction be not hence drawen? And whether this Iurifdiction which in thefe Epiftles is maintained, concerning appellation : was not repreffed, and vtterly denied by Saint *Augustine*, and the reft of thofe auncients in the Cartheginian, Affrican, and Mileuitan Councels? Perhaps it is not hard for a man of a leaden heart, and a brafen forehead to rufh through thefe difficulties after the Romane Catholike maner without blufhing ; but let a man in humility and good confcience, fet himfelfe to feeke the truth herein, and to giue God the glory ; and it will bee impoffible for him to wraftle out of thefe nets, but by confeffing the forgerie, and reiecting the Iurifdiction forged.

13. Moreouer that it may it further appeare, that this Iurifdiction is efteemed all in all, and more then all by thefe men : and that all other parts of their religion, are not fo deare to them, as this : we may further obferue, that as the Pope ouer-ruled the Councell of Trent, fo the thing that fwayed the Pope, and forced him to refolue vpon this courfe which now is eftablifhed by the Court of Rome, in the Councell of Trent, was onely the feare of loofing, and care of maintaining this Iurifdiction. For before the Councell of Trent (which thing we fhall hereafter by Gods helpe more manifeft at good opportunity) the Church of Rome ftood fo indifferently affected in the chiefe points of religion : that if the refpect and practife of the Pope had not
                                                              mifled

misled them, it may bee well iudged, they would haue beene more ready to assent to the conclusions of Master *Luther*, and *Iohn Caluin*, then to those that are established in the Councell of Trent : so indifferent stood the world before that Councell. For after that time that they had begun to challenge this Iurisdiction, & before the Councell of Trent, the Popes were alwayes affrighted at the name of a generall Councell ; as *Paul. Iouius* winesseth, otherwise a flatterer of the Popes : for he saith thus. *Id vnum concily nomen supra cæteros in salices humanarum rerum casus, maximo terrori Pontificibus esse consuevit.* That is, [The onely name of a Councell, more then all other humane incident miseries is wont to be a great terrour to Popes.] He giueth the there, reason why the Popes were so much afraid of Councels, because saith he, in them questions of faith & religion are interpreted, & the Popes Iurisdictiõ censured & curbed. *Ad castigandam sacerdotum luxuriam censorias leges condunt, ipsi Pontificives Pontificio iure circumuenti eterare supremam dignitatem, seq̃, demum Pontificatu abdicare coguntur : hoc metu armati reges, Pontifices terrent.* That is, [Councels make lawes to chastise the luxuriousnesse of Priests. The Popes themselues circumuented by the Popish law are compelled to resigne the Supreame dignitie, and to relinguish the Papacie.

Paul. Iouius li.1. historiarum.

Iouius ibid.

14. So that before the Councell of Trent the Soueraigne Iurisdiction was neuer held to be in the Pope, seeing the Church being gathered together in a Councell did vse to exercise Iurisdiction vpon the Popes. For if the Popes were wont so much to feare and flie a generall Councell in regard of censuring and inhibiting their Iurisdiction ; then must these conclusions follow : That the Councell of Trent was not a generall Councell, because the Pope was not afraid of it : that the Popes themselues did acknowledge, that the Iurisdiction of a Councell was aboue their Iurisdiction : for otherwise why should the Pope be afraid of a free Councell ? So that if the Councell of Trent had beene like to those Councels which the Popes did so much feare ; it might haue giuen as good satisfaction to true Christians, as now it doth to the followers and flatterers of the Court of Rome. And before that Councell, there was great hope that

it

it might haue bin so. For the minds of al good men were marueilously prepared to peace, and to a mutuall consent. And for the points of doctrine, if the Friars and such as were by them infected, had not troubled all, the truth might haue preuailed. For

Card. Contaren.
tract. de iustifi-
oatione.

Cardinall *Contaren* made a good preparation to the doctrine of iustification : which being the greatest point in controuersie, is handled by him conformable to the doctrine of *Luther* & *Caluin*, and directly against that which was concluded in the Councell of Trent : this he wrote in the yeere one thousand fiue hundred fourtie and one, a little before that Councell. The Cardinall therein teacheth nothing, but that which was before him the knowen doctrine of the Church of Rome : from which because the Councell of Trent swarued., therefore they made the separation, and not we. This wisdome and moderation of Cardinall *Contaren* and others of that side, gaue great hope to Master *Bucer*, and some other of this side ; to labour for an agreement and mutuall consent : and assuredly there was great reason to hope it. For if the rest had beene of that spirit and moderation which Cardinall *Contaren*, *Georgius Cassander*, *Iohn Ferus*, Master *Antonius Flaminius*, *Espenceus* and many others, a mutuall consent would haue beene obtained. But will yee haue the truth ? the points of faith and doctrine, were not the things which most hindered this concord ; for in these things many of that side were very conformable, and moe might haue beene drawen : but there was another thing which crossed all peaceable purposes ; this was the Popes Iurisdiction. If it had not bene for this Iurisdiction, the doctrine of *Luther* might haue beene easily granted : for what taught he, which was not before him taught in the Church of Rome ? I graunt that the contrary was also taught by Friars : for in the Church of Rome before the Councell of Trent, some taught after the manner of the new deuised doctrines which Friars brought in: others taught the truth preseruing the auncient doctrines in most points, till that time, as by their writings extant appeareth. So that if the Councell of Trent had beene indifferently chosen of learned men then liuing : and if their voyces had not bene forced and forestalled by an oath of obedience to the Pope, and to satisfie his lust : (a
desperate

desperate practise declaring a desperate cause) things might
might haue beene aswell concluded against the Iurisdiction of
the Pope, and faction of Friars, as now all is for them.

15. And because wee haue so often mentioned, and are so
often to mention the Councell of Trent, seeing we wholly reiect it, and our aduersaries wholly rest vpon it : it may bee expected that wee should giue some reasons why we disable it so
much : I may answere, the reasons are in the doctrines and con-
clusions themselues, which are throughly and worthily examined by Master *Chemnisius* and others. But ouer and besides the
falshood of doctrines, which are concluded there directly against
the manifest truth of holy Scriptures, we haue also these iust exceptions; that, that Councell was neither a generall, nor a free,
nor a lawfull Councell. Generall it was not, because if we consider these Westerne parts of Christendome, for the benefite
whereof that Councell is pretended to be gathered, the greatest
part was excluded from that Councell. For all England, Scotland, Ireland, all France, and all Germanie that are Protestants,
will make a farre greater part, then all the rest that consented to
that Councell : so that it was a Councell held of a small part against the greater part. The King of England by publicke writing, protested against it, when first it was appointed by the
Pope to be held at Mantua, the reasons which King *Henry* alleaged against it are these: [That it belonged not to the Pope to cal
Councels, but to the Emperor & to the Kings of Christendom :
that the Pope himselfe was to be censured by the Councell, and
therefore Italy was no fit place for it : that there was no caution
made to him and his Embassadours, and Bishops for their safe
conduct : that though there were publike caution giuen, yet the
practise of Popes in breaking their faith, and violating publike
cautions, and sucking the blood of innocent men was too well
knowen. In fine the King giueth aduise to all other Princes,
and Magistrates, to gouerne their owne people, to establish
true religion, to reiect the Popes tyrannie, as hee had
done.]

16. The French King made like Protestation against this
Councell of Trent, for the Abbot of Bellosan the French Kings

The Councell of Trent.

Not a generall Councell.

Iohn Sleidan. lib. 11.

Embassa-

Embaſſadour, obtaining admittance into the Councell (though not without great difficultie) in the middeſt of that aſſembly, a-gainſt the expectation of many, deliuered the Kings proteſtati-on thus : [That it was neither ſafe nor fit for him to ſend his Bi-ſhops to Trent, that he held not that aſſembly for a publike and generall Councell, but rather for a priuate conuenticle; ga-thered not for the common good, but for the pleaſure and pro-fite of ſome few : that heither he himſelfe, nor any of his king-dome ſhould be bound by thoſe decrees : and if need required that he would vſe ſuch remedie to reſtraine the Popes, as his Aunceſtours had vſed before.] Thus did theſe Kings then pro-teſt againſt that Councell eſpecially becauſe it was called by the Popes authoritie, who had no right to call generall Councels. And both theſe kingdomes, and the Churches therein, haue withſtood the authoritie of this Councell : yea the French Church of Papiſts would neuer admit the Councell of Trent: ſo that it is not onely diſallowed of vs, but by a number of them who profeſſing to follow the auncient Church of Rome, yet vtterly reiect this Councell of Trent, as ſwaruing from the Church of Rome. Of the Princes of Germanie there is no doubt made, but that they would neuer yeelde conſent to it. Then generall it cannot be, when as ſo many and ſo great a part haue withſtood it : yea a farre greater part then they can make who held it.

The Councell of Trent not free.

17. And whereas in all ancient generall Councels the free-dome and libertie of Biſhops, and of all that had voices in Councels was neuer impeached : in this Councell of Trent it was quite otherwiſe, for none might be admitted to haue voice therein, but only ſuch as ſhould be bound in an oath of bondage and ſlauerie to the Pope. And therefore when the Embaſſa-dours of *Maurice* Duke of Saxony came to the Councell and propoſed from their Maſter theſe petitions ; [That the forme of ſafe conduct might be made for his Diuines, according to the forme which the councell of Baſill graunted to the Bohemians, that is to ſay, that theſe particulars might be expreſſed therein, that they alſo with other might haue deciding power, that in euery controuerſie the holy Scriptures, the practiſe of the aun-cient

Sleidan.lib.22.

Sleidan.lib.23

cient Church, the ancient Councels and Fathers agreeing with Scriptures, and founding them vpon Scriptures ; might be admitted and receiued for the most true and indifferent iudge : (for thus much was contained in the safe conduct graunted by the Councell of Basill to the Bohemians) that there might bee no proceeding till his Diuines came : that when they were come, all things precedent might be recalled, that the Councell might be free for all nations : that the Bishop of Rome might submit himselfe to the Councell, and remit that oath which he had taken of the Bishops which were of the Councell ; that their voyces might be free, and without such euident partiality and preiudice as they brought with them, who were bound by oath to doe nothing against the pleasure of the Pope : these petitions were reiected, freedome vtterly excluded ; partiality and preiudice maintained with resolution.

Lex diuina,
praxis Christi, A-
postolica, & Ec-
clesiæ primitiuæ,
vna cum consilys
doctoribu(q, fun-
dantibus se ve-
raciter in eadem
pro verissimo &
indifferente iu-
dico in hoc Basi-
liensi consilio ad
mittentur. consi-
li. Basil. sess. t.
Epist.4.

18. And that the same Councell of Trent was not a lawfull assembly, it is no lesse euident ; because it was not called by lawfull authoritie : for it was called onely by the Popes authoritie, who neuer had authoritie to call generall Councels. And though *Charles* the fift then Emperour, was at the first drewen to yeeld a consent, yet the Pope would neuer allow that the Emperour should haue the authoritie to call the Councell, and to appoint the place (as alwayes it was the Emperours Iurisdiction in auncient Councels) but this Iurisdiction the Pope by vsurpation drew to himselfe in the Councell of Trent : Insomuch that when the Emperour vtterly disallowing the translation of the same Councell to *Bononia*, wrote to them and sent his Embassadour *Vargas* to protest against them that he would hold all as vaine, friuilous and vnlawfull whatsoeuer they did, tearming them not a Councell, but a Conuenticle : *Montanus* the Popes Legat answered, that it should neuer be indured that the Ciuill Magistrate should haue authority to call Councels, or to appoint the place thereof. To this purpose the Pope also writeth to *Charles*, that the Emperour hath no right herein, but the Pope himselfe is the man : *Qui solus iure diuino & humano cogendi concilia, & decernendi de rebus sacris potestatem obtinuet.* This authoritie then being vtterly denied to the Emperour

The Councell
of Trent not a
lawfull Coun-
cell.

Sleidan.lib.19.

Sleidan.lib.:6

perout for calling the Councell of Trent : we say that Councell
was an vnlawfull assembly, because it was not gathered by the
authority of the Emperour, and of Christian Kings. And when
it was thus gathered, neither a generall Councell, nor a free,
nor a lawfull Councell ; yet as it was with all these foule faults,
it could not serue the Popes turne, vnlesse singular fraud and
deceit had bene practised. *Olaus Magnus* was intituled Archbishop of Vpsala, and blinde Sir *Robert* a Scottishman was intituled Archbishop of Armach in Ireland : so that for want of true
Bishops, some were set vp onely in name to fill vp the number,
and giue voices.

19. And when all other shifts would not serue, the Pope
still reserued one for the last cast. The greatest part of them
that were present, had a purpose to curb the Popes Iurisdiction,
especially the Spanish Bishops, who saith *Sleidan* were most diligent in this Councell. These combined with those few Germane Bishops which were there, resolued saith he, *Pontificis*
Sleidan. lib. 23. *Romani potestatem intra certos fines includere, nec illius aulæ tan-*
tum facultatis in omnes prouincias attribuere. That is, [To reduce
the Popes authority within some bounds, and not to yeeld such
power to that Court ouer all Prouinces.] The Pope fearing
such a thing afore, prouided that the greatest part of Bishops,
should be Italians : none might be admitted of any other Nation, but such as were made obnoxious to the Pope, aswell by
some other respects as by an oath. If any were obserued to
speake in the Councell, with some freedome (as some did)
especiall marke was taken of such : these were withdrawen and
recalled thence, that other might take their place. Of this the
Protestant Princes complaine to *Charles* : *Fuerunt in eo concessu*
Sleidan. lib. 17. *pauci quidem aliquanto liberiores in dicendo, sed inuenta ratio fuit,*
vt ijs renocatis atq; summotis, alij summitterentur nequiores. That
is, [Some were in that company who vsed some freedome of
speech : but a meanes was inuented to remoue and recall them
that other more seruile might be in their places.] The Pope
thus giuing continuall direction to the Councell, and appointing by intercourse of messages cõtinually trauelling betweene
Rome and Trent, what should be concluded : (insomuch that a
common

common prouerbe was then taken vp among them, that the holy Ghoſt trauelled from Rome to Trent in a packet) and finding that after all this, his purpoſes were croſſed by a certaine number of voyces, the number being preciſely brought vnto him: began to flie to his laſt reſerued ſhift. For of a ſuddaine he created thirteene Cardinals in one day, all Italians; to whom hauing giuen vncertaine titles, but certaine inſtruction, he ſent them to the Councell: whom the other Fathers of the Councell welcomed not knowing their end. At the next meeting the matters being propoſed as before, it was found that the voices of theſe that were come ſo lately, did alter all; and caſt it at the Popes pleaſure: and yet their wretched pollicies reſted not thus. If any were ſuppoſed to excell in knowledge, grauitie, learning, and godlineſſe, they were (ſome before the Councell, that their preſence ſhould not hinder or diſturbe the Popes purpoſes: ſome afterward) ſecretly taken away by poyſon: this was the end of that worthy Cardinall *Contaren*, and others: who for their eminency in vertue, were ſuſpected of Lutheraniſme. And that the world might know and take full notice of the Popes end and ſcope in calling this Councell, that it was not the true faith and religion of the Germanes that hee ſought, but their blood, it is euident by his practiſe. For whileſt thus they held the Germanes, and all the world in expectation of a Councell; the Pope in the meane time, raiſed an army and ſent it againſt the Proteſtants, to be ioyned with other armies prepared for their vtter deſtruction. The generall of the Popes armie, *Octauius Farneſius* (Graundchild to Pope *Paulus* the third, by whom hee was ſent) departing out of Italy was obſerued to ſay, [That he would deſtroy ſo many Germanes, that his horſe might ſwimme in the blood of Lutherans. This is their holy Councell of Trent, conſiſting of a fewe, and thoſe fewe bound by an oath to the Pope, reſtrained, prohibited, poyſoned, and at laſt with many ſhifts drawen to ſerue a purpoſe: aſſembled without lawfull authority, called by the vſurped power of the Pope, drawen and pulled by fraud and ſubtiltie, ending in blood and warres: and remaining the onely cauſe of all the warres, which haue beene raiſed within

Sleidan. lib. 14.

Sleidan. lib. 17.

Q   theſe

these westerne parts of Christendome since that time to this day.

§. II.

Of Friars, by whom this Iurisdiction was maintained.

20.   MY purpose being to note the meanes by which this Iurisdiction hath beene aduanced: I thinke it needfull after forgeries to speake of Friars. For they haue beene the chiefe aduancers of this Iurisdiction, and the fittest instruments that the Pope hath found for his purpose: *Iohn Wiclife* in diuers places declareth (out of assured knowledge of storie, himselfe being neere those times, and therefore more able to iudge therof) that before the yeere of Christ one thousand two hundred, there were no Friars in the world. About which time *Dominicus* a Spaniard, and *Francis* an Italian began their new orders. *Fasciculus temporum* setteth their beginning about the yeere one thousand two hundred and foure: and that they were confirmed by Pope *Honorius* the third, about the yeere one thousand two hundred and fourteene. *Ordines quatuor mendicantium* (saith he) *videlicet Prædicatorum, Minorum, Augustinensium, & Carmelitarum confirmantur ab Honorio, præponuntur Prædicatores Minoribus in literis Papalibus, quia sex mensibus ante eos confirmati fuerunt. Matthæus Palmerius* setteth the confirmation of the Dominicans in the yere one thousand two hundred and sixteene. Of the Franciscanes, in the yeere one thousand two hundred twentie and three: so that *Wiclife* hath a good ground for that assertion, that Friars were neuer known in the world before the yeere one thousand two hundred.

21.   This was the first thing that made the alteration of the Church of Rome famous. For before the institution of Friars, the doctrines of the Church of Rome stood sound and vnchanged in most things. The alteration was afterward wrought especially by these Friars, both in doctrine & Iurisdiction. For at the first Friars were set vp to oppresse the old Priests, to alter

the

VViclifes complaint to the King and Parliament, art.1.

Fasciculus temp.

the auncient religion, and to exalt the Popes power in a greater meafure then it was before. In which bufineffe they haue not beene idle, but taking directions onely from the Pope, haue brought in a great chaunge in all things. *Wiclife* obferued, that Friars purfued, imprifoned, and burned Priefts onely for reprouing their finnes. So that then queftions of doctrine made not the quarrell betweene Priefts and Friars, but only the reproofe of the corrupt and vncleane liues of Friars : as in corruption they began, fo they continue. And this is teftified by others alfo, that the firft caufe of the Popes perfecutions was not for doctrine, but onely for the Popes Iurifdiction. *Reinerius* writing againft the Waldenfes, teftifieth thus much : that they differed from the Church of Rome in no point of doctrine, but onely they denied the Popes Iurifdiction. *Hæc fecta Leoniftarum* (for fo they were called) *magnam habet fpeciem pietatis* (faith he) *eo quod coram hominibus iufte viuant, & bene omnia de Deo credant, & omnes articulos qui in Symbolo continentur; folam Romanam Ecclefiam blafphemant & oderunt.* So that all the herefie which then was found in them, was onely againft the Popes Iurifdiction, they fwarued not from the doctrines of the Church of Rome, but the Friars made the alteration from that auncient doctrine. Then howfoeuer fince that time fome Popifh writers, vpon humour and partialitie haue charged them in points of doctrine : yet the writers of that age, and neere it, euen their aduerfaries, do therin iuftifie them, and fhew that the quarrell was not for points of doctrine, but only for the Popes Iurifdiction. And it is worth obferuation, that the fame *Reinerius* confeffeth that there was no origin of this fect knowen, fome, faith he, affirme that this fect hath continued from the time of *Siluefter* : others thinke it continued from the time of the Apoftles, himfelfe concludeth that out of queftion, it is ancienter then any other fect. Then out of doubt, they were much more auncient then Friars, and Friars were raifed vp, partly to this end, to pull them downe.

22. And that this was an end of the inftitution of thefe orders: to make fome chaunge in that ancient religion, which before ftood in the Church of Rome in fome tollerable meafure,

The firft caufe of perfecution by Popes: not for doctrine, but for Iurifdiction.
Reinerius

and

and to vexe and perfecute the profeffors thereof, and especially to bring in a new Iurifdiction of the Pope: it will better appeare if wee confider what hath bene in the beginning of their inftitution, and fince obferued of their innouations, libertie, luxurioufnefle, and what defolation they haue brought into the Church. That thefe men may better be knowen, I will note what *Iohn Wiclife* and fome others haue obferued.

VViclife lib.de fundam.legum Angl.cap.36. pag.424. Companit. pag.9

Friars taught (faith *Wiclife*) that the King of England is not Lord of the Clargie, but that the Pope is their Lord.

Friars fo ftreitched the priuiledges of the Clargie, that though an Abbot and all his couent ben open traitours confpiring vnto death of the King and Queene, and other Lords; and inforce them to deftroy all the Realme: the King may not take fro them an half-penny, ne farthing worth.

Ibid.pag.14.

When Parifh-churches ben appropred to men of fingular religion (that is to Friars) fuch appropriation is made by falfe fuggeftion, that fuch religious men han not ynough for lifelode and healing, but in truth they han ou: rmuch.

Let me obferue this by the way, as being now better inftructed in the opinion of *Iohn Wiclife,* concerning tithes. Whereas he feemeth to be againft tithes, it is to be vnderftood (as he doth in diuers places open himfelfe) againft tithes as then they were abufed by Fryars. For Fryers then had power from the Pope to appropriate tithes to their Couents, by which meanes tithes came into their poffeffion. This thing *Wiclife* thought vnlawfull, and would haue had tithes reduced to their ancient vfe againe.: now let vs returne to his obferuations. Fryers

Treat.againft Friars pag.19.

p.24.

p.28.

fayen, that their religion (founden on finfull men) is more perfit then that religion or order which Chrift himfelfe made. They fayen alfo that begging is lawfull, the which is damned of God, both in the old Teftament and in the new. Fryers after they had procured impropriations, and left a poore Curat in place, drewe alfo from Curats their office and Sacraments: they got

p.55.

p.30.

the confeffion of Lords and Ladies. They purfuen true Priefts, and letten them to preach the Gofpell. Chrift chargeth all his Priefts to preach the Gofpell truely, and they purfuen them for this deed; yea, to the fire: they will flea Priefts, for they
doe

doe Gods bidding. When the King by his officers prisons a   *p. 40.*
man, that is commonly done for great and open trespasse, and
that is good warning to other misdoers, & some profit comes
of the Kings Ministers : but when Friars prisonen their brethren, the paine is not knowen to men, though the sinne were
neuer so open and slaunderous, and that does harme to other
Liegemen. Friars sayen, that they han more power then the   *p. 28.*
Curat, and thus they make dissention and discord among Christian men. Friars labour to roote out true Priests that preach   *p. 30*
Chrifts Gospel, themselues han their chamber and seruice like
Lords or Kings, and senden out idiots full of couetise, to preach
not the Gospell, but Chronicles, Fables, and leefings to please
the people, & to rob them. And yet for sending of those coue-
tous fooles that ben limitors goes much Symonie, enuy, & much
foule Marchandise. And who can best rob the poore people by
false begging and other deceits , that shall haue this *Iudas* office and so a nest of Antichrifts Clarkes is maintained.

. They shew not to the people their great sinnes, and namely   *p. 31.*
to mighty men of the world, but pursuen other true preachers,
for they will not glose mighty men, and comfort them in their
sins. Thus mighty men hire by great costs, a false traitour to   *p. 32.*
lead them to hell. Friars deceiuen the people in faith, and robben them of Temporall goods , & make the people trust more
in dead parchment, sealed with leefings, and in vaine prayers of
hypocrites, that in case ben damned deuils, then in the holy
helpe of God and their owne good liuing. Friars peruert the   *p. 33.*
right faith of the Sacrament of the Auter, & bringing in a new
herefie, saying there is an accident withouten subieʒt : which
herefie neuer came into the Church , till the foule fende Satan
was vnbounden after a thousand yeeres. Friars vndoe Parish   *p. 35.*
Churches, by building other needlesse (meaning Abbeyes, and
Priories, &c.) They destroy the obedience of Gods law, & mag-   *p. 36.*
nifien singular obedience made to sinfull men, and in case to diuels, (this is blind obedience brought in by them) which obedience Chrift insampled neuer, ne in himselfe, ne in his Apoftles.

Friars being made Bishops robben men by extorsion , as in
punishing of sin for money, and suffren men to lie in sinne, they   *p. 37.*
Q 3   beare

p. 38.

p. 41.

p. 42.

p. 45.

Ibid.

p. 47.

p. 50.

p. 52.

p. 53.

p. 54.

p. 57.

beare out the gold of our land to Aliens, and sometimes to our enemies, to get, of Antichrist false exemptions. They teach Lords and Ladies, that if they die in *Francis* habite, they shall neuer come to hell. They are neither ruled by Gods law, ne lawes of the Church, ne lawes of the King. They ben the cause and procuratours of all warres. They say apertly, that if the King and Lords, and other standen thus against their false begging, &c. they will goe out of the land, and come againe with bright heads: and looke whether this be treason or none. They teach and maintaine that holy writ is false, and so they putten falsnesse vpon our Lord Iesus Christ, and vpon the holy Ghost, and vpon the blessed Trinitie. Friars teach that it is not lawfull to a Priest, or any other man to keepe the Gospell in his bounds and cleannesse, without errour of sinnefull men, but if he haue leaue thereto of Antichrist. Friars by hypocrisie binden them to impossible things; that they may not doe, for they binden them ouer the commaundements of God, as they say themselues: (hence are works of supererogation.) They burne Priests and the Gospell of Christ, written in English to most honour of our Nation. They call the curse of God, the lesse curse; and the curse of sinfull men, the more curse. They distroyen this Article of Christian mens faith: I beleeue a common or generall Church. For they teachen, that tho men that shall be damned, be members of holy Church: and thus they wedden Christ and the diuell together. They waste the treasures of the land, for dispensations and vaine Pardons. They ben most subtill and priuy procurators of Symonie, and most priuily make Lords to maintaine the Pope and his robbing our land of treasure by his Pardons, Priuiledges, first fruits of Benefices in our land; and Dismes, and Subsidies.

23. By this wee may in part see those innouations, which Friars brought into the Church, raysing a new Iurisdiction to the Pope, defrauding and robbing the King of his auncient Iurisdiction: these are they who first taught, and practised obedience to another Soueraigne then the King, conspiracy against the life of Princes: impropriations, turning tithes first from their true and auncient vse: persecution for preaching the Gospell;

exemptions,

exemptions ; the vſe of Legends in the Church, and reading of fables to the people : Symonie, flattery, pardons, indulgences : the hereſie of an accident without a ſubiect : ſingular and blind obedience ; the vſe of commutation of penance into money : they were inſtruments of warres and bloodſhed, they inuented works of ſupererogation, the doctrin that reprobates are members of the Catholike Church : to robbe the land of money. Theſe are the things in part which are obſerued by *Wiclife* to haue beene firſt inuented by Friars. Now whereas *Iohn Wiclife* was reputed an hereticke, wee finde that this imputation was laid vpon him eſpecially by Friars. For he was a profeſſed enemie to them, and to their innouations, holding with the Church of Rome, and maintaining no other doctrine, then that which he found publikely maintained and receiued in the world, before Friars altered it. Still he pleadeth the cauſe of the Prieſts againſt Friars, which ſheweth that he taught no otherwiſe then thoſe Prieſts did teach. And albeit the Friars did marueilouſlly diſorder the Church in his time, yet hee witneſſeth that the third part of the Clergie of England defended the truth againſt Friars. Then the Friars being ſet vp to alter the auncient doctrine and Iuriſdiction, and to induce new : did labour herein throughly imploying their beſt ſkill and power, for the aduancement of the Pope, and ſuppreſſing of the truth. Heerein the Ieſuites ſucceed their forefathes, in this inheritance of innouation, daily adding ſome new monſters, to thoſe which theſe old Friars left to their hands.

Confeſſ. de Sacram. pag. 64.

24. The Vniuerſitie of Paris hath likewiſe declared their iudgement againſt Friars, ſomewhat before this time wherein *Wiclife* liued. They gathered ſeuen Articles againſt Friars, which becauſe they proue Friars to be the authors & introducers of innouation in the Church, I will here ſet them downe. [Firſt, we ſay, that Friars are not to be admitted into our Scholaſticall ſocietie, except by our conſent : becauſe the ſociety ought not to be coact but voluntarie. Secondly, becauſe wee haue found by experience, that their fellowſhip hath beene many wayes hurtfull and dangerous to vs. Thirdly, ſeeing they are of a diuerſe profeſſion from ours : for they are regulars, and wee ſchollers ;

Extat catalog. teſt. veritat. Tom. 2. p. 798.

schollers; we ought not to be ioined or mingled together in one
scholafticall office. For the Spaniſh Councell ſaith, Thou ſhalt
not plow with an Oxe & an Aſſe, that is, thou ſhalt not aſſociate
men of diuers profeſſions together in one office : for how can
they agree together, whoſe ſtudies, vowes, and purpoſes are diuers? Fourthly, becauſe they raiſe diſſentions & offences, but the
Apoſtle ſaith : we beſeech you brethren that you obſerue them,
that is, that you diſcerne ſuch as make diſſentions for the doctrine which you haue learned of the Apoſtles, and eſchewe
them; for they ſerue not the Lord, but their belly. Gloſſ. for
they flatter ſome, they backbite others, that they may fill their
bellies : and by gloſing words and their benedictions they beguile the hearts of the ſimple. Fiftly, becauſe we feare leaſt
they bee ſuch as enter into houſes, becauſe they thruſt themſelues into euery mans houſe ; they ſearch and ſift the conſci-
ences of men : & ſeduce ſuch as they find like women ready to
be ſeduced. And whō they haue once ſeduced, them they draw
from the Councels of their owne Prelates, to their Councels :
for they bind them by oath to their Councels, ſuch the Apoſtle
commaundeth to eſchew. Sixtly, becauſe we feare they are
falſe Prophets, for they are not Biſhops, nor Pariſh-prieſts, nor
their Vicars, nor by them inuited : yet they preach, being not
ſent, againſt the Apoſtle ſaying, *Rom.* 10. How ſhall they preach
except they be ſent. For they worke no miracles, thereby to
witneſſe that they may preach: the Church then ought to auoid
ſuch men, being ſo dangerous. Seuenthly, becauſe they are
curious, and hauing no lawfull calling in the Church, they buſie
themſelues with other mens buſineſſe, & thruſt themſelues into
other mens callings: and yet they are neither Apoſtles, nor their
ſucceſſours; that is, Biſhops, neither are they of the ſeuenty and
two Diſciples of the Lord, neither their helpers, or Vicars, as
before is ſaid. Now the Apoſtle commaundeth vs to eſchewe
ſuch as will liue ſo : ſaying, 2. *Theſſ. vlt.* We declare brethren
to you in the name of the Lord Ieſus Chriſt, that you withdraw your ſelues from euery brother that walketh inordinately, and not according to that tradition which they haue receiued of vs, &c.]

22. Thus

25. Thus haue we fet downe the fincere iudgement of that Vniuerfitie, before it was corrupted and infeted with Friars. They haue prooued that Friars haue no lawfull calling in the Church to preach, or adminifter the Sacraments; becaufe they haue no inftitution of Chrift or his Apoftles. And howfoeuer fince thofe times the iudgement of that Vniuerfitie was chaunged, after they had once receiued thefe ferpents into their bofomes: yet the reafons which they haue brought againft Friars, are vnchaungeably true, and will alwayes prooue that which then they prooued, that neither the old Friars, nor the new Iefuits, haue any lawfull calling in the Church. As thus they haue beene the bane of the Church in chaunging the old bounds: fo they haue beene the ruine of Princes, and the caufe of great warres and bloodfhed, yea of all the perfecutions that haue bene fince. For before that time that the orders of Friars were brought foorth by a new and monftrous birth in the Church; there was no bloodfhed nor perfecution offered by the Pope, nor the Church of Rome, for matters of Religion. *Berengarius* was forced to a Recantation before, but no blood was fhed. But after that *Dominicke* had inftituted the order of the Iacobites, or preaching Friars; and *Francis* the order of the Minorites, profeffed beggars: then began great bloodfhed and perfecution to be pratifed vpon men, that did not allow the Popes Iurifdiction: in blood was it firft founded, and fo it hath beene euer fince maintained.

26. The firft perfecution began againft them, that were called *Albingenfes:* whofe opinions are made hainous by fome that write affectionately fince that time; but by the writers of that time there appeareth no other thing wherewith they were charged: but onely that they withftood the Popes pride and Iurifdiction; for which they were perfecuted. The Earle of Tholoufe who fauoured them, was depriued of his Earledome, his landes were giuen to *Simon Monford:* the forces of the French and the Pope were raifed againft him: when they were not able to vanquifh him by force, by fraud and falfhood of the Friars and Popifh Bifhops, they ouerthrew him. In this ouerthrow of the Earle, the induftry and valour of *Dominicke* is much

*Albegefij, quorū dogma nemo ad hunc diem notus fcriptor reliquit: & cum hæreticos eos vocent, genus tamen hæreseos prætereunt. Naucler. generat.*41,

R

much celebrated by the ſtories of this time. Inſomuch, as the whole praiſe is attributed to him: of him *Platina* witneſſeth Platin. Inno-cent. 3. thus much. *Quos*(Albingenſes)*Dominicus mira celeritate compe-ſcuit,adiuuante etiá Simone Monteforti: non enim diſputationibus verum armis opus fuit, adeo inoleuerat tanta hereſis.* That is, [Whom *Dominicke* did ſpeedily ouercome, by the helpe of *Si-mon Monford:* for there was not ſo much neede of diſputation, as of armes, that hereſie was ſo rooted.] Then we vnderſtand the end why Friars were inſtituted,by their firſt and chiefe im-ployment: they were founded in blood, in treacherous practi-ſes againſt Princes, for the ſeruice of the Pope. Wherein wee behold the endes of ſuch Councels as the Pope calleth, and wherein he is Preſident: as the Councell of Lateran, and the Councell of Trent. For as vpon the time of holding the Late-ran Councell, the firſt Friars were ordained, and allowed by the Pope ; ſo vpon the time of the Councell of Trent were the Ieſuites confirmed to be an order by Pope *Paul* the third : after both Councels, great warres and bloodſhed followed through Chriſtendome ; wherein the Friars were the Popes inſtruments, and the procurators of the warres at both times, and euer ſince.

27. As theſe firſt orders of Friars increaſed in number,ſwar-ming like Locuſts vnder the Popes protection ; he like an ex-perienced Captaine, prouidently ordered his troupes, and ſet them to their ſeuerall taskes:ſome to writing of books,ſome to the practiſes of ſtate againſt Princes. By thoſe that were ſet to write, as *Aquinas,Scotus,* and ſuch like, the alterations of do-ctrines were brought into the Church of Rome firſt : ſo that herein appeareth their full & finall end,in raiſing vp rebellions; firſt againſt God,and corrupting of the truth : and then againſt Princes, by impugning their ſoueraigne authoritie and Iuriſ-diction. In both which practiſes, the Friars take continuall di-rection from the Pope, by whoſe power they were created, by whoſe authoritie they ſtand,from whoſe ſpirit they breath, and for whoſe ſeruice they are deuoted, and reſolued to ſpend their breath and blood. In theſe practiſes,the Ieſuites being the laſt brood, ſtriue to ſurpaſſe all other, for their audacious corrupting

ting of the truth, and outragious interprifes againft the liues of Princes. For which in the end, they will vndoubtedly drawe vpon themfelues the anger of God, and of the Princes of Chriftendome. I haue ftayed the longer in thefe defcriptions, for the honour of the Iefuits, that their defcent and progenie, may be knowen: that we may behold the aduancers of the Popes Iurifdiction: which Iurifdiction will the better appeare, if the firft and chiefe aduancers of it, might be well knowen.

§. III.
Of Oathes exacted by the Pope.

28.   ANother efpeciall meanes of aduauncing this Iurifdiction, was practifed by exacting Oathes : which is alfo much practifed now; becaufe by experience they finde great vfe of it; an Oath being the greateft bond of humane focietie, and the fitteft meanes to ingage men throughly in any caufe : the firft exacting of Oathes, was from Archbifhops, and Bifhops, by which meanes their Allegeance was ftrangely withdrawen from their Soueraigne Princes. Whereas then firft princes for their owne fafetie, and for the fafetie of their Countrey, vfed to exact an Oath of Allegeance, afwell of the Ecclefiafticall, as Temporall fubiects : The Popes began to withdraw the Clergie from this obedience, and Allegeance; and fo farre they preuailed, that the Friars taught, that the King of England was not lord of the Clergie, but that the Pope was their lord : as we haue declared from *Ioh. Wiclife*. And now the Pope beginneth in thefe defperate dayes, to forbidde them of the laity, to take the Oath of Allegeance to their Soueraigne : whereby as they began to fteale away the hearts of the Clergie firft, from the true and lawfull obedience of their Soueraignes; fo now proceeding in the fame courfe with the laity, what will they leaue to Kings in the end? And becaufe this containeth an efpeciall myfterie of Iurifdiction, therefore we thinke it needfull to be plainely opened.

29. That Kings did out of dutie and Allegeance, exact an Oath of their fubiects, euen of Bifhops; and had the fame yeel-

ded as a due homage to them, and confirmed also by decrees
of Councels : it is well and worthily obserued of late, by that
booke written most learnedly and exactly, intituled, *Triplici*
nodo triplex cuneus. Where this vse is confirmed from the practise of the fourth *Toletan* Councell, held in the yeere sixe hundred and thirtie: and from the fift *Toletan* Councell, held about
the same time. And from the sixt *Toletan* Councell held in the
yeere sixe hundred seuentie and sixe. And from the tenth *Tole-*
tan Councell, gathered in the yeere, sixe hundred ninetie and
foure: as also from the Councel of Aquisgrane, in the yere eight
hundred thirtie and sixe. We may adde (though it be needlesse)
some fewe and small obseruations thereto. It appeareth, that
this practise of taking an Oath of Allegeance of subiects, is
drawen from the law of nature, as necessary for the preseruation of States, and it seemeth to be as auncient as the gouerne-

Plutarch,Ly-
curgo.

ment of States. For *Lycurgus* the first founder of the State of
Lacedemon, hauing once well ordered that State by good
lawes : tooke an Oath of them all that they should preserue
those orders till his returne from the Oracle : that is alwayes. If
any thinke that this was not an Oath of Allegeance to the
State, I suppose it will be hard to distinguish betweene an Oath
to preserue the lawes, or to be true to the lawes ; and an Oath
to be true to the State. For it is certaine, that the State of Lacedemon, was preserued by those lawes in great honour and fe-
licitie, for the space of fiue hundred yeeres, as the same Author

Plutarch,ibid.
Plut.Agesil.

reporteth : Or as hee saith in another place, for sixe hundred
yeeres ; and vpon the breach of those lawes came in the ruine
of that State, as the same Author doth often obserue. This declareth the antiquitie of this Oath, as proceeding from the law
of nature ; which yeeldeth this helpe to States for the necessarie
preseruation of themselues. For which cause it hath bene practised, whensoeuer the State thought it needful: for after the kings
were driuen out of Rome, L. *Brutus*, and *Collatinus Tarquinius*
being chosen Consuls : *Valerius Publicola* grew so offended, because himselfe was not respected in that choise, that he retired
from the Senate, & from all publick action to a priuate life. This
thing drewe the Senate into some suspicion of his Allegeance.
Wherfore *Brutus* the Consul called all the Senate to a solemne
                                                              Oath

Oath of Allegance: which Oath *Valerius* firſt of al others took *Plutarch.Publicola.* moſt cheerefully. Thus in the danger of the State, they had recourſe to this practiſe as the moſt lawfull, and aſſured helpe of States. And *Scipio Africanus* is much commended in the Ro- *Liui.Plutarch. Scip.* mane ſtories, for vſing this practiſe in the danger of that State: for when hee vnderſtood that ſome had a purpoſe to forſake the State, hee cauſed them to take an Oath to bee true to the State, and not to forſake it. After the ſame manner was this Oath of Allegeance yeelded by the Church of the Iewes of old. For *Ioſephus* reporteth, that *Auguſtus Cæſar* required an Oath of Allegeance ; which Oath, ſaith he, all the nation of the Iewes did take, ſauing orely the Phariſes. And therefore theſe Phariſes, he deſcribeth to be ſeditious and intollerable ſtirrers in States, euen ſuch as the Friars prooued afterward. The words of *Ioſephus*, though they be long, yet I will ſet downe; becauſe they open the practiſe of this Oath of Allegance, the conſent of the auncient Church of the Iewes, and the ſeditious and peſtiferous practiſe of the Phariſes, that the Ieſuites the broode of theſe Vipers may the better be knowen : his words are theſe.

[There was a ſort of men among the Iewes, glorying in *Ioſeph. antiquit. lib.17.cap.3.* the ſcrupuloſitie and ſubtiltie of the law, by hypocriſie and ſimulation, counterfeiting the holy worſhip of God, by whom women were much moued and drawen, &c. Theſe were called Phariſes, who had great power, either to helpe, or to hurt the kings State. For they were troubleſome, ſeditious, the ſtirrers of wars, iniurious and immoderate prouokers of trouble without cauſe or ground. For when the whole nation of the Iewes bound themſelues by an Oath to be faithfull and true to *Cæſar*, and to obey him, only theſe Phariſes did not ſweare: theſe were in number ſomewhat aboue ſixe thouſand, whom the King puniſhed with a mulct pecuniarie : which ſumme of money the wife of *Pherora* disburſed for them. But they, to recompence this her great liberalitie, tooke vpon them the foretelling of things to come, as men forſooth indued with diuine inſpiration: they propheſied that K. *Herods* end was at hand, decreed by the diuine Maieſtie, and the end of all his iſſue, and kinred: and that this woman their Benefactour with her husband *Pherora*, and

R 3   the

the children defcending of them,fhould be Kings. When this practife of the Pharifes, came to the Kings knowledge, he killed them as ftirrers of fedition and traitours to the State.] Thus farre *Iofephus*, Whereby we vnderftand that this Oath of Allegeance, was well approoued of the Church of the Iewes, and onely denied by the feditious Pharifes,who then inueigled women and weake men, and by fuch meanes ftirred rebellions, as now their fucceffors the Iefuites doe. In like manner was this Oath practifed in the Church of Chriftians,as appeareth by the teftimonies before cited, and by thefe that followe. The fecond Synode of Rhemes was gathered about the yeere nine

Synod. Rheme cap.5.

hundred and ninetie: againft *Arnulphus* Archbifhop of Rhemes, where it was witneffed of that Archbifhop ; that in the prefence of the Kings,and Bifhops andClergie,and people, he was of his owne confent bound by an Oath, that to the vtmoft of his skill and power, he would be true and faithfull in Councell and aide to his Prince : the manner and forme of his Oath is fet

Ibid.cap.6.

downe thus. *Ego Arnulphus gratia Dei praeueniente Rhemorum Archiepifcopus promitto regibus Francorum Hugoni, & Rotberto me fidem puriffimam feruaturum, confilium & auxilium fecundum meum fcire & poffe in omnibus negotijs praebiturum : inimicos eorũ nec confilio nec auxilio ad eorũ infidelitatem fcienter adiuturum.* And fo it proceedeth with a long execration vpon the breaker.

30. *Nauclerus* doth likewife obferue, that *Fredericke Barbaroffa* Emperour, perceiuing that the Pope by his excommunications practifed fecret confpiracies, drawing fubiects from Allegeance, from faith and obedience ; to preuent thefe new and fubtill practifes did exact an Oath of Allegeance of all Bifhops vnder his Dominions : commaunding the Popes Agents to bee excluded from Germany, vnleffe hee fent for them. The fame exclufion of the Papall Legats was often vfed by the Kings of England and France, after that thefe Princes perceiued, that the end of fuch Legacies was to ftrengthen the Popes excommunications, and to ftirre the people to rebellions, or to robbe the land of treafure. The fame *Fredericke* did alfo forbid his fubiects to appeale to Rome,and to goe thither.

Naucler.Vol.2. generat.39.

By

By this iniunction of *Fredericke*, the Popes Legate being forced to trudge home, returning to Pope *Hadrian*, made a grieuous complaint; the Pope hereupon wrote a letter to the Emperour; which becaufe it openeth the Popes meaning concerning the Oath of Allegeance, I will here fet it downe.

Hadrian *the fourth, feruant of Gods feruants, to* Fredericke *Emperour of Romanes, health and Apoftolicall bleffing.*

31. THe law of God promifeth a long life to them that honour their parents, and threatneth the fentence of death to fuch as curfe their Father or Mother. *And we are taught by the voice of the truth it felfe, that hee that exalteth himfelfe, fhall be brought lowe. Wherfore my fonne beloued in the Lord, we maruaile not a little at your wifedome, for that you feeme not to yeeld fo much reuerence to S. Peter, and the Church of Rome, as you ought to doe : for in the letters which you wrote to vs, you fet your name before ours : wherein you doe incurre the note of infolency, that I may not fay arrogancie. What fhall I fay of the Allegeance by you promifed and fworne to S.* Peter *and to vs? How can you keepe that Allegeance, feeing that you your felfe require homage & Allegeance of thofe that are Gods? That are the fons of the moft high? (that is Bifhops) and you haue held their hallowed hands in your hands: & manifeftly declaring your felfe contrary to vs, you fhut out our Cardinals, not onely out of your Churches, but euen out of your Cities : Repent therfore, repent we aduife you: for whilft you feeke the Crown and Confecration at our hands, we feare that feeking more, you will loofe that which you haue.*

Naucler. 2. generat. 39.

The Popes fingular humilitie.

32. By

32. By this wee perceiue the Popes meaning, in denying that Kings ought to exact an Oath of Allegeance of Clarkes: eſpecially of Biſhops, for they finding that the Oath of Allegeance draweth ſubiects to the obedience of Princes, reſiſt it by all poſſible meanes: becauſe the Popes ſeeke Soueraigne Allegeance: which cannot be performed both to the Pope, and to Princes: ſo that if the Popes purpoſes ſtand, ciuill obedience to Princes cannot ſtand. And howſoeuer the Ieſuites cauill at the late Oath of Allegeance by Parliament enacted, quarrelling againſt it, as if it were not a meere Ciuill Oath: yet this is but their friuoulous exception, for it is euident by this Epiſtle of the Pope, that an Oath of meere Ciuill Allegeance, ſtandeth a-gainſt the Popes purpoſes. For this Oath which *Fredericke* exacteth, was for meere Ciuill Allegeance; and yet the Pope denieth that the Emperour ought to take ſuch an Oath of Biſhops: the reaſon was that which *Iohn Wiclife* deſcried, becauſe Biſhops muſt be the Popes ſubiects, not the Kings. This was alſo a part of that quarrell, wherewith *Thomas Becket* troubled the State in his time; for he hauing firſt taken the Oath of Allegeance to King *Henrie* the ſecond; afterward repenting, ſought to be abſolued of the Pope.

The like Oath was exacted of all the Cities of Italy, vnder the Empire, by *Henry* the fift Emperour. *Naucler.2. gener.38. Houeden.part poſter.*

33. Then this Oath of Allegeance to Kings, was in vſe before we finde it exacted by the Pope: the Pope did firſt exact it of Archbiſhops. The firſt that I can find to binde himſelfe in an Oath to the Pope, was *Boniface* tearmed the Germane Apoſtle, Archbiſhop of Mentz, an Engliſh man by birth named *Winefride*. For Pope *Gregorie* the ſecond, deſirous to draw the Germanes vnder the yoake of his ceremonies (the Chriſtian religion being long before planted among them) ſent this *Winefride*, otherwiſe called *Boniface*, to reduce all to the obedience of Rome as much as might be. For this purpoſe he exacted an Oath of *Boniface*, the forme of the Oath is extant in *Auentinus*, thus: [In the name of our Lord and Sauiour, *Leo* being Emperour, &c. I *Boniface* promiſe to thee S. *Peter*, which waſt the chiefe of Chriſts Apoſtles, and to *Gregorie* who now repreſenteth thy perſon, and to all thy ſucceſſours by the Father, the Sonne, and the holy Ghoſt, &c. I vow by this thy holy body,

Auentin.Ann. lib.3.

that

that I will follow the sincere truth of Christian pietie, as long
as my life and strength last, I will keepe concord, I will shunne
persons excommunicated, I will giue notise of lying sects, of
pestiferous errours against the decrees of our Elders, to the Bishop of Rome.] This Oath carrieth a shew of great moderation, being compared with the formes of those Oathes which
succeeding Popes exacted.

34. We declared before how *Hildebrand* caused the Emperour *Henrie* the fourth, to displace certaine Bishops: and presently after that he had made a breach betweene the Emperour and them, he restored them all to their seuerall places a-
gaine ; and exacted an Oath of them, to be true to him, the
forme of that Oath I find not : but it seemeth that then an Oath
was exacted much in preiudice of Princes. For *Anselme* Archbishop of Canterburie, by reason of that Oath which then the
Popes exacted, was enboldened to raise a contention with *William Rufus*, about inuestitures. And *Thomas Becket* by vertue
of the like Oath, contended with *Henry* the second : for that
vpon the quarrell for inuestitures, Bishops were strictly tied to
the Pope by an Oath, we finde in the contention which was
betweene Pope *Paschalis* the second, and *Henrie* the fift Emperour. For when *Henrie* the fift had bene set vp by the Pope,
to raise warres against his owne Father, and had at the Popes
instigation, robbed him of his Empire and life : he himselfe
found afterward the same measure at the Popes hands, which
his Father had found before him ; for claiming the right of inuestitures as belonging to the auncient right of the Empire, he
was denied : the matter brake out into a tumult, in which tumult Pope *Paschalis* was taken, and being in the Emperours
power, graunted and confirmed vnto him the right of inuestitures. From which graunt the Pope reuolted afterward, and
shewed himselfe more vehement in this quarrell, then any before him. After some stirres and contention, the Pope held
a Synode at Trecæ in France : this Synode was held in the yeere
one thousand one hundred and seuen. Wherein the Bishops of
Germanie were suspended by the Pope, for doing any part of *Vspergens.*
Episcopall function, (saith *Vspergensis*) because, fauouring the

S   Empe-

Auentin.lib.5.

Emperor, they were not present in this Synode. And *Auentinus* saith , that all they that were present , were bound by an Oath to the Pope, to obey him herein : *A singulis Episcopis,* saith he, *iusiurandum exactum, futuros in potestate Romani Pontificis.* That is, [An Oath was exacted of euery Bishop, that they should be in the power, and at the pleasure of the Pope.]

35. Thus were Kings robbed of their strength , when Bishops were by an Oath so bound to the Pope , that what hee commaunded, they must doe. And if the Pope listed to quarrell Princes for their auncient rights and priuiledges , it was enough for him to say, those priuiledges of Princes were matters Ecclesiasticall or Spirituall , and must therefore belong to the Pope : and not to Temporall Princes. What thing could more weaken Princes, and bring them to that poore state, that the Pope might triumph ouer them, as he did , then this subtill practise whereby Bishops, who before with other subiects held their Allegeance inuiolated to their Soueraignes ; were now by a new policie of Popes , brought by Oath to the Popes subiection, and forced to violate their Allegeance to their Princes. Consider then what seruice Princes may expect from Popish-bishops, who are so bound by Oath to the Pope , that they can doe no seruice either to God, or their Prince (if it be against the Pope) but they must violate their Oathes. And this is the great bond of their spirituall Iurisdiction, as they call it. The Popes haue wrested from Princes their auncient right by violence, excommunications, warres, and great bloodshed : these rights of Princes thus withdrawen from them , the Popes hold as matters of their Iurisdiction : and to strengthen them herein they bind Bishops and other chiefe of the Clergy, by Oaths to themselues, against their owne Kings : these practises set the Pope in the possession of this Iurisdiction.

Onuphr.in Pio 4.

36. *Onuphrius* speaking of that Oath which all Doctors tooke that were to bee made Bishops, doth at large set downe the forme of it : and among other particulars, this : *Romano Pontifici B. Petri Apostolorum principis successori , ac Iesu Christi vicario, veram obedientiam spondeo, ac iuro.* This Oath was ministred to all that proceeded Doctors; which was the cause that
some

some men of great worth and learning, refused to take that degree in those dayes : for besides other daungers, it brought two great mischeifes vpon them, that tooke it. The first concerning Allegeance of subiects to their kings; the second concerning Bishops or Doctors that might be called to a Councell. For if a quarrell fall betweene the King and the Pope, it is hard for any man to be a true subiect to the King, that taketh such an Oath to the Pope. Especially when the Pope must interprete that obedience which is vowed and sworne to him, in such a sort, as that it includeth a contradiction to the faithfull seruice and Allegeance, which euery Subiect oweth to his King. Moreouer, if a Councell should bee called to determine Religious affaires, and to reforme the abuses of the Court of Rome, how can sinceritie and indifferencie bee expected of them, that are aforehand bound by Oath to the Pope, and ingaged so farre that as a Pope chargeth the Bishops of Germanie, they cannot speake the trueth against the Pope, but they breake their Oath. And therefore since this Oath was exacted of the Clergie, there were neuer such free, sincere, and holy Synodes held, like to those which were in former times. But of all Oathes or vowes, that is the most seruile, which the Iesuites by vertue of their Order professe to the Pope, that they will serue him, as Chrsts Vicar.

37. These Oathes by the Pope were first exacted of Archbishops, though in processe of time, they came to bee farther imposed. To this purpose there is a Canon in the Decretals of *Gregorie* the ninth, which Canon becaufe it openeth somewhat, both of the reason and antiquitie of this Oath, I will set downe the whole. Thus it is; *Significasti Reges & regni maiores admiratione permotos, &c.* That is: [You signified to me by your Letters, that the Princes and Barons of the Kingdome, were mooued with admiration, that the Pall was offered you by our Apocrisiaries, (that is *Chaplanes*) with this condition, that you should take that Oath which they brought you written from vs. Let them in like sort maruell at our Lord Iesus Christ in this cause : Who committing the charge of his sheepe to *Peter*, put thereto a condition: saying, If thou louest me, feed my sheepe.

Now

M. Gilpin.

Pius 2. ad Moguntin. capit.

Chemnit. exam. part. 1. cap. 1. Ex Andradio.

De elect. & elect. potest. cap. 4 Significasti. Apocrisiarius, id est, responsalis negotiorum Ecclesiasticorum. Hincmarus Epist. 3. Nostrates capellanum appellant. Idem ibid.

Now if the creator of confciences, and fearcher of fecrets vfed this condition, and that not once, but the fecond time and a-gaine, till he had made him forie: What care then ought we to haue that fo great a Prelatcfhip of the Church bee not by vs committed to our brethren, whofe confciences we know not. They obiect that all Oathes are prohibited by the Lord, and that this practife of exacting Oathes, is not found either efta-blifhed by the Apoftles of Chrift, or by Councels. What then is that which the Lord addeth as next following: That which is more then this is of euill. For euill compelleth and forceth vs (the Lord permitting) to exact this which is more. For is not this euil, to ftart from the Church, and obedience of the Sea A-poftolicke? And to breake out againft the conftitutions of Ca-nons? Which many haue done, after their Oath to the contra-rie. We are therefore compelled by this euill, and by neceffitie to exact an Oath for Fealtie, for Obedience and Vnitie. They obiect that this thing is not eftablifhed by Councels: as though any Councels may prefcribe a Law to the Romane Church, fee-ing all Councels are by the Authoritie of the Bifhops of Rome enacted, and haue their ftrength. And in their Canons the Popes Authoritie is manifeftly excepted.]

38. The Reader may be intreated hence to obferue: Firft, that this Oath in the time of *Pafchalis* the fecond, who wrote this (for *Gregorie* the ninth Collected it from him) was receiued with great admiration, both of Temporall Lords, and of the Archbifhop himfelfe, as a thing neuer practifed before that time. Then we haue the antiquitie of impofing fuch an Oath. Secondly, we obferue this curfed boldneffe of the Pope, in per-uerting Scriptures to ferue his pride and luft. Without which blafphemous abufe of holy Scriptures, this Iurifdiction could neither at firft haue beene impofed; nor fince maintained. Thus hee handleth all the Scriptures that he meeteth withall, as in thefe few words two diuers Scriptures. Thirdly, he graunteth that euill compelled him to this, God onely permitting, which is as if he fhould fay: The diuell compelleth and driueth him to it, God onely permitteth. He who acknowledgeth thus much, is wittingly and willingly the feruant of the diuell, and of that

euill

Hoc enim am-plius vt Exiga-mus, malum nos, illo permittente compellit.

Hoc nimirum malo, ac neceffi-tate compelli-mur, iuramen-tum pro fide, pro obedientia, pro vnitate requir-re.

Anno 1099.

euill which by his owne confeſſion compelleth him. Fourthly, he reiecteth the authoritie of the Apoſtles and Councels, as being himſelfe aboue them. Fifthly, his reaſon is to bee noted, drawen from Scripture : Chriſt ſaith, That which is more then this is of euill; therefore the Pope may exact an Oath of Archbiſhops. And the Popes Canons hauing once expounded this Scripture thus; it muſt alwayes be the true ſenſe of it : For that ſay they is the true ſenſe which the Pope giueth. Sixthly, where we find this Oath exacted of an Archbiſhop, accounted a thing ſo ſtrange by the Barons of the land: We collect that the Pope at the firſt required this Oath of Archbiſhops onely, which was the cauſe that mooued many Archbiſhops to ioyne with the Pope in the purſuite of this new Iuriſdiction againſt their owne Soueraignes. And hence we ſee a reaſon, why *Anſelme* withſtood the King againſt the liking and conſent of all the Biſhops of the land, as we ſhall hereafter declare: Becauſe this Oath was exacted of Archbiſhops, *Anſelme* had taken it. For (as by this Canon it appeareth) it was conueyed with the Pall to the Archbiſhops, if they will haue the Pall, beſides the other price, they muſt take this Oath. But the Biſhops as then had not taken the Oath, which made them freer to withſtand *Anſelm.* Seuenthly, and laſt of all, obſerue what kind of Oath the Pope required: An Oath of Allegeance, And therefore the ſumme and purpoſe of that former Canon, is thus ſet downe in the Edition of *Gregorie* the thirteenth. *Electo in Archiepiſcopum ſedes Apoſtolica Pallium non tradet, niſi prius præſtet fidelitatis & obedientiæ iuramentum.* That is, [The Sea Apoſtolike will not deliuer the Pall to any Elect for Archbiſhop, except he firſt take an Oath of Fidelitie and Obedience.] Then the Oath which the Pope requires, is an Oath of Allegeance. By this the purpoſe, reaſon, Antiquitie, and honeſtie of this Oath may the better appeare.

   39. Beſides this Oath which Popes haue exacted of the Clergie, they haue laboured to bring the Emperours alſo vnto their obedience by an Oath : There is the forme of an Oath ſet downe, *Diſt.63.* as exacted by Pope *Iohn* the twelfth, of *Otho* the firſt Emperour : but becauſe in that diſtinction there is much   *D.63.cap.33.*

      coun-

counterfeited ftuffe thruft in , as that Canon which beginneth *Ego Ludouicus,&c.*which *Carolus Molinæus* hath by irrefragable proofes manifefted to be forged; therfore this is to be fufpected to be of the fame kinde. And this thing feemeth fo vnlikely, that there is no reafon to receiue it, without better ftory, then the Popes Canons : For *Otho* the firft was a Prince of great worth, wife and valiant; and *Iohn* the twelfth, a Pope that deferueth no better Titles of the Hiftoriographers , then a Monfter and a Beaft. Neither was this Empegour at any time in the power of that Pope , but the Pope in his ; for *Iohn* the twelfth helped *Beringarius* and his fonne, againft *Otho* , which caufed *Otho* to bring an Armie againft him : And as *Luitprandus* faith, *Iuramentum Othoni Papa Iohannes fupra pretiofiffimum corpus Petri præftitit,fe nunq̃ Beringario & Aberto eius filio auxiliaturum.*Naucler faith,that this *Iohn* (whom he alfo calleth a Monfter and a Beaft)hauing intelligence that two Cardinals wrote to *Otho*,to call him to Rome , cut off the nofe from the one,and the hand from the other. Then for any Oath that *Otho* fhould take to the Pope,we finde nothing in Storie but the contrarie. True it is,that *Henry* the fourth Emperour was forced by *Hildebrand* to fuch an Oath : for this Emperour being by him excommunicated , his Nobles and Bifhops falling from his obedience,was driuen to come bare-foote with his wife and little fonne,in a fharpe froft to Canufium (where the Pope then lay) and to ftay at the gates of the Citie all night : and though in greateft humility he intreated pardon , yet *Hildebrand* was fo bufied(forfooth in company of his Harlots) that the Emperour was forced to attend three daies in this grieuous affliction, before he might haue acceffe to his holineffe. And when hee came before him,he muft be contented to be bound by an Oath to ftand to the Popes iudgement : that at the pleafure of the Pope,before the triall of his caufe , he fhould be ready either to leaue or to retaine his Kingdom : that he fhould vfe no Princely habite or ornament in the meane time : that hee fhould not vndertake any part of gouernement : that he fhould not exact an Oath of Allegeance of his owne fubiects : that hee fhould neuer reuenge this wrong vpon the Pope. When he had thus
hampered

Luitprand.lib.
6.cap.6.

Naucler.2.
Generat.33.

Naucl.Generat
36.
Schardius by-
pomn.

hampered the Emperour with an Oath, and with such strange
and mercilesse conditions(such is the Popes mercy where he is
Master)behold a stratagem,a president of humility, godlinesse,
patience,mildenesse of a Pope,he set vp *Rodolph* Duke of Sueuia
against him in battell.

    40. The Popes hauing once extorted an Oath of the Empe-
rour, were desirous vpon such presidents to make lawes: for
they had no other meanes to build vp their Iurisdiction : therefore when as first by force they extorted some Oathes , afterward they set such examples in their Canons, and last of all
they expounded those Oathes , which sometimes Emperours
tooke,to be Oathes of Allegeance to the Popes. For this purpose there is a Canon in the Clementines : *Clement* the first
confesseth that *Henry* the seuenth Emperour , refused the Oath
which he would haue imposed vpon him : and so doe other stories witnesse,that the Emperour refused to take that Oath.But
if we will beleeue *Clement* in his Canon,*Henry* afterward yeelded to that Oath,but would not acknwledge that it was an Oath
of Allegeance,because the Emperours neuer sweare Allegeance
to Popes,but Popes to Emperours : therefore *Clement* in that
Canon,declareth that these(which some Emperours yeelded to
some Popes)were Oathes of Allegeance. *Declaramus*(saith he)
iuramenta prædicta fidelitatis existere & censeri debere : That is,
[We declare that the foresaid Oathes are, and must be accounted to be,Oathes of Allegeance.]

Naucler.Ge-
ner.43.
Lib.2.tit.de
iuramentis.
See the an-
swer to this
Canon, cap.8.
by *Marsilius*
and *Occham.*

    41. By this we see how highly they would aduance the
hornes of this Iurisdiction. And still we finde this confirmed,
that the Oath which is giuen to the Pope,is vnderstood an Oath
of Allegeance. And to certifie vs yet more fully of their meaning ; it is set downe not onely as a law in their Decretals , but
publisbed as an ordinarie Ceremony,which al must take knowledge of. In the booke of their Ceremonies it is said that an
Oath is to be ministred to all Emperours, before their Coronation , and before they enter the territories of the Romane
Church. The Oath is there thus set downe: [I will exalt the
Pope,*secundum meum posse* , *& vitam :* hee shall neither loose
member nor honour by my will,councell, consent , or exhortation :

Sacrar.ceremon
lib.1.sect.5,cap.2

tion : In Rome I will make no Decree , or ordination of any thing that belongeth to his Holinesse without his councell.] In the same booke and place before cited , it is said that *Frederick* the third Emperour tooke that Oath.

42. In this Mysterie of Oathes they haue proceeded so far, as to exhibite an Oath not onely to the Clergie, but to the temporall subiects of other Princes , whom they may poyson and peruert, by reconciling them to the Pope; which as it, is a practise most dangerous to them that are so taken , and insnared as Birds in the net of their owne destruction , so is it no lesse pernitious for such Princes from whose obedience these are drawen : whereby the Pope seemeth to bring the question of Iurisdiction to an issue with the Princes of Christendome , whether he shall ouerthrow them, or they him : for it is not possible that both should stand vp together : for what is left to Princes, if their Crownes and the hearts of their subiects be taken from them? Or what is it , that Princes can haue a more tender feeling of, then of their Crownes , and of the hearts of their subiects? And what is more forcible to steale away the hearts of subiects from their Prince, then to binde them with an Oath of Allegeance to another Prince ? Then these men that haue bound themselues by an Oath to the Pope; how is it possible they should performe true Allegeance to the King ? For that the Oath which is exhibited to the Pope, is an Oath of Allegeance and fidelity; the Popes themselues by their Decretals haue assured vs.   And if you will seeke it out, this you shall finde to be the true reason , why Pope *Paulus* the fift in his late Breues hath forbidden the Recusants of this land, to take the Oath of Allegeance to the King , because they haue taken an Oath of Allegeance to the Pope. Now it is not possible that a man should performe Allegeance to two Soueraignes : if one be vassal to the other, happily one may hold Allegeance to two; as for example, a Tenant may sweare homage to his Land-lord, and to his Prince also : but this cannot be done to two Soueraignes. And if one shall take an Oath of Allegeance to diuers Lordes, it is concluded, that if the Pope be one of those Lords, he must be obeyed before all other whatsoeuer. Then it

Auguſt. Anco-nit. lib. de po-teſt. ecclef. q.22. art.3.& 4.

is

is not a Fatherhood in the Church, that the Pope ſtriueth for,
but a power ouer Princes, by weakning and vndermining their
authority, withdrawing the hearts of ſubiects: exacting an Oath
of Allegeance of all whom they can reconcile : and not permitting their Conuerts to take an Oath of Allegeance to their
owne Soueraigne Princes. And becauſe we find that moderate and conſcionable Papiſts, as Maſter *Hart* in the conference with Doctor *Reynolds*, and ſuch like, being driuen to vnderſtand the cauſe aright, cannot chuſe but iuſtifie our cauſe,
and will not yeeld to the Pope, a Princehood ouer the world,
but onely a Fatherhood of the Church : not graunting to him John Hart
a power to depoſe Princes : confeſsing alſo that the power Epiſt. to the
which we giue to Princes, is not vnderſtood of themſelues, for Reader, and
they, before they will vnderſtand our cauſe, thinke that wee chap. 7. diuiſ. 7.
meane to giue as much to the Prince, as they doe to the Pope :
therefore we haue reaſon to reſt herein aſſured, that if the Ieſu- Hart. chap. 10.
ites entred not into the Popes battels with a Pontificall furie, diuiſ. 2
the Pope would vtterly be forſaken in this, wherein all moderate ſpirits haue already forſaken him : or if hee would relin-
quiſh this part of the quarrell, which hee maintaineth againſt
temporall Princes, happily he might make himſelfe much more
ſtronger then he is, or poſsibly can be, by following this courſe;
But as the end is not Religion, but a worldly Principality that
they ſhoot at, ſo the meanes which they vſe, are not the courſes
of moderation, conſcience and religion, but of force and furie ;
they will haue all, or looſe all. Wherein the wiſedome of the
Ieſuites will be called into great queſtion, for ſetting the Pope
vpon ſuch deſperate courſes, at leaſt for being the onely inſtruments of theſe new and furious practiſes, which doubtleſſe will
in the end make an end of his Kingdome.

§. IIII.

Of Inueſtitures.

43.   HAuing ſpoken ſomewhat of the meanes, whereby
this Iuriſdiction was ſought, wee are now to
ſpeake of the partes of this Iuriſdiction, as wee finde the
T   ſame

same practised at this time, when it was at his height. The partes of this Iurisdiction so much pursued by Popes, we gather to be these: power ouer Bishops, power ouer generall Councels, Inuestitures, exemption of criminous Clerkes, the Popes power in giuing lawes, appellation; and last of all, a power to depose and depriue Kings: In all which the Pope hath proceeded *de facto*, to practise that power whereunto hee neuer had right. The two first we purpose not to speake of here, because of the first we haue spoken already, Chapt. 5. Of the second we purpose to speake in the last Chapter; the rest are here to be handled in Order: and first of Inuestitures.

44. The first Pope that claimed Inuestitures, was *Hildebrand. William Malmsbury* saith, *Hic (Hildebrandus) quod alij nusitauerant palam extulit, excommunicans electos qui Inuestituras Ecclesiarum de manu Laici per annulum & baculum acciperent*: That is [He openly by excommunication thrust out them that had taken Inuestitures of Churches from a Lay hand, by a Ring and a Staffe: which thing before *Hildebrand* other Popes had not done.] Whereunto all the Histories of this time giue consent, declaring that the first claime that the Popes made for Inuestitures, was begunne by *Hildebrand*: And because that the Popes were so peremptorie herein, raising and continuing so great and so long a contention about this thing, therefore it is thought by many that this right of Inuestitures was the Churches right, and consequently the Popes. And that Emperours and Kings did vsurpe it by inuasion and intrusion, first, priuately, and then more publiquely: We are therfore to seeke out this point, to whose right Inuestitures did aunciently belong, whether to Kings or to Popes. Now that they were a part of the auncient right of Emperours and Kings, it is witnessed by *Gratian*: for he bringeth an ancient testimonie which doth witnesse, That Pope *Hadrian* did intreat *Charles* the great to come to Rome, and defend the affaires of the Church; and that there the Emperour held a Synode, in which this auncient right was confirmed to him by Pope *Hadrian*: *Hadrianus autem Papa cum vniuersa Synodo, Carolo ius & potestatem eligendi pontificem, & ordinandi Apostolicam sedem, dignitatem quoque patri-*

tritiatus ei concesserunt: Et Episcopos per singulas prouincias ab eo Inuestituram accipere definiuit, vt nisi à rege laudetur & Inuestia- tur Episcopus, à nemine consecretur. That is, [Pope *Hadrian* with the whole Synode graunted to *Charles* the right and power of choosing the Pope, and ordaining the Sea Apostolike, and the priuiledge of the Romane Nobility ; and defined that Bi- shoppes through all Prouinces should take Inuestitures from him : that a Bishoppe should be consecrated by none, vnlesse he were first inuested by the Emperour.] Thus much is also te- stified by *Sigebert* and many moe. The same is confirmed by Pope *Leo,* who graunteth this to be the right of *Otho* the first, as *Hadrian* did to *Charles* : for thus saith *Leo : Othoni primo Teutonicorum Regi eiusq, successoribus , &c. perpetuam faculta- tem eligendi successorem, & summæ sedis Apostolicæ Pontificem, ac per hoc Archiepiscopos seu Episcopos, vt ipsi ab eo Inuestituram ac- cipiant.* [To *Otho* the first, Germane Emperour , and to his Suc- cessours, &c. We grant the chusing our successour, the Bishop of the chiefe Apostolicke Sea, and by this to chuse Archbishoppes and Bishoppes, that they may receiue Inuestitures from him.]

*Sigebert an.*774

*Leo.*7.
*Dist.*63.*cap.* 23.
In Synodo.

45. In both these Decrees, as wel of *Hadrian* as of *Leo,* there is *Anathema* denounced to the violators thereof : Now *Hilde- brand* was the first violator of them. The things which the Popes decree in their Consistory, in a full Synode , vnder *Ana- thema,* are things which must be vnchangeably kept, or els there may be errours and vncertainty in the Decrees of his Holines, which the Iesuites will not confesse. But some of late presume, that the Popes first graunted these Inuestitures to temporall Princes, and that they haue no greater right or Title to them, then from the Popes gift : and the same authority, say they, which gaue them, may reuoke this gift. We answere, this was yeelded to *Charles* when he was first made Emperour , as the auncient right of the Empire. This is proued first, because in the same Distinction of *Gratian* this is often called *antiqua consuetu- do,* and *prisca consuetudo :* and *cap.* 18. Pope *Stephen* answereth that he deferred the consecration of a Bishoppe, *Quod imperi- alem nobis , vt mos est, absolutionis minimè detulit Epistolam.* And a little after, *Vestra solertia, imperialis, vt prisca dictat consuetudo,*

*Dist.*63.*cap.* 18.
& 21.

T 2

percepta

percepta licentia, & nobis, quemadmodum vos scire credimus, imperiali directa Epistola, tunc voluntati vestre de hoc parebimus. And againe : *Non debet ordinari qui electus fuerit, nisi prius decretum generale introducatur in regiam vrbem, secundum antiquam consuetudinem, vt cum eius scientiâ & iussione debeat ordinatio prouenire.* Then the Bishops of Rome themselues graunt, that this was the auncient vse and custome of the Empire. The same is also confirmed from the reason that drew *Charles,* then from the siege of *Ticinum* to that Synod, it was to haue the auncient rights of the Empire confirmed to him. Which thing is declared by diuers Histories, especially by *Theodoricus de Niem,* who testifieth that the reason which drew *Charles* to Rome at that time was, to haue the right and auncient vses of the Empire clearely knowne. There was, saith he, a Synod holden by Pope *Hadrian,* and one hundred fifty three Bishops & Abbats, *exquirentibus vsus, leges, & mores eiusdem Ecclesia & Imperij* That is: [Making search of the vses, lawes, and customes of the same Church, and of the Empire.] For all that could bee proued to be the auncient priuiledges of the Empire, was *Charles* to haue then to be confirmed to him, but then were Inuestitures confirmed to him : therefore they were part of the auncient priuiledges of the Empire.

Theodor. de Niem de inuestituris.

46. *Hincmarus* Archbishop of Rhemes, liued and wrote about the yeare eight hundred sixtie. At what time without any question the auncient practise was continued of choosing Bishops by the consent of the King. For he writing to the Bishops of France, saith of the manner of choosing Bishops. *Consensu principis terra, qui res Ecclesiasticas diuino iudicio ad tuendas & defendendas suscepit, electione cleri atq́, plebis, quisq́, ad Ecclesiasticum regimen absq́, vlla venalitate prouehi debet.* That is : [By the consent of the Prince of the land, who by the Diuine ordinance hath vndertaken the defence and preseruation of Ecclesiasticall causes : and by the election of the Clergy and people ought euery one to be promoted to the Ecclesiasticall gouernment without Simony.] This then is the auncient right of euery Prince within his owne dominions. As the same *Hincmarus* saith afterward : *Principi terra magnoperè prouidendum est, ne in*

Epist.4.ad Episc. Franc.cap.5.

Ibid.

bis

his Deus offendatur, per quos religio Christiana consistere debet.
Marsilius Patauin. hath a testimony, which if it were of doubtlesse authority, might moue some doubt. For hee saith, that
Pope *Simplicius* did forbid Inuestitures to bee taken at a lay
hand, albeit, saith he, by that decree it is manifest, that his predecessours exhibiting all due and humble reuerence to Princes,
did vse to take Inuestitures from Lay-men. It is manifest by this,
that *Marsilius* had seene a decree of *Simplicius* to this purpose.
Which if it were the true decree of *Simplicius*, then were Inuestitures acknowledged the Princes right, long before *Charles*:
but if that decree were forged, as doubtlesse it was, with many
moe : Let the Romane forgery be acknowledged, and the Masters of that mint knowne. Howsoeuer, it is out of question that
Inuestitures were acknowledged the auncient right of the Empire by *Hadrian*: yeelded to *Charles* ; graunted also by diuers
Popes, as is apparant by their expresse confessions ; of whome
some were more auncient then *Charles* the great, and some
since.

Defensor. pac.
part.2.cap. 25.

Simplicius was
Pope an. 467.

47. The reason why it should belong to temporal Princes is
so great, that it moued Popes, Emperours, and Kings, to enter
into the greatest and hottest contentions, the one to purchase a
new title ; the other to retaine their auncient right. For vntill
the time of *Constantine*, wee finde little or no mention at all of
these things, because the Iurisdiction was then vnmixt, this power coactiue was not then practised by the gouernours of the
Church. But when *Constantine* had enriched the Church, giuen
place and authority to Bishops : adding vnto that power which
they had, a new part of Iurisdiction, which they had not before
(as we haue declared.) And by this example of *Constantine*, o-
ther Emperours and Kings adding thereto ; so that a temporall
Lordship was added in the end to a Bishoprick: (which thing
was first instituted by *Otho* the second Emperour, in the opinion of Cardinall *Cusanus*. For writing of this *Otho*, hee saith :
Credidit perpetuis temporibus imperio subiectis pacem dari posse, si
temporalia dominia tam Rom. Ecclesiæ, quam alijs adiungerentur,
cum certi seruitij obseruatione, tunc enim cultus diuinus augmenta-
retur, religionem in magnam reuerentiam exaltandam credidit,

Cap.5.

This *Otho* was
Emperour An.
967.
Cusan.de Cathol.
concordantia.
lib.3.ca.27.

T 3   *quando*

quando ſanctiſſimi Epiſcopi magna potentiæ alijs Principibus inter-
miſcerentur : A mixt Iuriſdiction thus being committed to Biſhops : Then was it good reaſon, that Biſhops hauing receiued
ſuch an externall coactiue power from temporall Princes ; that
theſe Princes ſhould bee well ſecured of their fidelity to them,
for ſo much of their authoritie, as they receiued from ſuch
Princes.

48. This example of gouernment, the firſt Chriſtian Princes
ſet vp in the Church , drawne from the gouernement of the
Church of Iewes, as we haue ſaid : ſo that Chriſtian Kings haue
the ſame power ouer Biſhops, which the godly Kings of Iſraell
had ouer the Prieſts in that ſtate. From this ground riſeth Eccleſiaſticall Iuriſdiction, which being taken by the firſt Chriſtian Emperours, from the example of the ſtate of Iſraell, was continued by them and their ſucceſſours, without queſtion or contradiction, till the time of *Hildebrand.* For *Gregory* the firſt,
ſpeaking of this auncient right which Emperours had in his
time and before, declareth that this right of theirs in placing of
Biſhops, was an order ſo auncient, ſo eſtabliſhed, that the contrary thereof was neuer knowne or heard of in the Church. And
therefore writing to *Conſtantia Auguſta,* he ſaith : *Salonitæ ciui-*
tatis Epiſcopus me ac reſponſali meo neſciente, ordinatus eſt : Et fa-
Lib.4.regiſt. in-
dict.13.cap.78. *cta res eſt, quæ ſub nullis anterioribus principibus euenit. Quod ego*
audiens, ad eundem præuaricatorem qui inordinate ordinatus eſt,
protinus miſi, vt omnino miſſarum ſolennia celebrare nullo modo
præſumeret, niſi prius à ſereniſſimis Dominis cognoſcerem, ſi hoc fi-
eri ipſi iuſſiſſent. That is : [The Biſhop of Salone, was ordained
without the knowledge of my ſelfe and my Chaplaine : And
that thing is done which neuer hapned vnder any of the former
Princes. Which when I vnderſtoode , I ſent preſently to that
Præuaricatour which was inordinately ordained, that he ſhould
not in any caſe preſume to celebrate Maſſe, vnleſſe firſt I might
vnderſtand of my moſt ſerene Lords (the Emperours) whither
they commaunded this.] Which teſtimonie is alſo cited *Deſt.*
63. to proue that the Emperors ought to chuſe Biſhops, as *Ha-*
drian acknowledged the right to *Charles,* and *Leo* to *Otho.*
Gregory ſaith, that the Biſhop who intruded vpon that Church
not

not onely without his knowledge, but also without the confent of the Emperour, should not be suffered to exercise his function, before that he might vnderstand whether the Bishoppe had the Emperours consent herein: he saith also, that this practise of intruding without the Emperours consent, was a thing neuer practised vnder any Prince before that time. *Facta res est qua sub nullis anterioribus principibus euenit.* For that these wordes are referred to that intrusion without the Emperours knowledge, it is euident, because he saith not that this was neuer practised vnder any Pope, but not practised vnder any Prince; and that he will send to the Prince, to know whether the Prince commanded this thing: and therefore hee calleth him a *Prauaricator* that presumed to crosse this auncient right of Princes.

Then he condemneth a number of his successours for *Prauaricators*. *Gregory* knew well what he wrote, hauing the perfect Register of things of this kinde, done betweene the time of *Constantine*, and his time; therefore his testimonie maketh faire and full euidence, that this was the right of Christian Magistrates, long before Pope *Hadrian* did yeeld it to *Charles*. The same thing is also witnessed by the twelfth Toletan Counsell, which was held in the time of Pope *Agatho* in the yeare sixe hundred and eightie, that is long before that time wherein *Hadrian* yeelded this right to *Charles*, as the olde right of the Empire.

Concil. Tolet. 12. *cap.* 6.

49. But Cardinall *Baronius* striken with a strange fury in this question of Inuestitures, ventureth vpon a new and desperat course, denieth all Antiquities, and bringeth a more shamelesse handling to these things, then euer was brought by any man before him: He denieth the whole, with all the parts of it, that is reported of *Hadrian* yeelding this to *Charles*: but most of all he breaketh all rules of patience and moderation against *Sigebert*, because among many, he also hath reported this Storie: *Sigebert* (saith he) like an Impostor, first deuised and forged this tale, that Pope *Hadrian* yeelded Inuestitures to *Charles*; and this he wrote in the fauour of a schismaticall Emperour. Why *Baronius* should put vpon *Sigebert* Imposture and

Baron. Annal. an. 774.

and fubornation , we fee no reafon ; vnleffe it be that he thin-keth, that if *Sigebert* could be put to filence herein, there could no proofe appeare in all Antiquity for Inueftitures. If this bee his meaning, he is much deceiued : for before this word Inue-ftiture was in vfe, the Princes right was alwaies acknowledged. Long before *Sigelert*, the twelfth Councel of Toledo remem-bred this thing, as we haue declared : and before that Coun-cell *Hincmarus* ; and before *Hincmarus* , *Gregory* the firft wit-neffeth, that it was a cuftome in his time fo auncient, that the contrary had neuer beene heard of vnder any Chriftian Princes. Then if we fhould admit that *Sigebert* had beene filent , yet the right of Princes in this thing, is fufficiently proued againft the Pope.

50. But let vs heare what the Cardinall can fay for himfelfe: We muft needes examine his proofes, becaufe diuers other doe reft vpon his iudgement, and deliuer it peremptorily, that *Sige-bert* hath deuifed this tale, and that there was no fuch thing in truth. Becaufe the Difcourfe of *Baronius* is long , I will gather his reafons, and will leaue out nothing materiall , that hee hath brought for himfelfe. Firft he telleth the Reader , that when he hath heard all the matter, he wil be forced to crie out, *O Sce-lus, O impoftura, O Fraus.* I fuppofe that this will proue true in the end, that when the Reader hath heard all, he will exclaime, O villany, O knauerie, O coufenage : But why? For, faith *Baro-nius* [*Sigebert* perceiuing that he could not proue this by former Hiftoriographers, what did he? Forfooth in the fauor of a fchif-maticall Emperour, who challenged Inueftitures, he thruft into his Chronography by fraud thefe wordes : *Poftea rediens Caro-lus, Papiam cepit, iterumque Romam redijt, Synodumque conftituit cum Hadriano Papa, alijsque 153. religiofis Epifcopis & abbatibus, in qua Hadrianus Papa cum vniuerfa Synodo tradidit ei ius eligen-di pontificem & ordinandi fedem Apoftolicam , dignitatemque pa-tritiatus : Infuper Archiepifcopos, Epifcopos per fingulas prouincias ab eo inueftituram accipere definiuit, vt nifi à rege laudetur & In-ueftiatur, a nemine confecretur.*] Is it any reafon that a man who for almoft fiue hundred yeares hath alwaies beene reputed an honeft man, fhould now be called by a pafsionate Cardinall a Knaue ?

Knaue ? Was there euer any man before *Baronius* that put this imputation vpon *Sigebert* ? His memory in all ages since hee wrote hath beene famous for his learning, grauity, wisedome, and integritie : *Sigebertus horum temporum scriptor* (saith *Auentinus* speaking of those times wherein he wrote)*vir alioquin etiam vt quisq̃ illa tempestate esse poterat,omnis diuini humaniq̃ iuris consultissimus.* That is [*Sigebert* a writer of these times, a man most skilfull in all humane and diuine Law, as any other whatsoeuer that could be found in that time.] Then it is not likely that he should now be found vnhonest,that in so many ages hath passed for an honest man : And if the testimony of others that witnesse with him the same thing, be sufficient to cleare him,he will be cleared by a great Iury, and a firme verdict.

Auentin.lib.5.

51. *Frosard* writing the French Storie,and collecting the actions of *Charles* the great,out of the ancient Stories of that nation(and where can the actions of the French Kings bee better knowne,then by the Stories of that nation?) saith thus[*Charles* came to Rome at the request of the Pope,and there kept Easter. And before he went away there was a Councell of one hundred,fiftie and three Bishoppes and Abbots : there Pope *Hadrian* by the consent of all the Councell, gaue him the honour to chuse the Pope,&c.and that Archbishoppes and Bishops should hold and haue their Seas by him.] *Functius* hath the same storie. *Huldericus Mutius* witnesseth as much. *Sabellicus* saith, *Hadriano autore decretum vt Carolus rex qui optimè esset de Romana Ecclesia & Italia meritus, Pontificem legeret, &c.Par illi potestas de patritiatu dando, de Episcopis prouinciatim eligendis,vt omnia demum irrita haberentur,nisi quæ Carolus probasset.* *Walthramus* Bishoppe of Naumburg saith, *Hadrianus Papa collaudantibus Romanis & plena Synodo &c. Carolo M. & eius successoribus &c.sub anathemate concessit patritiatum & inuestituras.*

Frosard.in Charlemain. fol.80.

Funct.comm.An 772. Mutius l.de Germanorum morib.7. Sabel.Ennead. 8.l.8.

VValthram.l.de Inuestitur.Episc.

52. I must entreat the Readers patience. For I am forced to cite these witnesses only for the iustifying of *Sigebert*, which otherwise might haue beene spared ; if *Baronius* had not brought *Sigebert*, as it were to holde vp his hand at the barre : vnreuerently raking vp the ashes of the dead, & disquieting the graue

V   of

of a man that was buried with honour, and hath reſted ſo many ages without diſturbance, ·vntill the profane hands of *Baronius* light vpon his graue. It would be a matter of iuſt reproofe and reprehenſion in vs, not to be as courteous to the dead, as they are cruell againſt them : not to be as carefull for preſeruing antiquities, as they are to deface all ancient monuments that ſtand againſt them : not to be as reſolute for the truth, as they·are impudent to maintaine falſhood. I muſt therefore proceed in producing witneſſes, who liued ſome ſince that time, and ſome before : that *Sigeberts* teſtimony may be iuſtified, his honeſty cleared: and that the world may ſee by what ſtrong faction and paſſion, Hiſtories are now written to defend the Popes Iuriſdiction by defacing all ancient records that ſtand againſt it. *Lupoldus de*

Lupold de iure
Regni & Imper.
ca. 1.
Faſcicul. tempor. an.784.

Babenberg hath written a booke, *de iure Regni & Imperij Romani,* in which he hath the ſame ſtory, that *Charles* came into Italy at the requeſt of Pope *Hadrian,* & that *Hadrian* graunted inueſtitures to *Charles* in a Synod held at Rome. *Faſciculus temporum* written by *Rollewinkins Warner,* ſaith likewiſe of *Hadrian*: *Iſte Hadrianus &c. ius Carolo ſuper ordinatione ſedis Apoſtolicæ & inſtitutione Epiſcoporum, Abbatum, &c. in generali concilio dedit.* *Marſilius Patauinus* in diuers places doth witneſſe the ſame

Marſil. de tranſlat. Imperij.

thing, but more expreſly in his booke *de tranſlatione Imperij,* where he ſaith thus : *Tunc Hadrianus beneficijs temporalibus dicti Principis allectus, 153 Epiſcoporum & Abbatum concilium Romæ congregauit ibiq, cum vniuerſa Synodo dedit ei ius, &c.* And ſo declareth the ſame thing, that inueſtitures were confirmed to *Charles.* *Rodulphus de Columna* writeth a booke of the ſame argument, wherein he witneſſeth the ſame thing. The Story which

Rodulph. de Columna lib. de tranſlat. Imp.
Hartman. Shedell.
Mat. Palmer. an. 776.
Ranulph. Polycron. lib. 5. ca. 6.
Martini Chronic. an. 779. extat Ms. in bibliothec : Mertonēſis Collegij Oxon.

is called *Regiſtrum mundi,* written by *Hartmannus Shedell,* ſaith that *Charles* went from the ſiege of Pauy to Rome. *Paſcha in vrbe celebrare conſtituit, aſſumptis ſecum Epiſcopis & Abbatibus &c. inde Synodum habuit.* *Mat. Palmerius* ſpeaketh to the ſame purpoſe. *Ranulphus* in his *Polychronicon* ſaith likewiſe, *Hadrianus cencilium celebrauit in vrbe Roma cum CL. patribus præſente Carolo cui conceſſum eſt tunc ius in electione Rom. Pontificis, & ordinandi ſedem Apoſtolicam, &c.* To the ſame purpoſe ſpeaketh *Martinus,* who is intituled *Papæ Primarius Capellanus.* *Vincentius*

tius in ſpeculo Hiſtoriali hath the ſame narration at full, of the ſiege of *Papia,* of *Charles* his comming to Rome, of the priuiledges graunted to *Charles* by Pope *Hadrian* in a councell, among which inueſtitures are expreſly named.

Vincent. in Speculo Hiſt. lib.23. ca.168.

53. *Nauclerus* hath the ſame Story at large, declaring that Pope *Hadrian* held a councel of one hundred and fifty three Biſhops and Abbats, by which Synod inueſtitures were yeelded to *Charles.* Vpon which graunt, ſaith he, the French Kings to this day hold the ſame priuiledges in diuers Prouinces, and namely *in Prouincys Cenomanenſi Rotomagenſi & Remenſi.* What greater euidence can we ſeeke to proue that this thing was done, then ſuch confirmation from ſuch witneſſes, and from ſuch priuiledges of the kingdome of Fraunce, that in the midſt of Popery continued from that firſt priuiledge. The ſame Author witneſſeth, that when *Henry* the fift Emperour came to Rome to appeaſe this controuerſie, for Inueſtitures between the Empire and the Papacy, which was firſt raiſed by *Hildebrand :* that the Emperour intreated no more, then that which in publique recordes was continued the cuſtome from *Charles* the great. *Imperator,* ſaith he, *volens vti conſuetudine & authoritate prædeceſſorum ſuorum, petebat ſibi ſeruari ea quæ priuilegys Carolo M. & ſucceſſoribus in Imperio iam per 300 annos & amplius conceſſa & obſernata fuerunt. Ex quibus priuilegys licitè per Inueſtituram annuli, & virgæ Epiſcopatus & Abbatias conferebant.* [The Emperour deſirous to vſe the cuſtome and authority of his predeceſſours, required that thoſe priuiledges ſhould bee reſerued for him which were granted to *Charles* the great, and to his ſucceſſours in the Empire, and obſerued now for 300 yeares and more. By which priuiledges it was lawfull for the Emperours to conferre Biſhopricks and Abbacies, by Inueſtiture of a ring and a ſtaffe.] When the Emperour did ſhew theſe priuiledges, and claimed nothing but that which by publique recordes was confirmed to him: did any man then obiect that *Sigebert* had corrupted thoſe euidences? When the Pope nor no man for him would or could plead this corruption then, it is too late and too groſſe for Cardinall *Baronius* now to bring that plea. Againſt theſe knowne priuiledges of the Empire, Pope *Paſchalis* at that time pleaded

Naucler. volum. 2.Gener. 23.

Naucle. gener. 38.

nothing but *Synodale decretum,*ſaith mine Author:a late decree that the Pope himſelfe had made.

54. Then we haue witneſſes of all ſorts,of all times ſince *Sigebert*. But if *Baronius* ſit as Iudge in this cauſe, he will ſay all theſe are not able to moue him. For all theſe wrote ſince the time of *Sigebert,* and had the narration from him,who by fraud and impoſture put it into his Chronography, as he is alſo charged to put the Hiſtory of Pope *Ioane* a woman into his booke. And I am perſwaded that the Cardinall is more paſſionate in this particular againſt *Sigebert,* becauſe he reciteth alſo the Storie of Pope *Ioane.* For if they can cóuince him of a lie in any one thing, his report may be iuſtly weakened for other things. For

Pope *Ioanes* matters I medle not,I leaue them to him who hath of late learnedly and painfully handled the ſame. I am now to cleare *Sigebert* from forgery in this point of Inueſtitures. And becauſe *Baronius* doth peremptorily aſſure vs , that no man before *Sigebert* did write it: we are to ſearch the times before him. A man would think that the Cardinal ſo skilfull in Story as *Baronius* is taken to be, affirming ſo confidently that before *Sigebert* none wrote thus : and thereupon charging *Sigebert* of forgery (the moſt hainous crime that can be committed by a vvriter of recordes) ſhould be ſure of one of theſe two things, that either in truth no Storie before *Sigebert* hath mentioned this ; or if any haue done it, to expunge them ſo, that the truth might neuer come to knowledge. And to ſay the truth, all his confidence (as likewiſe all the confidence of that ſide) conſiſteth in this new found vnbleſſed deuiſe of expunging ancient Authors. And yet for all their expurgatoriall tables and ſhameleſſe ſhifts, this truth will not be hid. We muſt theifore declare,who hath written the ſame thing before *Sigebert.*

55. Firſt, we produce *Gratian Diſt.63.ca.22.*who recordeth the ſame thing, as before wee declared. Nay, ſaith *Baronius,* *Gratian* wrote after *Sigebert,* and hath tranſcribed this narration word for word out of *Sigebert.* That *Gratian* wrote after him, it is not altogether ſo cleare;for there is ſome doubt of the time when *Gratian* wrote. And if he wrote after him, it was not long after, for they liued together in one time. And *Gratian*

tian ſo much reſpecting the Popes authority as he doth,ſo well read in antiquities as hee was, is very vnlikely to take a tale from *Sigebert*, which hee ſaw not confirmed by auncient writings, or to receiue a ſlight report from one of his owne time, and one of the Popes enemies, (as *Baronius* would make *Sigebert*.) But where he ſaith, that *Gratian* tranſcribed this from *Sigebert*, this wee vtterly denie : for that which *Gratian* ſaith hereof, if it be compared with that which *Sigebert* writeth, cannot appeare tranſcribed, becauſe there are diuers words in the one narration, which are not in the other. Moreouer, *Gratian* citeth another Author for it then *Sigebert*. Let *Baronius* bee Iudge, and *Gratian* the witneſſe. *Gratian* citeth the Eccleſiaſticall Hiſtory for this narration, thus : *Ex Hiſtoria Eccleſiaſtica,* and then hee ſetteth downe the Story. But *Sigebert* wrote no Eccleſiaſticall Story : therefore *Gratian* doth not tranſcribe this word for word out of *Sigebert*. The propoſition is euident in all Editions of *Gratian*, yea euen in the Edition of *Gregory* the thirteenth, which the ſame *Gregory* commaundeth to be preſerued without addition or change in any thing. *Ne cuiquam liceat eidem operi quicquam addere vel immutare, vel inuertere, nullaue interpretamenta adiungere, ſed prout in hac noſtra vrbe Roma nunc impreſſum fuit, ſemper & perpetuo integrum, & incorruptum conſeruetur.* In this Edition, that is with ſuch caution and authority ſet forth, this place of *Gratian* is cited, out of the Eccleſiaſticall Story. Now that *Sigebert* wrote no Eccleſiaſticall Hiſtory, all men know his booke is intituled thus, *Sigeberti Gemblacenſis Chronographia. Baronius* acknowledgeth ſo much, and calleth it *Sigeberts* Chronography. Neither was it his purpoſe to write an Eccleſiaſticall Hiſtory, but a ſhort and very ſuccinct Chronography : neither hath it euer beene taken and reputed for an Eccleſiaſticall Hiſtory. Then *Gratian* citing an Eccleſiaſticall Hiſtory, citeth not *Sigebert*, but ſome other. And this is enough to cleare the matter againſt *Baronius*, that *Gratian* did not tranſcribe it from *Sigebert*.

56. From whom then did *Gratian* tranſcribe it? I ſay *Baronius* is refuted, though I could not anſwere this queſtion. But if we muſt anſwere, and make a further ſearch : I anſwere, that

Gregorius 13.
Præfat. ad corpus iuris Canon.

Gratian cyted this aſſuredly from *Anaſtaſius Bibliothecarius*; who wrote the ſtory of the Church, and the Popes liues. *Anaſtaſius* is extant in Print, *Ann.* one thouſand, ſixe hundred and two, *Moguntia.* This was long after that *Baronius* had vndertaken, that none before *Sigebert* wrote thus. In this Edition of *Anaſtaſius* there are diuers references in the Margent to the Annals of *Baronius* : ſo that we are not to looke for any helpe from this Edition; *Baronius* hauing done his luſt vpon it, and ſo many eyes watching, and handes working, to ſee that nothing may come to light, which may diſproue that which *Baronius* hath once with ſuch confidence vndertaken. But theſe workes of darkeneſſe, though neuer ſo cautelouſly handled, will be found out, and bring ſhame vpon the workers. For

Platin. Paſcal. I. *Platina* witneſſeth that *Anaſtaſius Bibliothecarius* wrote this, that Pope *Hadrian* yeelded this right to *Charles* the great. His wordes are theſe : *Bibliothecarius ſcribit Lodouicum liberam eligendorum Epiſcoporum poteſtatem Paſchali dediſſe, cum antea ea quoq̄ in re Imperatores conſulerentur : quam poteſtatem ab Hadriano Pontiſice Carolo conceſſam, idem autor refert.* That is, [*Bibliothecarius* writeth that *Lodouic* graunted to *Paſcalis* the free choiſe of Biſhoppes, when as before that time the conſent of the Emperours was required in this thing: which power the ſame author *Bibliothecarius* declareth that Pope *Hadrian* gaue to *Charles.*] Then we are certified that *Anaſtaſius* wrote it. And though this late Printed *Anaſtaſius* haue it not, yet that dooth not impaire our cauſe, but our aduerſaries : and dooth teſtiſie before God, Angels and men, the execrable impietie of them who like Giants fight againſt God, and truth, expunging and defacing auncient Records. Then *Platina* aſſureth vs that *Anaſtaſius* wrote it, and therefore *Sigebert* was not the firſt reporter of it.

     57. *Theodericus de Niem* doth alſo witneſſe, that this ſame narration was tranſcribed by him, out of an auncient Copie written ſo long before his time, that for age the Bookes and places where they were kept were almoſt conſumed, *hæc ſcripta* Theodoric. de Niem. *reperiuntur* (ſaith he) *in antiquiſſimis Bibliothecis, & pæne præ nimia vetuſtate, conſumptis:* In which Bookes he found it written thus:

thus : *Carolus rex ingreſſus Italiam, Papiam obſedit &c. Poſt hæc reuerſus eſt Romam, vbi conſtituta eſt ſancta Synodus a beato Papa Hadriano in Palatio Lateranenſi, videlicet in Eccleſiæ ſanctiSalua toris, quæ reuerendiſſimè celebrata eſt ab* 153. *viris religioſis Epiſ copis, abbatibus &c. ab vniuerſis regionibus & ordinibus almæ vr bis, a cuncto etiam clero huius ſancta Rom. Eccleſia, exquirentibus vſus leges, & mores eiuſdem Eccleſia & imperij* : Where the ſame teſtimony for Inueſtitures followeth at large. This mans credite hath not beene called in queſtion, for ought that I could finde : and there can be no reaſon to except againſt him, being the Popes Regiſter, or in ſome chiefe place vnder him for wri ting. And the better to declare the truth and fidelity of this man, it is worth the obſeruing, that he hath with exact care re corded where he found theſe antiquities, naming the place where theſe bookes might haue beene ſeene of all men, at that time when he wrote, for before his booke he writeth thus : *In cipit deſcriptio de Inueſtitura Epiſcopatuum regum Teutonicorum ex quodam antiquiſſimo libro Florentino per me Theodoric um de Niem Litterarum Apoſtolicarum ſcriptorem & abbreuiatorem re perto, dum Dominus Papa Iohannes* 23. *illic cum curia ſua reſide ret, fideliter extracta, & ſequitur de verbo ad verbum prout in dicto libro videbatur ſcriptum.*

Theodoricus de Niem ſtiled Apoſtolicus ſcriptor by Cuſ pinian. Fred. 1.

The booke is extant in the Library of Queenes Col ledge, Oxon.

     58. This man then liuing in the time of *Iohn* the three and twentieth, being the Popes Regiſter or Secretary, or in ſome ſuch office, dealeth faithfully : For this extreame impudencie was not then knowen in the world, which is now ſo much pra ctiſed in the Court of Rome. We haue alſo declared from the teſtimonie of *Nauclerus* (whom *Iohn Reuclin*, a man ſo much reuerenced for learning in his time, did ſo much reuerence for fidelity, and diligence, as appeareth by that Preface which the ſame *Reuclin* hath ſet before *Nauclers* hiſtorie) that this queſti on of the Emperours right for Inueſtitures came to a hearing and examination, betweene *Henry* the fift Emperour, and Pope *Paſchalis* the ſecond, where the Emperor ſhewed records, proo uing for three hundred yeares before his time, the cuſtome of Inueſtitures to haue beene continued from *Charles* the great. On the other ſide for the Pope, there could nothing be ſhewed,

but

but *Synodale decretum*: Some decree which *Hildebrand* or ſome Pope after him did make. Moreouer vpon that Canon of *Gratian*, which before we cyted, there is reference to *Iuo Carnotenſis, Lib.8. de Election. Rom. Pent* So that it ſeemeth that *Iuo* alſo wrote this before *Gratian*. Howſoeuer it be, we haue witneſſes cnow to proue *Sigebert* an honeſt man, and yet haue wee iuſt cauſe to exclaime : *O ſcelus, O impoſtura, O fraus*. For when we finde the mouth of antiquity ſtopped, the teſtimoniés of approued writers partly reiected as impoſtures, only becauſe they make againſt the Popes Iuriſdiction : partly expunged by ſacrilegious hands, and malicious and cruell hearts, that the truth by all meanes may be defaced, and falſhood adored and maintained by a generation, framed and faſhioned to vanity and vntruth ; appearing with the countenance and haire of women, that is, of Harlots for their impudency, with the teeth of Lions for their cruelty, with the tailes of Scorpions, for their ſtinging and expunging of auncient Authours, leauing the Markes of their poyſoned ſtrokes in all bookes which they handle : haue we not then iuſt cauſe to exclaime, O profound villany, O admirable couſenage, O Antichriſtian impoſture, drawen from the depth of Sathans pollicies ! And what could make *Baronius* ſo confident to aſſure that none before *Sigebert* wrote thus ; but a ſure confidence and repoſe in the expunging of *Anaſtaſius* ? And yet hath he not ſo expunged that Authour, but that the true markes of that Narration remaine ſtill in his booke, as preſently we ſhal declare. But behold into what wretched times we are now fallen : for we cannot write for the truth without feares, leaſt we ſhould by conuincing falſhood giue an opportunity to falſifiers to worke more falſly. For who can warrant vs that this which we haue produced, ſhall not hereafter bee cleane expunged out of theſe Authors, that no memory in antiquitie may remaine againſt them? And when they haue corrupted all auncient Recordes, and their poſterity ſhall triumph in the wickedneſſe of their Fathers; then our hope is that Chriſt from heauen will ſhew himſelfe, and will not ſuffer that Kingdome long to indure, which ſtandeth vp by no other ſupporters then falſhood and vngodlineſſe. Theſe outragious practiſes

ſes

Apoc.9.

ſes againſt the truth, cannot but raiſe vp the ſpirits of G O D S children, to an earneſt longing and expectation of Chriſts comming to deliuer his truth, out of this captiuity and filthy priſon wherein vnrighteous men ſeeke to holde it downe ſuppreſſed.

59. *Baronius* proceedeth : and telleth vs that *Eginhardus* ſaith, that *Charles* came but foure times to Rome, then *Baronius* laboureth to proue, that this thing could not be done at any of thoſe times. We anſwere; It is enough for our purpoſe if *Charles* came but once to Rome : for all thoſe Authours which I haue cyted doe proue, that this was done in his firſt iourney to Rome, before he went to the Saxon warres. And if he thinketh reaſon to denie the truth of this Narration, becauſe *Eginhardus* doth not mention it : I anſwer, *Eginhardus* writeth very ſuccinctly, and had no purpoſe to record all particulars. For he doth not mention that *Charles* the great did erect the Vniuerſity of Paris by the helpe of *Alcwin* an Engliſh man, and *Iohn Mailroſe* a Scottiſh man, and yet this is recorded by others, whoſe credite is nothing impaired by the ſilence of *Eginhardus*. *Baronius* doth alſo obſerue, that all that wrote before him, did not refel *Sigebert* for an Impoſtor, but only ſay that thoſe things were graunted by *Hadrian*, but reuoked by other. We anſwer, it had beene much more for his credite, if he alſo had kept the ſame moderation, which all before him haue done. But now for an eſpeciall ſeruice to the Pope, hee hath by his owne confeſſion pulled vp an olde hedge, which no man ſtirred before him, and therefore it is no maruell if a Serpent bite him : and that in ſtead of a graue and faithfull Hiſtoriographer, hee purchaſe the iuſt imputation of a factious writer, ſtuffed with inuectiues, betraying, profeſſed partiality, an euill heart, a corrupt and pernitious reſolution, to deface all antiquity that ſtandeth againſt his purpoſes.

Eccleſ. 10.8.

60. But he proceedeth, and asketh how this Councel ſhould be called of a ſudden ? And whence ſhould ſo many Biſhoppes and Abbots be ſo ſoone gotten together ? A goodly queſtion. Theſe trifling obiections ſerue to no other end, but to helpe to conuince him, that dare contradict ſo many witneſſes with ſo ſmall ſhew of reaſon. But as in the examination of theeues

X　　　　　　　　　　　　and

and Felons many things fall from themſelues at vnawares, by which their falſhood is conuicted, ſo by this queſtion he draweth an ineuitable conuiction vpon himſelfe: for *Charles* purpoſing to hold a Councell, brought theſe Biſhoppes and Abbots with him to Rome. And thus *Anaſtaſius* witneſſeth; for they haue left ſuch markes in the Printed *Anaſtaſius*, as doe plainely ſhew where he was ſtunge with the Scorpions taile. For thus ſaith this printed *Anaſtaſius*: *Dum per ſex menſium ſpatium ipſe Françorū Rex Papia demoraretur, in obſidione ipſius ciuitatis, magnum deſiderium habens ad limina Apoſtolorum approperandi &c. Tunc abſtollens ſecum diuerſos Epiſcopos & Abbates, & iudices &c Cum pluribus exercitibus Romam per Thuſciæ partes properauit.* That is, Whilſt *Charles* ſtayed ſixe moneths in the ſiege of Pauie, hauing a great deſire to approach to the doors of the Apoſtles, &c. Then taking with him diuers Biſhoppes, and Abbots, and Iudges, &c. Hee came by the parts of Tiuſcia with many Armies to Rome.] Where we ſee, that they who expunged *Anaſtaſius* (as Theeues vſe to doe in the like caſe) haue left ſuch markes behinde them, as are ſufficient to conuince them: For to what end did *Charles* bring ſo many Biſhops, and Abbots, and Iudges with him to Rome? This ſheweth euidently that he had a purpoſe to hold a Councell. And becauſe *Baronius* asketh this queſtion, whence came ſo many Biſhoppes and Abbots of a ſudden? We can ſoone anſwere him: *Anaſtaſius* witneſſeth, that *Charles* brought them with him, as purpoſing this thing aforehand. But we aske him a queſtion which hee will neuer aſſoile vs, Why did *Charles* bring ſo many Biſhoppes and Abbots to Rome? *Anaſtaſius* witneſſeth, that hee brought a number of Biſhoppes and Abbots to Rome: ſo that either *Baronius* and the Expurgatours ſhould haue ſpared *Anaſtaſius*, and not expunged that which he had written of the holding of this Councell, or this ſhould haue beene alſo expunged, which he writeth of the preparation of that Councell. Againe theſe words which are left in *Bibliothecarius*, of *Charles* his comming from Pauy, doe further conuince *Baronius*, and detect the purpoſe of falſifying: for *Baronius* wil not admit that *Charles* came to Rome at this time from Pauie, becauſe *Eginhardus* ſaith, he

was

Anaſtaſ. Biblioth. ad An. 772.

was but foure times at Rome,and this could not be done at his firſt iourney,becauſe from the expugnation of Pauie , he went preſently to the Saxon warres : and thus he proceedeth,vexing his reader with winde, and wordes lighter then winde.Though he be deepely to be charged for this light and vaine reaſoning, yet his great and groſſe fault wherein he was ſo groſſely ouer-ſeene,is, that in cutting *Anaſtaſius,*he cut not deep enough:For *Anaſtaſius* in the wordes that are left,doth expreſly declare,that *Charles* came from the ſiege of Pauie to Rome, which *Baronius* denieth,and that he brought many Biſhops and Abbots with him. Thus both by cutting out of *Anaſtaſius* , that which *Platina* witneſſeth he wrote , and by leauing in *Anaſtaſius* that which doth proue ſo much,and teſtifie their falſhood : they are conuinced to be corrupters of antiquities , and new forgers of nouelties.

61. *Baronius* perceiuing that all this that he hath ſaid will not helpe him,vnleſſe he proceede further to refute likewiſe all that *Gratian* ſaith in the next Canon,*In Synodo* : goeth on , and vndertaketh alſo to refute it : For what other thing can he do, that hath once broken the bounds of modeſty and moderation, but proceede to a reſolutio n in impudency ? *Gratian* cyteth the Canon of Pope *Leo,*who gaue Inueſtitures to *Otho* as *Hadrian* did to *Charles. Baronius* denieth that Pope *Leo* wrote ſo , as *Gratian* cyteth him : what authority can be produced to ſatisfie theſe men ? VVe bring the teſtimonies of Popes,we bring them cyted by ſuch as were the greateſt maintainers of the Popes Iuriſdiction,and yet it will not ſatisfie : Why? No reaſon is brought,but it ſtandeth not with the liking of the Court of Rome in theſe daies. He ſaith , that the name of Inueſtitures was not knowen in that age,wherein *Charles* liued : But how doth he proue that ? No proofe is brought : and what neede he bring any proofe,ſeeing there are many that are readie, to take all that he ſaith without proofe ? Concerning the name of inueſtitures,the Ciuilians are herein reſolued,and peremptory, that it came from the Lawes of the Lumbards, as did alſo all the Lawes, *De feudis.* For of theſe things there is nothing found in the auncient Romane Lawes,nor in the later Imperiall
X 2   Lawes,

Lawes, vntill the gouernment of the Lumbards was raifed. And therefore it is certaine, that before the gouernement of the Lumbards was erected in Italy, this word Inueftiture, can not be proued to haue beene in vfe. But feeing by the Lumbards it came in, and the Lumbards were at their higheft before, and in the time of *Charles* the great (for they were ouerthrowne by *Charles*, after that they had raigned two hundred and foure

Palmerius An.
776.
Naucler. gener.
23.

yeares in Italy, and had poffeffed all Italy in a maner, except only the City of Rome, as diuers Authors doe witneffe) it can not be chofen but that in the time of *Charles* this word was in vfe. And when we haue of the one fide good reafon, the teftimonie of hiftories, the iudgment of Lawyers, concurring with the expreffe wordes of the Popes Canons which vfe the fame word: fhall it be thought a fufficient refutation on the other fide, to fay the word was not then vfed, and bring no reafon thereof? Then this thing was vfed in *Charles* his time, and the name of Inueftitures knowne. The fame thing was vfed long before *Charles* his time, but not vnder the name of Inueftitures. This name, and the ceremonie of a ftaffe and a ring came in by the Lumbards. Then whether we confider the thing without this new name and ceremony, or with it: wee finde it alwayes the Princes right. Thus *Sigebert* is iuftified, the truth tried, and the Knaue knowne.

62. Now to come to the Kings of England, as their authority was no leffe then the authority of other Princes in their Kingdomes, fo more we feeke not. And therefore whereas a

Anfwer to the
fift part of Reports.

certaine Catholique diuine, telleth vs, that *Henry* the firft chalenged Inueftitures, as vfed by his father and brother before him, whereof yet (faith he) we finde no expreffe proofe, or example in any of our Hiftories, that they had vfed them, much leffe that they were lawfully graunted: how ftrange is this dealing? befeeming none but fuch as he is. For is not this proofe good and fufficient, when the King chalengeth no more, then that which was in frefh memory and vfe in his brothers dayes, and fathers? When wee finde fo many teftimonies of Story, of Councels, of Popes, that there was no other right of giuing Inueftitures knowne through Chriftendome, then the right of
Princes,

Princes: fhall bafe perfons quarrell the teftimonie of a King, founded vpon fuch proofes? Let the world iudge of the learning of him who writing hee knoweth not what, will tell vs that the fenfe, deuotion, and iudgement of the world, was neuer to the contrary: fancying conclufions like a dreamer, not prouing like a difputer. Now touching the particular of *Henry* the firft, it is certaine that hee began no new cuftome, but Pope *Pafchalis* the fecond, began to debarre him from that ancient cuftome and right, which he and his Elders had alwayes vfed.

63. For thus *Roger Houeden* reporteth: In the yeare of Chrift one thoufand one hundred and three, a great diffention grew betweene King *Henry* and *Anfelme* Archbifhop of Canterbury: becaufe the Archbifhop would not confent that the King fhould giue Inueftitures of Churches. Neither would he confecrate thofe Bifhops to whom the King gaue them. Becaufe the Pope had forbid him & all the reft to do fo. *Quia Apoftolicus* (faith he) *fibi & omnibus interdixerat.* And againe he faith: *Quibufdam ad hoc nitentibus, vt Rex eas faceret more patris & fratris fui, non iuxta praceptum & obedientiam Apoftolici.* [Becaufe the Pope had forbidden him & the reft, &c. Some perfwaded that the king would make Inueftitures after the cuftome of his father and brother: and not according to the precept and obedience of the Pope.] Where note, that it is not the Kings allegation, that this was his fathers, and brothers right; but it is a truth acknowledged by *Houeden,* maintained by the Barons, denied by none. Againft which, there was nothing then known, but onely the new Precept of Pope *Pafchalis.* The fame Author declareth alfo, that thefe cuftomes and prerogatiues were not impofed by the King, but fought out with exact care & diligence by the Bifhops & Barons iointly. For fpeaking of thefe cuftomes in the time of *Henry* the fecond, he recordeth an Epiftle which the Bifhops of the Prouince of Canterbury wrote to *Thomas Becket,* wherein they teftifie thus much: *Ne fuper his contentionis funis traheretur in pofterum, noticia publica delegari, ad iuratis itaq, per fidem, & per eam qua in Deum fpes eft, maioribus natu Epifcopis, alyfq, Regni maioribus, retroacti temporis infinuato*

Houeden. Henric. 1.

Rog. Houeden. Henric. 2.

finuato

sinuato statu, dignitates requisitæ palam prolatæ sunt, & summorum in Regno virorum testimonijs propalata. [Least this occasion of contention should proceede any farther heereafter , it was brought to publique triall. Therefore the most auncient Bishops , and other Barons of the Kingdome, tooke an Oath by their faith, and by that hope which they haue in God to make a true search, whereupon looking into the times past, the priuiledges of the Kingdome were sought out, and published, and divulged by the testimonies of the greatest persons in the Kingdome.] Then these customes and auncient priuiledges of the Kings, were sought out by the grauest, and most learned of the Bishops and Barons : they were sworne to deliuer the trueth, as they should finde it in the auncient Records of the land. After all these expresse proofes a masked Romane Catholique telleth vs, that no proofe heereof is found in all our Stories. If this mans Catholique diuinity were examined (as when opportunity serueth it shal be)it will appeare, that it consisteth of extreme confidence and impudency patched vp with a fewe smooth words, without knowledge of Diuinity, or of solid learning.

64. After this *Calixtus* held a councell at Rhemes, wherein hee condemned all Inuestitures taken from a lay hand. With this Pope, *Henry* the second King of England , met in conference at *Gisars* in Fraunce. The King pressed the Pope, that he might not be disquieted in his auncient right, that the auncient Lawes and customes of his Kingdome , might be kept inuiolable, as in the time of his progenitours they were. The Pope hauing nothing to say against these auncient customes, drew the King into another matter, intreating the Kings fauour for *Thurstinus* Archbishop of Yorke, that he might be restored to his place, for the King had depriued him. The King answered, that he had sworne the contrary. The Pope replied; but I am Pope, and if you will doe as I bid you, I will absolue you from your Oath. *Ego Apostolicus sum, & si feceris quod ego postulo, ab hàc fidei sponsione te absoluam.* This was the olde practise of abusing Kings. And it was not much to be meruailed, if some kings were then blinded, when they were led by such guides. *Houeden* doth likewise declare, that the Decrees of that Councell of
Rhemes,

Houed. Henric. 2.

Rheines, were sent to the Emperour *Henry.* The Emperours answere was : *Nihil in his se prætermissurum quod sui iuris esset,* *suorumq̃, sibi contulit antiqua consuetudo progenitorum.* That is : [That he would loose no part of that his right, which the auncient custome of his progenitours had conferred vpon him.] And afterward, saith *Houeden,* other things he graunted ; *Vltimum vero, scilicet Inuestituram rerum Ecclesiasticarum, concedere noluit.* [The last thing, that is to say Inuestitures of Ecclesiasticall dignities, he would in no case graunt.] Then it appeareth that antiquity, custome, and the right of their progenitors stood for the Princes of this age, and against them was nothing but the bare will, and new commaundement of the present Popes, herein falling away not onely from the auncient vse before, but from the sense, knowledge, confession and iudgement of the auncient Popes.

This was *Henry* the fift.

65. I stay the longer vpon this point, and am more willing to search the truth herein, because it is a matter of especiall importance concerning this question of Iurisdiction, which wee seeke to know. For *Robert Persons* the masked Catholique diuine confesseth in effect thus much, that if wee can proue that Inuestitures belong to temporall Princes, we haue in his iudgement questionlesse obtained the cause for which we striue. Let me set downe his owne words. [Three things, saith he, do concurre in making of a Bishop by diuine and Canon law, to wit, election, confirmation, and consecration. The first, to wit election, when it is iustly made, doth giue right to the elected to pretend the second and third, &c. Yet can he not vpon his onely Election, exercise any part of his office of a Bishop either in Iurisdiction or order. But when he hath the second part which is confirmation, and induction to the benefice, which is properly called Inuestiture ; then hath he Iurisdiction vpon those people, and may exercise the Acts thereof by visiting, punishing, or the like : but not the Acts of order, vntill he haue consecration also, that is to say, he cannot make Priests, nor administer the Sacrament of confirmation, &c. And a little after he saith : the second which is confirmation and giuing of Iurisdiction, must onely proceede from him, that is the fountaine of all spirituall Iurisdi-

Answer to the fift part of Reports, pag.171.

Iurisdiction vnder Christ, which is the Bishoppe of Rome, or some Metropolitane or Bishoppe vnder him, that hath authority and Commission from him.   Thus much the Catholicke Diuine.]

66. I forgiue many particular escapes in this short discourse, not spending time in the examination of by-points, I would meete him there, where he thinketh himselfe strongest. For where he saith, confirmation, which also he calleth induction, or which properly, as he graunteth, may be called Inuestiture, giueth Iurisdiction: this we yeeld.   And then heere wee ioyne issue with olde Sir *Robert*, in that part of his Collection, whereon he layeth his greatest hold; and are content to trie the whole cause thereon: whether Inuestiture, which by his confession, and the doctrine of his Church, and the consent of all, giueth Iurisdiction, belong of ancient right to the Pope, or to temporall Princes. If he be able to proue by any auncient, full, cleare, vnsuspected witnesse, that the Popes within the space of the first thousand yeares, or before *Hildebrand*, either had that right, or did practise, or so much as challenge that right: I will for my part yeeld the cause, and will confesse mine errour, if thus much be euidently euicted. But seeing we haue proued by vndoubted Histories, by the consent of Popes themselues, by the Decrees established in Councels, that this was an auncient right of temporall Princes, called *Prisca consuetudo* by Pope *Stephen*, *Antiqua consuetudo* by another: that the contrarie was neuer heard of vnder any Christian Prince, confessed by *Gregory* the first: Then hath he reason either to yeelde vs the cause wholly, or to reuoke his wordes againe, that Inuestiture giueth Iurisdiction.

67. Then the right of Inuestitures standing as the auncient right of our Kings, being neuer questioned in Christendome, before the time of Pope *Gregory* the seuenth, neuer questioned in this land before the time of *Henry* the first, that King had reason to pleade the vse of his father and brother for himselfe; because it being a thing quietly possessed by them, was, out of doubt, peaceably inioyed before them, because before them the Popes neuer made title thereto. Now concerning the tumults, warres,

warres,blood,and confusion in Christendome , both in the
Church and temporall states,which for this quarrell the Popes
procured,for fistie yeares together,as *Malmsbury* witnesseth ;
of this it is not my purpose to speake. It is enough for mee to
open the time when it began,and before which time it was neuer challenged by any Pope,and to declare that the Popes late
practise is condemned by the Iudgement of the auncient
Church.

Malmsb.Hen.1.

§. V.

Exemption of criminous Clerkes.

68. OVr purpose being to take a suruey of that Iurisdiction which we finde challenged by Popes,at and
somewhat after the time of the Conquest of England, at what
time the Popes power was at the highest : we are to consider
in the next place Exemption of criminous Clerkes ; for as Inuestiture of Bishoppes began then to be claimed , so about these
times crept exemption of the Popes Clerkes, which is taken to
be another part of this Iurisdiction. My purpose is not to
speake of lawfull exemption of the Clergie : for both Diuine
and humane lawes approue such immunities , without which ;
how could the Clergie attend vpon their heauenly businesse ?
These immunities which Emperours and Princes haue giuen
to the Church,the Church ought to inioy without disturbance,
and to withdraw such immunities , were high sacriledge and
impiety against God and his Church: But the question is not
of these immunities which Christian Kings haue giuen to the
Church,but of those immunities, which the Pope without the
leaue or authoritie of Princes,hath bestowed out of his fulnesse
of power vpon the Clergie which liue vnder the gouernement
of other Princes , by which the Clergie inioyed a protection
from punishment for any sinne : This is the thing for which
they are not ashamed to striue euen at this day , as earnestly as
they did in the midst of blindenesse. This thing will be better
knowne if we search the originall foundation of this errour,
from the beginning,and the occasion by which it grew in the

Y

Church.

Church. For now this opinion is, and for some late hundred
yeeres hath beene so rooted in the Court of Rome (that the
Clergie though neuer so much offending by murther, treason,
theft, robberies, or such like, is priuiledged from all temporall
Courts of Princes, and punishment from the Laity, vnlesse first
the Church proceede against them, and make them no; Clerks)
that they are perswaded both of the truth and antiquity hereof,
as of a point of faith : the occasion grew thus.

69. The first auncient and famous Emperours did out of
their godly and zealous affections : and as we may well iudge,
vpon good reasons to helpe the Church, and to preserue discipline, ioyne the aide of their coactiue lawes, to the spirituall
censures of the Church : ordeining that whosoeuer by the gouernours of the Church could not be brought to obedience
and order, should by the seuerity of temporall punishment be
reduced to obedience.　　The vsuall punishment which Emperours did inflict vpon Clerkes, was deportation : So did *Con-*

Theodoret.lib.1. *stantine* the great punish *Eusebius* Bishop of Nicomedia, and
cap. 20. *Theognius* Bishoppe of Nice. And albeit some were threatned
Sozomen.lib.1, with capitall punishment, as appeareth by a Letter which *Con-*
cap.16. *stantine* wrote to the Bishoppes of the Nicen Councel, recorded
by *Socrates,* and inserted in the first Tome of Councels : yet the
vsuall censure of the Emperour was exile. This kind of punishment was often inflicted by other Emperors vpon Bishops : the
examples are famously knowne, and acknowledged, I need not
to speake of them.　　Insomuch that it began to be enacted by
Emperours to be a law, that all of the Clergie that offended
might know their punishment : for that *Constantine* by whose
authority the sixt Synode at Constantinople was held, in a De-
Synod.sexta. cree inserted in that Councell, saith : *Si quidem Episcopus est, vel*
actio.18. *Clericus, vel monachico circundatus habitu, deportationis pænam*
exsoluet. Carlomannus in a French Synode decreeth imprison-
Tom.2.Concil. ment : *Si ordinatus presbyter fuerit, duos annos in carcere perma-*
neat. These punishments were inflicted vpon such Clerkes, as
would not be ordered by Ecclesiasticall censures of their Bishoppes; for so *Guntranus* doth testifie, a French King, by whose
Concil.Matiscon authority the Councel of Matiscan was held: *Quicunq; Sacerda-*
tum

tum (faith he in a Writ added to that councell) *aut ſacularium in intentione mortifera perdurantes crebrius admoniti,ſi ſe emendare neglexerint,&c. alios canonica ſeueritas corrigat, alios ligatos pæna percellat.* And a little after he faith : *Conuenit vt iuſtitæ & æquitatis in omnibus vigore ſeruato , diſtringat legalis vltio iudicum,quos non corrigit canonica prædicatio Sacerdotum.*

70. Then the ancient practiſe was, that the temporall Magiſtrate ſhould puniſh ſuch as offended of the Clergy,as well as of the Laity. Concerning the antiquity of this exemption of Clerkes from temporall Courts : wee finde no preſident for it, all the while that the Emperours had any gouernement and commaund in Italy. But when the Pope was able to meet the Emperour in battell, and giue him the worſe, then began the authority of the ciuill Magiſtrate to decay in Rome, and fell at the laſt into contempt. And the Pope hauing caſt off the yoak of obedience,which before he held to the Emperour as to his Soueraigne, began to take an authority to himſelf,which neither God nor man had giuen him. Hence proceeded that vſurpation of power to giue Lawes to other. Pope *Nicholas* the firſt,in the eight hundred and threeſcore yeare of Chriſt, writeth in his Epiſtle to the Emperour *Michael,* in another ſtile,then his predeceſſours had vſed to write to Emperours before. Among other things contained in th   Epiſtle , whereas the Emperour had written for a Clarke that had offended him,and was fled to the Pope ; whom the Emperour required to be ſent back again to Conſtantinople, Pope *Nicholas* to this maketh this anſwere. [Wee haue from the great power of *Peter* and *Paul* right and power to call Clerkes from any other Dioceſſe, if wee thinke good,and to inuite them to vs. This is our right : but Chriſtian Emperours haue no right at all to make any inquiſition for Monks, vnleſſe it be in fauour to pity them.]

Palmer.Chron. An.726. Naucler.gener. 25.

Epiſtol.Nicolai. ad Michael. imperatorem.

71. Here we obſerue the difference betweene the ſpirits of Popes in this time, and the ſpirits of auncient Popes who held the doctrine of obedience , as the Fathers then did , drawing the doctrine from the Scripture and examples of Chriſt and his Apoſtles. Chriſt when he was vniuſtly condemned, exempted not himſelfe from the puniſhment of the ciuill Magiſtrate, and

yet he wanted no power to haue done so, if hee would. These
late Romane counterfait Catholiques, when by their rebellious
doctrine and bloudy practises, they haue iustly prouoked the
Magistrate against them, yet forsooth will denie him authority
to punish them. Saint *Paul* teacheth: Let euery soule be subiect to the higher powers. S.*Peter* teacheth the same doctrine,
Submit your selues to all manner ordinance of man. The Fathers receiued this doctrine from the Scriptures, and preserued
it faithfully in the Church. *Chrysostome*, and after him *Oecume-*
nius expounding that place of *Paul*, say thus: *Omnem animam*
instruens, siue Sacerdos sit quispiam, siue monachus, siue Apostolus,
vt Magistratibus subdatur: nam hæc subiectio non euertit pieta-
tem. A learned man of late (which also was Pope) speaking of
these words, *Omnis anima subdita sic, &c.* saith: *Nec animam*
Papæ excipit. So doth God sometimes draw testimonies for the
truth, out of the mouthes of them that oppugne it. The auncients helde this truth vp in great sincerity. *Gregory Nazianzen*
saith: *Homines cuncti &c.* All men are ordered in subiection
vnder the higher powers. Hee that saith all men includeth the
Pope and his Clarkes. *Augustine* saith: *Generale pactum est so-*
cietatis humanæ obedire gregibus suis. *Leo* the first saith: *Ad im-*
perialem pertinet potestatem vt perturbatores Ecclesiæ, pacis, &
reipub. quæ Christianis principibus merito gloriatur, inimici, solli-
citius comprimantur. These troublers of the peace of the Church
and state, of whom he speaketh were Clergy men. For in that
Epistle *Leo* writeth against certaine of the Clergy, who embra-
ced the errour of *Eutyches*. Then in the time of Pope *Leo*, this
was not the doctrine of the Church of Rome, which now these
Romane Libertines haue brought in. *Gregory* the first writeth
to the same purpose: *Potestas super omnes homines dominorum me-*
orum pietati cælitus data est, vt qui bona appetunt adiuuentur, vt cæ-
lorum via largius pateat, vt terrestre Regnum cælesti Regno famu-
letur. In the same Epistle, he induceth Christ thus speaking to
the Empeiour: *Sacerdotes meos tuæ manui commisi.* Then *Gre-*
gory knew no other doctrine but that Priests were subiect, & by
Christ subiected to the Magistrate. And whereas the Emperour
commanded a law to be executed, which *Gregory* misliked: hee
wri-

*Rom.*13.1.

1.*Pet.*2.13.

Chrysost.& Oe-
cum. in Epist. ad
*Rom.*13.1.

Aeneus Siluius
in gestis concil.
Basiliens.

In orat. ad sub-
dit. et imperat.
irasc.
*Lib.*3. *cap.* 8.
confess.
*Leon. Epist.*80.
ad Iulian. Coens.
Episcop.

*Lib.*2. *indict.*11.
cap. 100.

writeth thus to the Emperor. *Ego quidē iuſſioni tuæ ſubieĉtus ean-* *Ibidem.*
dem legem per diuerſas terrarum partes tranſmitti feci : That is,[I
being ſubieĉt to your cōmand, haue cauſed that law to be ſent
to diuers Prouinces : but becauſe the law conſenteth not with
the law of Almighty God, behold I haue ſignified the ſame by
my letters to your moſt excellent Lordſhip : ſo that on both
parts I haue payed what I ought, for I haue yeelded obedience
to the Emperor,& haue not cōcealed what I thought for God.]
Then *Gregory* knew no exemption, he accounteth himſelfe a-
mong them that owe ſubieĉtion and obedience to Emperors.

72. Concerning the puniſhment of Heretiques & Schiſma-
tiques that were criminous, there was no other means knowne
in S. *Auguſtines* time,then the coaĉtiue power of the ciuil Magi-
ſtrate.For thus he ſaith : *Si nec hoc volunt Donatiſta, &c.* [If the *Lib.1.cap.6.con-*
Donatiſts will not grant this power to the Emperour, why doe *tra Epiſt. Par-*
they acknowledge the force of the Lawes to be iuſtly executed *meniani.*
againſt other malefaĉtors,and deny the ſame to be done againſt
hereticks and Schiſmaticks,ſeeing by the Apoſtolicall authority
they are all alike numbred with the ſame fruits of iniquity?Muſt
not theſe humane ordināces regard ſuch things?Why then doth
he beare the ſword? &c.]Thus ſaith *Auguſtine*: And in the ſame
place he declareth that there is one law imperial general againſt
all that profeſſe thēſelues Chriſtians,but are not true Catholicks,
but keep priuate conuenticles,that either he that ordaineth ſuch
a Clerke,or the Clerke ſo ordained, ſhould looſe ten pounds of
gold,& the place where ſuch conuenticles were kept, ſhould be
forfeited to the Emperors Exchequer.And againe he ſaith thus. *In Euangel. Ioh.*
Mirantur quia cōmouentur poteſtates Chriſtianæ aduerſus deteſtā- *traĉtatu.2.*
dos diſſipatores Eccleſia.Si nō ergo mouerentur, quomodo redderent
ratiōe de Imperio ſuo,Deo? And much more he ſaith to this pur-
poſe.Frō theſe few places of *Auguſt.*we obſerue:Firſt,that in his
time there was no doubt made among Catholicks, but that the
Magiſtrate ſhould puniſh criminous Clarks, by his coaĉtiue po-
wer.Otherwiſe they could not rēder to God an account of their
gouernment:which ſtandeth full againſt the doĉtrine of the preſent court of Rome. 2.That they who firſt ſought priuiledges &
exemptions from the ſword of the Magiſtrate were Donatiſts.

Where-

wherein the Court of Rome succeedeth them, taking other errours from other filthie heretiques, and this from the Donatists.

73. This was the auncient Doctrine : but now at Rome they teach the contrary. *Bellarmine* saith, that such Clerkes as are within the Dominions of any King, are not subiects to that King, meaning that they are the Popes subiects, and therefore not the Kings. He saith also that Clerkes owe no obedience to Kings, neither by Gods law, nor mans. *Non sunt amplius Reges*

B. Varm. l. de Clericis. ca. 28.

Clericorum superiores, & proinde non tenentur iure Diuino, nec humano, eis parere, nisi quantum ad leges directiuas. That is [Kings are not now any more Soueraignes of Clerkes; and therefore Clerkes are not bound to obey them by Gods Lawe or mans law, vnlesse it be in respect of lawes directiue.] What his meaning is by lawes directiue, he expoundeth thus : That Princes haue no coactiue power ouer the Clergie, but onely power directiue. If the Prince direct some things for the good of the Common-wealth, Clerkes (saith he) are to obey such directions;

Ibid.

but he addeth : *Nec volumus dicere his legibus teneri Clericos obligatione coactiua, sed solum directiua, vt sunt leges principum : quanquam ijsdem legibus, vt ab Ecclesia approbantur, & rata habentur, etiam coactiua obligatione teneantur.* [Wee graunt not, saith he, that Clerkes are bound by these lawes of Princes, in a bond coactiue, but onely directiue, as they are lawes of Princes. Albeit the same Lawes being approoued and ratified by the Church, bindeth Clerkes in a bond coactiue.] By this new and admirable doctrine, Princes hane no coactiue power ouer their Clergy, but the Church hath coactiue power ouer them : by the Church he meaneth the Pope here : and therefore comparing the lawes of Princes with the Popes Canon lawes, he saith;

Ibid.

Legi Canonicæ etiam in causis criminalibus cedere debet lex imperialis. That is, The imperiall law ought in matters criminall to giue place to the Canon law : by which doctrine we finde, that they tread the pathes, and fil vp the measure of their forefathers the olde Friars : maintaining that which *Iohn Wiclife* obserueth was first begunne by Friars : that the King was not Lord of the Clergie, but the Pope was their Lord. Thus a new King is raised vp ouer the Popes Clerkes, and the Scripture is verified which

which faith: And they haue a King ouer them, which is the
Angell of the bottomlesse pit, whose name in Hebrew is *A-* *Apoc.9.11.*
baddon, and in Greeke he is named *Apollyon.*

74. The Laterané Councel was held in the yeare one thousand, twohundred, and fifteene. It is decreed in the same
Councell, That Heretickes being condemned, should be deliuered ouer to the secular power: from which time these pretended priuiledges haue growen so great, and swollen vp so bigge,
that not being able to holde together, they are burst in the
midst, hauing drawne vpon themselues the iust vengeance of
God, and of Magistrates, so procuring their owne ruine. But
because *Bellarmine* cyteth a few testimonies to prooue the exemption of Clerks from secular iudgements, we may first breef-
ly examine them, and so proceede. Hee cyteth thus ; *Concil.* *Ibid.cap.3.*
*Mileuitan.Can.*13.*& Matiscon.Can.*8. These places he quo-
teth, producing no words. He cyteth also other places thus:
Sulpitius lib.2.Sacra histor.refert.5. Martinum aliquando dixisse
nouum esse & inauditum nesas, vt causam Ecclesia iudex saculi iu-
dicaret. Item Ambrosius Epist.78. ad Theophilum. et August.
Epist.162. These places are cyted or quoted by *Bellarmine,*
barely without the Authours wordes. We answere in a word:
All this toucheth nothing our question, of exempting criminous
Clerkes from temporall Courts: for these places speake not
one word of this thing.

75. The first place, *Concil. Mileuit. can.*13. to preuent such
busie fellowes of the Clergy, which caried their causes to
Rome (as then some did) ordeyned, that euery Clerke should be
gouerned by his owne Superiour. What is this to the purpose?
This is all which that Canon faith. The next Canon of the Ma-
tiscon Councell faith, that if one Clerke had a matter against
another Clerke, he should not complaine to the secular Iudge,
but to the Bishoppe: This maketh as little to the purpose. Afterward he citeth for exemption from punishment, these places;
*Concil.Chalced.can.*9.*Si Clericus aduersus Clericum habet negoti-*
um non relinquat Episcopū suum, & ad sacularia iudicia non recur-
*rat,&c.Concil.Agathens.can.*32.*Clericum nullus prasumat apud*
sacularem iudicem, Episcopo non permittente pulsare, &c. Concil.
Car-

*Carthag.*3 *can* 9.*Toletan* 3.*can.*13.*Matiſcon.cap.* 8. Theſe teſtimonies ſpeake as little for him as the other. The 9. Canon of
the Chalced.Councell ſpeaketh not of the immunities of criminous Clerkes, but onely preſcribeth how one Clerke ſhould
accuſe another before the Biſhoppe ; and not before the ciuill
Iudge. And this is the purpoſe of all the other places cyted out
of *Concil.Agathenſ.Cartbag.Toletan,* and *Matiſcon,* all ſpeake
of one thing : Onely here, one part of their knowne knauery is
to be opened : for he cyteth *Concil.Agathenſ.can.*3 2. thus ; *Clericum nullus praſumat apud ſacularem iudicem Epiſcopo non permittente, pulſare.* Marke good Reader a worke of darkeneſſe,
an example of Romiſh impudency : by true, ſound, and vnſuſpe-
cted Recordes, theſe priuiledges which now are in queſtion betweene vs, cannot be proued to haue beene eſtabliſhed of old,
or to haue any teſtimonie of antiquity, but by vertue of their
expurgatoriall tables, they are able to ſhew vs this auncient Canon of the Councell of *Agatha,* corrupted by themſelues. For
the Canon which *Bellarmine* cyteth of this Councell , and the
masked Romiſh Catholicke Diuine taketh from *Bellarmine,* in
ſome later Editions hath theſe wordes as they are cyted by
him : but in the firſt incorrupt Edition of Councels , ſet forth
by *Peter Crab,* the wordes of that Canon are thus ſet downe :
*Clericus nec quenquam praſumat apud ſacularem iudicem Epiſco-
po non permitente, pulſare.* And thus it is read by them that aunciently cyte the ſame. Now this agreeth well with the ninth
Canon of the Chalced Councell , which ordeyneth that if one
Clerke will accuſe another, it muſt be before his Biſhoppe; if he
will accuſe the Biſhoppe, it muſt be in a prouinciall Synode : if
he will draw a Metropolitane to anſwer for ſome things which
he hath done, it muſt be either before the Primate, or before the
Biſhoppe of Conſtantinople. All this we graunt to be orderly
eſtabliſhed , the things intended are matters of Eccleſiaſticall
Cogniſance , which are to bee heard in ſuch Courts : but our
queſtion is of Clerks that are conuinced to be murtherers, or
Traytors, &c. VVhether ſuch are to bee exempt from triall at
Common Law : Of which exemptions theſe auncient Biſhops
neuer dreamed,

76. It

76. It is moreouer to be noted, that diuers of these places which he citeth, as that from *Sulpitius* of S. *Martin*, and from *Ambrose*, &c. are vnderstoode of another thing, and not of exemption of Clarkes at all. For the auncient Bishops, as before I haue declared, thought it not lawfull that matters of faith and doctrine should be determined in ciuill Courts by ciuill Magistrates. This is true: and this is that which those testimonies speake of; but what is this to criminous Clarks? that Robbers, Traytors, murtherers of the Clergy should be protected by reason of their Order from triall in Kings Courts: this is a doctrine neuer knowne to the auncients. It was first knowne in England in the dayes of *Henry* the second, stirred seditiously by *Thomas Becket* Archbishop of Canterbury, when as before that time it was neuer heard of in this land. The manner heereof I will briefly recite out of *Roger Houeden.*

77. In the yeare of Christ 1163. the contention concerning exemption of Clerkes, grew famous betweene King *Henry* the second and *Thomas Becket* Archbishop: *Rex volebat* (saith *Houeden*) *Presbyteros, Diaconos, Subdiaconos, & alios Ecclesiæ rectores, si comprehensi fuissent in latrocinio, vel murdra, vel felonia, vel iniqua combustione, vel in his similibus: ducere ad sacularia examina, & punire sicut & laicum. Contra quod Archiepiscopus dicebat, quod si Clericus in sacris ordinibus constitutus, vel quilibet alius rector Ecclesiæ calumniatus fuerit de aliqua re, per viros Ecclesiasticos & in curia Ecclesiastica debet iudicari. Et si conuictus fuerit, ordines suos amittere, & sic alienatus ab officio & beneficio Ecclesiastico, si postea forisfecerit, secundum voluntatem Regis & baliuorum suorum iudicetur.* That is: The King required that Priests, Deacons, Subdeacons, and other Rectors of Churches, if they were taken in murther, robbery, felony, burning of houses, or such like, should be brought to secular Courts, and there punished as Lay-men were. Against this the Archbishop affirmed, that if a Clerke being within holy Orders, or any other Parson of a Church were accused of any thing, he must be iudged by Ecclesiasticall Iudges in the Ecclesiasticall Court: and if he were conuict, he should loose his orders. And so being excluded from office and benefice Ecclesiasticall, if after this he incurred

Z

Houeden. Henric. 2.

Thomas Becket stood for this priuiledge of holy Church, that although one of the Clergy had committed felony, murther, or treason, yet might not the King put him to death as he did the Laymen. *Fabian. Part. 7. cap. 237.*

curred the like fault, then might he be iudged at the pleasure of
the King and his Officers. Thus farre *Houeden.*

78. This manner of degrading and afterward deliuering criminous Clarkes to the Secular power, crept in about the time
of the Conqueft. *Bellarmine* pretending greater antiquity for it,
can neither bring reafon nor teftimony for his opinion. For
whereas he faith, *Eufebius* Bifhop of *Nicomedia* was firft depofed by the Nicen Councell, and afterward banifhed by *Conftantine,* by this offering to proue, that they muft firft be deliuered
to the Secular power, before the Magiftrate may punifh, and
reproueth *Caluin* for not confidering thus much : We anfwere,
Bellarmine fheweth his skill in fhifting, and hiding the truth to
deceiue the fimple. For *Caluin* in that place which he citeth a-
gainft this Romifh immunitie, proueth two things. Firft, that
coactiue power is in the hand of the Prince, and not of the
Church. *Ecclefia cogendi non habet poteftatem, de ciuil coactione
loquor,* faith he. Secondly, that criminous Clarkes had no immunities from the ciuill Courts of Princes. Now that *Bellarmine* faith, *Eufebius* was firft depofed by the Councell, and then
banifhed, is nothing againft *Caluin,* but for him. For the Church
did not inflict the coactiue punifhment of banifhment, but the
Emperour. And *Caluin* proueth at large in the fame place, that
Kings and Emperours haue no authority to iudge in caufes of
faith; Producing the example of *Ambrofe,* who in fuch a caufe
refifted the Emperour *Valentinian.* Such a caufe was that of *Eufebius :* the Emperour knew not whether he was in fault or not,
before the Church had iudged the caufe. But *Caluines* iudgement, and our queftion ftandeth in two thinges, againft which
Bellarmine doth not fo much as fpeake one word. Firft, that
coactiue power was not then in the Church, but in the Emperour : Secondly, that criminous Clerkes were then punifhed
by the Magiftrate. *Eufebius* is not there propofed as a criminous
Clerke, but as an example wherein the coactiue power of the
Magiftrate appeared. But now they fay, if a Clerke bee proued to be a felon, murderer, traytor, &c. the Kings Courts may
not cenfure this man, before he be degraded. Againft thefe immunities wee fpeake, for which *Bellarmine* offereth not any
proofe.

*Bellarm.lib.de
Clericis cap. 28.*
*Theodoret.lib.1.
cap.20.*

*Inftitut.lib.4.ca.
11.§.15.*

proofe. Let the manner of *Bellarmines* anſwering bee conſide-
red : for it is eaſie for him thus to anſwere *Caluin*, and all Proteſtants, when he toucheth not the point in queſtion: but ſingling
out of ſome peece from the whole, wreſteth that alſo from the
true intent, that he may ſhape a miſ-ſhapen anſwere to it. Then
we ſay, that before thoſe deſperate times, wherein *Iohn Wiclife*
ſaith, and often affirmeth, that Satan was looſed : no man clay-
med ſuch a beaſtly priuiledge, as to be exempt from the Kings
Lawes for murder, treaſon and ſuch like. Godlineſſe, reaſon, and
the light of Nature ſeemeth to be extinguiſhed in theſe men,
that being contented to take the benefite of Lawes, will not be
contented to bee ordered by Lawes. This hath forced ſome
Princes and States to ordaine Lawes that ſuch ſhould be out of ┆ *Statut.25.Ed.3.*
the Kings protection. Thus did that noble Prince *Edward* the ┆ *de prouiſoribus.*
third, King of England. Wherein the King ſeemed to open
the true way to his ſucceſſors, to deale with theſe men, for ſeeing as then they did, ſo now they doe denie themſelues to ┆ *Bellarm.lib.de*
be the Kings ſubiects ; and affirme that neither by Diuine nor ┆ *clericis.cap.28*
humane right, they are bound to obey the King with his coac-
tiue Lawes : and that they are onely vnder the ſubiection of
the Pope : that for no crimes they are to bee examined in the
Kings Courts: is it not great reaſon that the protection of the
King, and of his Lawes ſhould bee denyed to them that reiect
both?

79. *Houeden* declareth alſo, that in the yeare one thouſand ┆ *Houed.Henry 2.*
one hundred ſixtie foure, the King called a Synod, and requi-
red the Biſhops vpon their allegeance, to receiue his Graund-
fathers Lawes, to vſe and obſerue them. *Thomas Becket* anſwered for him and the reſt, they would keepe all the Lawes of his
aunceſtours : *Salua in omnibus ordine ſuo, & honore dei, & ſancta
eccleſia*. This clauſe was thought new, ſcrupulous, and offenſiue.
The King would haue him yeeld without exception, but the
Archbiſhop would not. In this contention *Philippus* a Legat
from the Popes ſide, came into England, by him the Pope and
all the Cardinals commanded the Archbiſhop to yeeld to the
King without exception: whereupon hee did ſo, but afterward
reuolted from that promiſe. Hence a new contention began:

but

but being againe perſwaded , hee promiſed obedience to the
Kings·Lawes. The King to hold faſt this ſlippery Merchant,re-
quired all the Biſhops to ſet to their approbation, and ſeales to
thoſe Lawes. Hereunto when other aſſented, the Archbiſhop
ſwore that hee would neuer ſet his ſeale to them, nor allowe
them. Afterward the Archbiſhop ſuſpended himſelfe from ce-
lebrating Maſſe, and deſired to goe to Rome, but the King denied him. The Biſhop of London accuſed him of Magick. The
King perceiuing his rebellious diſpoſition, required the Barons
to giue iudgement of him, that being his ſubiect, would not be
ruled by his Lawes. *Cito facite mihi iuſticiam de illo , qui homo*

Houed.ibid.

meus ligius eſt, & ſtare iuri in curia mea recuſat. As the Barons
were attending this ſeruice , and now ready to giue ſentence:
I prohibite you (quoth the Archbiſhop) in the behalfe of Almighty God, to giue ſentence vpon me, for I haue appealed to

Houed.ibid.

the Pope. And ſo he departed, *Omnibus clamantibus,*ſaith mine
Author, *quo progrederis proditor ? exſpecta & audi iudicium tuum.*
The Archbiſhop after this ſtole away out of the land,changing
his apparrell and name, for hee called himſelfe *Deerman.* The
Archbiſhop thus conueying himſelfe out of the land , came to
the Pope, and ſhewed him a Copy of theſe Lawes, which the
King called his Grandfathers Lawes. When the Pope heard
them reade in the preſence of his Cardinals and diuers others,
he condemned the Lawes, and excommunicated all that maintained them. *Condemnauit illas in perpetuum , & anathematiza-*
*uit omnes, qui eas tenerent , & aliquo modo fauerent,*ſaith *Houe-*
den.

  80. Thus did the Popes then ſtirre to aduance their ſpirituall Iuriſdiction (as they called it) to ſuch an height, that the
Kings of the earth, who are ſet vp by God to iudge the world,
could not execute iuſtice and iudgement vpon offenders ; might
not be ſuffered according to the commaundements of God, to
take vengeance of murtherers, robbers, incendiaries, traytors ;
might not execute that office , for which onely they beare the
ſword. Now becauſe the deuotion,ſenſe, and iudgement of all
ages, is pretended to be for the Popes Iuriſdiction, and againſt
the Kings : let vs obſerue the iudgement of the men that liued

at.

at this time. We shall finde in all this question of Iurisdiction, and of these exemptions in particular, that the king was iustified and the Archbishop condemned. The Kings auncient Iurisdiction acknowledged, the Popes new Iurisdiction, and the Archbishops disobedience disallowed and abhorred of all. For all the Bishops of the Prouince of Canterbury, wrote a letter to the Archbishop, the letter is extant in *Houeden*. Therein they entreat him to yeeld to the King: they commend the Kings care and zeale for the Church. They testifie that the king requireth no more of him, then the due honour which his ancestours haue alwaies had. *Rex a Domino constitutus pacem prouidet subiectorum per omnia, vt hanc conseruet Ecclesijs, & commissis sibi populis, dignitates regibus ante se debitas & exhibitas sibi vult exhiberi & exigit.* [The King ordained by God, prouideth his subiects peace by all meanes, that he may preserue this in the Churches, and people vnder him, hee requireth and exacteth that Iurisdiction, which was due and exhibited to the Kings which were before him.] They charge him with rashnesse, and furious anger for suspending and condemning the Bishop of Salisbury and the Deane, before any question of their fault was moued. *Ordo iudiciorum nouus* (say they) *hic est, huc vsq̃ legibus & canonibus vt speramus incognitus, damnare primum, & de culpa postremo cognoscere.* [This is a new proceeding of iudgements, and as wee hope vnknowne in Lawes and Canons to this day; first to condemne a man, and last of all to know the fault.]

Houeden Annal. pag. 292.

81. And that the iustification of the King in this cause, and the condemnation of the Archbishoppe might be made more euident to all the world; the same Suffraganes, that is, all the Bishops of the Prouince of Canterbury, wrote to Pope *Alexander* the third, to whom they giue a worthy & famous testimonie of the Kings iustice, temperance, and chastitie: declaring that the King could not be suffred to execute his Princely office, nor effect his good and godly purposes in execution of Iustice, for the filthinesse of some of the Clergie. *Rex* (say they) *fide Christian ssimus, in copula coniugalis castimonij honestissimus, pacis & iusticiæ coseruator & dilatator incoparabiliter strenuissimus, hoc votis agit totis, in his feruet desiderijs, vt de regno suo tollantur scandala, cũ spur-*

citijs fuis eliminentur peccata,pax totum obtineat atq̃, inʃtitia &c.
Qui cum pacem regni ʃui enormi inʃolentium quorundam Clerico-
rum exceʃʃu , non mediocriter turbari cognoʃceret &c. That is,
[The King in faith moſt Chriſtian, in the bond of matrimoniall
chaſtity moſt honeſt, for preſeruation and dilatation of peace
and iuſtice, without compariſon the ſtouteſt, doeth with great
zeale and affections deſire this , that ſcandals may be remoued
out of his Kingdome, that ſinnes with their filth may be baniſhed,&c.and finding the peace of his Kingdome not a little troubled with the enormous exceſſe of ſome inſolent Clerks, &c.]
And thus they proceede , declaring wherein thoſe ſtrange exemptions ſtood , which then began firſt to bee knowne in the
world. For,ſay they, if a Clerke ſhould commit murder, &c.
the Archbiſhoppe would haue him puniſhed onely by degrading,but the King thought that puniſhment not ſufficient for
eſtabliſhing of peace and ordér , and for execution of iuſtice.
Hinc non dominationis ambitu, non opprimendæ Eccleʃiæ libertatis
intuitu,ʃed ʃolummodo pacis affectu eo Rex progreʃʃus eʃt , vt regni
ʃui conʃuetudines regibus ante ʃe in regno Angliæ à perʃonis Eccleʃi-
aʃticis obʃeruatas,& pacificè & reuerenter exhibitas Dominus no-
ʃter Rex deduci vellet in medium. That is , [Hereupon not
through ambition of Domination,not with any purpoſe to op-
preſſe the liberties of the Church , but onely in a zeale of peace
the King proceedeth thus farre, as that hee will haue the cuſtomes of his Kingdome now brought to open knowledge,
which Eccleſiaſticall perſons haue obſerued, and peaceably and
reuerently exhibited vnto the Kings of the kingdome of England before him.] And a little after, *Hæc eʃt Domini noʃtri regis*
in Eccleʃiam Dei toto orbe declamata crudelitas , hæc ab eo perʃecu-
tio. That is[Now this is the crueltie of our Lord the King,that
is ſo much ſpoken of through the world againſt the Church;
this is that perſecution that he raiſeth.] Then it is an auncient
complaint of theſe Romiſh Catholickes, to call the iuſt,lawfull,
godly,and neceſſary execution of iuſtice, crueltie and perſecution : this complaint hath beene euer ſince continued by them ;
and moſt of all where there is leaſt cauſe , euen in the milde and
mercifull gouernement of the late Queene of famous memory.
What

What crueltie did they impute to her? What persecution to her Gouernement? When they are not able to proue that one man was executed for Religion, but for treason : Which was so much the more dangerous, becauſe it was masked with the viſard of Religion : but Religion is not, nor euer was the cauſe why our Kings puniſhed the Popes Clerkes, but onely Iuriſdiction. For when the Pope will ſtretch his Iuriſdiction ſo farre, as to include coactiue power, and to exclude Kings from the gouernement of their Subiects, drawing the Clergie from the obedience of their Kings, to the obedience and ſubiection of the Pope; drawing the ſubiects of other Kings vnder his ſubiection by an Oath of Allegiance : and hereupon perſwading al that will hearken to him, that they may not yeelde an Oath of Alleageance to their owne Princes : the Popes Iuriſdiction being drawne to theſe points (as now by the confeſſion of themſelues they are) the queſtion betweene the Pope and Chriſtian Princes, is not of Religion, but of Iuriſdiction, of ciuill and coactiue Iuriſdiction; and the ſumme of all is this; Whether the Princes of Chriſtendome ſhall be free Princes, or the Popes Vaſſals?

The iſſue of exemptions.

82. By this which we haue declared, we ſee the cauſe of our Kings iuſtified againſt the Archbiſhoppe, and the exemption of Clerkes (for which the Archbiſhoppe ſtroue, and which ſince that time is claimed to be an eſpeciall priuilege of that Church) to be condemned by the chiefe of the Clergy, by all the Biſhops of that Prouince : and that euen to the Pope himſelfe. Which thing the Biſhoppes of the Engliſh Church would neuer haue done, vnleſſe they had beene well aſſured that the Kings cauſe was good, and that the contrary opinion was a pernicious nouelty, a late vpſtart deuice in the Church. But howſoeuer the Popes Clerkes pretended their new forged priuiledges, yet the Kings of this land held ..... their olde courſe in the auncient manner of execution of iuſtice againſt them that offended. And therefore *Henry* the ſecond by law commaunded, as *Houeden* ſaith, that the Biſhoppes of London and Norwich ſhould be ſummoned, that they might be before the Kings Iuſtices to anſwere, for that they againſt the ſtatutes of the Kingdome

Rog. Houed. Hen. 2.

kingdome did interdict the land of the Earle *Hugh*

83. This exemption of Clarks was a new practiſe in the time of *Marſilius* of Padua, and not ſo new as peſtiferous, occaſioning the ruine of States, and being as a furie ſent abroad from hell to diſorder all gouernment. For thus he complaineth of it.

Defenſor pacis part.2,cap.23.

Quibus non contenti,ſed ſæcularium contra Chriſti & Apoſtolorum præceptum, appetentes faſtigia, in legum Lationes ſeorſum ab ijs quæ Ciuium vniuerſitatis ſunt, proruperunt. Omnem clerum ab his decernentes exemptum,ciuile ſchiſma & principatuum ſupremorũ pluralitatem inducentes ex ipſis, &c. Hæc peſtilentiæ Italici regni radix eſt & origo,ex qua cuncta ſcandala germinauerunt, prodeunt, & qua ſtante nunquã ciuiles ibidem ceſſabunt diſcordiæ, &c. That is, [Not content herewith they (the Popes) ſeeking the honour of ſecular gouernement, againſt the commandement of Chriſt and his Apoſtles, haue taken vpon them the ordaining of Lawes and Canons,other then ſuch as ſerue for the common good.They decree that all the Clergie are exempt from temporall Princes,heereby inducing a pluralitie of Soueraignties,&c. This is the roote and ſpring of the peſtilence of the Empire, from whence all ſcandals grow,and which ſtanding, ciuill diſcord ſhall neuer haue an end,&c.] Thus were theſe exemptions then found,and acknowledged to be the peſtilence and ruine of all ſtates, eſpecially of the Empire : And his reaſon is well to be obſerued,becauſe,ſaith he,it bringeth in *Pluralitatem ſupremorum principatuum,quam velut impoſſibilem humanæ quieti demonſtrauimus:* he proueth the plurality of Soueraignty a thing impoſſible to ſtand with the quiet and peaceable Gouernement of the world.Now this exemption muſt eyther induce a plurality of Soueraignties,when the Pope is one Soueraigne, and the Prince another,which is impoſſible in nature(ſaith *Marſilius*) or elſe it denieth the Kings Soueraignty to eſtabliſh the Popes, which thing can neuer bee indured by any Prince.

Of

§. VI.

Of the Popes power in giuing lawes.

84. ANother thing whereby this new Iurisdiction of the Pope was so highly aduanced, was, giuing of Lawes to Princes, and their subiects; whereas before Princes had giuen lawes to him. *Marsilius* in the wordes last cyted in the end of the last Paragraffe, speaking of these laws, saith: They now break out into a practise of Iurisdiction, taking vpon them to make lawes, separat and distinct from such lawes, as are for the common and publique good of all: meaning the Canon lawes: which because they intend onely the priuate aduancement of the Pope, and not the publique good of the Church: being also made onely by the authority of the Pope, and not by the publique consent of the Church: therefore he doth not account them lawes, but Oligarchicall, and tyrannicall Decrees; these lawes are to be considered, because they make so great a shew of the Popes Iurisdiction.

85. The Church before, was gouerned by Bishoppes and Metropolitanes, in such order, that the affaires of euery particular Diocesse were ordered by the Bishoppe, or by a Synode of his calling: the affaires of the Prouince were determined by the Metropolitane, or by a Prouinciall Synode of his calling: from an Episcopall Synode, a man might appeale to a prouinciall Synode; and from a Prouinciall Synode, to a nationall: but from a prouinciall or from a nationall Synode, none might appeale to the Bishoppe of Rome: for which thing diuers Decrees were made in prouinciall Synodes, as we haue before declared. As the Bishoppes were Gouernours, so the lawes whereby they did then gouerne the Church, were the Canons of auncient Councels; especially of those foure most famous Councels of Nice, Constantinople, Ephesus, and Chalcedon: For that the Canons of these Councels were held for the lawes of the *Constitutio Iustiniani quint. Sy-* Church, it appeareth by a Constitution of *Iustinian*, extant in *nod.act.1.* the fift Synode, held at Constantinople: wherein *Iustinian* the *Memnæ Patri-* Emperour declareth that *Anthimus* was deposed from the Bi- *archæ.*

A a   shoprike shopricke of Conſtantinople by Pope *Agapetus* ,and a whole Synode with him conſenting,for that he had departed from the doctrines of thoſe foure holy Synodes, the Nicen,the Conſtantinopolitan,the Epheſian, and the Chalcedonian : The Emperor alſo declareth,that he being depoſed by the Church,ſhould be baniſhed by him,ioyning his coactiue power to the ſpirituall Iuriſdiction of the Church. This is the meaning of the imperiall Conſtitutions that are in this manner ſet forth by Emperors of religious and doctrinail matters : For the Emperours neuer tooke vpon them by their authority to define matters of faith and Religion; that they left to the Church : but when the Church had defined ſuch truthes againſt Heretiques, and had depoſed thoſe Heretiques ; then the Emperours concurring with the Church by their imperiall Conſtitutions, (*Sicq, Diuina pariter & humana concurrentia* (ſaith *Iuſtinian* in the ſame place)*vnam conſonantiam rectis ſententijs fecere* :) did by their coactiue power giue ſtrength to the Canons of the Church : And thus was the Church then gouerned , by the Canons of auncient approued Synodes for matters of faith and doctrine; and by the Conſtitutions of Chriſtian Princes for matters of externall coactiue Iuriſdiction. That *Conſtantine* by whoſe authority the ſixt Synod was held at Conſtantinople, declareth that the Canons of the fiue generall Councels (adding this ſecond Conſtantinopolitan,to the other foure) were the rules or Canons of the Church.

6.Synod.ſub-ſcriptio ſacræ. ante action. 1.

86. So long as thoſe Canons of auncient Councels ſtood for Church lawes, executed by the Biſhoppes who were the Gouernours,ſo long the Gouernement of the Church ſtood vp in peace,order and Godlineſſe ; one Biſhoppe incroached not vpon the Iuriſdiction of another : But after that the Pope had intruded vpon the Iuriſdiction of the Church , and was growen ſo great as that by coactiue power hee was able to maintaine his intruſion : then began hee to giue lawes , ſuch as are compriſed in the Decretals of *Gregory* the ninth,who was Pope in the yeare one thouſand,two hundred and thirty,the firſt publiſher of thoſe lawes , which were continued by *Boniface* the eight,*Clement* fift,*Iohn* the two and twentieth , and by ſome other

ther Popes vnto the yeare one thousand, foure hundred and eightie, for then liued *Sixtus* the fourth, whose Decrees are published in that part that is called *extrau. Commun.* since which times those lawes haue beene in some force in diuers nations, where they did not crosse the imperiall lawes of those nations, nor the Iurisdiction of the Kings thereof. Now seeing that the Popes Iurisdiction is so much set forth and aduanced by these Canon lawes, let vs in few wordes examine how he came to this Iurisdiction to giue lawes, and by what right he maintaineth it. If any man haue right to make and giue lawes, this right must either be from God giuen him, or from men, who haue had this right before in themselues: for euery man cannot giue this right, but onely such as haue it, and haue power to giue it: But the Pope receiued not this right of giuing lawes to all Churches from God ; for God hath no where giuen any such Commission to him. The ancient Bishops of Rome, either did not claime any such Iurisdiction, or if any were carried by leuity, and ambition out of their bounds, they were presently recalled and repressed by the godly Bishoppes of that age: As *Anicet* was by *Polycarp*, *Victor* by *Irenæus*, *Polycrates* and the other Bishoppes of Asia, *Zozimus*, *Boniface*, and *Celestinus* by S. *Augustine* and the Afftican Bishoppes: so that the Bishoppes of Rome could neuer be suffered to make lawes to the Church, for one thousand, or twelue hundred yeares after Christ : therefore this right was not from Christ.

87. For if it had beene from Christ, then should the Pope haue beene suffered to haue practised the same, before twelue hundreth yeares were expired. For the godly auncient Fathers did neuer withstand the Bishop of Rome, in any Iurisdiction which hee could claime from Christ. But in this thing it is knowne that they withstoode him: therefore this Iurisdiction whereunto after so many hundreth yeares, hee intruded himselfe, against the iudgement of the auncient Fathers (who resisted him heerein) is not from God. Neither can this right bee claimed from man, because they who chalenge it, will haue it to be a diuine right, not humane. And they quarrell vs for that we admit, that temporall Princes may haue such Iurisdiction: so

that they vtterly denie that this Iuriſdiction is deriued from any humane power. Now he who is found to execute Iuriſdiction which is neither giuen him from God, nor man : muſt needs be conuinced to be an intruder, and to come in his owne name, and conſequently to fulfill that Scripture : I came in my Fathers

Iohn.5.43.

name, and you receiue mee not. If another ſhall come in his owne name, him you will receiue. Which the auntient Fathers expound of the comming of Antichriſt in his owne name. And what more pregnant proofe can be brought of this his comming in his owne name, then is this intruding himſelfe into a Iuriſdiction,which he had neither from God,nor from the Princes of this world. And becauſe the Pope after one thouſand and two hundred yeares, had no more right to giue Lawes to the Church, then in former ages he had; therefore this Iuriſdiction is vnlawfull, which by theſe Lawes hee practiſeth. Wherein onely *de facto,* he is found to doe that, whereunto he neuer had right.

88. Moreouer, if *Bellarmine* haue declared the true conditions of iuſt and lawfull Lawes, it will followe that the Canon Lawes are no iuſt Lawes. *Bellarmine* confeſſeth that foure con-

Bellarm.lib.4.
cap.15.de Rom.
Pont.
Ariſt. Ethic.lib.
8.cap 10.

ditions are required in a Law,to make it iuſt : the firſt is drawne from the end, for it muſt be referred to the common good : for herein ſaith *Ariſtotle,* a King differeth from a tyrant; becauſe a King reſpecteth the common good of his ſubiects, but a tyrant looketh onely vpon his owne priuate profit : and thus ſaith *Bellarmine* doth a iuſt Law differ from a tyrannicall Law. Then are the Popes Canon Lawes proued tyrannicall and vniuſt, becauſe they reſpect not the common good, but the priuate wealth of the Pope, as all thoſe doe that draw all appellations to him. The ſecond condition, which in *Bellarmines* iudgement maketh a Law iuſt, is drawne from the efficient. For it muſt be from a

Bellar.ibid.

man that hath full authority. *Nemo enim poteſt legem imponere non ſibi ſubdito,* ſaith he. By this it will likewiſe follow, that the Popes Canons are no iuſt Lawes, becauſe the Pope hath no authority to make ſuch Canons, binding them that are not his ſubiects, as we haue declared before. The third condition that maketh a Law iuſt, is drawne from the matter, ſaith *Bellarmine,*

for

for it muſt not forbid vertue, nor commaund vice : but the Canon Lawes are ſuch as forbid vertue and commaund vice; as appeareth by all thoſe Canons that proceede with their *non obſtante.* I will note one example of many. There is a Canon that runneth thus. *Quum aliquibus recipiendi aliquem in Canonicum alicuius Ecclesiæ, non obſtantibus ciuſdem Ecclesiæ, priuilegijs, conſuetudinibus, vel ſtatutis iuramento, confirmatione Apoſtolica, vel quacunq̃ firmitate alia roboratis, per noſtras literas concedimus facultatem, &c.* That is : When wee graunt power to any by our letters to receiue any to be a Canon in ſome Church, notwithſtanding the priuiledges of that Church, the cuſtomes to the contrary, or ſtatutes confirmed either by Oath, or by Apoſtolicall confirmation, or by any other ſtrength, &c. By this Lawe, as by many other, it appeareth, that the Popes Canons allowe that men ſhould goe againſt their owne Oathes when the Popes letters doe commaund them ſo to doe. Which is a forbidding of things honeſt, iuſt, and godly, and commanding thinges euill and vnlawfull. Therefore theſe Lawes forbid vertue, and commaund vice, and are conſequently no iuſt Lawes in the iudgement of *Bellarmine.*

89. The laſt condition that in *Bellarmines* opinion is required to make a Law iuſt, is drawne from the forme : Becauſe ſaith hee, the Law muſt keepe that proportion in diſtributing honours, which the Subiects haue in the Common-wealth. For example ſaith he, if the Pope ſhould make a Law, that onely rich and noble men ſhould be made Biſhoppes, and not poore and meane men otherwiſe more learned and more worthy, this Law were ſimply vniuſt: but it is certaine that the Popes Lawes are ſuch. I ſpeake not here of their corrupt practiſe, which ſince the Canon lawes came in, was neuer found without ſtrong and ſtrange Simonie : but I ſpeake of their Lawes, which command it. For who made that Law which ſaith, *Pallium non datur niſi fortiter poſtulanti:* The Pall is not giuen to any man, vnleſſe he make a ſtrong ſuit. What is meant by a ſtrong ſuit, they know beſt that haue purchaſed Palls at the Popes hand. But it is certaine that a poore man did neuer purchaſe a Pall, therefore poore men, though more learned then the rich purchaſer, are

De Reſcriptis. cap. 14. 6. Decreta. lib. 1.

Diſt. 100. cap. 2.

A a 3　　　　　　excluded

excluded from this honour by the Law, that alloweth none to make suit, but such as can make strong suit, then the Law is vniust by *Bellarmines* confession. It is also an vniust and an vngodly Law, which saith : Though the Pope should draw innumerable soules with himselfe downe into hell, yet no mortall man may presume to say to him, Sir why do you so? It is an vncleane Law, which so strictly denying the mariage of Priests, yet, doth allow them to haue Concubines. Many other Lawes there be of this forme. So that by all those conditions which *Bellarmine* will haue to be requisite in all Lawes that bee iust, the Popes Lawes are found to be vniust. By all which is euinced, that the Pope commeth in his owne name, maketh Lawes to rule those Subiects, ouer whom he hath no authority; respecteth therein his owne ends, taketh vp a new Iurisdiction which hath beene denied by the auncient Bishops, and which was vnknowne in the world all the while, that the Popes liued vnder the obedience of the Emperours, as other Bishoppes did vnder seuerall Princes.

Dist. 40 Si Papa.

Dist. 34. cap. 4.

§ 7.

Of Appellation.

90. ANother part of this pretended Iurisdiction, stoode in appellation to the Pope. This they haue chalenged, but it hath alwayes beene denied by the Kings of this land, as being a thing preiudiciall to the auncient Lawes and customes of the Kingdome. The first question about appeales in this land, that I can finde, began by *Anselme* Archbishop of Canterburie, in the time of *William Rufus*. For after that some breach was made betweene the King and the Archbishop, the Archbishoppe *Anselme* desired leaue to depart the land, to goe to Rome for his Pall. The King perceiuing that hee had a purpose to appeale to the Pope, Aunswered, That if hee should appeale to Pope *Vrban*, or any other (for at that time two stroue for the Papacy) without his leaue, then should he falsifie his alleageance. The King reasoned thus, saith *Malmsbury*: *Consuetudo Regni mei est, à Patre meo instituta, vt nullus præter licentiam Regis appelletur Papa. Qui consuetudines Regni tollit, potestatem*

Malmsbury. lib. 1. de gestis Pontif. Angl.

teſtatem quoq̃, & coronam Regni violat, qui coronam mihi aufert inimicitias & infidelitatem in me agit. [It is a cuſtome of my Kingdome, preſerued by my Father, that no appeale be made to any Pope without the Kings licence : hee that taketh away the cuſtomes of my Kingdome, doth violate my power and crowne : he that robbeth me of my crowne, practiſeth enmity and vnfaithfulneſſe againſt me.] *Anſelme* his anſwer was, *Tu es Petrus & ſuper hanc Petram, &c,* And therfore (quoth he to the King) the obedience which I offer to S. *Peters* Vicar, is not againſt mine alleageance to the King. Thus had the Popes with a ſtrong kinde of poiſon, as it were ſo enchaunted thoſe words of holy Scripture, as to make them ſerue for a cloake of diſobedience, and breach of alleageance to temporall Princes. *Anſelme* being further vrged by the King, that he had promiſed to keepe all the cuſtomes of his Kingdome, and hee was bound to performe alleageance, anſwereth thus. [What doe you tell mee that I breake mine alleageance to the King, by appealing to the Sea Appoſtolique? I graunt I promiſed, but conditionally, that I would keepe thoſe cuſtomes which are agreeable to the lawes of God, and honeſty. And therefore where you tell me that I haue broken mine alleageance, by appealing to the Sea Appoſtolique; ſauing your honour it is not true, if another had ſpoken it. For the faith which I owe to the King, I haue it from the faith of God, whoſe Vicar is S. *Peter*, to whoſe Sea I appealer with much ſtirre and ſtrife to this effect *Anſelme* held his reſolution ſtifly.]

Malmsb.ibid.

91. Now let the Reader be entreated to compare theſe times with the times of the Affrican Councell, and *Anſelme* Archbiſhop of Canterbury with *Auguſtine* Biſhop of Hippo. S. *Auguſtine* with the reſt of the Affrican Councell condemned appellations to Rome, as ſtanding againſt godlineſſe, order, the freedome of the Church; as quenching the light of ſimplicity, as inducing darkneſſe, pride and ambition into the Church. Now that which in Saint *Auguſtines* time was vngodly, can it be made godly, and lawfull in *Anſelmes* time? Yet *Anſelme* we ſee maketh this thing the cauſe of God. *Auguſtine* condemned appellations to Rome ſimply, without conſideration of diſobedience

dience to Princes. What then would he haue done, if thereunto had beene added the commaundement of his Prince againſt
ſuch Appellations ? *Anſelme* ſtanding for Appellation to
Rome, which *Auguſtine* denied, and withſtanding the iuſt and
lawfull commaundement of his Soueraigne, hath no other colour to caſt ouer the matter, then the pretence of God and Saint
Peters Vicar. If this obedience had beene required of God to
Saint *Peters* Vicar in *Anſelmes* time, Why was not the ſame required and yeelded in Saint *Auguſtines* time ? This is the difference betweene the opinions brought in by men, and the
truths of God : that the one ſtandeth alwaies the ſame in the
Church without chaunge, the other hath his times of riſing and
falling. As this opinion of Appellation to the Pope, which was
ſo ſtrongly reiected by *Auguſtine*, found a time to riſe vp betweene the pride of the Popes, and the ſeruile flattery of
ſome Biſhoppes. And what greater ſigne of pride in the Pope,
and flattery in his ſeruants, then to reſume theſe old condemned Priuiledges, and therewithall to patch vp a Iuriſdiction
ſtanding ſo directly againſt the iudgement and practiſe of the
auncient godly Fathers !

92. And yet was *Anſelme* as reſolute in this, as *Auguſtine*
was in the contrary : But herein a great difference appeared
(which might much ſway the iudgement of indifferent readers,
if there were no other meanes to informe them) that Saint *Auguſtine* ſtanding againſt appellations to Rome, had herein the
full conſent of all his fellow Biſhoppes, not one diſſenting. But
Anſelme ſtanding for appellations to Rome, ſtood alone without the conſent of ſo much as one Biſhoppe : which thing I report for the honour of the Church of England, and of all the
Biſhoppes of England at this time; who herein reſiſted their
Archbiſhoppe, ſtanding for the ancient liberties of the Church.
William Malmsbury witneſſeth thus much : *In his exequendis*
(ſaith he) *omnes Epiſcopi Angliæ Primati ſuo ſuffragium negarunt.*
That is [In the execution of theſe things, all the Biſhoppes of
England denied their conſent to their Primate.] This ſheweth
that Archbiſhoppes were made the Popes ſeruants before Bi-
ſhoppes were : the reaſon was, becauſe the Archbiſhoppes vſed

to

to purchase a Pall from the Pope, which Pall *Anselme* had not yet at this time of his variance with the King, obtained ; for *Malmsbury* saith, he first asked leaue to goe to Rome for the Pall. Now the Pope in graunting the Pall conueyed an Oath of Alleageance with it, as before we haue obserued, which was the reason that moued our Archbishopps to stirre such rebellious tumults against the Kings of this land : Such was this faction which *Anselme* maintained for the Pope against the King, wherein he was condemned by all the Bishops of England in the question of Appellation, as *Thomas Becket* was after this time condemned by all the Bishoppes in like sort, in the question of Inuestitures.

93. And therefore *Henry* the second had iust cause to publish that law which *Roger Houeden* calleth *graue edictum & execrabile*, against the Pope, beginning, *Si quis inuentus fuerit literas vel mandatu ferens Domini Papa &c. c. piatur, & de eo sicut de regis traditore & regni, sine dilatione fiat iusticia.* That is [If any be found bringing in the Popes Letters or Mandat, &c. let him be apprehended, and let iustice be executed without delay vpon him, as vpon a traytor to the King and Kingdome.] In the same law it is said ; *Item generaliter interdictum est, ne quis appellet ad Dominum Papam.* That is [It is simply by law prohibited, that no man appeale to the Pope.] This was not a new law now inuented by *Henry* the second, but an auncient law now renued, and vpon a iust occasion put in execution : for *William Rufus*, as before we haue declared, vrged this law against *Anselme*, proouing it to be one of his Fathers lawes, and auerring that such appeales did stand against the auncient lawes and customes of his Kingdome ; so that the Kings Iurisdiction in such matters, was maintained by the auncient lawes of this land.

Houed. Henr. 2.

94. But because the antiquity of the lawes of our land is questioned by our aduersaries, though this thing belong not to my profession, yet let me in a few wordes declare what I haue met with in Stories concerning this point : that it may appeare, that the lawes of this land are much more auncient, then that Religion which now is called the Religion of the Church of Rome, King *William Rufus* the Conquerours sonne, declareth

Bb

Malmsb.l.de
gestis Pontif.
Ang or.

as *Malmsbury* witnesseth, that it was a custome of this kingdome confirmed by his father, that without the Kings licence no
man might appeale to the Pope. Now these lawes and customes
which *William* the Conquerour did publish and confirme, were
the auncient lawes and customes of the Saxons before him: not
first inuented by the Conquerour, though enacted and established by him. For *Roger Houeden* writing of these lawes which
the Conquerour enacted, saith, that the King being once in
minde to establish the lawes of the Danes, was after much and
earnest intreaty of the Barons, perswaded to yeelde that the
lawes of King *Edward* the Confessour, should be retained still.
The Barons (saith *Houeden*) vrged the King, *Pro anima regis Ed-*
uardi, qui ei post diem suum contesserat coronam & regnum, & cu-
ius erant Leges : Vnde Concilio habito precatui Baronum tandem
acquieuit, ex illa ergo die vsa authoritate venerata per vniuersam
Angliam corroborata & confirmata sunt pra ceteris patria legibus
leges Edwardi regis ; qua prius inuenta & Constituta erant in tem-
pore Adgari aui sui. [For King *Edwards* soule, who bequeathed
him his Crowne and Kingdome after his death : and whose
lawes they were : whereupon holding a Parliament, he yeelded
at last to the Barons request : from that day forward the lawes
of King *Edward* were by his authority honoured, established,
and confirmed through all England ; which lawes were before
found out, and enacted in the time of *Edgar*, Grandfather to
King *Edward.*] After this, *Houeden* entreth into a large discourse to proue, that the lawes which the Conquerour established, were King *Edwards* lawes, which lawes, saith he, were called King *Edwards* lawes, not because hee inuented them first,
but because after they had beene buried in some neglect, lying
vnregarded and not put in due execution for the space of three
score and eight yeares after *Edgars* death (for so many yeares
are betweene King *Edgars* death, and S. *Edwards* Coronation)
he reuiued them : And thus much he confirmeth that the lawes
established by the Conquerour, were S. *Edwards* lawes, and the
same which were in vse here in the daies of that peaceable King
Edgar.

     And it is not without good reason collected, that the
same

Houeden.Hen.2.

Pro visa autho-
ritate, legendum
fortasse, sua au-
thoritate.

fame lawes proceeded from King *Alphred*: for he, like another *Iuſtinian* is reported to haue compiled certaine volumes of ʙalæus.ᴄᴇɴt.ʒ. lawes, not onely from the lawes of the Britaines, Saxons, and Danes, but alſo of the ancient Grecians and other: Beſides that he tranſlated into the Saxon tongue thoſe lawes, which were called the Molmucin lawes, and alſo the Martian lawes, the one of *Dunwallo Molmucius* an auncient Brittiſh King, the other ſo named of *Martia Proba* an auncient Brittiſh Queene. And that *William* the Conquerour eſtabliſhed the Saxon lawes, it is likewiſe teſtified by *Henry Huntingdon*, who ſaith thus: *Saxones pro viribus paulatim terram bello capeſſentes, captam obtinebant, obtentam ædificabant, ædificatam legibus regebant: Nec non & Normanici cito & breuiter terram ſubdentes ſibi, victis vitam & libertatem legeſ́q́; antiquas regni iure conceſſerunt.* [The Saxons by a ſtrong hand ouercame the land in time by war, built as they o-uercame, and as they built gouerned it by lawes: The Normans alſo quickly ſubduing the land vnder them, yet graunted by the right of the Kingdome, life and libertie, and the auncient lawes to them whom they ſubdued.]

95. Then whereas *William Rufus* maintained the lawes and cuſtomes of his father, againſt the Pope, and *Henry* the firſt the lawes and cuſtomes of his brother and father, and *Henry* the ſecond, the lawes and cuſtomes of the Kingdome, vſed by his Grandfather *Henry* the firſt, or any other afterward referring themſelues to the ſame lawes: the lawes and cuſtomes of which they ſpeake, are the auncient lawes and priuiledges of this land, confirmed by the Conquerour, receiued from King *Edward*, proceeding from King *Edgar*, and before him from King *Al-phred*: And are therefore of much greater antiquity, then the Popiſh Religion lately concluded in the Councell of Trent, as many parts of that Religion were. Then it appeareth that the auncient lawes of this land did forbid an appeale to Rome: nei-ther is that to be much maruelled; for why ſhould it be thought ſtrange, that an appeale to Rome was vtterly forbidden by the Church and State of England, ſeeing long before that time we finde the ſame thing forbidden by the Church of Africa. After this time wherein Appeales to Rome were forbidden in Eng-

land,

land,we finde that in Fraunce the same thing was prohibited
by the law which the French call the pragmaticall Sanction:for
in the yeare one thousand,two hundred, threescore and eight,
Lewes the ninth French King, called S. *Lewes,* ordeined the
pragmatical Sanction,wherin all the oppressions of the Church
ofRome are vtterly forbidden,that none of those things be practised in Fraunce,vnlesse it be by the expresse and free consent
of the King,and Church of that Kingdome. Thus haue Kings
alwaies prescribed against the Pope in matters of Iurisdiction,
as the Church in like sort hath prescribed against the Pope , in
matters of faith and Religion , as hereafter in the last Chapter
shall be declared.

§. VIII.

Of deposing and depriuing Kings,and dissoluing the Oath of
Alleageance , wherein consisted the highest pitch of this
pretended Iurisdiction.

96.   THE last and greatest point of this Iurisdiction ,
wherein the strings of this authority were stretched vp to the highest,was that their practise of Deposing Kings,
and discharging Subiects from their Alleageance : By which
practise the Church was confounded,the States of the world o-
uerturned , Kings robbed of their right , subiects of their faith
and truth,euery nation scourged with warres and blood-shed :
and in the common vexation of all Christendome , onely the
Popes state,and worldly glory increased, who could not otherwise rise,but with the ruine of the Church and States. In this
place therefore I will,as breefely as I can, passe through by way
of short History,the practise of the Popes,in deposing of Kings.
That it may be apparant to the world,that we are so farre from
being afraid to confesse this power , which they so much boast
of;that we are rather readie to publish it to the world. For
hereby all men which haue any vnderstanding of that power
which Iesus Christ left to his Church,may know the Tyrannie,
vsurpation,pride,vaine-glory,ambition and madnesse of him
who

who exalteth himselfe in the Church againſt God, and againſt them that are called Gods. Wherein we may learne to be armed with patience to ſuffer for a time, whatſoeuer the luſt of proud and bloud-ſucking Popes haue leaue to do for the ſinnes of our Princes, and people, and Churches. For their time is ſet and drawing to an end, and nothing hath beene done, but that which is fore-warned in the Scripture. So that by theſe ambitious and bloudy practiſes, wee ſhall finde how the Scriptures are fulfilled.

97. For one Scripture ſaith, that a ſtarre muſt fall from heauen, who muſt be a King of the Locuſts, which is called alſo the Angell of the bottomleſſe pit, whoſe name in Hebrew is *Abaddon*, and in Greeke *Apollyon*, that is a deſtroyer. Which Propheſie of his deſtroying power, is verified moſt apparantly in this practiſe of excommunicating Kings, and looſing the knot of obedience. Whereby confuſion and deſtruction is brought vpon all Kingdomes of Chriſtendome. Hereby he is proued to be a deſtroyer, an exterminator, an excommunicator. Therefore the vulgar tranſlation addeth ſignificantly, *Latine habens nomen exterminans*. Another Scripture ſaith : The tenne Kings ſhall giue their power and authority to the beaſt. Though the Kings of Chriſtendome did neuer directly yeeld to the Pope this authority ouer their owne Kingdomes, and ouer themſelues, that the Popes might depoſe and diſplace them at his pleaſure: yet this they gaue him in effect, and by conſequence. For they gaue him ſo much, that he might vpon their owne graunt challenge this, and they who had graunted him ſo much, had no reaſon to except againſt his challenge. For though the King which was to be depriued, denied the Pope this power, yet ſuch Princes did yeeld it to him, to whom the Pope had giuen the Kingdom of the depoſed Prince: he did yeeld it, who ſhould vſe the benefit of the Popes vſurped power. For example : though the late Kings of France haue alwaies denied, that the Pope had any Authority to depoſe the French Kings, yet the Kings of France haue giuen him this power. For the former Kings yeelded it, as *Pipin*, and *Charles*. For they had no other title to the Kingdome, then from this power of the Pope. Therefore they

Apoc.9.1.11.

Apoc.17,13.

Bb 3   yeelded

yeelded that the Pope had power and authority to giue Kingdomes, and in that ſenſe gaue their power and authority to the
beaſt.So that when theſe firſt French Kings,honoured the Pope
with this vndue honour, though then they ſeemed to receiue
Kingdomes from him, yet the Scripture looketh farther into
theſe practiſes, then they did which practiſed them. For they
reſpected onely themſelues, their owne preſent greatneſſe : but
in receiuing ſuch power from the Popes, they gaue, in trueth,
their power and authority to the Popes. For how could they
in iuſtice denie, but that the ſame power which depoſed other
Kings to raiſe them, might as well haue depoſed them to raiſe
other. Thus moſt of the Kings of Chriſtendome gaue their
kingdomes to the Popes. That this new and ſtrange power of
Antichriſt may better appeare, I will open the beginning and
continuance of the Popes practiſe herein.

Leo Iconomachus.

98.   THe firſt Prince vpon whom the Pope began this practiſe, was *Leo* the Emperour, whom *Platina* calleth
Leo the third, he was called *Iconomachus* for defacing of Images. This Prince was depoſed by *Gregory* the third, who was
Pope in the yeare ſeuen hundred ninety ſixe. Pope *Gregory* the
ſecond prepared the way thus. When *Leo* the Emperour being
much offended at the ſuperſtitious and foule abuſe of Images,
which he ſaw daily then growing in the Church, did vtterly deface Images in Churches, and commaunded Pope *Gregory* the
Naucl. vol.2. ſecond, then Biſhop of Rome to doe the like, the Pope tooke
generat.25. his aduiſe in ſuch indignation, that he raiſed all Italy in rebellion againſt him. So the Emperour loſt his holde in Italy, and a
number of little States were raiſed in Italy, euery City ſtriuing
to make it ſelfe a free State. *Gregory* the ſecond hauing done
thus much died, and left the place to *Gregory* the third, who
Plat. Gregor. 3. ſucceeded him. This Pope as ſoone as euer he was choſen, by
Onupbr. the conſent of the Romane Clergy, depriued *Leo* the third Emperour, from the Empire,and from the communion of the faithfull,for the ſame cauſe : to wit, for defacing Images which were
                                                            ſet

set vp in Churches to be worshipped. This was the ground of the Popes proceeding against the Emperour, which is to be obserued. By this wee see the state of Rome cleane changed, for whereas the Emperours at the first were persecutours, and the Bishops of Rome were such as suffered for righteousnesse:Now had they changed places, for the Popes were become persecutours, and the Emperours were such as suffered for righteousnesse. For what was the Emperour *Leo* his fault in breaking downe and defacing Images, after that hee found that diuine worship was exhibited to them, other then that so much commended zeale of *Ezekias* in breaking downe the brasen Serpent? so that if we looke vpon this fact of the Emperour(which was the occasion why the Popes so proceeded against him) there can nothing appeare but the Popes persecution, and the Emperours suffering for righteousnesse.Pope *Gregory* the third, after this called a Synod in Rome, wherein the worship of Images was established, and all excommunicated that held the contrary. All Italy, saith *Onuphrius*, fell away from the obedience of *Leo* the Emperour, with the City of Rome, and other Westerne parts of the Empire, which were before subiect to the Emperour, excepting Sicily, and a part of Liguria, and a little corner of Calabria. All this the Emperour lost at once by the practise of Popes.

Platin. Greg.3.
Onuphr.annot.
ibid.

99. Now because wee consider these beginnings of the Popes persecutions, (for he began with the Emperour, whom thus he driued out of Italy, putting him from all gouernment in Rome, and after tooke vp his place and gouernement) let vs heere remember an auncient tradition of the auncient Fathers, who wrote before these times with freedom.For they are al resolued vpon this, as vpon an Apostolicall tradition, that Antichrist must driue the Emperour out of the gouernement of Rome and Italy,and take vp his place and seate.*Tertullian* doth often repeate this sentence, *Romanus status cedet Antichristo.* That is: [The Romane Empire must giue place to Antichrist.] And in another place he saith : *Qui nunc tenet teneat, donec de medio fiat. Quis? nisi Romanus status.* That is : [Hee that now with-holdeth, shall with-hold till he be taken out of the way:

Tertull.lib.3.
contra Marcion.
Lib.de resurr.
carnis.

Who

2.Theſſ.2.7.

Who is that? the Romane Empire.] And vpon thoſe words of the Apoſtle: [He that now with-holdeth, ſhall with-hold vntill he be taken away:] The auncient Fathers writing, doe with an admirable conſent agree vpon this, that the thing which the Apoſtle ſaith, did with-hold, and ſhould with-hold for a time, was the Romane Empire. For the Empire of Antichriſt muſt be raiſed vp in the ſame place, where that Empire ſtood that is in Rome. And therefore *Hierome* writing of thoſe wordes of the Apoſtle, except there come a departing firſt, & that that man be

Hieronim.Ad Algaſiam.

diſcloſed: ſaith, *Niſi venerit diſceſſio primum, vt omnes gentes quæ Romano Imperio ſubiacent, recedant ab eis.* That is: [Vnleſſe a departing firſt come, that all the Nations which now are ſub-iect to the Empire of Rome, may depart from that ſubiection.] Therefore he ſaith, that the Apoſtle left this tradition which he thought not good to commit to writing. Remember you not that when I was with you, I tolde you of theſe things, ſaith the Apoſtle. If any man aske why the Apoſtle thought good rather to commit this thing to their memory, then to writing: to this the ſame Author Saint *Hierome* aunſwereth in the ſame place: *Si apertè audaĉtérq̃, dixiſſet, non veniet Antichriſtus, niſi prius Romanum deleatur Imperium, iuſta cauſa perſecu.ionis in orientem tunc Eccleſiam conſurgere videbatur.* That is: [If Saint *Paul* had ſaid plainly and boldly, Antichriſt ſhall not come, vnleſſe the Romane Empire be firſt deſtroyed, this might haue miniſtred a iuſt cauſe of perſecution to the Church then riſing.] Then the Apoſtle would not ſpeake this thing directly for feare of drawing a perſecution vpon the Church, but committed it to their memories: Remember you not that when I was yet with you, I told you? If any man demaund this queſtion; why then, doe you admit ſome Apoſtolicall traditions? I anſwer.

100. Let theſe two limitations be remembred, and then I know not why Apoſtolicall traditions may not bee admitted. Firſt, it muſt haue an euident ground in the Scripture: Secondly, it muſt haue the conſenting teſtimonie of auncient Fathers, con-firming it to be an Apoſtolicall tradition. Theſe two conditi-ons are both kept, in this particular which now I ſpeake of; and in the baptiſing of Infants. But to take a tradition from the
bare

bare teſtimony of any Church, without a ground of Scripture, and the teſtimonie of the ancient Fathers, bearing witneſſe that it was an Apoſtolicall tradition : this wee vtterly refuſe as vn-warrantable. Concerning this particular, the reſt of the Fathers yeeld the like conſent to theſe. *Ambroſe* ſaith : *Non prius veniet Antichriſtus quam Regni Romani fiat defectio.* *Auguſtine* ſaith : *Quidam putant hoc de Imperio dictum fuiſſe Romano, & proptereà Paulum Apoſtolum non id aperte ſcribere voluiſſe, ne calumniam videlicet incurreret, quaſi Romano Imperio malè optauerit.* And in the ſame place : *Tantum qui modo tenet teneat, donec de medio tollatur : non abſurdè de ipſo Romano Imperio creditur.* Another of the aunciens ſaith thus : *Vt qui tenet nunc teneat donec de medio fiat. Donec Regnum quod nunc tenet de medio auferatur, priuſquam Antichriſtus reueletur.* *Iohn Chryſoſtome,* and *Oecumenius,* ſumming his words, ſay thns, writing vpon that Scripture. 2. *Theſſ.2. Solum eſt qui modo retinet. Thronus videlicet, & Regnum Romanorum, quod nunc impedimento eſt donec ceſſet, finemq́, accipiat, tunc reuelabitur iniquus ille, hoc eſt Antichriſtus. Vbi enim Imperium Rom. fuerit diſſolutum, tunc Antichriſtus rebellione irruet, ac obtinere conabitur non hominum ſolum, verum Dei Imperium. Romanorum autem Imperium ipſe Antichriſtus perfectè abolebit. Quemadmodum enim Medorum Imperium à Babylonijs diſſolutum eſt, & Babyloniorum à Perſis, Perſarum quoq́, à Macedonibus, & Macedonum à Romanis ; ita & Romanorum ab Antichriſto, & Antichriſti à Domino noſtro.* [That thing which with-holdeth, is the Romane Empire, which now ſtayeth the matter till it ceaſe and come to an end. Then ſhall that wicked man be reuealed, that is, Antichriſt. For when the Romane Empire ſhall be deſtroyed, then ſhall Antichriſt by rebellion inuade, and ſhall ſeeke to draw to himſelfe not onely the power of men, but of God alſo. And Antichriſt ſhall vtterly make an end of the Romane Empire. For as the Empire of the Medes was deſtroyed by the Babylonians, and that of the Babylonians by the Perſians, and that of the Perſians by the Macedonians, and that of the Macedonians by the Romanes : ſo ſhal that of the Romanes be deſtroyed by Antichriſt, and that of Antichriſt by our Lord Ieſus Chriſt.

Ambr. in 2. Theſſ.1.

Auguſt. lib.20. ca.19. de Ciuit. Dei.

Comm. in 2. Theſſ. 2. ſub nomine Hieronymi.

101. By all which wee finde by the confenting iudgement of the Fathers, that Antichrift muft rife vp vpon the ruine of the Romane Empire. And finding the power and gouernement of the auncient Romane Emperours to be vtterly ruinated by *Gregory* the fecond, the title of the Empire to be taken away from thofe Emperours by *Gregory* the third : the rule of the City of Rome (which was the auncient feate of the Empire) taken vp and furprifed by the Pope : the Cities of the Empire neere ad-ioyning to Rome, to bee brought vnder the fubiection of the Pope : by conferring the Prophefies of Scripture interpreted by the Fathers, with thefe euents which by Hiftory are truly re-corded, laying one thing to another, the conclufion is euident. My purpofe is not to fpeake of Antichrift ; but onely paffing through thefe Stories of the Popes temporall exaltation, I thought it a fmall labour for the Reader to compare the Pro-phefies of Scripture, and the iudgement of auncient Fathers with the euent, which fell out in the time of the two *Gregories*, the fecond and third. Before which time the Popes neuer en-tred into fuch furious attempts againft their Soueraigne Lords the Emperours. For they yeelded exact obedience to Empe-rours from the time of the firft Chriftian Emperour, vntill the time of *Gregory* the firft. All which while they refufed not to be ruled, commaunded, directed by the Emperours as by their Soueraignes, not onely in ciuill affaires, but euen in matters concerning the externall Difcipline of the Church, as calling of Councels, and confirming them : punifhing and cenfuring diforderous Clarkes and Bifhops, that offended the Imperiall Lawes, and fuch like. In fuch things the Emperours ruled, the Popes obeyed : no ftriuing, no threatning, no cafting off of the yoake appeared all this while. But after that *Phocas* had gran-ted to *Boniface* the third Pope, the title of Oecumenicall Bifhop, and that the Church of Rome fhould be head of all other Chur-ches : then began that ftarre to fall from heauen, falling from the fimplicity of truth & from fincerity of obedience, into pride, ambition, and noyfome lufts ; and neuer ceafed rolling down-wards till at laft it fell into the deepe practifes of the bottom-leffe pit. Thus when they began to fall, they had one fall after

*Apoc.*8.10.&
9.1.

ano-

another. They fell not into the practife of depofing Princes, *Anno* 733. vntill the time of *Gregory* the third.

Childeric or Chilperic.

102. THe Popes hauing proceeded thus farre in depofing the Emperour, thought all their labour loft,
vnleffe they might haue thofe Territories made fubiect to themfelues, from which they had expulfed the Emperor : Their feare
was, that either the feuerall Cities would procure their owne
Freedome, or that fome that were ftrongeft would furprife all
the reft, and fo a fmall part might come to the Popes fhare. The
Lumbards were then ftrongeft in Italy, and had foone gotten
the reft vnder their Dominion : To preuent their rifing, and to
inrich S. *Peter* with a new Patrimonie, the Popes after they
had vfed the power of the Lumbards againft the Emperour, fo
now againft the Lumbards begin to call new aides into Italie,
drawing firft *Pipin,* and then *Charles* againft the Lumbards, by
whofe meanes they obteyned their purpofe : *Pipin* was made *Harman. An.752.*
King of Fraunce for this feruice, and *Childeric* the right
King was depofed by Pope *Stephen* faith *Harmannus Contra-*
ctus : other attribute this to Pope *Zachary. Childeric* was fha-
uen and thruft into a Monaftery. After all this there ftuck a fcruple in the confcience of *Pipin,* for he had taken an Oath of Allegeance to *Childeric* his Soueraigne; this fcruple the Pope vn- *Vfperg.An.753.*
dertooke to remoue : For, faith *Vfpergenfis,* Pope *Stephen* abfolued him of his Oath, which in former times he had taken to
his Soueraigne *Childeric.* Thus were thefe great affaires ordered and difordered, the Emperour depofed, his fubiects raifed in
rebellion againft him, the Pope exalted and inriched by the
fpoiles of the Empire, the French king depofed, his fubiects abfolued from their Oathes and Alleageance, another fet vp in the
kingdome. Thefe were practifes which before this time were
neuer attempted by Popes : From thefe beginnings and examples the fucceeding Popes tooke light, and made rules of their
Gouernement; and therefore after this, the world could take
no reft for the Popes. Moreouer after thefe examples of *Pipin*
Cc 2 and

and *Charles*, they who through ambition aſpired without right or Title to kingdomes, haue deuoted their ſeruice wholly to the Pope. And what holdeth the Spaniard ſo ſtiffe in Popery, but onely an hope that by the Popes authority he may inlarge his Dominions in the ſame ſort? It is to be noted alſo, that they who thus offer their ſeruice to the Pope, are honoured by him, as the onely defenders of the Church, whereas none haue ſpoiled the Church more then theſe: for *Paulus Æmylius* recordeth, that *Carolus Martellus* (father to *Pipin*) being then Conſtable of France, robbed the Churches and Monaſteries of France at his pleaſure, promiſing that if he ſhould obtain victorie againſt the Sarracins, he would bountifully repay all: But after moſt great and rich victories, he not onely repayed nothing, but thruſt alſo the Biſhpppes from their Seas, held the Seas empty to pay ſouldiers; which thing brought a foule confuſion vpon the Church of Fraunce: yet this man for his ſeruice to the Pope was accounted a great defendor of the Church.

Henry the fourth Emperour.

103.　THe auncient manner of chooſing Popes, was by the Emperours conſent, after that Emperours became Chriſtian: This was practiſed from the time of *Conſtantine*, till *Hadrian* the third, ſaith *Platina*, who maketh this *Hadrian* the firſt, who altred this auncient manner: he tooke the opportunity of the abſenſe of *Charles* the groſſe then Emperor; who was ſo incumbred with the warres of the Normanes that he could not attend this buſineſſe. But *Onuphrius* in his Chronicle of Popes, ſetteth *Iohn* the fift to be the firſt Pope that was choſen without the Emperours commaundem̄nt and appointing: both may be well reconciled: for *Onuphrius* ſpeaketh of the Popes vnder the auncient Emperours: *Platina* of the Popes vnder the French and Germane Emperours, for from *Conſtantine* till *Iohn* the fift Pope, no Pope was choſen without the Emperours conſent: from *Iohn* the fift Pope, till *Charles* the firſt, no Pope was choſen by the Emperours conſent: *Charles* the firſt recouered the auncient rights of the Empire, as before we declared: from his time till *Hadrian* the third, no Pope was

choſen

Anno 884.
Platin.Hadrian 3.

Anno 685.

choſen without the Emperours conſent : from *Hadrian* the third, the conſent of the Emperour was not required, if *Platina* ſay true : others witneſſe, that the Popes were alwaies choſen by the conſent of the Emperor, till *Hildebrand.* The Popes thus ſtriuing to caſt off the ancient yoake, when *Gregory* the ſeuenth was choſen Pope, he added vnto this practiſe of reiecting the Emperours conſent, many moe practiſes, by blood, fraud, diue-liſh pride and Necromancy aſpiring to the Papacy, and was at laſt made Pope, not onely without the conſent of the Emperor, but without the conſent of the Cardinals alſo, onely a company of armed men with ſome few of the Clergie, gaue out that *Hil-debrand* was choſen Pope by S. *Peter,* he was much furthered by one *Maude* a Gentlewoman of great riches then in Italy, with whom he had great familiarity. *Beno.*

Naucl.gener.36

104. *Henry* the fourth Emperour called a Councell at Wormes to repreſſe *Hildebrand* : The Biſhops of that Councell condemned *Hildebrand* for intruding into the Papacy, & for his infamous & prodigious conuerſation, & adiudged him to be de-poſed. *Hildebrand* vpon the knowledg of theſe news excommu-nicated the Emperor, depriued him of Gouernement, abſolued his ſubiects from their Oath of Alleageance. The Emperor of a ſudden being robbed of his friends & ſubiects by the practiſe of them whom *Hildebrad* had ſet to negotiate this matter, was dri-uen to the greateſt debaſement of himſelſe, that hath bin heard of, bare-foot in a ſharp Froſt in deepe Winter, three daies atten-ding at Canuſium with his wife & child before he was admitted to the Popes preſence : when he was admitted, and had craued pardon : his cenſure was, to ſtand at the mercy of *Hildebrand* : Which when he had confirmed by an Oath, the Pope abſolued him, but afterward ſet vp *Rodolph* Duke of Sueuia in warre a-gainſt him. *Rodolph* being thus ſtirred vp to Rebellion againſt his Soueraigne, was ſo wounded in a battell, that being carried to Merſeburge without hope of life, called the Nobles and Bi-ſhoppes that had fauoured him; and in their preſence behold-ing his right hand which was ſmitten off in the battell, This, quoth he, is that hand by which I confirmed an Oath of mine Alleageance to my Maſter *Henry* : this haue I gotten by follo-

Auent.l.5.

Vſperg.An.
1080.
Naucl.gener.37

wing your Councell, returne you to your Mafter, and keep your firft faith, as for me, I goe to my Fathers.

105. The Emperour after this, gathered a Synode at Brixia : The Bifhoppes of Italy, Lumbardy, Germany meeting there, condemned *Hildebrand* for a difturber of Chriftendome, a diforderer of the Church, a periurous, facrilegious Incendiary, a Witch and Necromancer. The Emperour befieged him in the Caftle of S. *Peter*, but *Hildebrand* vnderftanding that the Emperour vfed to refort to S. *Maries* Church to pray, fet a knaue aboue the place where he vfed to pray, to throw downe a great ftone vpon him, and to kill him. VVhilft the varlet was fetting the ftone for that purpofe, downe comes the ftone and the traytor with it, who was crufhed to peeces therewith. After that *Hildebrand* had fet vp many fuch practifes againft the Emperour without effect, he betooke himfelfe to flight : And wandring like a Vagabond without comfort, without helpe, without hope, though brought to a moft pitifull eftate, yet pitied of no man, trauelling vnder the vnfupportable burden of a reftleffe confcience, he died for griefe at Salernum. By all which we fee, that this new and monftrous practife of depofing Kings, was refifted by the Emperour, as peftiferous againft his eftate, difclaimed by Bifhoppes, as a thing ftrangely difordering the Church and ciuill States, and iuftly reuenged by God, as a thing abhominable. The Chronicles obferue, as it is noted in *Vfpergenfis, Fol.* 226. that this *Henry* the fourth had fought threefcore and two pitched battels, in number furpaffing M. *Marcellus* and *Iulius Cæfar*, of whom the one fought thirty, the other fiftie.

Auent.l. 5.
Vfperg.

Henry the fift.

106. WHen *Hildebrand* and *Rodolph* both confpiring againft *Henry* the fourth, were both ouerthrowne, the fucceeding Popes maintaining the fame policy and practife (for it were pittie but that thefe Apoftolicall practifes were well knowne) raifed *Henry* the fift in armes againft his father *Henry* the fourth : this old Emperour being wearie of troubles, and defirous to haue fome repofe, made his

Nauel.gener. 37

pur-

purpoſe knowne, that hee would reſigne all gouernment to his
ſonne, and goe himſelfe in perſon to viſite the Sepulcher of
Chriſt : but the ſonne was ſtirred vp by the Popes to rebell a-
gainſt his Father, before hee had vndertaken that iourney. To
colour his rebellion, hee proteſted that hee ſought not his Fathers Throne for deſire of dominion, neither wiſhed he the de-
priuation of his Lord and Father : but if his Father would bee
ſubiect to Saint *Peter* and his Succeſſours, then would he yeeld
him the Empire. The end of this contention was this. The old
Emperour was ſurpriſed, impriſoned by his ſonne, and ſo died.
There is an Epiſtle of this Emperour extant in *Naucler*, wherein he complaineth that he was betrayed againſt all humane and
diuine Lawes, being inuited by his ſonne to a Treaty of peace,
after faith and aſſurance giuen for his life and honour, comming
peaceably to Mentz, was ſurpriſed treacherouſly. After all this
Henry the fift comming to Rome, found no more fauour then
his Father had done. For *Paſchalis* the ſecond contended with
him ſo earneſtly for Inueſtitures (which was the quarrell for
which his Father felt ſo much the Popes anger) that thereupon
a tumult was raiſed, in that tumult Pope *Paſchalis* was taken.
Who being in the Emperours power, confirmed the Emperors
Iuriſdiction, and diſclaimed the right of Inueſtitures, yeelding
it to the Emperour in that ſort, as his aunceſtours had vſed the
ſame in former times.

107. At this time the Cities of Italy tooke an Oath of alea-
geance to the ſame Emperour. But after all this grant of Pope
Paſchalis, no bond being ſufficient to hold faſt a Pope, he called a Councell at Rome; wherein he condemned all that himſelfe had done in yeelding Inueſtitures to the Emperour : and
excommunicated the Emperour. The Emperor to preuent the
dangers that might enſue, came again into Italy : and ſent Am-
baſſadors to the Pope, to try if theſe matters might be brought
to a peaceable end. The Pope in the mean time calleth a Councell at the Lateran. In this Councell Pope *Paſchalis* excuſing
that fact of his for yeelding Inueſtitures to the Emperour, deſired all that were preſent to pray for him, that God would forgiue him. For, ſaith he, that writing which I made, which is
called

Nauc'er.gener. 38.

Naucler. ibid.

called a priuiledge, I doe heere condemne vnder an euerlaſting
curſe, and pray that all you will doe the ſame. There followed
a generall acclamation, *Fiat, fiat:* that is, be it ſo. Then *Bruno*
Biſhop of Signinum, ſaid : We haue cauſe to thanke God that
we haue heard the Pope from his owne mouth condemne this
priuiledge. Which is not a priuiledge, but rather a prauiledge,
becauſe it containeth prauity and hereſie. Whereupon another
ſtood vp and ſaid : If that priuiledge containe hereſie, then hee
who made it is an heretique. *Caietan* being moued with the
ſharpneſſe of that ſpeach, anſwered : What? doſt thou in this
Councell, in the hearing of vs all, call the Pope an heretique?
that writing was not hereſie, but it was euill. Nay, quoth another, it was not euill, &c. *Paſchalis* by his hand commaunding
ſilence, appeaſed the clamour, and tolde them that hereſie neuer entred into the Church of Rome. This I haue declared,
that the Reader may vnderſtand, what graue matters are handled in ſome Popiſh Councels. In this Councell the excommunication againſt the Emperour was renued. Whereupon ſuch
a ruine and vaſtation of Italy followed, that nothing could bee
ſeene there for a time, but bloud-ſhed, burnings, robberies :
the State and Church confounded, the true heires turned out of
their poſſeſſions, robbers and oppreſſours thruſt in. All this moued not the Popes, to remit Inueſtitures. The Emperour perceiuing that nothing could moue the Popes, to looſe ſo benefi-
ciall a Pray, no not the common calamity of Chriſtendome :
was perſwaded to yeeld to the Pope in the end, in reſpect of the
miſeries that followed this contention. And ſo reſigned Inueſtitures to the Pope. Whereupon peace followed for a time.

Frederick Barbaroſſa.

108. *FRederick* the firſt, ſirnamed *Barbaroſſa* is highly commended by the Writers of that age, and of them that
followed, for a Prince of great worth, wiſedome, and valour.
When he came into Italy the Pope met him, not with a purpoſe
to honor him, but by him to be reuenged vpon the King of *Si-*
cily, with whom the Pope was at variance. *Frederick* receiued
the

Funct. lib.10. Chron.

the Pope with great reuerence, and as he lighted from his horſe, held the left ſtirrope. This was made a great quarrell againſt *Frederick*, and though he made his reaſonable excuſe, that this was the firſt time that euer hee ſerued in that ſort, and might therefore be pardoned for any thing vnskilfully done : that the office proceeding from good will, it made not much matter on which ſide he came, that came to reuerence him : yet the Pope would not be ſatisfied; but ſhewed himſelfe ſo much offended, that the Emperour began to be ſomewhat moued; ſo that the parting was with ſome ſtomacke on both ſides. The next day the Emperour meeting the Pope, helde the right ſtirrope, to pleaſe him : and when they were ſet, the Pope thus began. The Princes of auncient times your predeceſſours, when they came to make petition for the Imperiall crowne, were wont by ſome worthy office to promerit the fauour of the Church of Rome; that by preuenting the bleſſing, they might declare by ſome e-gregious ſeruice that the Crowne was due to them. Thus did *Charles* by ouerthrowing the Lumbards, Thus did *Otho* by de-feating the Berengarij, Thus did *Lotharius* by repreſſing the Normanes. So muſt you doe, and repreſſe the King of Sicily with the Normanes, and reſtore *Apulia* to vs and the Church : and then you ſhall ſee what we will doe for our part. The Em-perour vnderſtanding well how vnreaſonable the motion was, that *Apulia*, which was by right a part of the Empire ſhould be taken from the King of Sicily at the Emperors charges, and be-ſtowed vpon the Pope; yet for that time did giue a moderate anſwer, that he would goe into Germany & returne with freſh forces for that ſeruice, becauſe theſe which were with him were much decayed.

109. This mention of the King of Sicily, draweth vs to ſpeake ſomewhat of him, our purpoſe being to obſerue the pra-ctiſe of Popes in depoſing of Kings. *William* King of Sicilia, held alſo Apulia, as hee receiued it from his Father *Roger*, to whom it came from *Robert Guiſcard*, who firſt draue out the Moores from thence, and wonne the poſſeſſion thereof. This *William* becauſe he would not giue Apulia to the Pope, for in-larging of Saint *Peters* Patrimonie, was excommunicated by

King *William* of Sicily depo-ſed.

D d   Pope

Pope *Hadrian* the fourth depofed from his Kingdome, his fubiects difcharged of their Oath and Alleageance. And becaufe
William ftood vpon his ftrength in his owne iuft defence againft
the Pope, therefore the Pope would gladly haue fet *Frederick*

Naucler.gen.
39.

the Emperour againft him. In the end *William* in feare partly of
Frederick, but efpecially of *Immanuel* the Greeke Emperour
(whofe Orator *Palæologus*,promifed to driue *William* out of Italy, and to giue the Pope fiue thoufand pound weight of gold, if
three Hauen Townes of Apulia might be giuen to his Mafter by
couenant after the victory) was driuen to compound with the
Pope : and being thus forced thereto, did acknowledge that he

An. 1155.

held both thofe Kingdomes of the Pope.

110. When *Frederick* the Emperour vnderftoode that the
Pope had made a league with *William*, and confirmed him in
both the Kingdomes, after that he had moued *Frederick* to vndertake the warres againft him : was not a little greeued there-
at, confidering alfo other greeuances and oppreffions of Germany. Whereupon he began to execute fome feuere difcipline
againft certaine diffolute perfons of the Clergy, at which the
Pope grew highly offended : hereupon fome fharpe letters paffed betweene them, as before we declared. But when the Em-

§.3.

perour prepared a iourney into Italy with an Army, the Pope
fearing the worft, made meanes, and was reconciled to him. A
little after when *Frederick* befieged Crema,fome Cities of Italy
confpiring againft him, the Pope followed the firft opportunity
of rebellion, and excommunicated the Emperour and curfed
him. *Naucler* declareth the motiue that drew the Pope to ex-

Naucler.gene-
rat.39.

communicate the Emperour. *Data pecunia immenfa Domino
Hadriano Papa vt imperatorem excommunicaret.* A huge fumme
of money was giuen to Pope *Hadrian*, to excommunicate the
Emperour. Thefe be the Apoftolicall cenfures, and thefe be the
meanes that draw his holineffe to depofe Princes. Pope *Hadrian* fhortly after at Anagnia, walking abroad to take the ayre,
as he would haue drunke a little water in a fpring, a flie falling
into his mouth, ftucke fo faft in his throate, that no helpe of
Phyficke preuailing to remoue her, he was choaked therewith,
and died.

111. I may

III. I may not omit what *Iohannes Flasborienfis*, a Writer Naucle. ibid.
in this time, obferueth of this *Hadrian*, as from him *Naucler*
reporteth. This *Iohn* affirmeth, that he heard *Hadrian* confeffe
thus much : [No man liueth in the world more miferable then
the Pope of Rome: In this Sea haue I found fo many miferies;
that in refpect of this prefent eftate, all the bitterneffe of my for-
mer life feemeth pleafure & happineffe : This ambition to feek *Eft Romulo fuc-cedere in Parri-cidijs, non Petro in ouibus paf-cendis.*
the Papacy, euen by fhedding our brothers bloud, this is to fuc-
ceed *Romulus* in Paricide, not *Peter* in feeding.] By this auten-
tick teftimonie of Pope *Hadrian* a witneffe without exception,
we fee what it is to be a Pope. *Marcellus* the fecód as *Onuphrius* *Onuphr. vita Marcelli.2.*
reporteth in his life: gaue the like cenfure of the Papacy, adding
thus much : [That hee faw no meanes how any Pope could be
faued.] Thefe are the teftimonies of the Popes themfelues,
who deferue to be belecued fpeaking of a matter whereof they
had fo great experience. After the death of *Hadrian*, *Alexander* the fift being chofen Pope , renueth the excommunication
againft *Frederick*, thundering out great curfes vpon him, and
fent letters abroad to all Princes and people to raife tumults a-
gainft him. The Emperour to pacifie the troubles of Chriftendome which were growing by the Schifme, which then began
betweene this *Alexander* and *Victor* the fourth, entreated the
French King in fome conuenient place to meete him, and to
bring *Alexander*, as he would alfo bring *Victor* to this meeting,
that matters might be compofed, if it might be , and troubles
preuented. The meeting was appointed at *Diuion*. Thither
came *Frederick* and *Victor*. Thither came *Henry* the fecond
King of England, and *William* King of Scotland. But *Alexander*
was fo much afraid of this meeting, that hee perfwaded *Philip*
the French King , who had promifed to meete the Emperour
here, to practife a trick which better befeemed a fhifting Pope,
then an honourable Prince. The deuife was, that the French
King fhould come to the place before the Emperor was come,
& wafh his hands in the Riuer that ran by the place ; and by the
voice of a Criar, fhould call the Emperour three times, and as if
this were the keeping of his promife, afterward hee fhould depart. When the Emperour and the Kings of England and Scot-

land were come to the place, and heard what the French King had done: they were much offended that the King fhould fo Popifhly difappoint his promife, therefore they willed *Victor* to returne to Rome, and went their waies.

    112. I paffe by *Fredericks* iourney to the holy land, his warres there, how Pope *Alexander* fent his Image to the Souldian; how being taken prifoner when he would haue diffimulated his eftate, he was knowne by his picture : how after his returne he raifed an Army, and led the fame into Italy againft *Alexander* : how againft the Venetians, who tooke part with *Alexander*, he fent his fonne *Otho* : how his fonne was taken prifoner : which eftate of his fonne gaue *Alexander* the aduantage, and made the Emperour content to yeelde. The conclufion was : The Emperour muft come into Saint *Marke* his Church in Venice, and there humbly feeke abfolution at the Popes handes. *Fredericke* did fo : The Pope commaunded him to afke pardon proftrate on the ground ; the Emperour fufpecting no contumely, did fo. The humble, milde, and mortified Vicar of Chrift, hauing the Emperor thus proftrate before him, fet his foote vpon the Emperours necke, vfing thofe wordes : *Super Afpidem & Bafilifcum ambulabis, & conculcabis Leonem & Draconem* : The Emperours anfwere was, *Non tibi, fed Petro* : The Pope replied, *Et mihi & Petro*. Thefe be examples of the Popes power in excommunicating Emperours : from which examples they draw the claim of a right which they pretend to haue. The Popifh writers hope that men will be perfwaded by the examples of the Popes power, that this power was giuen to S. *Peter*, and in him to all Popes, becaufe there appeareth fuch Chriftian moderation, humility, and mildeneffe therein. Though there be nothing in Scripture for them, but all againft them ; though the auncient fathers exprefly denied the Popes to haue Iurifdiction ouer other Bifhpopes, yet they doubt not but they fhall finde fome that will reft perfwaded, that Chrift left this fulneffe of power to the Popes, which conteineth Soueraigne Iurifdiction, not onely ouer all Bifhoppes, but ouer all temporall Princes alfo.

                                          Henry

Naucl. gener. 40 reporteth this as done before *Fredericke* his expedition to the holy land.

Pfal. 91. 13. Thou fhalt walke vpon the Afpe and Serpent, thou fhalt tread vnder feete the Lion and Dragon. Not to thee, but to *Peter*. Both to me and to *Peter*.

Henry the fixt, and Philip.

113.   **H**Enry the fixt Emperour fucceeded *Frederic.* This Henry left a young fonne *Frederic* an Infant, yet elect to be Emperour, and committed his education and weldoing to the truft of Pope *Innocens* the third, leauing the Empire to his brother *Philip* vntill the childe fhould growe to age. Pope *Innocent* this truftie tutor, purpofing the deftruction both of *Philip* and young *Fredericke* fet vp another Emperour, which procured great vexation and trouble to them, and to all Germany. And firft he quarrelled *Philip,* that he ftood vnder an old excommunication of *Celeftinus*; but afterward making femblance of fauour and reconciliation with him, hee fent the Bifhoppe of Sutrium, to demand pledges (certaine men whofe eyes his brother *Henry* had plucked out). The Bifhoppe came and receiued the blinde pledges, and at the earneft requeft of *Philip,* abfolued him from the excommunication. The Pope when he had gotten thefe blinde men, made publicke fhew of them to moue enuie againft *Philip*: that done, he excommunicated the Bifhoppe of Sutrium for abfoluing *Philip* without his commaundement: the Bifhoppe was depriued, and fo ftood depriued all the daies of his life. Then laboured the Pope to ftirre vp *Bertholdus* Duke of Zaringia againft *Philip,* whom he would haue obtruded to the Electours: But *Berthold* vtterly refufing to rebell, fent his Nephewes to *Philip* for Hoftages of his Faith and Alleageance, and came himfelfe and fware Alleageance to him: at which the Pope taking great indignation, brake out into thefe wordes: Either fhall the Pope pull the Crown from *Philip,* or *Philip* fhal pull the Miter from the Pope. And fent therefore to *Otho* fonne to *Henry Leo*, a Prince more noted for boldneffe, pride and ambition, then for wifedome and moderation.

114.   To this man the Pope *Innocent* fent a Crowne, and fet him vp againft *Philippe* for the Empire, excommunicating *Philippe*, and pulling all helpes from him that poffible hee could, and fo filled the world with warres. As *Philip* and

Naucl.gener.40.
Cufpinian vita
Henrici & Phi-
lippi.

D.d 3   *Otho*

Otho were thus plunged in warres, all Princes and people troubled; there was not a Bifhopricke, or Ecclefiafticall dignity, or
Parifh-Church which was not made litigious; and in the common miferies of Chriftendome, and confufion of the Church,
the Pope onely reioyced, increafing his wealth by the ruines of
the Church: the calamity of all men was turned to his happineffe. To expreffe this true felicity of the Pope, and the Court
of Rome, in the mifery and vexation of all the world, mine Authour breaketh out into thefe wordes: [O our mother Rome,
reioyce, becaufe the Cataracts of earthly treafures are opened, that vnto thee Riuers may flow, and Mountaines of filuer
may be brought in great abundance to thee: be thou ioyfull
for the iniquity of the fonnes of men, becaufe in recompence
of fo much mifchiefe as from thee proceedeth, the price retur-
neth to thee. Let thine heart be merry for the difcord and diffention that troubleth all other, but helpeth thee; for out of
the infernall pit it breaketh to heape vp much money as a reward to thee. Thou haft that which alwaies thou haft thirfted
after, and longed for: Now maift thou fing this fong, that thou
haft ouercome the world, not by thy Religion, but by the mali-
tioufneffe of men. That which draweth men to thee, is not thy
deuotion, or a pure confcience, but impudency and boldneffe,
to commit all wickednes, and hope of impunity: for their hope
is to defend and maintaine any wickedneffe where thou art
the Iudge, and when the price is prepared.] Thus farre *Vf-*
pergenfis, making fomewhat bold with that innocent Pope *In-*
nocentius.   In this contention which the Pope raifed, *Otho* had
the helpes of the King of Bohemia, the Lantgraue of Thuring,
the Bifhoppe of Colon: thefe inclined to him being drawne
as well by the Popes curfing of *Philip*, as alfo for that they faw
that *Otho* was ftrong by meanes of his Vncle *Richard* King of
England. But at laft *Otho* being wearied with the warres, and
perceiuing *Philips* affaires to profper, was content to heare of
peace.

    115. The Pope himfelfe after all his malice thus fpent,
made a motion of reconciliation betweene them, vpon this
condition, that *Philips* daughter fhould be giuen in marriage to
                                                    Richard

Abbas Vfper-
genf.Philippo.1.

Richard the Popes brothers ſonne, newly created Earle of Thuſcia, Spoletum, and Marchia Anconitana, hoping that theſe lands and Titles which then his Nephew inioyed onely by the Popes fauour, and at his will, might by this meanes afterward paſſe by right of inheritance. The Pope ſeemed to be ſo earneſt for this match, that *Uſpergenſis* ſaith it was promiſed. Here is deſcried one end of the Popes excommunications and abſolutions, and of raiſing warres in Chriſtendome, that they might by troubling Chriſtendome drawe ſome aduantages to themſelues. The Popes motion was ſcorned of the Princes, and the daughter of *Philip* was giuen in marriage to *Otho*, and Articles agreed on that *Philip* during his life ſhould gouerne, and after him *Otho*.

Otho the fourth.

116. **P**Hilip the laſt Emperour being murdered by the practiſe and hand of the Countie *Palatin Wittleſpach*, Germany fell within the power of the Popes vexation more then before : *Hoc vno Philippo perempto* (ſaith *Naucler*) *Germania ſummis inſidijs Pontificis Romani agitata, vires pene ſuas omnes in ſeſe experta eſt truculenter* : That is, This one Prince *Philip* being dead, Germany vexed with the great and moſt fraudulent deceits of the Pope, did feele in a manner all his force and power againſt it. *Otho* after this, comming to Rome, *Innocentius* the third who had ſet him vp in armes againſt *Philip*, entertained him with great ſhew of fauor, but this loue was turned ſhortly into greater hatred : For whilſt Pope *Innocent* was ſomewhat too buſie in exacting an Oath of *Otho*, and ſtirred vp or heartned ſome of the Citizens of Rome againſt the Germanes, the Romanes drew to a tumult, and killed one thouſand and a hundred Germanes, who ſuſpected no harme. *Otho* being much moued at this Romiſh entertainment, firſt moued that in ſome peaceable manner mends might be made : but perceiuing them to be inraged, that they ſeemed more ready to giue him a new on-ſet, then to offer or to accept peace : hee departed out of the Citie, and finding by ſuſpitions and preſumpti-

Naucl.gener.41.

Suſpectum habens Rom. Pontificem, ne quid in eo tumultu occaſionis ciuibus preſtitiſſet. Naucler.

ſumptions that Pope *Innocent* had giuen ſome occaſion and heartning to the Citizens in that tumult: he reſolued to be re-uenged vpon the Pope, and entred into the lands of S. *Peters* Patrimony, making great waſt and deſolation where he came. Wherefore Pope *Innocent* excommunicated him, and abſolued all Prelates, Lordes, and all the people that were ſubiect to the Empire from that Oath of Alleageance, which they had taken to *Otho*, commanding all men not to call him or account him Emperour, nor in any thing to yeelde obedience to him.

117. *Otho* being thus excommunicated and curſed by the Pope, proceeded on in the ſame courſe, denying that the Pope had any power ouer the Emperour, or to diſpoſe of the Empire, and therefore notwithſtanding all that the Pope had done, ſtill he did beare himſelfe as Emperour. And comming into Germany, he held a Diet at Norinberge, where he opened to the Princes of Germanie, the manifold and fraudulent practiſes of the Pope againſt him: and mine Authour reporteth, that there he made this ſpeech: [Now is the time come, O Princes, for you to ſhew your courage and care of the Empire, and for the adminiſtration thereof; for to you, onely to you, belongeth this right of diſpoſing of the Germane Empire: therefore it muſt be your care to preuent theſe troubles. This we confeſſe to be in your power, and of your right to create an Emperour, or to depoſe him, to ſet him vp or pull him downe, and that herein the Pope hath no Iuriſdiction: when any trouble ariſeth in the Empire, you haue the power and right to redreſſe it. Now then like true Germanes defend your owne right, ſhew your courage and ſtrength in the maintenance of your Country lawes, and of the imperiall dignity: either now maintaine your owne right, or elſe you ſhall looſe all: for if by your facility you permit the Pope to diſpoſe of the Empire at his pleaſure, you ſhall ſoone finde moſt aſſuredly that your power in the choiſe of an Emperour ſhall be vtterly ouerthrowne and brought to nothing.] Thus did *Otho* then reiect the Popes power: but the Pope was too ſubtill and too ſtrong for him, for he ſet vp *Fredericke* the ſon of *Henry* the ſixt againſt him, to whom the Princes of Germany were bound in an auncient Oath of Allea-geance.

Multiplices Rom. Pòntificis contra ſe oſtenſas callidetates exponens, quàm iniuſtè ab illo inſectaretur, de-clarauit. Naucl. Naucl. gener. 41.

geance. The memory of which bond did ſo preiudice *Otbo* that he was forſaken, and *Frederick* was made Emperour.

Frederick the ſecond.

118. FRederick the ſecond, purpoſing to demerit the Popes fauour, and to aſſwage the inſatiable thirſt of bloud and warres: gaue many great and rich gifts to the Pope, granted much land, and many territories in Italy to the Church of Rome: but nothing could aſſwage the ſpirit that ruled in the Popes. For after all this kindneſſe of the Emperour, the Pope (then *Honorius* the third) gaue fauour and encouragement to two Earles of Thuſcia, *Richard* (or as *Vſpergenſis* calleth him *Mathew*) and *Thomas*, notorious enemies of the Emperour, and conuict of Treaſon againſt him. Whom when *Frederick* purſued in battell, they betooke themſelues to the protection of the Pope as their ſureſt refuge. The Emperor followed them within the Popes territories: he declared alſo his right to Sicily and Apulia, and the auncient Priuiledges which thoſe Kings had alwaies vſed for Inueſtitures, which priuiledges in his nonage *Naucl.gener.41.* (who was left to *Innocent* the third, as to a faithfull Tutor) were ſurpriſed by the ſame *Innocent*, taken from his mother *Conſtantia*, himſelfe being yong & not able to make reſiſtance. As thus *Frederick* ſought to maintaine his right, *Honorius* draweth out this new and ſtrange weapon againſt him, excommunicating, and depriuing him, raiſing vp his ſubiects againſt him, perſwading them to ſhake off their faith, Oath, Alleageance, and all reſpect of the Emperor. The Lumbards he ſtirred vp in rebellion againſt the Emperour, procuring thereby great preiudice to the Empire (ſaith *Naucler*) and defeating the purpoſe of the iourney, which *Frederick* intended to the holy land; and in the beginning of theſe furious attempts, hee was cutte ſhort by Death.

119. *Gregory* the ninth who ſucceeded, began there, where *Honorius* left. And becauſe he ſought a pretence for his fury, he accuſed the Emperour, for that he had not performed his vowe *Naucl.gener.41* of that iourney to Ieruſalem, whereunto he was drawne by *Ho-* *Cuſpinian. vita* *norius* *Frederici.2.*

Ee

norius (Though this iourney he performed afterward) Thus the Pope neither conuicting him, nor conuenting him, nor once hearing him, thundred out his bolt of excommunication. When the Emperours Ambassadours entreated that they might be admitted to reder reasons of his stay, they could not be admitted, but the Pope doubled & redoubled his excommunication. *Frederick* to mitigate this monstrous rage, vndertooke the iourney to Ierusalem, and performed the seruice with great labour and no lesse glory. But now behold the true reach of the Popes excommunications, and exhortations to the holy seruice. As soone as euer the Emperour was gone to Asia, then the Pope declaring why he so much desired his absence, raised forces and sent them to subdue Apulia to bring it vnder his subiection. The Souldiers which were signed with the Crosse for the holy wars he stayed, and them he spoiled of their prouision. *Frederick* in the meane time recouered Hierusalem, Nazareth, Ioppe from the Soldan, with other Townes, and wrote to the Pope of his successe: but the Pope suppressed those newes, and gaue forth that *Frederick* was slaine, to the end that he might with greater ease surprise certaine Cities of Apulia, which stood faithfull to *Frederick*. He slew with barbarous cruelty the Germane and French souldiers newly returned from the Easterne warres, least they should tell the truth of the Emperours good successe. And when *Frederick* sent to him to be absolued for his seruice (as the Pope had promised to absolue him, if once hee would take that iourney) this now hee vtterly denied. And moreouer as *Naucler* reporteth, hee enioyned the Knights that were called Templarians and Hospitularians, with a strict commandement, to vse *Frederick* no otherwise then a publique enemie. This practise of turning the Souldiers which were crossed for the holy warres to the Popes purposes, was much vsed by the Popes, and the common vse of it made the Princes of Christendome vnderstand, that the Popes vsed the pretence of the holy warres, when they would bring to effect some particular of their own. Thus were great preparations of the French and Germanes gathered by *Innocent* the third and *Honorius* the third, vnder pretence of the warres of Ierusalem: but turned wholly against the

Cuspinian. Fred. 2.

Naucler. gen. 41.

the Emperour of Conſtantinople : to reduce that Church to the obedience of Rome. Thus were other preparations and much money collected: pretended for the holy warres : but turned by *Martin* the fourth againſt *Peter* King of Arragon. Thus were the like preparations pretended for the ſame warres, but imployed by *Iohn* the two and twentieth againſt *Lodowick* Duke of Bauare. *Præſcriptio ſacrorum armorum alio ſpectauit* (ſayeth *Æmylius*) *Pontifex hoſtem iudicarat Lodouicum Bauaria ducem.*

Paulus Aemyl. in vita Philippi Longi.

120. *Frederick* returning into Italy from the Eaſt, after all theſe wrongs hauing both cauſe and means, opportunely offering it ſelfe to reuenge his wrongs : yet reſolued not to bee drawne from his milde courſe. He made meanes to be reconciled to the Pope : the Pope would not heare of reconciliation, vnleſſe he would giue him one hundred and twenty thouſand ounces of gold. This was the price of his abſolution. That the Princes of the world might know, that his excommunications ſtand in bloud, cruelty and ambition : his abſolutions in couetouſneſſe. *Frederick* being thus abſolued, was receiued by the Pope in a banquet, but all was counterfeit cheere. For no ſooner was *Frederick* returned into Germany, but preſently hee vnderſtood that the Princes of Germany had receiued directions from the Pope, to chuſe none of his family Emperour after him ; that the Pope had conſpired with his enemies to deiect him from the Empire. *Frederick* prepared an Army to repreſſe the Lumbards ; who had conſpired againſt him, and tooke many Cities in Lumbardy, Vmbria, and Hetruria. The Pope (being one of the ſame conſpiracy) was ſo offended at *Frederick*, that he thundred out now the third time his excommunication againſt him, diſcharging all his Subiects from their faith and alleageance. He made a league with the Venetians ; and hee called the Lateran Councell, wherein the purpoſe was to depoſe *Frederick*. Hee commaunded alſo the heads of *Peter* and *Paul* to be caried through the City in ſolemne Proceſſion. And calling the people together in Saint *Peters* Minſter, hee made an Oration to them full of commiſeration, ſtirring them vp to fight againſt the Emperour, and to take the ſigne of the Croſſe as

againft an enemie of Chrift, promifing euerlafting life to all that tooke Armes againft him.

121. The Emperour (in whom it appeared that the greateft patience once broken is turned into the greateft furie) vnder-ftanding that the Pope, whom he had alwayes fought to miti-gate, was not to be drawne by kindneffe or faire meanes, hea-ring alfo that againft himfelfe as againft a Turke or Sarracine the Croffe was giuen: brought his Army before the City of Rome; and ioyning battell againft his enemies, put them to an ouerthrow, but efpecially hee declared his indignation againft fuch as had taken the Croffe. For hee commaunded that they fhould be cut in the manner of a Croffe. Some had their heads clouen in foure quarters croffe-wife. The Clergie had firft a crowne cut off to the quicke, and then were deepely croffed with a fword; that as they were called, fo they might bee in truth figned with a Croffe. The Emperour alfo vnderftanding that the Popes Legates were fent out to call the Bifhops of England and Fraunce to the Councell, kept watch in all the wayes that none might come to the Councell. He tooke diuers Cardinals and Bifhops that were comming by fhippe: fome he drowned, others he hanged; among whom was the Popes bro-ther. Pope *Gregory* hauing thus raifed vp the quiet fpirit of this Prince into fuch a rage, and knowing no way how to appeafe him, or to rid himfelfe out of thefe troubles, which himfelfe had procured, for griefe died.

122. *Caleftinus* the fourth fucceeding, would alfo haue fuc-ceeded *Gregory* in the fame hereditary fpirit of rebellion, and fa-uage crueltie, but a fudden death and fhort gouernment would not fuffer him to performe his purpofe: for within eighteene daies of his Election he was poifoned. In his place came *Inno-centius* the fourth, who of a moft inward friend of the Emperor, became a moft mortall foe, and furpaffed all his predeceffours in fpirituall fury againft the good Emperour: for when *Bald-win* King of Ierufalem, and *Raymond* Earle of Tholous labou-red to eftablifh peace betweene the Empire and Papacy, and had procured for that purpofe a meeting: the Pope aided by the Fleete of Genua, gaue them the flippe and came to Lyons

in

in Fr ance, where he called a Synode. In this Synode the Pope caufed *Fred ericke* to be cyted perfonally to appeare, and to an-fwere to fuch things as fhould be obiected againft him. The Emperour appeared not, but fent thither *Thaddaus Sueffanus* a famous Lawyer in thofe daies : among other that the Empe-rour fent, *Naucler* nameth alfo *Petrum de Vineis*, a learned and eloquent man at that time. Thefe pleading for the Emperor, declared that he was hindred by fuch impediments, that perfo-nally he could not be prefent, and therefore they required with great fubmifnes on the Emperours behalfe, that a conuenient time might be affigned to him, wherein he might come and an-fwere. This reafonable petition was denied : the Pope drew out his terrible toole, excommunicating the Emperour, abfol-uing all Princes of the Empire from their Oath and faith, mo-ued them to make choice of a new Emperour, alleaging many caufes falfly deuifed, as blafphemy, periury, facriledge, and fuch like.

123. *Fredericke* after he heard of thefe proceedings againft him, made readie for a iourney to Lyons : but as he was in the way, ynderftanding that they whom he had banifhed from Par-ma, were returned thither by the Popes practife, and taking the Towne by force, had giuen a great ouerthrow to the other Ci-tizens : fearing leaft this example might draw other Cities to the like reuolt : he gaue ouer the iourney to Lions, and wrote Letters to the French King, and all Prelates refuting the Popes friuolous obiections, declaring the iuftice of his caufe and his innocency. *Innocentius* regarding neither iuftice nor innocen-cy, purfued him by violence, malice, open warres, fecret confpi-racies, feeking all meanes that his vnholy head could inuent to take away the life of *Fredericke*. As he was taking his recrea-tion in hauking at Groffetum by the Sea fhore, neare to Sien, the Pope drew his owne feruants to a confpiracy : the confpi-racy was detected, and the traytors had the reward of their treafon. *Innocentius* who could not reft till he had done fome Pontificall exploit againft the life of this Prince, ftirred vp the Princes of Germany to thruft downe *Fredericke*, and to fet vp another : firft was fet vp *Henry* Lantgraue of Thuringia; this

Pet. de Vineis l. 2. Ep. 10. & 20 Cufpinian. vit. Fred. 2.

Anno 1247.

man befieging Vlmes was. wounded by the fhot of an Arrow, and fhortly after refigned both his life and the Empire. After this was *William* Earle of Holland fet vp : this man was flaine in the warres which he had gaged againft the Frifians : neither of thefe faith *Naucler*, were numbred among the Emperours. At laft after fo many fecret traps laid for the life of this Prince, (behold the end of the Popes malice, where ftrength faileth)the Emperour was deftroyed by poifon.

King Iohn of England.

124: THe King of England fped no better then others, for by this vnbridled power of vfurped Iurifdicti-on King *Iohn* with the whole Kingdome was brought into great trouble and perplexity: thefe troubles grew vpon a quar-rell of Election betweene the Monkes of Canterbury, and the Suffraganes, in the feuenth yeare of King *Iohn* : for after the death of *Hubert* Archbifhoppe of Canterbury, the Monkes without the knowledge of the King, or refpect of the Suffra-ganes, chofe *Reynold* the Subpriour of the houfe, to be Arch-bifhoppe,who fecretly went to Rome to haue this his electi-on confirmed by the Pope:but ftay was made at Rome,becaufe he fhewed not Letters commendatory from the King.   The Monkes perceiuing that without thofe letters commendatory, they could not proceede,made requeft to the King that they might chufe another whom the King might commend:this the King liked well, and commended *Iohn Gray* the Bifhoppe of Norwich,being his Chaplaine, and Prefident of his Counfell (as *Hollinfhed* faith,but *Mat. Paris* whom he cyteth, hath not fo much)The Monkes gladly obeyed the Kings requeft, and made choife of this man : but the Pope refufing both, thruft vpon them *Stephen Langton*, commanding and compelling fo many of thofe Monkes of that Couent, as were then at Rome, to chufe him : the King was herewith much moued, becaufe *Stephen Langton* was brought vp vnder the French King, and bound to him : betweene whom and King *Iohn* there was at that time much warre and diffention, wherefore the King ba-nifhed nished the Monkes that had chosen *Stephen*, and wrote to the Pope, that he had no reason to admit *Stephen* to such a place in his Kingdome, a man promoted by the French King, and at his commaund. This contention continuing, the Pope sent to the Bishoppes of England, commaunding them to put the King and his land vnder the sentence of interdiction, denouncing him and his land accursed. The Bishoppes to whom the Pope wrote (being by this time become the Popes subiects and seruants and not the Kings, which is the end which the Pope seeketh by his Iurisdiction) denounced the interdiction, and then fledde to Rome : King *Iohn* seeing many fall from his obedience to the obedience of the Pope, drewe his people to an Oath of Alleageance, After this came *Pandulph* Legat from the Pope, who after that he had beene here a while, was commaunded by the Pope to repaire to the French King, there with *Stephen Langton* to take Councell, and to stirre vp the French to make warres vpon King *Iohn*. Thus King *Iohn* was depriued of his Gouernement, his subiects absolued from their Alleageance, by which practise many reuolted from him; so that he was left weake; and when the Pope had thus weakned him, then he set vp the French King in armes against him. The issue was this : The King circumuented by these practises of the Pope and oppressed, being also bereaued of all helpe, was forced to deliuer his Crowne to *Pandulph*, and receiued it from him againe, as from the Popes hands. And thus was *Stephen Langton* made Archbishoppe : this was done in the fifteenth yeare of King *Iohn*. *An. Dom.* 1213.

The Earle of Tholous.

125.   WHen *Frederick* the second liued, so persecuted by the Pope, as we haue declared : a new and strange generation rose vp of a suddaine, neuer seene in the world before, starting vp like those armed Souldiers, which the Poets faine to haue sprung vp suddenly of the Serpents teeth being sowed by *Cadmus*. Such a serpentine generation of Friars were newly hatched at this time : the first founders of them
were

were *Francis* and *Dominick*. For the Popes hauing a purpose to raise themselues aboue the Church, and aboue Kings and Emperours; as both by their profession and claime in the Canon Law, and by their practise was apparant; and for this purpose thundring out their excommunications vpon euery occasion, practising this power in deposing Princes: found themselues much crossed in these courses by Bishops, and especially by the Bishops of Germany; who stood out for a long time faithfull in the Church, and couragious against the Popes tyranny. *Auentinus* giueth many testimonies of the courage of the German Bishops (as else-where also we haue obserued of the English Bishops) for he writing of the times of *Frederick* the second, the Bishops then saith he, were not as now they are addict to the seruice of the Pope, giuen to idlenesse and pleasure, but learned, industrious, louing Christ, and declaring their loue by feeding their flockes diligently. These were not for the Popes purpose. For in diuers Synodes they censured the Popes folly and ambition freely, and withstood his tyrannie. Then was the Church so gouerned by Bishops, all matters so iudged and determined, that the Pope might aduise, but hee could not by authority attempt any thing in the Prouince of any Bishop: thinges being guided by truth, law, the iudgement of che wiseft and beft learned in the Prouince; and by the Councel and common consent of the Clergy of that Prouince. Who had reason to know the estate of their Church and Prouince, better then the Pope, or any stranger could doe. This godly order in the Church, the Pope had a purpose to confound: to oppresse the Bishops authority, and to draw all power to himselfe. *Hoc institutum* (to vse the words of *Auentinus*) *tollere & antiquare, Episcoporum autoritatem Labefactare, ad vnius cuncta potestatem redigere complacitum est.*

126. This being the purpose of Popes: for the better effecting of it, it was thought fit & expedient to raise vp new Sects of Friars, which might be wholly at the deuotion and direction of the Pope; to dissolue the discipline of the Church; to mollifie and corrupt the auncient rigour of Bishops, to alter the auncient doctrines, and bend them to the Popes purposes: and to
be

be refolute and defperate Minifters for eftablifhing the Popes authority and Iurifdiction ouer Kings; though it were to the wrack and common difordering of Chriftendome. For thefe purpofes were Friars eftablifhed at this time. And they wrought effectually to thefe ends. For the grauity, integrity, true honor, courage, conftancy, and reputation of Bifhops was neuer vtterly ouerthrowne, till Friars became Bifhoppes, then came thefe corruptions into Bifhops Courts. Then and neuer before, came in thefe fordidous cenfures to punifh finne with pecuniary mulcts in Bifhops Courts, as *Iohn Wiclif* doth witneffe, then and by them crept in the great corruptions of doctrine. And becaufe when the Pope had excommunicated and depofed Princes, the Bifhops in former times were not onely cold in executing the Popes fury, but fometimes withftoode thofe attempts as new, rafh, and bloudy: the Friars were created to bee the firebrandes of Chriftendome for all the Popes furious enterprifes.

127. The firft feruice which the Friars did performe to the Pope, was in the execution of his excommunication againft the Earle of Tholoufe. The manner thereof by *Mathew Paris*, and other Writers, is defcribed thus. *Raimundus* Earle of Tholoufe was much enuied by the Pope, for fauouring them who then were called *Albigenfes*. The Pope without examination of his caufe, without iudiciall proceeding againft the Earle, excommunicated him, and gaue his lands to *Simon Montford*. Which gift when *Simon* claimed in a parly before the Popes Legate: the Earle defended his right, and entreated the Cardinall the Popes Legat, to come to his Cities. And if hee found any that held any erroneous point of doctrine, he promifed it fhould be reformed. And heerein the Earle promifed his beft helpe and affiftance to the Cardinall. So confident was the Earle, knowing that no errour in doctrine could be found in his people, knowing alfo that the quarrell was not then for doctrine, but onely for Iurifdiction. And this thing the Cardinall well vnderftanding, would not make any examination of their Doctrines. Onely it was concluded, that the Earle and his people muft be vndone, and no other agreement might be admitted but this:

The Earle of Tholous.

Simon Montford Earle of Leifter, when peace was concluded betweene *Henry* the third King of England & the Barons, fledde from England to France, and put himfelfe in the feruice of the French King. *Fabian. Anno 1245.*

that

that the Earle muſt depart from his inheritance, and ſuffer his people to be at the Popes pleaſure. The Legat hauing a purpoſe to raiſe great ſummes of money through Fraunce for this ſeruice, applied that buſineſſe, and in the meane time this new generation of Friars were ſent and diſperſed in euery corner of France, to incite men tō take the Croſſe, and fight againſt the Albigenſes.

128. But eſpecially and aboue all other the new ſtart-vp S. *Dominick* was a man of great vſe & imployment in this ſeruice. He went like a fire-brand through France, and ſtirred vp both Princes and people to take the Croſſe, and to fight againſt the Earle and his people, as againſt Turks & Saracines. The French King himſelfe tooke the Croſſe. The King and the Cardinall raiſed an Army of fifty thouſand fighting men beſides Wagganers, Victualers, &c. And came before Auinion the Earles chiefe City. In the ſiege there were two and twenty thouſand of French ſlaine and drowned; the Citizens valiantly defending the City. In the meane time King *Philip* died, and King *Lewes* who ſucceeded him, died alſo in the Camp before Auinion. The Cardinall perceiuing that the City was ſo well defended, that all the loſſe fell on the beſiegers; ſeeing that by direct meanes he could not preuaile: he put of the Lyons skinne, and put on the skinne of the Fox, and ſo preuailed by falſhood in the end. For he tooke a ſolemne Oath, that if the people would let him in, and the Biſhops who were with him: they would onely examine them of their faith and Religion, and would attempt no other thing. The people being well aſſured, that for matters of faith and Religion, nothing could be found againſt them: aſſented to the motion of the Cardinall. Whereupon the gates were ſet open to the Cardinall, and ſo the City was betrayed. For with the Cardinall and Biſhops, the French Souldiers thruſt in, and tooke the City. By this meanes was Auinion brought firſt vnder the Popes yoake; and made afterward the chiefe City of his reſidence for a time. For *Clement* the fift in the yeare one thouſand three hundred and fiue, tranſlated the Popes ſeate to Auinion from Rome: where it remained for the ſpace of threeſcore and fourteene yeares.

129. Though

129. Though afterward the Earle repairing his Armie gaue the French diuers ouerthrowes, yet could he neuer recouer this great losse. *Fasciculus Temporum* witnesseth, that because the Albigenses were ouerthrowne by them that bare the Crosse, therefore the Pope instituted a new Order of Friars, called *Cruciferi*. In all this action the industry and valour of *Dominick* is much celebrated by the Stories of this time: the whole praise of this ouerthrow is attributed to him: Of him *Platina* witnesseth thus much; *Quos (Albingenses) Dominicus mira celeritate compescuit, adiuuante etiam Simone Montiforti: non enim disputationibus verum armis opus fuit, adeo inoleuerat tanta haeresis.* That is, *Dominick* did tame the Albingenses in a maruellous short time, by meanes of the Armie which *Simon Montford* brought: For that heresie was so rooted, that there was no vse of Disputation, but of armed prouision against them. Then we see that the first Order and Institution of Friars, was founded in blood and treacherous practises, against the State of Princes that withstood the Popes Iurisdiction. And herein the Popes end may appeare in aduancing Friars, not by disputations to search out a truth, but by force and armes to oppresse the Popes aduersaries, and so to fill Christendome full of blood and rebellions.

Platin. Innocent.
3.

Conradus and Mamphred Kings of Sicily.

130. THe next Prince that felt the stroake of the Popes Thunderbolt, was *Mamphred* King of Sicily: Sicily with Naples being the auncient right of the Empire; the Popes hauing gotten so much of that which before was the Emperours, were desirous to haue this also to helpe the patrimonie of poore Saint *Peter.* After the fall of the Empire, the Moores had taken Apulia and Sicily, and held those landes by force, vntill one *Robert Guiscard* comming out of Fraunce with an Army, draue out the Moores, and first wonne the Dominion of Apulia, and after in like sort of Sicily. The Kingdome of Sicily he gaue to his brother *Roger: Roger* left it to *William.* These men possessed it by the right of Conquest, driuing thence the

barians and Infidels : But the Pope, hauing no other Title , but becaufe he muft fucceede the Emperor in Italy ; firft excommunicated and depofed *William*. After this *Otho* the fourth , whom the Pope raifed vp in rebellion againft *Philip* , got the Dominion of Sicily : for which hee was alfo excommunicated by the Pope, and depofed. After him *Conradus* fonne to *Frederic* the fecond obtained the Kingdome of Sicily, and Apulia : for which Pope *Innocent* the fourth depofed him from the Empire, and fet vp *Guilliam*, Lantgraue of Thuring, commanding the Princes to make choice of him. *Conrad* being excommunicate and depofed, maintained his right by ftrength of armes, but was fecretly taken away by the practife of poifon. This was fuppofed to be the practife of *Mamphred*.

131. *Mamphred* the baftard fonne of *Fredericke* the fecond, tooke and held poffeffion of thefe Kingdomes after the death of *Conradus*. This man was alfo excommunicated by the Pope, and depofed : the Pope feeking alwaies to bring this Kingdome vnder the obedience of the Church of Rome. Pope *Vrban* the fourth, a French-man borne , finding his owne power too weake to effect this Maftery ouer Sicily and Apulia , gaue thefe Kingdomes (which neuer were his to giue) to *Charles* brother to the French King *Lewes* the ninth, who was called S. *Lewes* : This was the beginning of thofe troubles , which afterward brought fo great warres and bloud-fhed, and thereby wel-nigh the vtter ruine of Italy.

Anno 1263.

Charles King of Sicily, and Conradinus.

132. FOR *Charles* comming with an Army into Italy, at the Popes motion , ioyning battell with *Mamphred*, ouerthrew him , and flew him in battell neare to Beneuentum. Pope *Clement* the fourth fucceeding *Vrban* the fourth, vnderftanding that after the death of *Mamphred Conradinus* the fonne of *Conradus*, then but yong, prepared forces in Germany to recouer his inheritance of Sicily : made *Charles* brother to the French King the Vicar of the Empire to giue him ftrength againft *Conradinus* ; and wrote Letters to all Chriftians,

ans, forbidding all men to write to *Conradinus* as to the King
of Sicily. And to the Princes of Germany hee wrote likewise,
forbidding them vnder the terrible paine of excommunication
to chuse *Conradinus* Emperour : by which meanes the Empire
was without a Soueraigne Magistrate for the space of two and
twenty yeares : In which time *Alphonsus* King of Spaine, and
Richard Earle of Cornewall brother to *Henry* the third King of
England contended for the Empire. These had the titles of the
Emperour bestowed vpon them by their friends, but the Emperour was not placed till *Rodolph* Count of Habspurge was
chosen. In the meane time *Charles* grew strong in Italy, being
made by the Pope, Vicar generall of the Empire.

133. When *Conradinus* vnderstood these practises of the Pope
against him, perceiuing that the Popes had a resolution to roote
out the seede, and vtterly to extinguish the blood of *Frederic*, he
wrote a lamentable Epistle, deploring his owne fortunes, and
the Popes iniquities. [*Innocent* the fourth (saith he) hath o-
uerthrowne me an innocent man : for *Conradus* my father, King
of Sicily left me yong and tender in the custody of the Church :
then Pope *Innocentius* pretending my wealth, professing himselfe a trusty Tutor, inuaded the whole Kingdome, and when
once he had gotten the possession thereof, he sought vnmercifully to extinguish my name and blood, deuiding my lands and
Countries, and distributing the same among his owne kinsemen
and Nephewes. After his death *Alexander* succeeding, inuited others into the possession of that Kingdom, excluding me.
After his death *Vrbanus* dealt very inurbanely : for hee drewe
Mamphred in, excluding my selfe the true heyre. The same
Pope disanulling that match with *Mamphred*, drew *Charles* to
vndertake the businesse against my selfe. After his death *Clement* vsed all inclemency against me, setting vp another King :
and not content herewith, thundreth out his Processes against
me, thinking it a small matter that against God and against
Iustice, he hath robbed me of my Kingdome ; vnlesse he proceede also to take the title from me. Last of all, he hath established *Charles* Vicar of the Empire to preiudice and defeat me by
all meanes.] Thus doth he complaine : by which complaint we
may

Epist. Conradin. apud Nauslerũ Generat. 43.

Quem cum
Pontifex tranfe-
untem vidiſſet,
prophetica voce
vſus,adoleſcens
dixit,hic tan-
quam victimam
ad cædem duci-
tur.Naucler.

may vnderſtand ſomewhat of the Popes purpoſes. *Conradinus* gathered an Army,and came into Italy: the Pope as he paſſed by (as ſome doe witneſſe) did propheſie his death, which was not hard for him to doe, when hee had ſo ſtrongly prepared the meanes thereof : *Conradinus* therefore was ouerthrowne by *Charles* : and ſo was all the bloud of *Frederick*. And thus was that noble line of the Dukes of Sueuia vtterly extinguiſhed.

134. When *Charles* had at the Popes ſuggeſtion made this diſtruction in the houſe of Sueuia: the Popes not knowing how to liue in peace and quietneſſe, began to turn their malice vpon *Charles*. And firſt Pope *Nicholas* the third , onely fearing that *Charles* ſhould be too great in Italy, hauing no quarrell againſt him, tooke from him the office of Deputy of Hetruria : preten-ding that, *Rodolph* Emperour was therewith ſo much offended, that vnleſſe *Charles* would deliuer vp into his handes that re-giment, he would not vndertake the iourney to the holy land, ſeeing that place belonged to the Emperour by right. But when the Pope had gotten this both from the Emperor & from *Charles*, together with *Flaminia, Bononia,* the Exarch of Rauen-na : he kept all, ſaith *Platina,* in his owne cuſtody, and thither he

Platin.Nichol.3.
Naucl.gener.43

ſent his Nephew. Thus muſt all the world be troubled that principalities may bee procured to the Popes baſtards. This Pope, ſaith *Platina,* had a deſire to create two Kings in Italy of the Vrſini : one of Hetruria againſt the French forces now pla-ced in Sicily and Naples : the other to be King of Lumbards a-gainſt the Germanes and imperiall forces. But firſt for the more ſpeedy ouerthrow of *Charles* , whom the former Popes had drawen into Italy as into a trap , he conſpired againſt him, labouring by all his power to throw him out; and therefore gaue his Kingdomes to *Peter* King of Arragon. The great of-fence between Pope *Nicholas* and *Charles* grew (ſaith *Naucler*) *quia Carolus aſſentiri noluit vt ſuus conſanguineus contraheret cum conſanguineis Pontificis.* [*Charles* would not agree, that his kin-red ſhould match with the Popes kinred.]

Peter

Peter King of Aragon.

135. **P**Eter King of Aragon, being thus drawne in, to the quarrell of Sicily by Pope *Nicholas* the third, (For faith *Naucler* the Pope, perswaded *Peter* to take the Kingdom of Sicily in the right of his wife *Conſtance*, who was the daughter of *Mamphred*, and Niece to *Conradinus*) brought an Army into Sicily and inuaded the Kingdome. But *Martin* the fourth, who ſucceeded Pope *Nicholas*, excommunicated *Peter*, depoſed him, depriuing him alſo of the Kingdome of Aragon. Thus were theſe Princes firſt drawne into bloudy wars by the Popes, who ſometimes inuited them, and laughed vpon them as louing friends, ſometimes plunged them in bloud as taking a delite in their deſtruction. Let the Princes of Chriſtendom once awake and conſider the ſauage nature of this wilde beaſt, that is not onely drunk with the bloud of Saints, but fed alſo fat with the bloud of Princes. Thus the Popes filled all Chriſtendome full of bloud with their excommunications. Are theſe Chriſts Vicars? are theſe the cenſures of Chriſtes Church? *Martin* then excommunicated *Peter*, gaue his Kingdome to ſuch as would inuade it, abſolued his Subiects from their faith & alleageance, *Platin. Mart.4.* drew thoſe that had taken the Croſſe for the warres of Ieruſalem, to fight againſt *Peter*. And when *Martin* was dead, *Honorius* the fourth did redouble his curſes vpon *Peter*. After all theſe curſes, and ſo much bloud and warres procured by the Popes to the vexation of Chriſtendome, yet *Peter* maintained his chalenge and held thoſe Kingdomes.

Philip the French King.

136. **B**Onface the eight, pretending to aduance the holy warres, (for this was not the leaſt pollicy of that Sea to ſend Princes abroad, that in the meane time they might ſuck their Kingdomes, and draw the ſinewes thereof to Rome) for this purpoſe ſent the Biſhop of Ariminum to *Philip* the faire, the French King. The Biſhop hauing vſed all perſwaſions hee

could

could by faire meanes , and finding the King nothing mooued with all that he alleadged,from perswasions hee fell to threatnings. The King being much offended at his threatnings : and because as some adde,the Bishoppe had rauished an ingenuous maid,threw the Bishoppe in prison : Others say he apprehended the Bishoppe , *Quod esset paterinus hæreticus.* Whatsoeuer the cause was of the Kings offence,*Boniface* was highly displeased,and sent the Archdeacon of Narbon,to command the King to acknowledge that he held his Kingdome of the Church of Rome,or else to denounce the Anathema against him, and obsolue all French men from their Oath of Alleageance. When the Archdeacon arriued at Paris,the King would not permit his Bulles to be published. The Popes letters were taken from him,and burned with fire.The King also vnderstanding the end of the Popes earnest motion for his iourney to Ierusalem, to be that in his absence he might draw great treasures out of France to Rome; published an Edict wherein it was made vnlawfull for any to depart out of France to Rome , or thither to carry money. Whereupon *Boniface* cursed *Philip* to the fourth generation,absolued his Nobles,and gaue his Kingdome to *Albert* the Emperour , inuesting *Albert* by his letters into the Kingdome of France : but *Albert* protested that he would not stirre against the King , vnlesse hee might haue that Kingdome confirmed to him and to his heyres. No,quoth the Pope, that may not be as long as *Iezebell* liueth : meaning *Elizabeth* wife to *Albert*,a woman of great fame and honour, whom he hated for no other cause,but for that her brethren and aunceſtors had done valiantly against the Sea of Rome.

137. Against this furious attempt of *Boniface* , *Philip* the French King in an Assembly at Paris appealed from the Pope to a generall Councell : this appeale is diuersly reported: All agree that he appealed from the Pope. *Platina* confoundeth the Narration thus : *Ad sedem Apostolicam tum, vt ipse dicebat , vacantem futurumque Concilium appellauit.* That is, [He appealed to the Sea Apoſtolicke then vacant as he said,and to a Councell which should after this be held.] *Naucler* deliuereth it thus : *Rex Franciæ congregari fecit Paritijs omnes Prælatos Franciæ,nec*

non

non Barones,& facto Concilio,pro sui iustificatione appellauit ab il-
la sentētia se excusando, & contra Bonifacium inuehendo,&c. That
is[The French King gathered a Councell at Paris of Prelates
and Barons,and for his owne iustification hee appealed from
that sentence,excusing himself,& inueighing againſt *Boniface.*]
This man then hath nothing of any appellation to the emptie
Sea : but the appellation was as diuers were about these times,
from the Pope to a generall Councell : this appeale was sent
by *Sarra Columna* a Nobleman of Rome , and one *Nogarelius* a
French Knight,a man faithfull to the King. The pretence was
diuulged that they should goe to publish the Kings appeale a- *Naucl.gener.44.*
gainſt the Popes Decree,but *Sarra* hauing another secret pur- *Plat.Bonif.8.*
pose came into Italy in the habite of a seruant : gathered close-
ly by the helpe of his friends a band of souldiers,and with great
secresie and silence came to Anagnia where the Pope lodged
then in his fathers house. *Sarra* breaking vp the doores,tooke
Boniface in bed,bound him,and brought him to Rome; where
after a few daies in great sorrow and desperation , he ended his
wretched life. *Ranulphus* saith,that he was set vpon an Horse
vnbridled,with his face turned to the horse taile,and so running *Polychron.l.7.*
to and fro,was famished with hunger , and died like a Dogge : *cap.39.*
as the common saying was of him, that he entred like a Foxe ,
raigned like a Lion, and died like a Dogge. It may be truely
said of all the Popes that liued since the yeare of Chriſt one
thousand,which *Naucler* obserueth of this Pope : *Imperatori-*
bus,Regibus,Principibus,nationibusque terrorem potius quam reli-
gionem inijcere conabatur,dare regna & auferre pro arbitrio, &c.
[He sought not so much to plant Religion, as terrour in Emperours,Kings,Princes and nations : to giue and take away kingdomes at his pleasure.] Where hee doth truely describe the
fruite of the Popes excommunications : it is not for planting of
Religion, but for ſtriking a terrour in Princes , and breeding a
confusion in the world : and therfore it is no censure of Chriſts
Church ; because all these censures plant Religion without confusion of Princes , and disordering of the world.

    138. Finding in Story two Epiſtles , one from *Boniface* to
         this

this *Philip*, the other from *Philip* to *Boniface*, I thought good to set them downe, they are but short.

Boniface feruant of Gods feruants, to *Philip* the
French King: feare God and keepe
his commandements.

WEe will haue you to vnderſtand, that you are ſubieCt to vs, both in ſpirituall and temporall affaires: No collation of Beneſices or Prebends belongeth to you: and if you haue the vacation of any, reſcrue the fruits thereof to the ſucceſſours: if you haue made any collation, we iudge that ſuch ſhall be of no validity that are to come, and thoſe that are paſt we reuoke: reputing all Hereticks that thinke otherwiſe. Dated at Lateran, &c. The anſwere was thus returned:

Philip by the grace of God, King of France, to *Boniface* bearing himſelfe as Pope, health
little or none at all.

Fatuitas veſtra. YOur ſingular fooleſhip may vnderſtand, that in temporall affaires we are ſubieCt to none: that the collation of Churches and Prebends perteineth to vs by royall prerogatiue, and the fruits thereof during the Vacation: that the collation already made, or hereafter to bee made, are of iuſt force and validity; and that we will defend the poſſeſſours thereof againſt all men: reputing all fooliſh and madde men that thinke otherwiſe.

Henry

Henry the feuenth.

139. **H**Enry the feuenth Emperor was much fauoured at the first by *Clement* 5. Pope, for that *Clement* was highly offended with *Philip* the French King, who then fought the Empire : the hatred of *Philip* drew fauour to *Henry*; but as paſſion ruled the Pope, fo pride ouer-ruled the paſſion, and turned this fauour into greater hatred : for when *Henry* came to order the State of Italy, at that time greeuouſly troubled and vexed for want of the Emperors preſence, and had twiſe ouerthrown *Rupert*(or as ſome call him *Robert*) King of Sicily, the fon of *Charles* (whence grewe a new vexation of Italy betweene theſe two Princes, and, as *Platina* faith, the blame was laid vpon *Clement*, who had called the Emperour with an Armie into Italy) hee came to Rome for the Emperiall Crowne, as *Clement* had inuited him thereto. But becauſe the Popes muſt bee alwaies like themſelues, *Clement* firſt denied his Coronation, afterward hee conſented vpon condition, that *Henry* ſhould take an Oath of Alleageance to the Pope. This the Emperour refuſed as being a thing ſtrange, and without example. Heere is deſcried an other end of theſe excommunications : the Popes purpoſe to bring Kings and Emperours vnder them in reſpect of temporall Iuriſdiction, therefore they required of Emperours an Oath of Alleageance. *Clement* the fift in one of his Canons, maketh a long proceſſe to proue that *Henry* tooke an Oath of Alleageance, and that ſuch an Oath is due to the Pope from Emperours.

140. *Clement* purſuing his hatred againſt *Henry*, aduanced the Title of *Robert* to Sicily, whom the Emperour had by an ordinary proceſſe of law condemned for Treaſon, and declared an enemy to the Empire. The Popes exception againſt *Henry* was, that the Kingdome of Sicily belonged not to the Empire; but he alleaged, faith *Platina*, that it was the Popes right to beſtow the Kingdome of Sicily on this ſide and beyond Pharus , vpon whom he pleaſed, or to take it from whom hee would : hence began great ſtirres to grow betweene the Pope and Emperor :

Anno 1038.

Platin. Clem. 7.

Clem. de ſent. & re iudic. paſtoralis.

The Emperour pursuing his right, brought an Armie into Italy; and comming to Bonauentum, his purpose was there to rest himselfe a few daies, and to betake himselfe to prayer and fasting, and other good workes, that his lawfull labours and purposes might be blessed of God, intending on the feast of the assumption to take the holy Sacrament. The Bishoppe of Trent his Confessour was absent at that time, being sent to Pope *Clement* : but there was one sent backe in his roome a Iacobin Friar of S. *Dominicks* Order, suborned for to worke a feate : this man at that time administring the Sacrament, hauing mingled Adamantin dust, which is thought to be the strongest poyson, in the flower whereof the Eucharist was made, gaue it so prepared to the Emperour : the poyson was so strong, that the Emperour presently perceiued the danger; and when the Masse was ended, he called the Friar, and said to him; O Sir, depart quickly, for if my seruants shall knowe what a mischiefe you haue done vpon me, you should die a miserable death: but God forgiue you. And so the Friar escaped, and the Emperour died.

Lodouicus Bauarus.

141.   AFter the death of *Henry* the seuenth, the Princes Electors were at variance for a successour : some were for *Frederike* Duke of Austria, others for *Lodouich* Duke of Bauare : *Iohn* the two and twentieth Pope, apprehended the occasion to dash one of these Princes against the other. First he reiected *Fredericke* with great contumely ; for when *Fredericke* had sent a Bishoppe to moue the Pope to ratifie his Election, and the Bishoppe eloquently declared the Nobility of *Fredericke*, and his valiant Progenitours, vsing that speech; *Fortes creantur fortibus & bonis* : the Pope with Pontificall arrogancy, answered, that *Solomon* the wisest man that euer was, begot a most foolish sonne. Against *Lodouicke* likewise hee pretended a quarrel, for that he tooke more vpon him then belonged to his place : and sometimes seeming to fauour the one, and sometimes the other, at last he promised *Fredericke* that hee
would

Anno 1313.

Cuspinian. Nausler. Plat.

Naucl. gener. 45

would make him Emperour, if hee would bring an Army into Italy to reueng him of *Maphæus* and of his sonnes called Vicounts. By this means great warres were raised vp in Italy, and in Germany: the two Princes *Lodouicke* and *Fredericke* met also in a battell fought from Sunne rising to Sunne setting, wherein *Lodouicke* had the victory; *Fredericke* was taken prisoner.

142. Whereupon Pope *Iohn* without lawfull processe, excommunicated *Lodouicke* in his Consistory at Auinion, and declared him to be schismaticall, hereticall, and rebellious against the Church; and depriued not onely *Fredericke* himselfe of all his Dominions as much as in him lay, but depriued also all Clerkes that should giue him councell or aide. Against this excommunication the Emperour appealed: the forme of which Appellation *is* to be well obserued; for albeit some write that he appealed from the Pope mis-informed, to the Pope truly informed, and to a generall Councell; yet *this* is but the relation of such as fauoured the Popes Iurisdiction, thinking that no appeale could be made from the Pope simply: And therefore no relation of others can satisfie vs in this point so well, as the very authenticke writ of *Lodouicke* himselfe, wherein hee declareth his appeale: which writ or declaration is set downe at large in *Naucler*, from whence I would obserue some things which the Emperour declareth concerning the Popes Iurisdiction; for therein he toucheth many points of his Iurisdiction, and taketh exception against such partes of Iurisdiction which the Pope claimed, partly in preiudice of the temporall Magistrate, partly in preiudice of the Church. For the question of Iurisdiction was better studied by learned men in the time of this Emperor, then euer it was since.

143. *Lodouick* then vnderstanding by men of greate learning in humane and diuine lawes, which that age brought forth, that the Pope had incroached vpon the right of temporall Princes, and vpon the Iurisdiction of the Church: and that hee ought to be gouerned in temporall affaires by the Emperour, in spirituall affaires by the Church, appealed from the Pope to a generall Councel, and to the Catholicke Church: thus the Emperour

perour

perour declareth his appeale ; *appellauimus ad futurum generale Concilium, & ad ſanctam Catholicam Eccleſiam.* This was done in an Aſſembly held at Franckfort , publiſhed as a Decree a-gainſt the Proceſſes of *Iohn* the two and twentieth : which De-cree though it be ſomewhat large, yet becauſe it conteineth the iuſt claime of the temporall Magiſtrate , againſt the pretended Iuriſdiction of the Pope, I muſt draw at leaſt the ſumme of it to giue ſome ſatisfaction to the Reader : He declareth the Popes claime, for he claimed that hee had temporall Iuriſdiction ouer Princes : that the imperiall power was from the Pope : that he that is choſen King of the Romanes hath no Iuriſdiction by his ſole Election vntill he be annointed, conſecrated and crowned : that in temporall matters the Pope hath a fulneſſe of power. This was firſt the Popes claime ; whereunto the Emperour an-ſwereth[That this ſtandeth againſt the auncient Canons of the Church, againſt law, and againſt reaſon.] Hee cyteth for this diuers Canons, to proue that the Emperour hath not his pow-er from the Pope , but from God alone. Againſt each of the foreſaid Poſitions he cyteth diuers Canons out of the Decrete of *Gratian.* Secondly, Pope *Iohn* the two and twentieth obie-cted againſt the Emperour, that hee the ſaid Pope had annihi-lated the Emperours Election ; and that therefore the Emperor had no right to adminiſter the imperiall lawes, but that this ad-miniſtration belonged by right to the Pope. To this the Em-perour anſwereth : [That this ſtandeth againſt the liberties of the Empire, and againſt the liberties of them that are Electors, againſt the lawes and liberties of all the Princes and ſubiects of Germany.]

144. And whereas thirdly the Pope obiecteth, that he hath excommunicated all that ſhall adhære, performe obedience and reuerence to the Emperour , and ſaith that the iudgement of the Paſtor, whether it be iuſt or vniuſt is to be obſerued. To this the Emperor anſwereth[That theſe denunciations are of none effect : for it is a rule, that if a Prelat in commaunding or for-bidding, ſhall not keepe the forme preſcribed by the Canons, they who diſobey him, doe not incurre the ſentence of excom-munication. Now the Canons, and the Church doe take from

the

the Pope power in temporalities, which power *Iohn* the two and twentieth vsurpeth: this is one of those cases wherein the sentence of a Prelat is not to be feared.   Another reason is, because by law that sentence is of no force, where there is an expresse errour in the sentence: as if a subiect should be commanded not to obey his Superiour: or if something should be commaunded againft God, or againft holy Scripture.   Now it is manifest that *Iohn* the two and twentieth hath commaunded the subiects of the Empire, not to obey vs, whom they are bound to obey by the lawes of God and man.   Another reason is, because it is a thing confessed, that the sentence which is giuen after a lawfull appeale, is void and of no strength: but it is well knowne that from *Iohn* the two and twentieth, and his Processes againft God, and iuftice, we appealed to a generall Councell, and to the holy Catholicke Church: which appellation was brought to the knowledge of the said *Iohn* before he published Excommunication againft them that fauour vs.]

145. If it be said the Pope hath no Superiour, and therefore no man may appeale from him.   To this the Emperour answereth thus: [It is manifest by the Catholicke doctrine, that the Pope in matters of faith is subiect to Councels. 1 6. *diff. ficut in tex. & in Gloff. 25.q.2. funt quidam.* 1 9. *di. Anaftafius. 40. di. Si Papa.*   Moreouer in matters of diuine right, a Councell is aboue the Pope.   Thus then we haue appealed to a Superiour, that is to a generall Councell, againft our aduerfaries who impugne vs, the Empire, the Catholicke faith, which the holy Church of Rome handleth.] This is the fumme of that Decree which the Emperour publifhed againft the Pope: it was dated at Franckfort the eighth of Auguft, *Anno* one thousand three hundred thirty and eight.   The processe of this worthy Prince giueth vs occafion to confider some things which declare the fenfe, iudgement and Religion of the Church of Rome at this time. By the Church of Rome I vnderftand thefe Wefterne parts of Chriftendome, for fo I find it tearmed heere, and other-where feparate and diftinct from the Pope.

146. For firft by this appeale from the Pope to a generall Councell, we finde that it was the iudgement and common receiued

ceiued sentence of that age, that a general Councel is aboue the Pope, may iudge the Pope, censure and depose him: this is here declared and confirmed : this was not onely the doctrine of the Church then, but long after it continued, and was neuer denied by the Church of Rome, before the Councell of Trent , as hereafter we shall declare. Moreouer we finde a distinction obserued by the learned men that held this Assembly : that is by the Prelates of the Empire, for so the Decree runneth, *De concilio ac assensu Prælatorum omnium, &c.* And many other learned men of Christendome, yea many Friars which were here assembled, especially the Minorites , who were then oppressed by the Pope) The distinction, I say, betweene the Pope and his flatterers on the one side, and the Church of Rome on the other side. For the Emperour appealeth from the Pope, to the Church: and this was a practise vsed by diuers, as hereafter we shall obserue. Then the Pope and his flatterers did not represent the Church of Rome , as now they pretend to doe. Againe wee obserue that the Emperour being defamed for heresie and appealing to a generall Councell, as he denieth the Pope to be his Iudge, so he refuseth not to be iudged by the Church : for as S. *Ambrose* saith, *Imperator intra Ecclesiam , non supra Ecclesiam est.* Then

Ora..in Auxent. the authority of the Church bindeth the greatest members thereof, euen Kings and Emperours. If our aduersaries obiect against vs and our Church : why then doe you giue to the King the Title of supreame head or Gouernour of the Church? We answere, such obiections proceede from an obstinate and wilfull ignorance in mistaking of our doctrine. For when the question is of Iurisdiction externall coactiue , wee giue to the King the place of a supreame Iudge: but if the question bee of faith and Religion, we say the King is no Iudge, but to be iudged by the Church : as we see godly Princes haue beene , and namely this worthy Prince *Lodouicke,* who being accused of heresie by the Pope, appealeth to the Church.

147. Last of all we obserue in the sense and iudgement of this Emperour, and of the learned men that were assembled with him, that in the point of Iurisdiction no such thing is left to the Pope as he claimeth. For in matters of faith , the Iurisdiction

ction is in the Church, as here it is acknowledged: in matters of coactiue power the Iurisdiction is in the Emperor; as all these learned men did yeelde in this Councell, and after the Councell did maintaine by their writings. For wee finde the same trueth maintained by *William Ockham, Marsilius Patauinus , Michael Cæsina,* and many moe, who with great courage and learning did maintaine the Emperours Iurisdiction heerein against the Popes vsurpation. This wisedome and moderation of the Emperour in defending his right, not onely by force of Armes, but by learning and iudgement, moued the Pope who succeeded *Iohn* the two & twentieth; that is, *Benedict* the twelfth, in spite of malice to giue him many honorable testimonies: to promise to restore him by absolution againe to this place. But the Pope did but fraudulently put him off from day to day :which thing when the Emperour perceiued, he called a Diet of the Empire at Rensium, where he did with that wisedome , courtesie, and liberality binde the Princes Electours to him, that they tooke a solemne Oath to maintaine the liberties of the Empire, and decreede that all the processes of *Iohn* once Pope, against *Lodouick* were of no force : and that the Pope ought not to attempt such things against the Emperour, seeing their Iurisdictions were so much distinct.

148. *Clement* the sixth succeeded *Benedict* the twelfth : this *Clement* falling into deeper fits of rage against the Emperour, then his Predecessours had done , commaunded Letters to bee fixed vpon the Church doors, filled with threatnings and curses against *Lodouicke,* if within three daies he did not make satisfaction to God and the Church (by the Church vnderstanding himselfe) & vtterly desist fró administration of the Empire. When three daies were expired , hee pronounced him contumacious, and thundred out his excommunication. The Emperour sent his Ambassadours, crauing pardon, promising satisfaction for any thing he had done amisse to the vtmost of his power: whereupon the Pope prescribed him a forme of reconciliation : hard, shamefull, dishonourable; that he shall confesse against himselfe all heresies and errours : that hee shall relinquish the Empire, and commit himselfe, his children, & all his goods to the Popes

Cuspinian.
Naucler.

Hh   mercy.

mercy. This the Embassadours sealed and confirmed : But when this forme of reconciliation prescribed by the Pope, came to the Emperours sight, he sent copies thereof abroad to all the Princes : and presently called a Diet at Franckfort : the Princes iudged the presumption and pride of the Pope to be intollerable, and therefore reiected this prescribed forme of his , as being deuised to the bane and ruine of the Empire ; and promised the Emperour assured and faithfull aide , if he would maintaine the liberties of the Empire , as hee had done. The Pope like a Tyger disappointed of his prey, entred into a deeper conspiracy against *Lodouicke*, purposing an vtter extirpation of him and his posterity, as the Popes his predecessours had done before, to the house of Sueuia, exterminating all the seed and posterity of the *Frederickes*.

149. And therefore this *Clement* at Masse curseth *Frederick* againe, renueth all the processes of *Iohn* the two and twentieth against him, declareth him to be hereticall and schismaticall : deposeth him from the Empire, and commaundeth the Princes to proceede to a new Election. To effect his purpose the better, he remoueth *Henry de Wirtenberg* from the Archbishopricke of Mentz ; this man was deposed because he fauoured *Lodouick*, and in his place he set *Gerlac* his Chaplaine. *Gerlac* the newe Archbishoppe calleth the Princes to Rhenes : and to goe thorough with his businesse which the Pope had giuen him in charge, corrupted the Archbishoppe of Colon , and the Duke of Saxony with great summes of money, to consent to the Election of *Charles* sonne to the King of Bohemia. They did so : and *Charles* was elected at Rhenes : and afterward crowned at Bonna. But after this, when *Lodouicke* summoned the Princes of Germany to Spire, there was not one found in all the Cities of Rhene , Sueuia , Franconia that regarded the election of *Charles*, or the Popes processe. The administration of Mentz was by *Lodouicke* committed to another. After that *Lodouicke* had thus with great moderation and courage maintained his estate, against the Pope and *Charles*, so that his aduersaries had no hope to preuaile against him by force ; the next newes was, *Lodouicke* was of a sudden found dead. This is the singular lucke

Anno 1346.
Nauclgener. 45

Paralipom.
Vsperg. Au. 1346

luke of thofe Princes, that falling into the offence of the Pope, will not be ouercome by force. Some write that he was poyfoned as he was to goe on hunting, that by the agitation of his body, the poyfon might worke more effectually.

Charles the fourth.

150. AFter the death of *Lodouicke*, *Charles* the fourth, whom the Pope aduanced to the vtter ruine, not of *Lodouicke* only, but of that Empire, did by the inftinct of his Ghoftly father lay the Empire in the duft fo lowe, that it neuer rofe vp to any fuch height, as before him it held. At his Coronation the Pope bound him with an Oath neuer to come to Rome, nor to make longer abode in Italy then the Pope himfelfe thought good. Now to make *Charles* to wafte and confume the reuennues of the Empire, this cunning was vfed: diuers competitours of the Empire were fet vp againft him: to *Guntherus* one competitor hee gaue two and twenty thoufand Markes, and two imperiall Towns in Thuringia : to *Fredericke* Marqueffe of Mifna, tenne thoufand Markes. There were at Millain at this time, they who were called Vicounts, who grew great and practifed their tyranny, oppreffing the Cities of the Empire. The Pope defired that they fhould be repreffed, but fo that himfelfe might be aduanced: and therfore by the helpe of *Charles* he got many Cities out of their handes : *Charles* being thus drawne to dilapidate the reuennues of the Empire, dealt alfo fecretly with thefe Vicounts, to whom for a great fumme of money he fold Millain, and confirmed them in a perpetuall Office, to be Vicars of the Empire : after which time, thefe Vicounts rofe to a great Dominion in Italy. The Kingdome of Arles which *Otho* the firft had conferred vpon the Empire, hee deliuered to the French King for a great dinner at a Towne neere to Auinion. Sixteene Cities of Sueuia part of the Empire he fold to the neighbour Princes : Bopardia and Wefalia imperiall Cities, he morgaged to *Cuno* Archbifhoppe of Triers. *Lufatia* hee confirmed to the Kingdome of Bohemia for euer, corrupting the Archbifhoppe of Magdeburg for a

Cuffpinian.vita Guntheri.

Cuffpin.in vita Caroli.
Vicecomites.

Auentin.l.7.
Naucl.gener.46

H h 2   great

great summe of money to sell the right of his Church: for the Archbishop before that time, held Lusatia of the Empire. That *Wenceslaus* his sonne, a man giuen to idlenesse, ryot, and pleasure, might be chosen Emperour after him, he practised a newe example, promising to euery Electour an hundreth thousand Crownes: and wanting money to performe this promise, to some he morgaged the reuennues of the Empire : to the Palatine of Rhene he morgaged Cæsarea, Luthrea, Oppenheim, Odenheim, Ingolheim for an hundreth thousand crowns : By this meanes the Maiesty of the Empire was throwne so flatte on ground, that since it could neuer holde vp the head. This the Pope long sought, and at last by meanes of his vnblessed sonne *Charles* effected.

Naucl.gener.46
AEneas Siluius.
hist.Bohem.cap.
33.

Wenceslaus.

151.   AT this time began a schisme in the Church of Rome betweene *Vrban* the sixt, and *Clement* the seuenth. This was the greatest schisme, the most terrible, and longest that euer was in that Church : it held fiftie yeares, and could scarce be appeased by two generall Councels of Pisa and Constance. In this schisme *Wencestlaus* fauoured *Vrban* : in whose behalfe he sent his Ambassadours to *Clement*, whom *Clement* vsed without all clemency ; for in a sauage manner he tortured them with exquisit tortures. After this *Boniface* the ninth deuised a new practise to robbe the Churches of Christendome, imposing the vse of Annates vpon all Benefices : that whosoeuer obtained a Benefice, should pay one halfe years profite to the Pope : some say that *Iohn* the two and twentieth first deuised this robbery. Whosoeuer inuented it, the Popes like vnsatiable Harpyes deuising all meanes to bring confusion and misery vpon the Church, to satisfie the Horse-leach that will neuer be filled, increasing in couetousnesse, increased these Annates in times, and brought them to first fruites : raking one whole yeares profite away from the Incumbents : Wherein of these Harpyes we may say, as the Poet saith of those other Harpyes : *Vestigia fæda relinquunt* : But the godly Princes of Christendome

Anno 1379.

Naucler.

Anno 1400.
Naucl.gener.47.

Virgil.AEn.li.3.

ſtendome are to be intreated in the behalfe of God, to remoue theſe greeuances from the Church, which the inſatiable coue-touſneſſe of Popes brought in. And ſeeing they haue remoued the Harpyes themſelues, why ſhould they leaue the markes of their abhominable couetouſneſſe to the eternall oppreſſion of the Church? Why ſhould theſe vncleane ſpoiles be found in the hands of godly Princes? It would be the eternall honour of our Princes, not to chaunge the oppreſſour, but to remoue the op-preſſion. It was the honour of this land, that when the Pope had oppreſſed all other Churches, onely the Church of England was free: *Hanc conſuetudinem omnes admiſere, præter Anglos*, ſaith *Naucler*. It was firſt impoſed in the yeare one thouſand and foure hundred: it was not vſed in England when *Naucler* wrote, as he witneſſeth: that is not before the yeare one thou-ſand fiue hundred, ſo odious an abuſe, ſo lately bred might ſoone be remoued, if the cup of theſe ſweete wines, wherein the Pope began, had not beguiled many men.

152. When *Boniface* the ninth had begun this oppreſſion: much money was thereby gathered from the Clergie through-out the Emperours Dominions: the money being thus collec-ted, was deteined by the greedy Emperour *Wenceſlaus* from the more greedy Popes. This turned the hearts of the Popes againſt him: therefore *Gregory* the ninth depoſed him and ſet vp *Ru-pertus* Count Palatine of Rhene againſt him.

George King of Bohemia.

153. AFter the death of *Ladiſlaus* King of Bohemia, who died without iſſue, two great Kingdomes of Bohemia and Hungaria, with the Duchy of Auſtria being va-cant: many Princes ſought the Kingdome of Bohemia: *Charles* Naucler. King of Fraunce, whoſe daughter *Ladiſlaus* married, would haue placed one of his ſonnes. *Caſimire* King of Polonia hau-ing married a ſiſter, ſought it in her right: ſo did *Guilliam* Duke of Saxony, who married the elder ſiſter of *Ladiſlaus*: *Sigiſmund* and *Albert* Dukes of Auſtria were in good hope: and *Frederick* the Emperour would haue had the adminiſtration of the King-

dome, becaufe the homage due to the Empire had beene neglected. When the day of Election came, *Georgius Pogebratius*
was chofen King, and afterward confirmed by *Fredericke* the
Emperour; but *Paul* the fecond, finding that this *George* fauo-
Platin.Paul.2. red the Hufsites, or as *Platina* faith, daily withdrew himfelfe
from the body of Chriftianity (meaning from the obedience of
the Pope) did excommunicate and depofe him, fetting vp *Ma-*
thias King of Hungary againft him. *Mathias* gaue the Bohe-
Palmer. mians a great ouerthrow in the yeare one thoufand, foure hundred and feuentie : and with fuch mortall hatred was Pope
Paulus fet againft this King, that he fent many Bifhoppes to ne-
gociate thefe warres, and to raife vp the Hungarians and Germanes againft him; and fo farre preuailed, that he extinguifhed
all the pofterity and difcent of *George*, and would, faith *Platina*,
vtterly haue rooted out all the name and memory of the Here-
Platin.Paul.2. tickes, vnleffe the Polonians had ftayed *Mathias*. For the Polonians claimed the Kingdome of Bohemia as due to them :
Mathias being already bufied enough with the warres of the
Turke, thought good not to draw new troubles vpon himfelfe
by prouoking the Polonians. Thus the Pope refted at that
time contented with the blood of *George*, and his children, feeing the power of his malice could then proceed no further.

King Iohn of Nauarre.

154. POpe *Iulius* the fecond, the fcourge of Chriftendome in his time, vfed the like courtefie to *Iohn*
King of Nauarre; for when this Vicar of Chrift *Iulius* raifed
warres againft the French King, *Iohn* King of Nauarre held, as
he had reafon, with the French King, being a French-man by
birth, and hauing the greateft part of his patrimony in Fraunce.
Ferdinand King of Arragon then fauoured the Pope. This *Fer-*
dinand prepared warre againft the French King; and to turne
the mindes and fpeech of all men vpon the French warres from
that purpofe, which fecretly hee intended, hee intreated *Henry*
the eighth King of England, to fend him an Army to helpe him
in the warres of France. King *Henry* hauing maried the daughter

ter of *Ferdinand*, ſent him ſixe thouſand footmen: theſe came to
the Frontiers of France, and there ſtayed long for the army of
Ferdinand: who for his better paſſage into Fraunce, required
of *Iohn* King of Nauarre (through whoſe Dominions hee was
to paſſe) that he would deliuer vp to his hands, three of the
ſtrongeſt Caſtles that he would demaund; the requeſt as vniuſt
was denied by the King of Nauarre : *Ferdinand* referreth the
matter to the Pope. The Pope *Iulius* not regarding the iuſtice
or iniuſtice of the cauſe, pronounceth the King of Nauarre a
Schiſmaticke and Hereticke, for fauouring the French King:
and therefore depriueth him of his kingdome, and giueth his
right to *Ferdinand*. Who thereupon ſent his army of a ſuddaine againſt the King of Nauarre, who fled into France. Thus
was the kingdome of Nauarre ſurpriſed, and no title pretended
ſauing onely the Popes excommunication.

Nebreſſ.lib 1.
cap. 3.

The ſtate of Venice.

155. IT were too long to recompt all the miſchiefes and
miſeries, that the Popes Excommunications haue
brought vpon Chriſtendome ; I haue collected the chiefe and
moſt eminent, and will end this diſcourſe with the memory of
that affliction and deſolation which the Pope brought vpon
the Venetians. *Iulius* the ſecond, following the ſteppes of his
predeceſſours, brought an armie before Bononia, beſieged the
towne, and tooke it. The familie of the Bentiuoli he vtterly
ruinated, killing ſome, baniſhing other : When thus hee had
ouerthrowne the Bentiuoli. Then he ſet himſelfe in like ſort,
to root out the Venetian name : *Ad veneti nominis excidium,*
ſaith *Onuphrius.* The better to effect the malice againſt the
Venetians, he drew *Maximilian* the Emperour, the French
King, the King of Spaine, the Duke of Ferrara, and the Duke
of Mantua into a league: when firſt himſelfe had excommunicated and curſed them, hee ſet all theſe vpon them at once.
The Pope made choice of a fit time to doe them the greateſt
hurt he could : for a little before this the ſtate of Venice was
brought ſo low, that a weake enemie might ſoone haue indan-
gered

Onuphr.Iul.2.

gered them; hauing had their whole army brought vnto Inter-
necion at Abdua : after that ouerthrowen in a great battell,
by *Lewes* the French King ; their chiefe generals , *Liuianus* taken prifoner ; *Petilianus* put to flight. The Pope tooke the aduantage of this their weakeneſſe, and ſeeing them falling, labored to thruſt them headlong, that they might neuer be able to
riſe againe. *Maximilian* tooke Verona, Vicetia, Padway, Carni;
the French King ſurpriſed Bergamum, Brixia, Cremona, & Crema : the Spaniard wan Tranum, Monopolis, and Barletta in A-
pulia. The Popes ſhare was Rauenna, Ariminum, & all Aemilia.
The Duke of Ferrara got Rodigium : and the Duke of Mantua
Aſula. Thus was that noble ſtate brought in manner to vtter
ruine.

156. *Iulius* hauing thus ſatisfied his malice , and obtained
his purpoſe in ſome meaſure againſt the Venetians, being ledde
by a ſpirit that would giue him no reſt, began to turne his furious wrath in like ſort againſt *Maximilian*, contrary to his faith
often promiſed , and confirmed in the publike aſſembly of the
States. And ſo furious was this Vicar of Chriſt , that himſelfe
led the Army, vſing theſe words, as hee went out of Rome :
that ſeeing Saint *Peters* keyes would not preuaile , hee would
trie what Saint *Pauls* ſword could doe : and ſo hee threw the
keyes into Tiber.

157. And thus when the Princes of Chriſtendome ſhall recompt their miſeries, the ſpoile and deſolation of their kingdomes, the ruine of auncient houſes, the vexation of their ſubiects, the circumuention of their perſons, the extirpation and
extermination of many noble families, the bloody warre, and
by reaſon of warres, all the troubles and calamities of Chriſtendome : then muſt the Pope come to remembrance (with his
excommunication as a firebrand in his hand, taken out of the
infernall pit, and carried in the handes of theſe furies) who
onely hath brought all theſe troubles vpon the Princes of the
earth : ſo that ſince the time that hee began to exerciſe his excommunication againſt Princes, there hath not beene much
warres in theſe weſterne parts of Chriſtendome; but ſuch as the
Pope himſelfe hath raiſed, daſhing one Prince againſt another ;

when

when firſt he had caſt them into a deadly ſleepe to make them
inſenſible of the wrongs which hee hath done them : but when
they are awaked out of their ſleepe, they will remember all.
For the Popes as the great conſpiratours againſt the States of
Princes, haue ſet Friars their reſolute creatures to practiſe all ſecret treaſons againſt the perſons of Princes. And becauſe this
cannot be done without great bloodſhed, they come reſolued
to ſhed blood like hungry wolues : ſo headlong are they carried
herein, ſeeking a temporall Iuriſdiction ouer Princes, ſecretly
by the conſpiracie of Friars, openly by their excommunications : that if the world ſhould ſtand long; before the Pope with
his Babylon be ouerthrowen, wee haue reaſon to thinke that
the Popes will in time vtterly caſt off and reiect the maske of
religion, wherewith they couer their practiſes now, and will in
plaine teatmes quarrell the Princes of Chriſtendome, for their
Temporall right and Iuriſdiction. And then will the Princes
thinke it is time for them to awake.

CHAP. VIII.

*wherein is declared what oppoſition this Iuriſdiction found
in the Church, after it was thus eſtabliſhed by Popes : It
was confuted firſt by particular learned men : then by generall Councels.*

1. Fter that this Iuriſdiction, thus deuiſed and
maintained, began to bee well knowen in
Chriſtendome : men of learning and iudgement began to be mooued with the noueltie,
and examined the whole matter with care and
induſtrie : the occaſion which firſt moued them to examine this
queſtion, was the defence of this ſtrange Iuriſdiction : firſt claimed by the Popes, and afterward more fully diſputed and maintained by *Auguſtinus Triumphus Anconitan* : who was ſet on
worke vpon this taske by the Pope. For in the end of his booke

we

we finde this written : *Explicit summa de potestate Ecclesiastica edita à fratre Augustino Triumpho Anconitano, in sacra Theologia magistro , ordinis Eremitarum sancti Augusti, iubente Iohanne 22. Pontifice M.An.Dom.1 3 2 0.* Where we find from what spirit this defence of this new Iurisdiction proceedeth, comming from the especiall direction of the Pope.   This Friar proceedeth herein according to his direction , concluding all Iurisdiction both Spirituall and Temporall , to be from the Pope.

2. Which thing though it seemed straunge, newe, absurd : yet in truth *Triumphus* could no lesse then publish (for he laboureth not so much to prooue it, as to publish it) the Popes challenge hauing vndertaken the businesse.   For the Popes before this had begunne to prescribe in their Canons so much, that their flatterers had their rules now prescribed to them, how farre they must stretch their consciences for the maintenance of Iurisdiction. For either they must maintaine all that the Popes had taken vpon them, or else giue ouer the cause as desperate.   From this spirit and direction , *Triumphus* entreth into this cause , as an hireling speaking for his fee : taking this ground, that the Pope is as directly lord of the whole world in *Temporalibus :* as hee is the head of the vniuersall Church in *Spiritualibus ;* and that he hath directly Soueraigne authoritie in respect of such his worldly Dominion ouer all Emperours, Kings and Princes to dispose of them and their kingdomes. This opinion is now strongly maintained by the Iesuits , and hath beene of late by *Tho. Bozius, Francisc. Bozius , Card. Baronius, Zecchus Carerius ,* and other.   But because *Triumphus* is, as I take it, the first Friar that hath handled this question on the Popes behalfe ; and the learned men that first wrote against the Popes Iurisdiction , haue beene mooued thereto by his writings, as also because the booke is rare to bee had : I will set downe some of his proofelesse positions ; that the Reader may the better vnderstand what it is which they seeke , and what is that against which these learned men that I am hereafter to produce, doe oppose themselues.

Qu.1.art.1.   3. One position of *Triumphus* is this : *Potestas temporalis Imperatorum & regum est in ministerium data à Deo Papæ & alijs Prælatis*

Prælatis Ecclesiæ in quibus residet potestas spiritualis: which he proueth by such reasons, as need no other refutation, sauing only the
recitall thereof. For it was truely said of *Iustin Martyr*, that to
know and truely to vnderstand an absurd reason, is a sufficient
refutation thereof. His reason is : *illa potestas est data in mini-*
sterium alteri, per quam habet institui, regulari, ordinari atque con-
firmari si bona sit : & per quam habet iudicari si non bona sit : sed
talis est potestas sæcularium Imperatorum, regum, &c. Quia per
potestatem Papæ habet institui, regulari, ordinari si bona sit, & per
ipsam habet condemnari & iudicari si mala sit. | That power is gi-
uen for seruice to another, by which it must be instituted, ordered and confirmed being good, and iudged being euill: but such
is the power of secular Emperours and Princes &c. For by the
Pope it must be instituted, ruled, and ordered being good, and
by him it must be condemned and iudged being euill.] All the
proofe that he bringeth for this, is : that Pope *Zachary* deposed the French King *Chilperic* and set vp *Pipin* in his place. An
other reason is this : *Illa potestas est in ministerium data alteri, cui*
iuramentum fidelitatis præstat, & ab ea cognoscit esse omne quod
habet : sed omnis potestas sæcularium Principum, Imperatorum, &
aliorum est talis. Dist. 63. Can. cum tibi Domine. [That power
is giuen and subiected for seruice to another, to whom it yeeldeth an Oath of Alleageance, acknowledging all that it hath
from the same : but such is all the power of temporall Princes,
Emperours, and such like.] Againe he saith thus : *Si inuenia-*
tur quandoque aliquos Imperatores dedisse aliqua temporalia sum-
mis Pontificibus, sicut Constantinus dedit Siluestro: hoc non est intel-
ligendum, eos dare quod suum est, sed restituere quod iniuste & ty-
rannice ablatum est. [If sometimes we finde that some Emperours haue giuen some temporalities to Popes, as *Constantine*
gaue to *Siluester* : wee must not thinke that they gaue that
which was their owne, but onely restored that which vniustly
and tyrannically was taken from Popes.] These things are such
that in the iudgement of all men, that are not destitute of iudgment, need no refutation. He saith also in the same place: *Po-*
testas omnis Imperatorum & regum est subdelegata resp. ctu pote-
statis Papæ. [All power of Emperours and Kings, is to them de-
legated

Ii 2

ἱκανὸς εἰς
ἔλεγχον τῦ
ἀσυςάτυ λό'γ
αὐτος ὁ λόγε
νοουμενος. Iu
stin. ἐρωτης.
πρὸς ἕλλην.

legated by the Popes power.] This is the Iurisdiction which is
fought, a temporall Iurisdiction ouer Princes : this doctrine was
deuised onely to maintaine the practise of the Popes excommuni-
nication. And as this new and strange doctrine was found out
for the defence of that new and strange practise, so the manner
of the defence is no lesse strange : for he declareth that this Iurisdiction for which he pleadeth so much , is not in the Pope as
he is a Priest or Bishoppe , but as he is a Prince. It followeth
then in his confession that this Iurisdiction is proper to Princes,
and not to Priests. For thus he saith : *Papatus est nomen Iuris-*
Q.4. Artic.2. *dictionis, & non ordinis.* That is [The Papacy is a name of Iurisdiction, and not of Order.] And againe, *Potest Papa habere omnem*
potestatem pertinentem ad Papam, & tamen carere potestate ordinis.
That is [The Pope may haue all Iurisdiction belonging to the
Pope, and yet be no Priest.] This new doctrine teacheth great
wonders : that the Pope may haue all Iurisdiction , and bee no
Priest. The Iesuites, and our owne Popish Countrie-men crye
out against vs, for giuing Iurisdiction to such as are no Priests,
but onely temporall Princes. It will be hard for them to accuse
vs, and defend their owne Doctors.

4. Because this manner of maintaining the Popes Iurisdiction is grosse to set him aboue temporall Princes in temporall Iurisdiction, therefore diuers since this time haue sought
to mollifie this harsh manner of speech , by a distinction which
they haue found out of late, betweene Power direct ouer Princes and indirect : These men say that the Pope hath power to
depose Princes, not directly, but indirectly , in respect of some
spirituall good. But when they come to the application of
this distinction, it appeareth nothing but a Miste to dazzle the
eyes of men, wherein there is no simplicity or truth. *Bellarmine*
is one of those that admitteth this Distinction , vpon which
Distinction graunted by Cardinall *Bellarmine*, Master *Blackwel*
thinketh he hath a good ground for taking the Oath of Alleageance. And when *Bellarmine* reproueth him for that , he answereth him by his owne Distinction : a reasonable answere;
and yet such is the Mist of this Distinction, that you can hardly
tell whether of these two speaketh more cunningly. For *Bel-*
larmine

larmine saith, that the Pope hath power to depose Princes not direcły, but in respect of some spirituall good: but when Master *Blackwell* saith, that in his particular case the spirituall good of Catholickes was respected. This *Bellarmine* will denie: for he will say that no priuate man must be iudge of this spirituall good, but onely the Pope. Now let the Pope bee Iudge, and then this Distinction is as good as nothing: for whensoeuer the Pope deposeth a Prince, or dischargeth his subiects from their Oath of Alleageance, he will iudge it to be for some spirituall good. So that in this vnderstanding, and sense of *Bellarmine* there is no reall difference betweene direct power and indirect.

In ordine ad spirituale bonum. l.5.c.6.de Rome Pont.

5. In like sort when Master *Blackwell* saith, the Pope hath power to depose Princes indirectly, or in respect of some spirituall good, and iudgeth the taking of the Oath of Alleageance to respect a spirituall good end, giuing this reason: because the refusal of this Oth wold bring vpon vs the ruines of Catholicke families & the lamentable extirpation of the whole Catholicke estate among vs: We say the case of this man, and of those that depend vpon him, is much better then the case of them that refuse the Oath: but yet to drawe them a little further into the loue of obedience, let vs note the imperfection of his defence. We commend his action, and speake here onely of his manner of defending it; for the reason that draweth him to obedience, and to take this Oath, is not a conscience of that commaundement of God, which commaundeth obedience to Magistrates: but the danger of Catholickes, and of himselfe; which proueth an indirect obedience. So that in pleading for a verball distinction of power, direct or indirect, they descry a reall distinction of obedience direct or indirect. Now there is not much difference betweene these three opinions of them that holde the Popes direct power, and his indirect power, and that say his power is to respect the present danger of the Catholickes. For whatsoeuer *Triumphus* bringeth vnder his direct power, that Cardinall *Bellarmine* will reduce vnder indirect power: so that though they differ in the manner how this power commeth to the Pope, direcły or indirecły, yet they both are agreed that

Examination of M. George Blackwell. Epist to Bellarmine.

Ii 3   the

the Pope hath this power; and this is also Master *Blackwels* iudgement. For remooue the danger of his Catholickes, and then he hath nothing to say against this power of thePópe, so that the question is not how he hath it, but whether he hath this power or not? Vnto which question all Romane Catholickes answer affirmatiuely, and we negatiuely.

6. Thus did those learned men conceiue the question that first began to handle it : these later distinctions came in by such as would hide themselues in a miste, and seeme to say something when they say nothing. Now let vs declare the iudgement of those men that first came to the handling of this question of the Popes power, after that it was fully made knowen to the world, by the Popes decrees, and the writings of *eAugustinus Triumphus.* The first occasion that set men on worke vpon the studie of this question, was partly, as I haue said, the writings of *Triumphus*; but this occasion was notoriously promoted by the vniust vexations which the Popes offered to *Lodouicke* Duke of Bauare Emperour, in prosecuting of their pretended Iurisdiction ouer Kings, and Emperours. This Emperour being persecuted by the Popes, as before wee haue declared, was desirous to know the iudgements of the best learned men that then liued in the world; who with industry did search out, and by learning did ouerthrowe this new sophisticate Iurisdiction : giuing to Emperours and Kings their auncient right. The chiefe of them who then wrote against the Popes Iurisdiction was *Marsilius Patauinus*, and *Guilielmus Occham.* Of these and of some other that in one part or other haue confuted this Iurisdiction of Popes, I am now to speake in order.

§. I.

Obseruations out of the writings of Marsilius Pat.
against the Popes Iurisdiction.

7.   **M**Arsilius about the yeere of Christ, one thousand three hundred twentie and foure, set out that booke
which

which he Intituleth, *Defensorem pacis,* wherein hee shaketh the
rotten and ruinous reasons of such as maintained this Iurisdiction: because the booke is written with great learning and
iudgement, I will record heere some obseruations of his: for it
seemeth that he had a purpose to refute that former worke of
Triumphus, though the truth is, hee nameth not *Triumphus*
throughout all his booke: concerning this point of Iurisdiction, one especiall ground which hee layeth, is this. *Ab officio* Part.2.cap.4.
*principatus siue contentiosae iurisdictionis, regiminis, seu coactiui iu-
dicy cuiuslibet in hoc saeculo, Christus seipsum & Apostolos exclusit,
& excludere voluit.* That is, [Christ hath excluded, and purposed to exclude himselfe and his Apostles from principalitie, or
contentious iurisdiction, or regiment or any coactiue iudgment
in this world.]Which thing he proueth at large, both by Scriptures & Fathers: because Christ saith, his kingdome is not of this
world; by which words coactiue Iurisdiction is excluded: as was
the doctrine of Christ, such was his example of obedience: for he
was alwayes subiect to the coactiue power of the Magistrate.
Thus by the sound and cleere Scriptures, with the expositions
and iudgement of the ancient Fathers, he refuteth that noueltie
which had no other ground then the Popes decretals.

8. Therefore he examineth the authority of the Popes decretals, and giueth a learned and iuditious distinction, declaring thereby how the Pope may bee obeyed or not obeyed,
commaunding against the Emperour: for saith he, if the Emperour commaund any thing against the law of God, and the
Pope commaund things agreeable to that law: thou must out
of doubt obey the Pope, and not the Emperour. But if the
Emperour commaund something according to his imperial law
& the Pope command somthing according to his decretals a-
gainst the imperiall lawes: no man subiect to the Emperour,
ought in such things to obey the Pope. Which thing he proueth at large, because the ciuill Magistrate beareth the sword;
because he is the Minister of God, the reuenger of disobedience:
because euery soule is subiect to him. Which things saith hee,
are not spoken of any spirituall Gouernour but of the Temporall
Magistrate. For the Gouernours to whom in coactiue Iurisdiction

ćtion we muſt obey, are ſuch as by armed power defend their
Countries and people, which in no caſe can agree to a Biſhop
or Prieſt.

    9.   By ſuch reaſons he proceedeth, and proueth infallibly
his purpoſe, and concluſion that no ſpirituall Gouernour hath
from Chriſt any Iuriſdiction coactiue ; but this power is left
wholly in the hands of the ciuill Magiſtrate. And thus doth cut
in ſunder the ſinewes of their diſputations, who plead for the
Popes Iuriſdiction: which Iuriſdiction they make to conſiſt in
power coactiue. Of the Popes decretals (which then were
lately deuiſed Lawes againſt the auncient Iuriſdiction of the
Church, as alſo againſt the Iuriſdiction of Princes) he ſaith : *Vt*
Part.2.cap.5. *ipſi fabulantur in ſuis decretalibus, quæ ſecundum veritatem nihil
aliud ſunt, quàm ordinationes quædam Oligarchicæ, quibus in nullo
obedire tenentur Chrſti fideles, in quantum huiſuſmodi.* That is,
[As they bable in their decretals, which in truth are nothing
but certaine Oligarchicall ordinations, to which Chriſtians are
in no caſe bound to obey, as they proceed from the Pope.]
Wherein he deliuereth thus much, that theſe Canon lawes or
decretals, ought to haue no force among Chriſtians, vnleſſe
they be confirmed by the lawes of the land, and by Princes in
their Dominions : ſo many as Princes ſhall thinke fit for the
gouernment of the Church in their proper Dominions, may be
eſtabliſhed, & being eſtabliſhed ought to be obeyed, but not as
the Popes laws vſe, but as the laws of thoſe Princes: for that is it
which *Marſilius* ſaith, the decretals are not to be obeyed, *in quã-
tũ huiſuſmodi.* Now that all coactiue power is by God deliuered
to the Temporall Magiſtrate, hee prooueth ſolidly from theſe
Rom.13.4. words; he is the Miniſter of God to take vengeance : by vengeance all coactiue power is vnderſtood. Neither doth he denie but that the Church gouernours may execute coactiue
power : but then they muſt haue it from Princes, and from ſuch
Temporall powers which haue the ſame. Which being ex-
preſly and diſtinctly written by him three hundred yeres agoe,
is no other thing then that which we now maintaine : at which
our aduerſaries ſeeme to wonder, as at ſome new doctrine neuer heard before; when the ſame truth, after the ſame manner
                                     hath

beene maintained by the learned men that haue handled this
question before vs. *Nec in quenquam presbyterum* (saith he) *aut* *Part.2.cap.5.*
non presbyterum conuenit coactiuam in hoc saeculo Iurisdictionem
habere, quenquam Episcopum, siue Papam, nisi eadem sibi per hu-
manum legislatorem concessa fuerit, in cuius potestate semper est hanc
ab ipsis reuocare: That is, [No man, Priest or not Priest, can
haue Iurisdiction coactiue in this world, Bishop or Pope : vnlesse it be granted to them by the humane law-maker, in whose
power it is at his pleasure to recall it from them.]

10. Concerning the right of calling Councels, his determination is this : If a cause of religion rise in question, the Pope,
saith he, may signifie the same to the chiefe Temporall Gouernour : but the authority of gathering and calling the Councell,
belongeth to him that hath coactiue Iurisdiction ; and ought to
bee gathered by his coactiue precept. When it is gathered,
he leaueth the first and chiefe seat therein to the Bishop of
Rome : hee giueth him the honour to propose the matter; to
collect all together that is spoken : to communicate the things
determined to others ; and to excommunicate the transgres-
sors. And all this to doe, not at his owne pleasure, or vpon his
owne head; *sed ex concilij sententia:* onely by the direction of
the Councell. This principality he yeeldeth to the Bishop of
Rome, and to that Church, so long as thus it standeth, and so
long as it doth nothing to the contrary whereby this honour
may be iustly withdrawen. *Secundum quem modum* (saith hee) *Part. 2. cap. 22.*
Romanae vrbis quamdiu extiterit, obicemq, ad hoc non apposuerit
populus ille &c. poterit licitè ac debebit iam dicta principalitas in E-
piscopo & Ecclesia continue reseruari. That is, [According to
which maner this principality may lawfully and ought to be reserued alwayes, for that Bishop and that Church as long as it
thus standeth, and doth nothing to the contrary. This honour
(if the Pope would haue held himselfe contented therewith)
might long time enough beene reserued vnto him. But when
this could not content him, but he must haue all Iurisdiction o-
uer the Church, and ouer secular Princes : if he finde not that
honour yeelded to him which hee expecteth, he may thanke
himselfe ; because he hath procured his owne contempt, and by

Kk   vsur-

vsurpation of vndue honour, he hath lost that, which though it was not due to him, yet from some custome was giuen, & might haue beene continued to this day, if himselfe had not caused the Church to withdraw it : For (saith mine Author,) *Licet circa initium Ecclesiæ, reliqui Episcopi & Ecclesiæ fidelium neq, diuina neq humana lege aliqua obligarentur obedire mandatis aut institutis Ecclesiæ vel Episcopi Romanorum, plusquam è conuerso : inualescente tamen hac vtili & rationabili consuetudine, qua fideles in vnitate amplius seruabuntur, eo quod tunc fideli caruerunt legislatore ipsos in ordine reducente, ac in vnitate seruante, &c.* That is, [Albeit about the beginning of the Church, other Bishops and Churches of beleeuers were not bound by any diuine or humane law, to obey the mandates of the Church or Bishop of Rome, rather then the contrary : yet this profitable and reasonable custome preuailing, by which beleeuers were better kept in vnitie, because they wanted then a Christian Magistrate to reduce them to order and preserue them in vnitie : therefore they were afterward bound, as by a diuine law to this obedience, in things honest and lawfull.]

11. But because the Popes and their flatterers did couer all their practises with *plenitudo potestatis*, as with a mist : therfore he doth with great light of learning and truth, dispell that mist : This saith he is, *Locus Sophisticus, vnde etiã paralogismus, quo reges & principantes ac singulos coactiua sibi Iurisdictione subiectos nituntur concludere traxit originem.* That is, [This is a Sophisme, whence that Paralogisme drew his beginning, by which they striue to draw Kings and Princes, and all other vnder their subiection by coactiue Iurisdiction.] And therfore it he belaboreth exactly and at full to open this fallacion of fulnesse of power : the summe whereof is this. By a pretended fulnesse of power the Pope without ground or reason, onely led thereto by pride and ambition, intruded vpon the right of Iesus Christ, and vpon the right of the Church, and vpon the right of Temporall Princes, wresting all authority to himselfe, & this he calleth fulnes of power. For if by fulnes of power be vnderstood that power wherby all men and all creatures are commanded and directed to what end the commaunder will : this power is giuen

only

onely to Iesus Christ, and to no other man : according to that Scripture ; all power is giuen vnto me in heauen and in earth. Mat.28.18. But if by fulnesse of power, be vnderstood power to preach, to excommunicate, to binde, to loose, to interpret Scripture, to determine controuersies ; this power is in the Church : partly in Bishops, partly in doctors, partly in Councels, and not more in the Pope then in another Bishop. Last of all, if by this fulnesse of power be vnderstood Soueraigne Iurisdiction coactiue, then it is in Temporall Princes. *Marsilius* maketh moe parts hereof ; but I draw him summarily, and presume that to these three heads all that he saith may be reduced.

12. And therefore whereas the Pope claimeth such a power, intruding vpon the right of each of these, he saith : *Ex vna* Part. 2. cap.23. *præsumptione in aliam transiuit Romanus Pontifex.* That is, [The Pope hath from one presumption passed into another. The same Author declareth how the Popes proceeded in these their incroachings vpon Iurisdiction. First, saith he, they made some constitutions to gouerne the Clergie : then they proceeded by Ibid. way of exhortation & intreaty, to perswade the laitie to keepe fastes, & to abstaine from meats. When they saw that laymen did willingly receiue such obseruations, the they proceeded to ordaine the same things as laws, & to denounce excomunicatio against the transgressours thereof. And all this was done, saith Ibid. he, *Sub pietatis & diuini cultus specie.* That is, [Vnder a shewe of godlinesse, and the worship of God.] The same Author addeth, *Crescente autem consequenter ipsis appetitu amplius dominandi, attendentibus deuotos fidelium huiusmodi verbis terreri propter ignauiam & diuini cultus imperitiam, qui ad ea quæ per sacerdotes indicebantur obligari credebant metu damnationis æternæ ; præsumpserunt vlterius Episcopi Romani, cum suo clericorum cœtu oligarchica quædam edicta circa ciuiles actus statuere, &c.* That is, [But as the appetite of ruling, farther continually increased in them, when they sawe that deuote Christians were kept in feare with such proceedings, through slothfulnesse and ignorance of Gods worship : which (Christians ignorant) thought themselues bound vnder the paine of eternall damnation, to all that was inioyned them of the Priests : then the Bishops of

Rome with their Clergie presuming further made certaine Oligarchicall Edicts concerning ciuill actions.   Thus saith hee,
the Bishoppe of Rome began first to practise expempti-
ons. And that hee might draw a number of the Laiety into the
loue of those practises, he extended these exemptions to diuers
companies of Lay persons, and so defrauded the Magistrate of
due honour and obedience, and brought in that confusion
whereof the same Authour complaineth thus: *Hæc est pestilentiæ
Italici regni radix & origo, ex qua cuncta scandala germinauerunt
prodeunt &c. Quæ stante, nunquam ciuiles ibidem cessabuut discor-
diæ, potestatem enim hanc ad quam paulatim & latenti præuaricati-
one subintrauit ex consuetudine aut abusione verius, dudum deti-
nuit Rom. Episcopus, eandem sibi per principem reuocari formidans,
& merito propter commissos excessus : creationem atque promotio-
nem Rom. Principis omni maligna sollicitudine vetat.* That is [This is
the roote and fountaine of the pestilence which troubleth the
Empire, from whence all scandals growe and proceede, and
which standing, ciuill discords shall neuer cease in Italy, for the
Pope fearing that this power may be reuoked by the Emperor,
and that deseruedly for the excesse committed therein : into
which power he hath by little and little stolne by secret preua-
rication of custome, or to say more truely, of abuse, hauing holden it some while : he hindreth the creation and promotion of
the Emperor by all malice and spite.] Wherupon, saith he, some
Popes haue broken out into such impudency, as in their Decretals is to be seene, that they auouch that the Emperor is bound
to them in an Oath of Alleageance, as if the Emperour were vnder them subiected by coactiue Iurisdiction.

  13.   Then *Marsilius* hath discouered the reason why the
Popes haue so much opposed themselues against the Emperors,
to be, because they were affraid least the Emperours should call
them to a reckoning for their Exemptions, for the abuse of
their excommunications, for intruding themselues into the office of the ciuill Magistrate, and taking a newe authority vpon
themselues from themselues without warrant of the Emperour.
This is that thing which caused them to stirre so much against
Emperours, and at last to procure the decay of the Empire so
                                                              much,

much, as at this day they haue made it so weake, that now they are out of the feare thereof. Other things for breuities sake I omit: this is sufficient to vnderstand what reason learned men had then to withstand the Popes Iurisdiction. This booke of *Marsilius* was neuer answered, and hereafter is not like to be. But *Iohn* the two and twentieth, against whom this booke was intended, did in stead of aunswering, condemne this worthy Writer: which thing was much more easie for him to doe.

§. II.

William Occham and Michael Cezena.

14. BVT the truth could not be suppressed thus. For other learned men deuoted to the seruice of the truth, entred into a further search of this Iurisdiction, among whom *Michael Cezena* and *William Occham* were famous. The occasion which stirred them vp to make search of this point, was this: *Michael Cezena* Generall of the Order of the Minorites refuted three Constitutions of Pope *Iohn* the two and twentieth; *Ad conditorem Canonum: Cum inter: &, Quia quorundam.* These hee refuted and sent his bookes abroad against these Constitutions; whereupon *Iohn* the two and twentieth depriued him, and disabled him from taking any other dignity. But *Michael* appealed from the Pope.

15. Here arose the question, whether a Christian might appeale from the Pope. *William Occham* once a worthy fellow of Merton Colledg in Oxford, vndertooke this question, & disputeth it throughly, in that booke which he intitleth *Opus nonaginta dierum.* He concludeth that a man may and might appeale from the Pope, and that a Councell is aboue the Pope. And saith, that many moe learned men wrote diuers bookes at that time, for confirmation of the same truth, wherein they alleadge strong reasons to proue their purpose, and answere all doubts. *De ista materia* (saith he) *plures libri prolixi sunt editi, in quibus* Cap.1. *prædicti impugnatores motiua adducunt quam plurima, obiectiones refellunt, & quæ possunt oriri dubia, declarare nituntur.* That is [Of

Kk 3   this

this matter many long bookes set forth, wherein these foresaid Disputers, alledge many reasons, refute obiections, and seeke to cleare all doubts that can rise.] Of the Pope he saith thus : *Iohannes 22. conscius errorum suorum ad iudicium generalis concilij venire recusat.* That is [Pope *Iohn* the two and twentieth, his owne conscience accusing himselfe of his errours, refuseth to come to the iudgement of a Generall Councel.] Thus the Pope hath euer bin affraid of a General Councell, since the time that first he vsurped Iurisdiction.   The same Author confuteth the

Cap. 2.

Constitutions of *Iohn* the two and twentieth, first by Scriptures, then by Canons of Councels, and testimonies of holy Fathers, and last of al by the determination of the Church of Rome. And for this question of Iurisdiction, because the Popes then began

Cap 93.

to chalenge temporall Iurisdiction ouer Princes, his assertion is : *Beatus Petrus non fuit vicarius Christi, quantum ad officium regni temporalis, nec in temporalibus quibuscunque.* That is [S. *Peter* was not Christs Vicar in respect of a temporall Kingdome, nor in respect of any temporalities whatsoeuer.] Which Assertion he proueth thus : If it were so that S. *Peter* were Christs Vicar in temporall Dominion, then should S. *Peter* haue Iurisdiction ouer Emperours and Kings : but this the Popes themselues denie, for Pope *Nicholas* saith thus : *Quum ad verum ven-*

Dist. 96. cap. cum ad verum

tum est, nec Imperator iura sibi Pontificatus, &c. That is : When we come to know the truth, neither hath the Emperour taken vpon him the right of the Pope, nor the Pope vsurped the title of the Emperour, for one Mediator of God and man Iesus Christ hath distinguished the Offices of both these powers by their proper actions and distinct dignities. *Ex his* (saith *Ocham*) *datur intelligi quod Rom. Pontifex ex successione Petri non habet Iurisdictionem temporalem super Imperatorem.* That is, [Hence we may vnderstand, that the Pope by succeeding *Peter* hath no temporall Iurisdiction ouer the Emperour.

16. Against this determination he moueth some obiections or rather taketh the reasons of *Augustinus Triumphus*, and maketh them his obiections, though he suppresse the name of *Triumphus.* The obiections are these : First, The Pope deposeth Kings, *15. qu. 6. cap. alius.* Secondly, The Pope translated the
Empire,

Empire, *Extra.de Elect.cap.venerabilem.* Thirdly, The Emperor *Cap 93.*
taketh an Oath of Alleageance. These are the reasons of *Au-*
guftin Triumphus, whereunto he aunswereth thus. To the first
he saith : *Ratione criminis habet fpiritualem Iurifdictionem, non*
temporalem. That is [In respect of some fault hee hath spirituall
Iurisdiction, but not temporall.] Then all the Iurisdiction which
the Pope or any other Bifhoppe hath, is onely spirituall in his
opinion, in respect of sinne which may be censured by spirituall
censures. But a power to depose Kings includeth temporall Iurisdiction. To the second he saith : The Pope translated the
Empire : *Non in quantum fucceffor Petri, fed authoritate Romano-*
rum qui fibi poteftatem huiufmodi conceferant : That is [Not as
the succeffour of *Peter,* but by the authority of the Romanes,
who graunted him that power.] To the third he saith ; the Emperour that first tooke an Oath of Alleageance, did it from deuotion and humility, and therefore afterward refused it. *Mar-*
filius answereth to this last obiection somewhat otherwise, for
he vtterly reiecteth the testimony of that Canon, that witnes-
feth that the Emperour tooke an Oath of Alleageance. *In tan-* *Part.2.cap.22.*
tum vero ipforum quidam prerupit audaciam (faith *Marfil.*) *vt in*
fuis edectis expreferit, Romanum Principem fibi iuramento fideli-
tatis aftringi tanquam coactiua Iurifdictione fubiectum, vt ex fua-
rum narrationum quas decretales appellant derifibili & contempto
*prorfus inuolucro * feptimo de Sent. & re iudicata palam fe infpici-* * *feptimo de*
entibus offert. That is [One of them (to wit *Clement* the fift) *Sent.&c.lege*
hath broken out in such impudency in his Edicts, that he affir- *fecund. de Sent.*
meth the Emperor is bound to him by an Oath of Alleageance,
as fubiect to him in coactiue Iurifdiction, as is openly to bee
feene in *2.de Sent.& re iudic.* out of that ridiculous and most
contemptible collection of their Narrations, which they call
Decretals.]

17. But to returne to *William Occham* and *Michael Cezena*
in whofe caufe *Occham* was ingaged : *Michael* was depofed by This Narrati-
Iohn the two and twentieth, in Iune in the yeare of Chrift, one on is written
thoufand three hundred twentie and eight : in his behalfe let- by *Occhem,* &
ters were directed to the Chapter of the Minorites, affembled extant in his
in Parpinian and Auinion in the yeare one thoufand three hun- workes.
dred

dred thirty and one. These letters were subscribed by *Henricus
de Chalchem, Franciscus de Esculo* , and *Guilielmus de Occham* :
not onely these men fauoured his cause, but those two famous
Vniuersities Oxford and Paris did approue the same. Whereup-
pon *Michael* being arrested by the Pope did appeale from the
Pope. Consider the nature of his appeale : for it openeth the
sense and iudgement of learned men then liuing , being approued by the greatest learned men then liuing ; and by all the learned men of that order in England and in Paris , for so it is said
there. *Quæ determinatio fuit etiam ab omnibus Magistris & bac-
calarijs in sacra pagina de Parisys & de Anglia dicti ordinis appro-
bata, & Vniuersis Christi fidelibus destinata.* That is [Which determination was also approued of all the Masters and Bache-
lours in Diuinity of the said order of Paris and England , and
directed to all Christians:] I will set downe the forme of his

*Literæ recitato-
riæ gestorum
fratris Michae-
lis Cezenæ, inter
opera Guilielm.
Occham.*

appeale as in the same place I finde it expressed , and thus it is :
*Habito prius magno & maturo consilio, ab ipso Domino Iohanne, &
à dicta eius assertione, & arrestatione infra tempus Legitimum meo
nomine, & omnium fratrum mihi adhærentium Volentium, ac dicti
ordinis, secundum quod tradunt Canonicæ sanctiones , ad sanctam
Romanam Ecclesiam Catholicam & Apostolicam appello.* That is,
[After great and mature deliberation first had , I appeale from
the same Pope *Iohn,* and from his said assertion, and arrest, within lawfull time for my selfe, and for all my brethren that do adhære or will hereafter adhære to me, and for the said Order according as the Canonicall Constitutions doe allow , vnto the
holy Romane Catholicke and Apostolicke Church.] In which
place he professeth that he doth this by the example of diuers
other who had done the like before.

  18. From whence I would obserue some things declaring
the sense, iudgement and religion of the men that then liued.
And first where he saith, that he doth this by great and mature
deliberation, and that herein he hath the approbation of diuers
learned men, of diuers Vniuersities , and that hee doth it by the
examples of such as were before him : we note that this is not
the iudgement of one man, but of the most famous learned men
of this age. For farther confirmation hereof, we obserue also
                                                            that

that *Naucler* speaking of this particular, and of the cause of *Lo-* *Naucl. gener.45*
douicke Emperour, saith, that many learned and godly men of
Chriftendome held that Pope *Iohn* the two and twentieth was
an Hereticke, conuict of affured errours: *Iohannem Papam*, faith
he, *magni & multi theologi fcientia & vita probati dogmatizabant
effe hareticum, propter certos errores.* And fpeaking of the learned
men that wrote againft the fame Pope, he nameth *Dantes* and
Occham among other. This agreeth with that which *Occhã* witneffeth of this Pope, that his own confcience accufing himfelfe
of his errors, he durft not come to the iudgement of a generall
Councell. Then I note not here onely the iudgement of thefe
learned men, but the fenfe and iudgement of Chriftendome, of
a generall Councell, of the Church of Rome. For *Cezena* and
Occham(who was combined with *Cezena* in this caufe) would
neuer haue appealed to the Church of Rome, or to a generall
Councell then reprefenting that Church, vnleffe they had been
fully feeured herein, that the Church to which they appealed
had condemned the errours of the Pope from whom they appealed. They then knowing the fenfe and iudgement of that
Church, appealed from the Pope to it : which thing is further
alfo confirmed by that which he faith in his appeale, *Secundum
quod tradunt Canonicæ fanctiones:* as the Canonicall Conftitutions deliuer: then the Canons of the Church allow and approue
fuch an appeale, howfoeuer fince this time the Popes haue altered the Canons and difcipline of the Church, yet then this difcipline was in force , and acknowledged through Chriftendome, that the Pope might be cenfured in a generall Councell.

19. Another thing which we obferue in this appeale, is a re-
markeable diftinction famoufly obferued in the fenfe, iudgement and religion of the men of this age betweene the Church
of Rome and the Court of Rome. For *Cezena* after that hee
hath appealed from the Pope to the Church of Rome, complaineth much of the Court of Rome, as being wholly gouerned by
the Pope: from whence he appealing to the Church of Rome,
declareth euidently that by the Church of Rome, he vnderftood
another thing, then that which our aduerfaries now cal by that

L l name,

name, an aſſembly whereof the Pope is the heade , which are wholly to be guided, gouerned and directed by the Pope. This is now commonly called the Church of Rome : but at this time wherein *Cezena* liued, the Church of Rome was vnderſtood to be a free, lawfull , holy generall Councell aſſembled of the Churches of theſe Weſterne parts of Chriſtendome. This is the Church of Rome which our forefathers haue ſo much honoured. The ſentence of this Church they reuerence, the authority of this Church they acknowledge, appealing from the Popes ſentence as vniuſt, reiecting his authority as vnlawfull, ſtill reſting in the iudgement of the Church of Rome. This declareth that the Pope may bee ſeparated from the Church of Rome, though not from the Court of Rome. Now ſeparate once the Pope from the Church of Rome, as by theſe appeales it muſt ſo be vnderſtood, and then it followeth by infallible inference, that the Church of Rome (as now it is commonly knowne by that name) is no other thing then that which theſe learned men called the Court of Rome : and that this preſent Church of Rome is not that which our fathers called the Church of Rome.   It is not the ſame thing : for from that Church of Rome the Pope might be ſeparated, from this he cannot. From the Pope to that Church a Chriſtian might appeale, which ſentence was iuſtified by the moſt learned that then liued : From the Pope to this Church there is no appeale. Thus much I obſerue from this appeale, and from the appeale of *Lodowicke* the fourth Emperour, which before we haue declared , being to the ſame end, and agreeing in the ſame forme with this, being from the Pope to a generall Councell, which alſo he calleth the holy Church of Rome. In which ſame manner did *Philip* King of Fraunce appeale from Pope *Boniface*, beſides diuers other who vſed the ſame courſe, as *Michael Cezena* witneſſeth.

20. Hence riſeth this Corollary, that the reformed Churches haue made no ſeparation from the Church of Rome , but onely from the Court of Rome: And that the Pope and his Court, that is Friars and Canoniſts who depend wholly vpon him , terming themſelues now the Church of Rome, haue made the ſeparation, and haue altred the auncient bounds of the Church, and
plucked

plucked vp the old hedge which was the partition between the Church and Court of Rome. Thus they reteyning onely the name, haue chaunged all things and turned them vpside down. So that albeit that which I shall say, may seeme a strange Paradox, yet it is a truth which will euery day bee more and more *Paradox.* knowne and confessed. The auncient Church of Rome, yea euen that Church of Rome which stood in the world before the Councell of Trent, can now bee found no where in the world but among Protestants. *Marsilius Pat.* obserued the beginning of this alteration, thus : *Apud Modernos Ecclesiæ nomen importat* *Part.2.cap.2.* *ministros Presbyteros Episcopos &c. Quemadmodum Ecclesia Rom. vrbis hoc dudum obtinuit, cuius ministri & præsidentes sunt Papa Romanus & Cardinales ipsius, qui iam ex vsu quodam obtinuerunt dici Ecclesia.* [The Church importeth as much as Ministers, Priests, Bishoppes in late vse, &c. as the Church of the Citie of Rome hath now obtained this name, whose Ministers and Gouernours are the Pope and his Cardinals, who now from a certaine vse are called the Church.] But that vse was but late brought in, especially by Friars : for the auncient vse of this, which was also long continued among many, and the best in the Church of Rome, he declareth to be thus : *Secundum aliam significationem dicitur hoc nomen Ecclesia, & omnium verissime & proprissime secundum primam inpositionem huius nominis, &c. de Vniuersitate fidelium credentium & inuocantium nomen Christi.* [But according to another signification, and that most truely and properly, & answering to the first imposition of this name : the Church is called the Vniuersall company of all faithfull beleeuers which call vpon the name of Christ.] Then the Church of Rome, as the Pope is the Gouernour thereof, was obserued to be but a particular Church, and not the Catholicke Church which conteineth all Beleeuers.

21. *Occham* hath also written another Booke, Intituled. *Super potestate summi Pontificis octo quæstionum decisiones.* From whence I will obserue some things concerning our question of Iurisdiction : disputing of that which the Friars and flatterers of Popes called *Plenitudinem potestatis:* he handleth it so, that in the conclusion, he putteth the Pope downe as low, as the flat-

terers

terers extolled him vp on high: For thus he saith. *Principatui*

Quest.3.cap.5.
optimo repugnare videtur, quod principans illam habeat plenitudi-
nem potestatis &c. Nam omnes subditi habenti talem plenitudi-
nem sunt serui secundum strictissimam significationem vocabuli, ser-
ui. That is, [It seemeth to be vtterly against the nature of the
best Gouernment, that the Gouernour should haue this fulnes
of power, &c. For all that are subiects to him that hath such
fulnesse, are his slaues according to the most strict vnderstanding of a bondslaue.] And because the Pope then began to
flatter himselfe strangely, and to swell with those words of
pride: that he was to iudge all men, but no man might iudge
him; no man might accuse him: *Occham* represseth this swel-

Quest. 3. cap.6.
ling vanitie thus. *Papa potest ab homine accusari, destitui, & de-*
poni: omnis enim accusatio est coram iudice facienda. Nec de hoc
debet Papa perturbari, ne contra doctrinam Christi Apostolis pro se
& pro prælatis Ecclesiæ traditam velit tanquam sal infatuatum
mitti foras & ab omnibus conculcari, ne contra præceptum eiusdem
velit pro salute eius corporis mystici vt membrum putridum ampu-
tari, ne desideret ipse potestatem qua se ex charitate correptum
quamuis etiam Ecclesiam non audiret, tanquam Ethnicus & publi-
canus non sinat se vt carnes putridas resecari, & vt ouem scabiosam
repellendam à stabulis, & expurgandum vt fermentum quod to-
tam massam corrumpit: sed velit vt sibi parcatur, vt vniuersa Ec-
clesia ad interitum perducatur. Quæ omnia à desiderio Papæ qui
animam suam tenetur pro subditis ponere, conuenit exulari. That
is, [The Pope may be accused, forsaken, deposed by a man: for
all accusation must be before the iudge. Neither must this thing
trouble the Pope, otherwise he might seeme to make himselfe
vnprofitable salt, good for nothing but to be trod vnderfoot a-
gainst the doctrine of Christ deliuered to his Apostles for themselues, and for the Prelates of the Church: and against the commaundement of Christ, to be cut off like a rotten member, for
the preseruation of his mysticall body. And so he might seeme
to desire such a power, by which being reprooued in charitie,
albeit like an heathen and Publican he should not heare the
Church, yet he would not suffer himselfe to be cut of like dead
flesh, and like a scabbed sheepe to be driuen from the folds, and
to be purged like leauen that corrupteth the whole lumpe. But
                                    he

he fhould by this feeke that for fparing him, the whole Church
might be brought to ruine. All which ought to be farre from
the Pope, who ought to giue his life for his flocke.] Then this
man forefaw, and in fome fort foretold all that mifchiefe which
fell vpon the Church by the Popes claime of this ftrange Iurifdiction : which Iurifdiction, if once it fhould be obtained by
the Pope ; then hath *Occham* plainely foretolde, that which
fince this time by too great experience we haue found, that
the Pope would hereby prooue vnfauery falt good for nothing
but to be troden vnderfoot of men ; a rotten member cut off
from the body of the true Church : as rotten flefh to be cut off
for the preferuation of the whole, as a fcabbed fheepe to bee
kept from the fold, as old leauen to be purged from corrupting
and infecting the whole lumpe. And that for fparing him the
vniuerfall Church muft bee brought to defolation and ouerthrow. All this *William Occham* forefaw, all this we haue
found by lamentable experience too true : and all this followed vpon his intrufion into this Iurifdiction.

22. Through this booke *William Occham* was driuen to carry himfelfe cunningly for feare of the Popes greatneffe, mouing
many queftions and doubts, and reafoning after the manner of
the fchooles on both fides, making no profeffed determination
or conclufion : but he leaueth fuch ftrength of reafon on the
one fide, and taketh away all obiections on the other fide, that
any man may inferre the conclufion, and vnderftand the reafon
why himfelfe did not conclude. For thus he faith in the end of
that booke. *Hæc breuiter conferendo, allegendo, & difputando
funt dicta ; non vt certa veritas in dubium reuocetur, fed vt aliqua
habeatur occafio,&c. Quid autem fentiam de prædictis, non ex-
preffi, quia hoc (vt puto) veritati non prodeffet.* That is, [Thefe
things haue we faid, by conferring, alleadging, difputing ; not
that a knowen truth fhould be called into queftion, but to giue
an occafion, &c. I haue not declared what mine opinion is of
thefe things ; becaufe (as I take it) that would not helpe the
truth.] Another booke *William Occham* Intituleth, *Dialogus :*
from whence I will cite onely one Sillogifme, contained in few
words, but fo ftrongly and foundly collected, that it may make
an end of all this controuerfie : his words are thefe. *Papa non*

Lib.3.tract.2.
cap.33.

est magis exemptus à Iurisdictione imperatoris & aliorũ seculariũ iudicum quam fuerat Christus & Apostoli: sed Christus & Apostoli fuerunt ab imperatore quantũ ad Iurisdictionẽ coactiuam iudicati. That is, [The Pope is no more exempt from the Iurisdiction of the Emperors, & other secular iudges then Chrift & his Apoftles were: but Chrift & his Apoftles were iudged by the Emperor, in refpect of coactiue Iurisdictiõ: therfore fo the Pope ought to be iudged.] This Syllogiſme to this day was neuer anſwered. In refpect of which found and pithy handling of theſe things, as *Occham* was furnamed Doctor *inuincibilis in argumento* : fo the

Ex regiſtro collegij Mertonenſ.

ſenſe and iudgement of learned men was wholly for *Occham.* Infomuch that *Naucler* witneſſeth, that this worthy *William Occham* threw downe all the Popes Temporall Dominion in the duft, and carried the glory in all theſe difputations : wherin many learned men followed him. For he fpeaking of *Dantes* that learned Florentine , faith that this *Dantes* alſo wrote a Booke, *De Monarchia;* wherein he prooueth that the Empire hath no dependance of the Pope : which opinion *Antoninus* reprooueth for an error. But *Occham* hath confirmed this which *Antoninus* tooke to be an error. *Quem errorem ſecun-*

Naucl.gener.45.

dum ipſum Antoninum, magis diffuſe proſecutus eſt Occham *ordinis minorum, quaſi ad nihilum deducens poteſtatem Papa & Prælatorum, in temporali dominio , quamobrem multi verè doctiſsimi tunc queſtiones diſputabant de poteſtate Eccleſiaſtica.* That is, [Which error as *Antoninus* taketh it, *Occham* a Minorite hath moft largely handled, reducing the power of the Pope and of Prelates, concerning Temporall dominion, as it were to nothing. Wherefore many men of greateft learning, did then difpute of Iurisdiction Eccleſiaſticall.]

23. By all which we fee the Popes Iurisdiction ouerthrown by men of the greateft learning, euen then when hee thought himſelfe ftrongeft : for this part of his pretended Iurisdiction which toucheth the depoſing of Princes was neuer better handled , then at this time in the middes of the Popes kingdome, by theſe men. And ſhall it be thought ftrange in vs now, to maintaine the ſame truth , which then theſe worthy men durft maintaine? Or ſhall it not be imputed either as damnable
ble

ble ignorance in vs not to know, or as extreame weakenesse and want of courage, not to professe and maintaine as much now against the Pope, as these worthy men did then? More we cannot say, then they haue said in this point of Iurisdiction: For they haue prooued by inuincible reasons, that *in temporalibus*, in temporalties the Pope hath no Iurisdiction ouer Princes: that *in spiritualibus*, in spiritualties the Pope is subiect to the censure of a generall Councell. This is the truth which euer hath beene maintained against the Pope : more then this wee seeke not.

§. III.

Robert Grosthead and Iohn Wiclife.

24. AFter *William Occham*, let vs come to that famous Bishop of Lincolne, *Robert Grosthead* : It is to bee lamented that more of his writings were not preserued; by so much as we haue extant, it appeareth that with great courage, learning, & integritie he withstood the Popes pretended Iurisdictiō: for his learning *I. Wiclif*. calleth him the true great Clark. The contention which exercised him most, was about the Popes prouisions : for the Pope would by his prouisions (and this was also a part of his Iurisdiction proceeding out of the pretended fulnesse of power) place strangers, commonly some of his owne bastardes, vnder the name of his Nephewes, and of these sometimes young children. Thus in the best and greatest Ecclesiasticall charges and benefices, as they became void he thrust in such as had neither learning nor honestie, will or skill to discharge the duetie which that place required by preaching. This being of it selfe a thing hatefull and abhominable : *Grosthead* conceiuing of the thing as it was in truth, resolued in his Diocesse to admit no such vngratious practise. And therfore when the Pope had written to him in this sort for one of his Nephews: *Grosthead* withstood the Pope, and would not place him. And hereupon he wrote to the Pope: the letter is extant in *Mat. Paris*, out of which I will rehearse some things, that the excellent spirit of that man may be the better obserued:

VViclif: complaint. pag. 14.

ued : and his zeale against the intollerable practise of the Popes
Iurisdiction. For these prouisions were then defended by flatterers as proceeding from the fulnesse of power , the fountaine
as they called it of all Iurisdiction against which *Grosthead* disputeth thus.

*Mat.Paris.Henric.3.37.an.
1253.*

25. *Apostolica mandata non sunt nec esse possunt alia quam A-
postolorum doctrina & ipsius Domini nostri Iesu Christi, Apostolorum magistri ac Domini.* That is, [The Apostolicall mandates
are no other :neither may they be any other then the doctrines
of the Apostles, and of our Lord Iesus Christ, master and Lord
of the Apostles.] By this rule which *Grosthead* prescribeth to
the Pope, we are ready to receiue any mandate from him. And
the things which we reiect , we reiect vpon no other ground,
then as this worthy Bishop did, because they are not consonant
to the Apostolicall doctrines. And whereas the Pope had written to him for a prouision to be sped in his Diocesse , hee proceedeth thus. *Ipse Dominus noster Iesus Christus ait , qui non est
mecum , contra me est : contra ipsum autem non est nec esse potest
Apostolica sedis sanctitas diuinissima : non est igitur prædicta literæ
tenor Apostolicæ sanctitati consonus , sed absonum & plurimum dis-
cors. Primo quia de illius litera & ei consimilium superacucmula-
to non obstante, nec ex legis naturalis obseruandæ necessitate indu-
cto patet cataclysmus. inconstanciæ, audaciæ, inuerecundiæ, mentiendi
fallendi, &c. Præterea post peccatum Luciferi, quod idem erit in fine
temporum ipsius fily perditionis Antichristi, quem interficiet Dominus spiritu oris sui, nec est, nec esse potest alterum genus peccati tam
aduersum & contrarium Apostolorum doctrinæ, & Euangelicæ, &
ipsi Domino Iesu Christo tam odibile , & tam abominabile , quam
animas curæ pastoralis officy & ministery defraudatione mortificare
& perdere.* That is, [Our Lord Iesus Christ himselfe saith , hee
that is not with me, is against me : now against him the most
diuine holinesse of the Apostolicke sea is not, nor cannot bee :
therefore the tenor of the foresaid letter is not consonant to the
Apostolicall holinesse, but dissonant, and altogether repugnant,
First, because the way is opened to an inundation of inconstan-
cy presumption, shamelesnesse, lying, cousening, &c. By reason of the *non obstante* in that and such like letters often heaped

vp,

vp, not proceeding from any necessitie of the obseruation of the naturall law : Moreouer, after the sinne of *Lucifer*, which also shall be the sinne of Antichrist, the sonne of perdition in the end of the world, whom the Lord shall kill with the spirit of his mouth: there is not, nor can be any other kind of sinne so repugnant & contrary to the Apostolical & Euangelical doctrin, to our Lord Iesus Christ, so odious, and so abominable, as this sinne is to kill and destroy the soules of men by defrauding them of the care of the pastorall office and ministery.]

26. The beginnings of M. *Luther* with Pope *Leo* the tenth, were much more mild then this : but he proceedeth and condemneth this sinne, and the Popes letters by Scriptures ; declaring that they bring in such confusion into the Church : which could be practised by none, but such as are vnder the same condemnation with *Lucifer* and Antichrist. *Peiores sunt Lucifero*, saith he, *& Antichristo proximiores ; & in hac peioritate gradatim quanto magis superexcellentes, qui ex maiori & diuinori potestate sibi diuinitus in ædificationem non in destructionem tradita, magis tenentur ab Ecclesia dei tales interemptores pessimos excludere & extirpare.* That is, [They are worse then *Lucifer*, and next to Antichrist : and in this badnesse they rise in a greater degree of euill so much the more, by how much they are more excellent, who from the greater and more diuine power that is giuen them for edification, not for destruction, are bound the more to exclude and root out these wicked distroyers from the Church of God.] And therefore hee auerreth that the Pope cannot commaund such a sinne as this, to be done, [So hatefull and detestable, so abhominable to Christ, so pernicious to man. For this were an vtter defection from power and Iurisdiction, a corruption, and abuse thereof, and a remotion from the throne of glory ; and a session in the chaire of pestilence, and in eternall shame in hell, next in place to those two great Princes of darkenesse, *Lucifer* and Antichrist.] And because in such things no man ought to yeeld his obedience, but is bound to disobey : therefore he saith thus, [Out of duety and obedience, and out of the loue of vnion with the bodie of Christ ; I vtterly reiect and resist these letters, especially because

Mm   they

they vrge me to fuch a finne, as is euidently abhominable to God, and pernicious to man; and becaufe they are contrary to the holineffe of the fea Apoftolike, and againft the Catholicke faith : *Filialiter & obedienter non obedio, contradico, rebello.* And vnto that Sophifticall fhift of *plenitudo poteftatis,* whereby they vfed to caft a colour ouer thefe practifes, he aunfwereth in fuch a fort, as giueth a fhort rule of vnderftanding this fulneffe of power, for thus he faith. *Breuiter autem recolligens dico, A- poftolicæ fedis fanctitas non poteft nifi quæ in ædificationem funt & non in deftructionem: hæc eft enim poteftatis plenitudo, omnia poffe in ædificationem.* That is, [Briefely recollecting what we haue faid, we fay, the holineffe of the fea Apoftolicke cannot doe any thing: but that which is for edification, and not for deftructi- on : for this is fulneffe of power, to be able to doe all things for edification.] In which fenfe who would haue denied the Pope a fulneffe.

27. When this letter came to the Pope, *Non fe capiens præ ira* (faith mine Author) *quis ait eft ifte fenex delirus, furdus, ab- furdus, qui facta audax & temerarius iudicat? Per Petrum & Paulum nifi me moueret innata ingenuitas, ipfum in tantam confufi- onem præcipitarem, vt toti mundo fabula foret, ftupor, exemplum & prodigium. Nonne rex Anglorum nofter eft vaffallus? & vt plus dicam, mancipium, qui poteft eum nutu noftro incarcerare & igno- miniæ mancipare?* That is, [The Pope not being able to hold for anger, faid, who is this foolifh, deafe, abfurd old man, that with fuch rafh prefumption iudgeth our acts? By Saint *Peter* and Saint *Paul,* if mine ingenuous good nature did not ftay me, I fhould hurle him into fuch a confufion, that he fhould be the fable of the world, an aftonifhment, an example, a monfter. Is not the King of England our vaffall, or to fay more, our flaue? who is able at our becke to imprifon him, and to appoint him to ignominie? But the Cardinals appeafed his holineffe, efpe- cially Cardinall *Egidius Hifpanus,* who fearing that the Pope might profecute fome courfes of extremitie againft him (as af- terward hee did) tolde him, that it was not fit to vfe that man hardly. [The things which he writeth (quoth the Cardinall) are true, we cannot denie them, or condemne him : he is a Ca- tholicke

tholicke and holy man : more religious, more holy, of a more excellent life then we are : there is not thought to be a greater Prelate this day liuing, no nor comparable to him. All the Clergie of France and England know this to bee true : hee is esteemed also a great Philosopher, in the Latine and Greeke languages famously learned, a man zealous of iustice, a reader of Diuinitie in the schooles, a preacher to the people, a louer of chastitie, a hater of Symonie, &c.] The Cardinals therefore ad-uised the Pope to dissimulate the matter, least some tumult might arise, saith mine Author.   *Mat. Paris.*

28. And marke well, why they feared that a tumult might rise in the Church about this matter, this reason *Mat. Paris* relateth in these words. *Consilium dederunt Cardinales Domino Papæ, vt omnia hæc conniuentibus oculis sub dissimulatione transire permitteret, ne super hoc tumultus excitaretur, maxime propter hoc quia scitur quod quandoq́, discessio sit ventura.* That is, [The Cardinals gaue this aduise to the Lord Pope, that hee would winke at all these things, and passe by them as dissimu-lating, least a tumult might arise : especially for this cause, be-cause it is well knowen that once there shal come a departure.] Let this be obserued, It was written long before M. *Luther* was borne. The Pope and the Cardinals knew long before, that once a departure should bee made from the obedience of the Pope : and therefore *Robert Grosthead* did put them in great feare, least he might be the man that might worke this depar-ture. Then it seemeth in the iudgement of the Cardinals, that he who first should worke this departure, must be an excellent godly and learned man, such one as *Grosthead* was then know-en to be. But if *Grosthead* had done that thing then, which vp-on the like occasion *Luther* did afterward : wee should haue heard him reuiled for the rankest hereticke, the most wicked and vngratious man that euer liued : as now *Luther* is by them, who vse to curse where God blesseth, and to blesse where God curseth. Then they were in feare of *Grosthead*, & thought that this departure could not bee done but by some such excellent man. And what hath M. *Luther* done, but that which *Grosthead* was prouoked to do? or who could doe otherwise that keepeth *Grostheads* principles.   Mm 2   29. The

Mat.Parif.ibid. 29. The godly zeale of this man is further declared by *Mat. Paris*, who recordeth certaine Difcourfes and actions of his a-gainft the Popifh practifes. *Improbos Romaniftas*, faith he, *præceptum habentes Papale vt eis prouideretur, quafi venenum odit ferpentium Dicebat enim quod fi animarum cuftodiam ipfis traderet, Satanizaret: vnde fæpius proiectis literis Papalibus bullatis, talibus mandatis præcife contradixit.* [The wicked Romanifts that brought the Popes letters for prouifions, he hated as the poyfon of ferpents; for he faid, if he fhould commit the cuftody of foules to them, that then he fhould play the diuels part. Wherfore often he threw away the Popes bulled Letters, precifely contradicting fuch commaundements.] The fame Authour noteth a memorable faying that *Grofthead* was wont to vfe: *Non liberabitur Ecclefia ab Ægyptiaca feruitute nifi in ore gladij cruentandi.* That is [The Church fhall not be deliuered from this Egytian bondage, but by the edge of the bloody fword.] By all which we fee the excellent fpirit of this man againft the fpirit that ruled in the Popes, and againft their Iurifdiction: neither are we to thinke that *Grofthead* followed any other religion then that which his fathers followed before him: this is the religion, fenfe and iudgement of the world then, that is, of all godly and iudicious that then liued.

30. But was not Bifhoppe *Grofthead* of the fame faith and Religion with the Church of Rome? Yes verily, and fo will I be, if you grant me his conditions & exceptions: for he putteth two claufes very memorable, by which he will condition with the Church of Rome, or any other particular Church whatfoeuer. Firft, That the doctrines of that Church, be the doctrines of Chrift and his Apoftles: Secondly, That fo wee may regard the Church of Rome, that wee be fure to hold vnity with the true Church, the body of Chrift. Thefe excellent and famous men that haue heretofore liued in the vnity of the Church of Rome, haue beene willing, wee confeffe, to yeelde fo much to the Pope, and that particular Church, as they might doe holding vnity with the true body of Chrift. But if the vnity with the Romane Church doe draw them away from the vnity with Chrifts body: then haue they alwaies beene refolued to giue

ouer

ouer the vnity with that particular Church. This confirmeth that which before I obferued in the Diftinction betweene the Church of Rome and the Court of Rome, becaufe we fee many learned and worthy men of our forefathers were of the Church of Rome, that is, held the bond of vnity with it, who were pro-feffed enemies to the Court of Rome. Now the Pope and his flatterers haue forfaken that vnity with the Church of Rome which ftood in Apoftolicall doctrines and vnity with the true body of Chrift, howfoeuer they boaft of the name, and haue no-thing now to fhew for themfelues but the pride and faction of the Court of Rome.

31. Now come we to the time wherein liued *Iohn Wiclif*, another of the worthies of Merton Colledge in Oxford : his aduerfaries would blot him with the name of an Hereticke: fome things are vntrue wherewith they iniurioufly charge him ; fome things are true, which they vniuftly call Herefie. In this queftion of Iurifdiction, as he receiued the truth from *Oc-cham*, his Senior in Merton Colledge, fo he deliuered the fame faithfully. Speaking of the Kings Iurifdiction as well ouer the Clergie as Laity, he faith, [The chiefe Lordfhippe in this land of all temporalties both of fecular men and religious pertaine to the King of his generall Gouernement: for elfe hee were not King of all England, but of a little part thereof. Therefore the men that bufien them to take away this Lordfhippe from the King, as don Friars, and their fautors, in this point beene fhar-per enemies and Traytors, then French men, and all other nati-ons.] *Wiclif* labored worthily to defcry & refute the errors con-cerning Iurifdiction that in his time came creeping in, introdu-ced by Friars. For he witneffeth that the Friars taught thus : *Rex Angliæ, non eft rex totius Angliæ, fed regulus paruæ partis, fu-per refiduum vero mortificatum eft Papa Dominus; Veruntamen non eft difputandum (inquiunt) de hac materia, quoufque fuerit in effectu potentius ftabilita: fed toleranda funt iniuriæ dominorum fæ-cularium quoufque arriferit opportunitas temporis.* That is [The King of England is not King of all England, but Lord of a little part : ouer the refidue in a dead hand the Pope is Lord, but, fay they, there is no difputing of this matter, vntill it be powerfully

Wiclifs com-plaint. Artic. 2.

Lib. de fundam. legum. Angliæ ca.36.pag. 424.

brought

brought in effect; In the meane time they say, the iniuries of temporall Lords must be borne, vntill an opportunity fauour them.] This is plaine dealing : The Friars declare, what is that thing at which they haue long aimed. For what other meaning haue their pretended exemptions, then by making a reuolt from the obedience of their soueraigns, to become wholly the Popes seruants and creatures?

32. But this late generation of Friars, I meane the Iesuites exceeding these olde Friars in admirable practises in the blood and destruction of Princes and states ; are yet so confident in their wit and eloquence, that they thinke themselues able to perswade the Kings of the earth to account them among good and loyall subiects. The old Friars dealt more plainely ; they professed not obedience to Princes : these professe more and would colour their deepe deuises in destruction of Princes with impudency and dissimulation, as if they meant not the same things which daily they practise. Now that which *Wiclif* taught against these wicked and prophane opinions of these olde Friars, was no other thing then the iudgement of the learned Diuines which liued before, and in his time : for he brought in no nouelties, but the Friars introduced the nouelties in Religion and Iurisdiction. And that Distinction which before we obserued betweene the Church of Rome, and the Court of Rome, he confirmeth as a thing notoriously marked in his time ; for of the Church of Rome he saith thus : *Protestor publice quod amando & venerando Romanam Ecclesiam, matrem meam, desidero &*

De veritat.
Scriptur.pa.196

procuro defensionem omnium priuilegiorum suorum. That is [I protest publiquely, that louing and honouring the Church of Rome, I reuerence my mother, and procure the defence of all her priuiledges.] But of the Court of Rome, or that particular Church of Rome which was gouerned by the Pope, hee saith much otherwise, not doubting but that the iudgement of the particular Church of England might in many things be preferred, before that particular Church of Rome guided by the Pope.

Ibid.

Fieri potest (saith he) quod Dominus Papa foret ignarus legis scripturæ, & quod Anglicana Ecclesia foret longe præstantior in iudicio veritatis Catholicæ, quam tota ista Romana Ecclesia collecta de istis

               Papa

Papa & Cardinalibus. That is [It may come to passe that the Lord Pope may be ignorant of the law of Scripture, and that the Church of England may be more excellent in the iudgment of the Catholicke truth then all this Romane Church collected of the Pope and Cardinals.] Then in those dayes there was not much attributed to the Popes not erring iudgement, or to the authority of that Church which was wholly gouerned by the Pope; seeing the Pope might be ignorant of the lawe of God, and the Church of England might haue a more excellent iudgement in the truth, then that particular Church of Rome. That which *Wiclif* saith might come to passe, the world seeth and acknowledgeth that since that time it is come to passe: That Friars were the introducers of Nouelties, we haue already shewed out of *Iohn Wiclifes* obseruations. In this sorte things stood vntill the time of the Councell of Pisa which was helde some twentie yeares after *Iohn Wiclifes* death.

Chapt.7.§.2:

§. IIII.

The Popes Iurisdiction ouerthrowne by Councels.

33. THus haue we heard the iudgement of learned men against the Popes Iurisdiction, after that the same Iurisdiction began to be practised: these haue refuted especially that part of his claime, which was in *temporalibus.* Now we will consider another part of his pretended Iurisdiction, which was in *spiritualibus* : in this we finde his feathers as well pulled, as in the former; so that when both temporall and spirituall Iurisdiction is pulled from him, and when Princes take their owne right in temporalties, and Councels in spirituall Iurisdiction : the Bird will be left naked betweene them, that was so glorious with the feathers of others.

34. Before the time of the Councell of Trent, this hath bin alwaies acknowledged and preserued a trueth in the Church, that the authority of a Councell is aboue any particular whatsoeuer, whether he be the Bishop of Rome or any other. This was neuer once brought in question the first thousand yeares :
but

but when the Popes had framed a Ladder of their supposed Iurisdiction to clime aboue Princes; and Friars began to puffe vp the Sailes of the Popes pride by the winde of their flatterie: then began some question to bee made of the authority of a Councell: The Friars hoisted vp the Pope aboue the Councel, but there were alwaies in the Church of Rome some remaining, yea a great number, and sometimes as the best part so the strongest, who held and maintained the auncient true Iurisdiction of a lawfull, free generall Councell to be aboue the Pope, and to haue authority to depose the Pope, or otherwise to censure him, as in their wisedome they thought meete. This question of the Iurisdiction of a Councell had often beene moued, as we finde by the appeales of Emperours and Kings, and others from the Pope to a generall Councell: but it came not to be put in execution before the Councell of Pisa, which was gathered vppon this occasion.

Naucl.gener.47. 35. After a long schisme in the Church of Rome, *Gregory* the twelfth was chusing during the schisme; *Gregory* tooke an Oath as soone as he was elected, to take away the schisme by all possible meanes, and wrote to *Benedict* the thirteenth, inuiting him to a mutuall abdication for peace: *Benedict* returned an answere to the same words backe again: As the Popes colluded together without any sincere purpose of abdication, the question began to be mooued of the authority of the Church, which might order them both, because the Church is aboue all; euen the Popes are subiect to this power: and therefore it was thought fit that a generall Councell should be called, representing the Church of these Westerne parts. The Councell was summoned to meete at Pisa: the Bishops, Prelates and Princes being orderly summoned, and meeting heere in the yeare one thousand foure hundred and eight, proceeded against both the Popes, deposed and depriued them; condemning them both for Heretickes and Schismatickes, commanding all Christians not to take them for Popes, or yeelde obedience to them. In this Councell there was great disputation of the authority of a Councell: and it was determined, none contradicting, sayeth mine Authour, that the Councell had authority to depose the

Popes

Popes perfifting in a fcandall, and to chufe another. This was the ground and occafion of calling the Councell of Conftance not long after this.

36. This Councell of Pifa is much commended by *Iohn Gerfon,* and by the Councell of Conftance, as the fame Authour *Gerfon* doth witnefle; Where he faith alfo that the Church of England fent learned men to that Synode at Pifa : who as they came through Paris were entertained with an Oration of the fame *Gerfon* then Chauncellor of the Vniuerfity of Paris, declaring the confent of that Vniuerfity with them. Then wee haue the Councell of Pifa, and herein the iudgement of the Church of England concurring with many other Churches againft the Popes Iurifdiction. The fame will likewife appeare by the Councell of Conftance.

Ioh. Gerfon lib. de auferibilitate Papæ.

37. The Councell of Conftance was called by the commandement of *Sigifmund* Emperor, in the yeare one thoufand foure hundred and fourteene, for the fame end. For the Synode of Pifa had depofed the two Popes that maintained the fchifme, and chofen a new Pope *Alexander* the fift, but the other two helde their places by force, and there were now three Popes: after *Alexander* 5. death, *Iohn* the three and twentieth was chofen: this man came to Conftance, and fhewed himfelfe willing to be depofed, fo that the other two in fchifme might be ordered and pulled downe from the places which they held : but this *Iohn* finding that the Councell had a purpofe after that he was depofed to chufe another, and not himfelfe ; fled away from the Councell, and refufed to be ordered by it : but hee was apprehended and brought backe againe : fo his life and conuerfation being examined by the Councell, he was depofed: but when he fent *Charles Malatefta* to approue the fentence of the Synode, and to make for him, and in his name a free abdication of the Papacy : he died for griefe that *Malatefta* had performed that commiffion fo roundly and fo quickly.

38. The other two Popes *Gregory* and *Benedict* ftood vp mainteining the fchifme all this while. To order them *Sigifmund* Emperor tooke great paines with the Kings of England, Fraunce and Arragon. *Gregory* yeelded to be ruled by the Synode,

Nn

node,

node,but *Benedict* ftood out ftiffely a long time,who in the end
alfo was depriued,and pronounced an Hereticke and Schifma-
ticke. It is obferued that there was nothing concluded in
this Councell without the confent of the fiue Nations.The Synode hauing thus depofed all thofe other Popes, made choyce
of *Martin* the fift : And to preuent fuch fchifmes and the troubles which grewe by them,it was decreed in the fame Synode,
that fuch Synodes fhould be often called ; the firft fhould bee
called fiue yeares after this : the fecond feauen yeares after the
firft ; the third tenne yeares after the fecond;and fo from tenne
yeares to tenne yeares continually. This order and Iurifdiction of the Church declared in Synodes,did fo terrifie the Popes
that they fought by all meanes to defeat it, they could not indure fuch a Iurifdiction aboue themfelues,to call them,cenfure
them, depofe them,as this Synode had throwen downe three
Popes at once. Therefore the Popes after this laboured by all
meanes how they might oppreffe the authority of a Councell,
(which they could neuer doe before the Councell of Trent)
and all thefe partes of Chriftendome on the other fide laboured to maintaine the authority of the Councell aboue the
Pope.

Seff.5.

39. For the better confirmation hereof, this Synode declareth the authority and Iurifdiction of a generall Councell thus:
*Declarat(hac fancta Synodus)quod ipfa in fpiritu fancto legitime
congregata,Concilium generale faciens,& Ecclefia Catholicam re-
prefentans,poteftatem a Chrifto immediate habet,cui quilibet cuiuf-
cunque fuerit ftatus vel dignitatis, etiam fi Papalis exiftat,obedire
tenetur in his qua pertinent ad fidem & extirpationem dicti fchifmatis & reformatione dicta Ecclefia in capite & in membris.*That
is[This holy Synode declareth,that they being gathered in the
Holy Ghoft,making a generall Councell, and reprefenting the
Catholicke Church, haue power immediately from Chrift, to
which euery man of what ftate and dignity foeuer, though he
be a Pope,is bound to obey in thofe things which pertaine to
faith, and the extirpation of fchifme, and reformation of the
Church in the head and members.] And prefently after this,
they declare and define thefe points, that euery man of what
con-

condition foeuer, though he be a Pope, that fhall not obey the
ordinances, ftatutes, or precepts of the Synode fhal be duly corrected and punifhed : that Pope *Iohn* the three and twentie (for
this was decreed at the beginning before *Iohn* was depriued)
fhall not transferre the Court of Rome, or any other publicke
officers therof, or compell them directly or indirectly to follow
him, without the confent of this Synode. And if he fhall ful-
minate any cenfures Ecclefiafticall againft fuch officers, or any
other adhæring to this Synode; all fhall be voide and of none
effect : neither fhall it be lawfull for any man to obey any fuch
cenfures : That all Tranflations of Prelates, all depriuations, re-
uocations, monitions, Ecclefiafticall cenfures, all proceffes and
whatfoeuer is done or fhall be done by the faid Pope in preiudice of the faid Councell, &c. fhall be voide, vaine, and of none
effect.

40. According to the Decree of this Synode, Pope *Martin*
the fift, after fiue yeares called a Synode at *Pauie* : thither came
they that were fent by the Pope, and expected the nations
without whofe prefence a generall Councell could not bee
held. But the plague increafing greatly in that towne, they
changed the place of this Synode to *Sene* : where Pope *Martin* perceiuing that *Benedict* began to ftirre againe; to preuent
troubles, diffolued this Synode, and according to the Decree of
the Synode of *Conftance*, appointed the place of another Councell after feuen yeares to be holden at *Bafil*; and when the appointed time came, hee fent Cardinall *Iulianus* to *Bafil* for the   *Anno* 1430.
furthering of the fame. This is the onely Pope of late that was
not affraide of a generall Councell; he was elected by a Councell, he kept the Decrees of that Councell with great commen-
dation, and liued in that moderation, that he feemed not to be
affraide of the cenfure of a Councell. *Martin* hauing proceeded thus farre, onely to fhew himfelfe willing to call the Councell of *Bafil*, died. *Eugenius* the fourth fucceeded, who did
ftriue by all meanes to defeate the Councell of *Bafil* : but by the
authority of *Sigifmund* the Emperour that Synode proceeded;
thither came the Prelates of thofe nations, without whofe confent a generall Councell of thefe parts of Chriftendome cannot
be held.   Nn 2   41. This

41. This Synode of Bafil thus gathered, among other things agreed vpon certaine conclufions concerning this Iurifdiction; the Conclufions are thefe :

Seff. 38.

1. *Veritas hæc de poteftate Concilij generalis, vniuerfalem Eccle-fiam reprefentantis fuper Papam & quemlibet alterum, declarata per Conftantienfe & hoc Bafilienfe generalia Concilia, eft veritas fidei Catholicæ.*

2. *Veritas hæc quod Papa Concilium generale, &c. actu legiti-mè Congregatum &c. nullatenus fine eius confenfu poteft diffoluere, aut ad aliudtempus prorogare, aut de loco ad locum transferre, eft veritas fidei Catholicæ.*

3. *Veritatibus duabus prædictis pertinaciter repugnans, eft cen-fendus hæreticus.* That is,

1. [This truth of the Iurifdiction of a generall Councell re-prefenting the Catholicke Church that is aboue the Pope or a-ny other, as it is declared by the general Councels, that of Con-ftance and this of Bafil, is a truth of the Catholicke faith.

2. This truth that the Pope cannot in any cafe without the confent thereof diffolue a generall Councell, &c. lawfully and actually gathered &c. or proroge it to another time, or transfer it from one place to another, is a truth of the Catholicke faith.

3. Whofoeuer doth with pertinacy, refift thefe two forefaid truths, is to be adiudged an hereticke.]

Thefe conclufions they fet downe againft that Iurifdiction which the Pope claimed, whom they called *Gabriel Condelme-rius*, otherwife called *Eugenius* the fourth, againft which con-clufions no man then contended, fauing the Pope and his flat-terers, who are therefore adiudged Heretickes by the Coun-cell. In the fiue and fortieth Seffion of this Synode of Bafil there are other conclufions added, to declare the pertinacy of *Eugenius* the fourth, condemned by that Councell: and firft they declare or teftifie that not in their owne iudgements one-ly, but in the iudgements of all that before them were men of knowledge and learning in the Church; this was euer main-tained, that the Pope muft be fubiect to a generall Councell :

Seff. 45. decre-tum quinq, con-clufionum.

Nec vnquam aliquis peritorum dubitauit (faith that Synode) *fum-mum Pontificem in his quæ fidem concernunt, iudicio eorundem*

Conci

Conciliorum vniuersalium esse subiectum. Then they declare how *Eugenius* first laboured to dissolue this Synode without the consent of the Synode. But after many admonitions he reuoked that dissolution, declaring it to be voide and of none effect: and so gaue great hope of peace to the Church. But after this againe, he attempted the second dissolution of the same Councell, which after many admonitions hee would not reuoke: wherefore these fiue conclusions are declared against him: First, The first dissolution of this holy Synode of Basil, pretended by *Eugenius* the present Pope, from the fulnesse of Apostolicall power (as he saith) attempted, is repugnant to the two foresaid truths. Secondly, *Eugenius* the present Pope, did in forme of law prescribed vnto him, iudicially reuoke all errours repugnant to the two foresaid truths, after the first pretensed dissolution or translation, being admonished, and commaunded by the Synode so to doe. Thirdly, The pretensed dissolution or translation of this holy Synode of Basil repugnant to the two foresaid truths, attempted by *Eugenius* after he was cyted vpon the point of reformation, proceeding (as he saith) out of the fulnesse of power, in case it should proceede against himselfe, or any of his Legates Presidents: this should conteine an inexcusable errour in faith: Fourthly, The second pretensed dissolution or translation of this Synode, repugnant to the two foresaid truthes, doth proue the said *Eugenius* to be a relapse, falling againe into his reuoked and condemned errour: Fiftly, This second dissolution or translation repugnant to the two foresaid truthes, as also the contumacy of *Eugenius*, and his long perseuerance therein, and the open rebellion of the said *Eugenius*, after that he was admonished by the Synode to reuoke that pretensed dissolution or translation; and also the erection of another Congregation vnder the name of a generall Councell to fortifie that pretensed dissolution, and that during the time of this holy Councell of Basil: all these are euident testimonies of the pertinacy of the same *Eugenius*, and so euident that they neede not the clamor of any other accuser.

42. Vpon these grounds this Councell deposed *Eugenius* the fourth, and elected *Amadeus* Duke of Sauoy, who was cal-

Nn 3   led

led *Felix* the fifth. But *Eugenius* resisted by force, and helde himselfe as Pope, the Synode not being strong enough for him by coactiue power, though in spirituall Iurisdiction it was aboue him: yet would not this Councell acknowledge *Eugenius* to be the Pope, but *Felix*. In the meane time *Eugenius* dieth, and *Nicolaus* the fift was chosen in his place. All this while the Councell of Basil stood vp: so that a new Schisme was like to rise; but all was compounded thus: *Felix* the fift should abdicate the office which he was content to doe, seeing *Eugenius* was dead who was deposed by the Synode: *Nicolaus* should be acknowledged and confirmed Pope. This *Nicolaus* thus confirmed, should by his bull approue and confirme all the things done and concluded in the Councell of Basill: all this was performed, and Pope *Nicolaus* by his *Bull* maketh a solemne confirmation and approbation of this Synode: which *Bull* is annexed to the Synode: bearing date *Calend. Iul.* 1449. But the Synode seemed not much to respect this confirmation, because they rested vpon that authority which the Church hath from Christ.

43. Now let vs consider how this Synode prescribed against the Popes Iurisdiction so much, that if the reformed Churches by the power and godly labours of their Princes, might once obtaine that which they haue so long wished, a generall, free, lawfull holy Councell: they would not desire much more freedome therein then was practised in this Synod of Basill. For first concerning the safe conduct for comming to the Councell, and manner of proceeding, there is so much graunted by this Councell to the Bohemians, whom the Councell inuited to a disputation, that more then this, none will desire. For besides the safe conduct for comming and going freely and safely, they are agreed vpon the iudge of controuersies: admitting that iudge which onely was alwayes acknowledged the iudge in all generall Councels: for the Pope was neuer acknowledged to be the iudge. This Synode of Basil admitting herein the manner of proceeding held in auncient Councels, reiecteth the Pope, and admitteth another iudge, in these words. *Lex diuina, praxis Christi Apostolica & Ecclesiæ primitiuæ vna cum concilijs*

Saluus conductus Boemorum conc. Basil.sess. 4.

concilijs doctoribusq́; fundantibus se veraciter in eadem, pro veris-
simo & indifferente iudice in hoc Basiliensi concilio admittentur.
That is, [The law of God, the practise of Christs Apostles,
and of the primitiue Church, together with Councels, and doctors founding themselues truely vpon the same, shall be admitted for the most true and indifferent iudge, in this Councell of
Basil.] Now this is far from the iudgement of our aduersaries,
who will admit no other iudge of controuersies, saue the Pope
onely. Wee haue the iudgement of the Church against them,
both of old time, and at this time of late: and before the Councell of Trent it was neuer otherwise.

44. Moreouer, whereas the Pope sent his Legates to this
Councell of Basil, requiring that they might be admitted as
Presidents of the Councell in his place: this the Councell granted, limiting the same graunt with these conditions : that these
who thus were admitted Presidents of the Councel in the place
of Pope *Eugenius*, should be in that place without all coactiue
Iurisdiction : that the manner of proceeding by disputations
should stand inuiolate : that all the Councell being equally deuided into foure deputations, nothing should be concluded but
that which was confirmed by three deputations at the least:
that the things thus confirmed should be inrolled by the Presidents or one of them : that if they refused to inroll such things,
then should it be lawfull for any other man, which was in one
of the deputations, to doe it : which must after this be brought
to the congregation, and read there and publikely approoued
before it be concluded. They condition also that all the Actes
of the Councell shall be done and dispatched in the name, and
vnder the seale of the Councell.

Ibid. sess. 17.
Sine omni Iuris-
dictione coacti-
ua.

45. Further in these late Councels there is no memorable
mention of the fiue nations. There was free accesse for all nations that would come, but there is especiall mention of fiue
nations, because these were the principall nations of these westerne parts: they are named in the first session of the Coungell
of Basill, Italy, Brittaine, Germanie, France, and Spaine : nothing might be concluded vnlesse it were first diuers times published in the presence of the fiue nations, and by the generall
consent

confent of them, confirmed. If things had paffed in this manner in the Councell of Trent, that free acceffe might be giuen to
all nations, that the Scriptures with the Fathers founding themfelues vpon Scriptures, might bee admitted the onely iudge of
controuerfies; that the Pope fhould haue no coactiue authoritie, that nothing fhould be concluded, but by the confent of
the fiue nations ; then would wee admit that Councell to bee
free and generall : but becaufe in ftead of thefe, the contrary
was practifed in Trent, that no iudge could be admitted there,
but the Pope; that none might haue acceffe to that Synod, but
they who were firft bound in an oath to the Pope; that therein the Pope practifed coactiue power, that nothing could there
be concluded but by the direction of the Pope: therefore when
we reiect the Councell of Trent, we doe no more then onr forefathers did in the Councell of Bafill, & before that in the Councell of Conftance, and before that in the Councell of Pifa. We
are the children of them that held thefe Councels : whom feeing we finde to be fo peremptor ily bent againft the Pope, and
againft the proceedings of the late Councell of Trent, haue we
not warrant following the footfteps of our forefathers, vtterly
to reiect and to condemne the Popes Iurifdiction which wee
haue now found to be fo late, fo bafely bred, without antiquitie, honour, honefty or libertie? Againft the Popes pretenfed
Iurifdiction, what can wee fay more, then hath beene already
concluded by thefe Councels ?

46. For they haue concluded that a Councell hath authoritie aboue the Pope : that the Church may correct and hath

Concili.Bafil.
feff.12.decretum
citat.contra
Papam.

corrected Popes: *Ecclefia Catholica Sapenumero fummos Pontifices, fiue à fide delirantes, fiue prauis moribus notorie Ecclefiam
fcandalizantes correxit, & iudicauit. Neq, vbi de fidei periculo aut
fcandalo religionis Chriftiana agebatur, Romanis Pontificibus pe-
percit.* They haue concluded that the Popes may erre as well
as other men. *Certum eft Papam errare poffe.* [It is certaine that

Ibid,
Refponfio Syno-
dal.de authorit.
concilij generalis
fuper Papam &
quoflibet.

the Pope may erre, and in the fame place it is faid : experience
prooueth it, for we haue often found and read that the Popes
haue erred : this Chrift declareth if thy brother offend againft
thee, *dic Ecclefia,* tell the Church, and if he heare not the
Church,

Church, let him bee to thee as an heathen or Publican : this comprifeth all men, euen *Peter* and his fuccessors. This *Paul* declareth, that refisted *Peter* to the face, and before all : then he faid it openly in the Church, and to the Church, which he faid before all. The Popes that haue not heard the Church, haue beene accompted as heathen and Publicanes, as we read of *Anastasius* and *Liberius*.] And a little after, answering to a teftimonie of *Thomas Aquinas*, who held the Pope, *Peters* fuccessor, and Paftor of the vniuersall Church, they fay thus : *De fingularibus Ecclefys & perfonis id intelligendum eft, non de vniuersali Ecclesia, quæ fæpe obedientiam iuftis de caufis Romanis Pontificibus fubtraxit: vt Marcellino, Anastasio, Liberio, Ioha. 12. Benedict. 9. Benedicto 13. Iohanni 23.* That is, [That is to be vnderftood of particular Churches & perfons, not of the Vniuersall Church; which many times vpon iuft occasions hath withdrawen obedience from the Bifhops of Rome: as for example, from *Marcellinus, Anastasius, Liberius, Iohn* the twelfth, *Benedict* the ninth, *Benedict* the thirteenth, *Iohn* the twentie three.] They haue in like fort concluded, that the Popes Gouernment in the Church is to be admitted, not that he rule at his pleafure, but according to the doctrine of Saint *Peter. Vt ipfe Ecclefiam Dei falubriter regat, non quidem vt pro libito voluntatis fuæ cuncta peragere velit, fpretis canonibus facrorum conciliorum, fed iuxta beatiff. Petri doctrinam, fic regat non vt dominans in clero, fed vt forma factus gregis: Romanus enim Pontifex eft vniuersalis Ecclesia minifter, non Dominus.* That is, [That he may foundly rule the Church of God, not that he fhould doe all things according to the luft of his owne will, reiecting the Canons of holy Councels ; but according to the doctrine of Saint *Peter* : let him fo rule, not as a lord ouer the Lords inheritance : but as examples to their flockes : for the Bifhop of Rome is the Minifter of the Vniuersall Church, and not the Lord.] They haue concluded, that if this Iurifdiction bee graunted to the Pope which he claimeth, and which his flatterers pretend for him, that by this meanes the way is laid wide open for Antichrift. *Aperite oculos & videte, qualis ex hóc daretur ingreffus Antichrifto.* That is, [Open your eyes and behold what an entrance by this meanes would

be

Epist. Synodal. refponfiua ad inuectiuam Eugenij.

Epiftola Synodal. ad vniuerf. Chrifti fidel. de obediendo concil. gener.

be made for Antichrist.] So that they who yeeld any authoritie and reuerence to these Councels, must needs acknowledge,
that the Popes Iurisdiction is laid downe in the dust.

47. Now let *Bellarmine* come with his fine distinctions, and
tell vs that these Councels are partly confirmed, partly reiected, *partim confirmata, partim reprobata:* these be pleasant heads
that can take of these Councels what pleaseth them, and reiect
all that is against them : but let them collude with their owne
consciences as they list, they are not able to answere that which
we vrge, or any way to shift vs off : for wee doe not vrge
these conclusions as decrees of Councels : (though against
them they may iustly stand for such, but wee doe not produce them to that end) but onely to declare the religion, sense,
and iudgement of Christendome, what it was at this time, and
before : what was the doctrine of the Church, concerning Iurisdiction: What the wisest, the most learned and best men in
Christendome then taught : What was the iudgement of the
Church of Rome then: This is euidently declared by these
Councels, and that we may vrge no more but this, by this wee
haue enough to proue that the Church of Rome then stood fully against the Popes Iurisdiction. If they tell vs that *Eugenius*
and they who followed him was the Church, and not these that
were gathered in Basil : I aunswere, this doth more and more
confirme that which I haue obserued betweene the Church of
Rome on the one side, and the Pope with his flatterers on the
other side : who albeit they haue gotten the vpper hand by
force and fraud, yet let them know the basenesse of their birth
and progeny : they are but a late vpstart generation, beginning when Friars began : lifted vp by the winde which themselues did raise, for increasing the Popes pride: crossed and contradicted, yea refuted and condemned by the learned and godly
that liued in the Church of Rome : neuer fully preuailing before
the Councell of Trent. Then let them not demaund of vs such
friuolous questions, where was our Church before M. *Luther* ?
for we are able to shew both our Church, and their Church, the
antiquitie and not interrupted continuance of the one, and the
base vpstart and late rising of the other.

Lib. 1. *de Concil.*
cap. 7.

Iohn

§. V.

Iohn Gerson.

48. HAuing thus farre declared the iudgement of the Church of Rome, assembled in diuers Councels : now let vs consider how in particular, the learned men of these ages stood affected in this question : and who they were that tooke part with these Councels to aduance the authoritie of the Church aboue the Pope : for they who followed the Pope in this faction were onely Friars and flatterers ; but on the other side were these, as then, the great lights of Christendome for learning, that I may of many remember a few.

49. First *Iohn Gerson*, a man of great authoritie in the Councell of Constance : who hath written diuers bookes, wherein he preferreth the authority of a Councell, before the Popes authoritie, and speaketh much otherwise of Iurisdiction, then the Court of Rome vseth now to speake. His booke *De potestate Ecclesiastica*, was pronounced and approued in the Councell of Constance, in the yeere of Christ, one thousand foure hundred and seuenteene ; as in the end thereof appeareth : from whence I will obserue some things, declaring his iudgement in our question of Iurisdiction. First he describeth that spirituall power which Christ hath left to his Church, thus : *Potestas Ecclesiastica* *Gerson de potest.* *est potestas quæ à Christo supernaturaliter & specialiter collata est* *Ecclef. consid. 1.* *suis Apostolis & discipulis, ac eorum successoribus legitimis vsq; ad finem seculi, ad ædificationem Ecclesiæ militantis secundum leges Euangelicas pro consecutione felicitatis æternæ.* That is, [Ecclesiasticall power, is a power supernaturally & especially giuen by Christ to his Apostles and Disciples, and their lawfull successors vnto the end of the world, for the edification of the Church Militant, according to the Euangelicall lawes, for the obteining of eternall life.] This power we acknowledge with *Gerson*, nay with all the auncients, who speake no otherwise of the power which Christ hath committed to his Church. But then we wish that our aduersaries might vnderstand how they wander in ignorance and confusion : confounding this power which is spiritu-

all,

all, executed *secundum leges Euangelicas,* with that power which
is coactiue and executed *secundum leges Canonicas.* It is their
common manner to confound these things, and thereby to per-
plexe themselues and their readers : but of all that euer I read,
he surpasseth ; who calleth himselfe the Catholike diuine : for
confused & vnlearned handling of these things. Then the power
which Christ left to his Church, is practised *secundum leges E-*
uangelicas : this is the true power of the Church. But our question hath beene altogether of Iurisdiction coactiue, executed not *secundum leges Euangelicas,* therefore not giuen by
Christ to his Church : but belonging to such lawes, to whom
all coactiue power peculiarly belongeth.

50. Of this coactiue power, the same *Gerson* saith thus :
Potestas Ecclesiastica Iurisdictionis in foro exteriori, est potestas Ec-
clesiastica coactiua, quæ valet exerceri in alterum etiam inuitum.
That is, [Ecclesiasticall power of Iurisdiction in the exteriour
Court, is an Ecclesiasticall power coactiue, which may be exercised against another, though it be against his will.] And a
little after, speaking of the same coactiue power, he saith : *Po-*
testas hæc Iurisdictionis Ecclesiasticæ adeo vicina est Iurisdictioni
sæculari & politicæ, quod laicis imò & mulieribus plerumq; & in
multis casibus communicari potest executio vel committi. That is,
[This power of Ecclesiasticall Iurisdiction, commeth so neere to
secular and Ciuill Iurisdiction, that the execution hereof may
be communicated or committed for the most part, and in many
cases to Lay-men, yea euen to women.] Then this power is not
from Christ directed to Church-gouernours, which may be executed by Lay-men, and women. For Christ gaue no Iurisdiction to his Church, which may be executed by such. Now if
this coactiue Iurisdiction may be executed by Lay-men : why
not by Magistrates ? If by women, (of which thing most of the
Popish writers are agreed) how then standeth it against the
lawes of nature, and grace, the Ciuill and the Canonicall
lawes, and I know not what other lawes, as the Catholicke
diuine telleth vs, that a woman should haue this Iurisdiction ?
for if a woman may be a Magistrate, it must needs follow that a
woman may haue that power which God hath giuen to Magistrates.

                                                      51. *Gerson*

51. *Gerson* speaking of the power of the Church, not this coactiue, but that which is giuen, *secundum leges Euangelicas,* declareth that it is founded vpon the text of *Mat.*18. *Dic Ec-* *Ibid.consid.*4. *clesiæ,&c.Fundatur in hoc textu,*saith he, *Plenitudo potestatis gladij spiritualis & executio eius in Ecclesia super quemlibet Christianum, qui est frater noster, etiam si Papa fuerit : nec accipiendum hic,dic Ecclesiæ, id est Papæ ; quia Christus Petro loquebatur qui non dixisset sibi ipsi.* That is, [The fulnesse of the spirituall sword aboue any Christian that is our brother, though he be a Pope, is founded vpon this Text : neither must we take it so, tell the Church, that is the Pope : for Christ spake this to *Peter,* who was not bidden to tell it to himselfe.] He declareth also, and much complaineth that the Ecclesiasticall Iurisdiction was by the practise of Popes, intruding vpon Ciuill Gouernment ; so strangely confounded, that a man could not in those dayes decerne the difference betweene the right of the Church and of Princes. *Potestatem Ecclesiasticam confundit magna caligine cupi-* *Ibid.consid.*8. *ditas ambitiosa,quærens quæ sua sunt, & quæ crescentibus beneficiorum dotationibus impudenter excreuit: Ita vt vix decerni modo possit,quid ex primaria institutione Christi,vel inuariabili iure diuino tenendum sit.* That is, [Ambitious coueteousnesse seeking her owne, and impudently inlarging her power as the dotation of benefices increased, hath confounded the Ecclesiasticall power with a great mist : So that now it may scarsely bee decerned, what we are to hold of the first institution of Christ, or by the inuariable diuine law.] Then this Iurisdiction was by the Popes hurled into such a confusion,that men of the best learning were much troubled with distinguishing this confused masse. And so farre did this confusion growe by meanes of the Canonistes extolling the Popes Iurisdiction without measure, that the same Author was forced to complaine bitterly thereof thus : *Hinc æquiuocatio per dominos iuristas,qui loquentes de plenitudine* *Ibid.consid.*10. *Ecclesiasticæ potestatis Papalis, solum loqui videntur de potestate Iurisdictionis : ex qua locutione videtur hæc absurditas sequi, quod pure Laicus,imo & fœmina posset esse Papa,& habere plenitudinem Ecclesiasticæ potestatis.* That is, [Hence commeth equiuocation induced by my masters the Canonists, who speaking of the ful-

nesse

nesse of the Papall Ecclesiasticall power, seeme to speake onely of the power of Iurisdiction: by which speech this absurdity seemeth to follow, that a pure Lay-man, yea a woman may be Pope, and haue the fulnesse of Ecclesiasticall power.

52. And thus, I trow, they will bring their Iurisdiction to a faire issue: that if wee should graunt it, as they claime it, this inference must also goe with it; that a Lay man or a woman may be Pope; were it not much better to giue to each his own right, to the Magistrate all power coactiue, to the Church power ouer the soules of men according to the lawes of the Gospell: then to follow all these absurd fancies, by taking away from the Church and Magistrates their distinct rights, and casting a new, vnlawfull, confounded Iurisdiction vpon the Pope? And that we may vnderstand how the Papal Iurisdiction grew onely by the Popes flatterers, of such knaues he saith thus: *A-*

Ibid. consid. 12.

dulatio negat Papā posse simoniacam committere, quoniam sua sunt omnia Ecclesiastica bona: concedit quod super ius est, potens ab altero ius suum tollere, & quod nec ab eo appellari, neq, eum iudicialiter euocari, nec obedientiam ab eo subtrahi: hic solus symbolum fidei condere, hic solus causas eiusdem fidei tractare potest. Solus definitiones, regulas, leges, & Canones condit: alioquin quicquid per alios definitur, statuitur &c. irritum est, fallor si non ante celebrationem huius Concily Constantiensis sic occupauerat mentes plurimorum ista traditio, vt oppositorum dogmatizatio fuisset de heretica prauitate vel notata, vel damnata. That is[Flatterie denieth that the Pope can commit Simony, becaufe al Ecclesiastical goods are his: it graunteth that the Pope is aboue law, able to take from a man his right, and that neither an appeale may be made from him, neither may he be called iudicially to triall, nor obedience be drawne from him: he onely must make Articles of faith: he onely must determine the caufes of faith: onely hee must make definitions, rules, laws, and Canons: otherwise whatsoeuer is defined, ordeined by other, &c. it is voide. I am deceiued if before the celebration of this Councell of Constance this tradition did not posseffe the mindes of most men, infomuch that they who taught otherwise, were noted, or condemned for hereticall prauity.]

53. In

53. In thefe words fome things are obferuable : Firft , That this vnlimited Iurifdiction is giuen to the Pope onely by bafe fellows, flattering knaues, againft the iudgement of the learned and graue men of the Church of Rome , and againft the iudgement of thefe Councels : Secondly, that the iudicious and graue men of this age, as *Gerfon* and fuch like, yea all that were affembled in this Councell, were noted by thefe bafe flatterers, and fufpected or condemned of herefie. The Pope and his flatterers wanted no good will then, to haue made them al hereticks. And it is to be obferued that the herefie which moft of all troubled the Pope with his flatterers, ftood in this pretenfed Iurifdiction : for this is the caufe wherefore flatterie, as *Gerfon* faith, would haue imputed hereticall prauity to the Councell : Thirdly, and laft of all, the diftinction betweene the Church of Rome and the Court of Rome, wherof we haue fo often fpoken, is here againe confirmed. For thefe flatterers ftood for the Popes Iurifdiction againft the Church of Rome heere affembled in a Councell : but howfoeuer they haue preuailed fince, wee fee heere that by the Church of Rome , they were accounted then but a bafe companie of flatterers. Thefe bee they who afterward preuailed in the Councell of Trent , lifting vp the priuiledges of the Pope aboue the Church : And this is that Church on the other fide, which then was in danger to be pronounced heretickes by the Pope, and thefe who are marked and branded, not by me, but by *Gerfon, Cufanus, Æneas Siluius,* and the reft of both thefe Councels of Conftance and Bafil, to bee no better then a generation of bafe flatterers.

54. Then there is no great thing done, or at which the world may maruel, when we fee the reformed Churches at this day accounted heretickes by the Pope and his flatterers : for this was a thing long looked for. The Church did beare the pride of the Pope, the ignorance and infolency of his flatterers, as long as fhe could indure it. And when there was no remedie, made a feparation indeede from the Pope , and his flatterers, holding on ftill in the auncient waies of our fathers , who haue from time to time made refiftance againft the Pope and his feruants : from which auncient way of our forefathers, from
their

their profeffion, fenfe, iudgement and religion, the Councell of Trent hath made a famous defection, hauing declined and turned afide from the ancient and conftant profeffion of the truth, in doctrine and Iurifdiction, vnto thefe new and ftraunge deuifes taken vp of late, and inuented by Friars and flatterers of the Court of Rome. This defection which the Pope hath made from the Church, and the Church from him, was long before looked for : and diuers did fpeake of it, before it came to paffe : as *Mat.Paris* declareth, that fome feared it might haue beene done by Bifhop *Grofthead*, fo Cardinall *Cufanus* declareth, as hereafter we are to fhew, how the Church may depart from the Pope.

Serm.pro viagio
*reg.Rom.direc.*I   55. The fame *Gerfon* faith alfo : *Concilium generale poteftatem à Chrifto immediatè habet, cui quilibet cuiufcunq́, ftatus etiamfi Papalis exiftat obedire tenetur, in his quæ ad fidem & extirpationem fchifmatis pertinent.* That is, [A generall Councell hath power immediatly from Chrift; whereunto euery man is bound to obey in things concerning faith, and the extirpation of Schifme, of what ftate foeuer he be, though a Pope.] And he addeth thus much: *Saluberima hæc determinatio lex fundamentalis & velut infallibilis aduerfus monftrofum horrendūq́, offendiculum, quod pofitum erat per multos determinantes ex texibus groſsè non ad regulam Euangelicam acceptis, &c. generale concilium totum à Papa robur immeditatè fumere.* That is, [This moft found determination is a fundamentall law, and as it were infallible againft that monftrous and horrible offence, which is giuen by many, concluding from texts groffely vnderftood, and not according to the Euangelicall rule, &c. That a generall Councell receiueth all ftrength immediatly from the Pope.] In which wordes hee obferueth that the Popes flatterers, who brought in this Papall Iurifdiction aboue the Church & Councels, did induce hereby a monftrous and horrible offence in the Church. This offence, faith hee, was giuen by fuch as would proue this Iurifdiction from certaine texts of Scripture, as: *Tu es Petrus, & fuper hanc Petram ædificabo Ecclefiam meam* : and, *oraui pro te Petre, &c.* And fuch like which are wire-drawen to countenance this Papall Iurifdiction. Which texts, faith *Gerfon,*

fon, are groſſely taken by theſe flatterers, and not according to the rule of the Goſpell. And ſeeing we finde that the Ieſuites at this day haue no other ground for the Popes Iuriſdiction, then the ſame texts by them and their forefathers diſtorted into a wrong ſenſe, as it is obſerued by our forefathers againſt them: let the Ieſuites know themſelues to be the generation of thoſe that haue diſtorted the holy Scriptures, and thereby brought a monſtrous and damnable offence into the Church. *Gerſon* preſenly after this declareth, that againſt theſe flatterers, the reuerend Cardinall *Cameracenſis* (whom he calleth his worthy maſter) did write in defence of the truth. *Scripſit* (ſaith he) *ſuper hanc materiam reuerendiſſ. pater dominus Cardinalis Cameracenſis praceptor meus inclytus* : which booke of *Cameracenſis*, if it be extant (for I could not ſee it, though I much deſired) I ſuppoſe might make theſe flatterers to be better knowen, and the right of the Church more ſtrongly confirmed.

56. *Gerſon* proceedeth, and of that Iuriſdiction which the Pope claimeth by impoſing his Canon lawes vpon other Princes, he ſaith: *Papa non debet conari vt Canones poſiti aut aliena traditiones humana inuariabiliter obſeruentur per omnes nationes.* That is, [The Pope ought not to ſtriue to impoſe his Canons, or that other humane traditions bee kept inuariable of all nations.] Where he declareth that this impoſing of the Popes Iuriſdiction vpon other nations, gaue occaſion to the Greekes to make a ſeparation from the Latins, and daily miniſtreth occaſions of contention through Chriſtendome. In the ſame Booke which he Intituleth, *De auferibilitate Papa,* he holdeth poſitiuely, that howſoeuer in ſome other reſpects there might be ſome vſe of a Pope, yet concerning this our queſtion of Iuriſdiction, the Pope with all his pretenſed Iuriſdiction might be vtterly remoued from the Church, his poſition is : *Auferibilis eſt Papa per generale concilium perpetuo, vel ad tempus, quoad ea omnia qua ſunt Iuriſdictionis.* That is, [The Pope may be remooued by a generall Councell, either for euer, or for a time, in reſpect of all things pertaining to Iuriſdiction.] Now if the Pope may be remoued from the Church, in reſpect of Iuriſdiction, then the Canoniſts are quite put downe, who hold that the very eſſence

Lib.de auferebi- lit.Papˡ.conſid.8.

Ibid.conſid.15.

P p   of

of the Papacy standeth in Iurisdiction. Further concerning this question of Iurisdiction, the same *Iohn Gerson* hath made a Treatise, wherein he handleth this question, *An liceat in causis fidei à summo Pontifice appellare?* Wherein he determineth, that a man may appeale from the Pope.

§. VI.
Cardinall Cusanus.

57. SOmewhat after this wrote *Cardinall Cusanus*, who offered his Booke *De concordantia Catholica*, to the Councell of Basil: submitting himselfe and his labours to the iudgement of that Councell. It appeareth that about this time there were some motions and consultations of a reuolt from the Pope and Court of Rome: which consultations were moderated then for a time, by such learned men as were in greatest estimation: but afterward vpon the like reasons it brake foorth. *Cusanus* disputeth this point in an Epistle written to *Roderic de Treuino*, Orator to the King of Castile. Wherein he seemeth first to disswade the separation, producing that out of *Augustine, Nullam posse causam dari ob quam necessarium sit ad schisma peruenire.* That is, [That no cause can bee giuen for which it may bee necessary to come to a schisme.] But after much dispute, at last hee resolueth that the case may be such, that the Church may well depart from the Pope: *Quando sacer Princeps* (saith he) *contra sanctorum patrum statuta aliquid praesumit, vbi non constat eum ex causa vtilitatis aut necessitatis moueri, sed ex aliqua particulari indigna causa, tunc ipse in priora Petri mandata offendit, exiens vires potestatis suae. Quapropter non esset inconueniens, si pertinaciter in hoc persisteret, Ab eo recedi posse per Ecclesiam.* That is, [When the holy Prince presumeth against the lawes of holy Fathers, where it appeareth that he is not moued thereto because of the publike good, or necessitie, but from some particular of his owne and an vnworthy cause; then hath he first offended against the former precepts of *Peter* going beyond the limits and strength of his power. Therfore if hee persist therein incorrigibly, it is nothing inconueni-
ent

Written, An. Dom. 1442.

ent for the Church to depart from him.

58. Then if a Pope make a departure firſt from the Mandates, Doctrines, and faith of Saint *Peter*, thus going out of the bounds of his power : in this caſe it is the iudgement of the graue Cardinals of Rome, who liued and wrote long before M. *Luther* was borne , that the Church might make a ſeparation from the Pope. *Iohn Gerſon* ſaith as before we heard, that this ſeparation may be for a time, or for euer. Now then whereas this ſeparation is made from the Pope by the reformed Churches, there is nothing done but that which the Church had in conſultation to doe long before, in caſe the Pope ſhould perſiſt in his pride and tranſgreſſions, and ſhew himſelfe incorrigible. So that it is no maruaile if the Church which hath ſo long before thought of this departure, being thereunto ſo much prouoked by the intollerable ambition of the Pope, hath once performed that thing, which was ſo long in conſultation : eſpecially ſeeing the Church hath for the ſame, both the warrant of holy Scriptures, which doth fully not only propheſie of this departure, which the Pope hath made from the truth, and conſequently which the Church was to make from the Pope : but alſo giueth expreſſe commaundement to the people of God to depart from thence; *Go out of her, my people.* And beſides this warrant of holy Scriptures they had alſo the iudgement of the Church before them : which Church whether we conſider it in particular members, as the learned men, principall inſtructours and preſeruers of doctrine : or in generall Councels; hath as we ſee oftentimes declared herſelfe to bee wearied with bearing the Popes proud and ambitious Iuriſdiction ; and hath beene in great conſultation to caſt off the yoake of this Aegyptian bondage. *Apoc.18.4.*

59. Now from that booke which this Cardinall *Cuſanus* wrote *De concordantia Catholica,* we will obſerue ſome things, wherein he declareth his iudgement againſt this Papall Iuriſdiction. And firſt he diſputeth againſt them that thinke the Pope hath more power then other Biſhops. *Oportet primum, ſi hoc verum foret, Petrum aliquid à Chriſto ſingularitatis recepiſſe, & Papam in hoc ſucceſſorem eſſe : ſed ſcimus quod Petrus nihil plus* *Lib.2.cap.13.de Cathol.Concord.*

poteſtatis

poteſtatis à Chriſto accepit, alijs Apoſtolis 21. *d. in nouo* 2 4. *q. loquitur.* That is, [Firſt if this be true, it muſt bee graunted that *Peter* receiued ſome ſingular power from Chriſt, and that herein the Pope is his ſucceſſor: but wee know that *Peter* receiued no more power from Chriſt, then the other Apoſtles. 21. *d. in nouo* 24. *q. loquitur.* And of this ſpirituall Iuriſdiction, he ſaith

Ibid.

thus: *Cum poteſtas ligandi & ſoluendi, in qua fundatur omnis Ecclefiaſtica Iuriſdictio, ſit immediate à Chriſto, quia ab illa poteſtate ligandi & ſoluendi, ſit diuina Iuriſdictionis poteſtas, patet omnes Epiſcopos & fortè etiam presbyteros æquales eſſe quoad Iuriſdictionem.* That is, [Seeing the power of binding and looſing, in which all Eccleſiaſticall Iuriſdiction is founded, is immediately from Chriſt: and becauſe the power of diuine Iuriſdiction is from this power of binding and looſing; it is euident that all Biſhops (perhaps alſo all Prieſts) are equall in reſpect of this Iuriſdiction.] And againe hee ſaith: *Quod vniuerſale concilium propriè captū ſcilicet quod vniuerſam Eccleſiā repreſentat, ſit ſupra Patriarchas & Roman. Pontificem, credo dubium eſſe non debere.* That is, [I hold it a truth not to bee doubted, that a generall Councell properly taken, that is as it repreſenteth the vniuerſall Church, is aboue Patriarches, and the Biſhop of Rome.]

*Ibid.cap.*17.

And againe, *Papa per Synodum in criminibus etiam alijs quam hæreſi iudicari poteſt.* That is, [The Pope may be iudged by a Synod

Ibid.

for other crimes alſo beſides hereſie.] Now for the Iuriſdiction of the ciuill Magiſtrate, the ſame Author ſpeaketh thus:

*Ibid.lib.*3.*cap.*5.

Imperator Chriſtianorum in ſua præſidentia eſt Chriſti vicarius. That is, [A Chriſtian Emperour in his office, is Chriſts Vicar.] And againe: *Omnis rex & Imperator habet officium Publicum ad Publicam vtilitatem ordinatum: Publica vtilitas eſt pax ad quam ordinantur iuſticia & iuſta prælia: principium autem pacis eſt ad finem æternum dirigere ſubditos, & media illum pertingendi ſunt ſacra inſtituta religionum: quare prima cura Imperialis in ijs obſeruandis verſatur.* That is, [Euery King and Emperour hath a publike office, ordinate to the publike good: the publike good is peace, whereunto iuſtice and iuſt warres are ordinated: the fountaine of peace to direct ſubiects to an eternall end; the meanes to obtaine that end the holy ordinances of religion:

where-wherfore the first and chiefe care Imperiall consisteth in the obseruation of those ordinances.] And therefore he saith : *Imperator curam custodiæ gerit* : And againe, *isto modo imperator dicitur aduocatus vniuersalis Ecclesiæ, & custos fidei orthodoxæ* : Which thing he proueth by the ancient practise of the Church, because in the Chalcedon Councell the Emperour *Martianus* is called, *custos fidei* : and the Emperour *Basilius* in the beginning of the eight Councell saith, that the gouernement of the Church was by the prouidence of God committed to his hands.

60. The same Author speaking further of the office of Kings, and of their Iurisdiction in Church affaires, and in Councels saith : *Debent reges & principes Synodos congregare iuxta admonitionem sancti Gregorij ad Theodoricum regem Francorum, ex registro, 273. It rata vos per vestram mercedem adhortatione pulsamus vt congregari Synodum iubeatis.* That is, [Kings and Princes ought to gather Synodes according to the admonition of *Gregory* writing to *Theodoricus* the French King ; *ex registro* 273. We moue you with our redoubled petition, that euen for that reward that is reserued for you, you will commaund that a Synode may bee gathered.] Another part of the office of a Prince, is saith he, *Confirmare & custodire in concilijs definita.* which thing hee proueth by diuerse auncient authorities : and concludeth that Emperours haue euer had this authoritie. Hee saith that in this thing hee had made diligent search, and had found this practise continued in all generall Councels vntill the eight Synode inclusiuely. In which search, saith hee, I finde by the acts of all generall Councels, aswell in Chalceon, as in Constantinople, Nice, Ephesus, that either the Emperour was present in person, or some iudges his Vicegerents : and those not aboue twentie, seldome fifteene : but when the Emperour himselfe was present in person, I finde saith he, that hee was alwayes Presedent of the Councell : no other secular Prince hath right to be present in the Councell, sauing the Emperour. Vnlesse the Emperour appoint some to be present : but being present they haue no voice in the Councell, but may sit onely to heare : this he proueth by that testimony of *Ambrose*, in the cause of faith, Bishops are the iudges and not the Emperours.

Ibid.

Ibid cap. 13.

Reperio eum semper presedisse. cap. 16.

Laici non habent vocem Synodalem sed tantum audire debent. lib. 3. cap. 17.

61. And

61. And whereas this aunci̇ent Iurifdiction of Princes was
fo difordered by the Pope, that by Papall intrufions and in-
croachments, the Princes had well-nigh loft their right, and
temporall Iurifdiction turned into fpiritual Iurifdiction; of this
he much complaineth, and openeth the true caufe of all this dif-
order to be in the infatiable couetoufnes of the Court of Rome:
for thus he faith: *Rabidus appetitus ad ipfa terrena Ecclefys an-*
nexa Dominia, Epifcopis ambitiofis hodie ineft &c. de temporalibus
omnis cura, de fpiritualibus nulla. Non fuit ifta intentio Imperato-
rum, non volebant fpiritualia à temporalibus abforberi &c. dum
vacant Ecclefiæ femper in periculo fchifmatis exiftunt &c. Si per e-
lectionem prouidendum eft, ambitio procurat diuifionem votorum.
Si per curiam facilius perfuadetur pro plus offerente : & omnia
ifta grauamina adueniunt pauperibus fubditis : curia attrahit
quicquid pingue eft, & id quod Imperium contulit, & pro
Dei cultu, & bono publico ordinauit fanctiffime, auaritia & cupidi-
tate exorta palleatis rationibus & nouis adinuentionibus totaliter
peruertitur : & Imperiale efficitur Papale, & fpirituale temporale.
That is[Such a rauenous appetite is in ambitious Bifhoppes at
this day, toward the temporall Dominions annexed to Churches, &c. all their care is for the temporalties, not for fpirituall
matters : this was not the meaning of Princes, they meant not
that the fpirituall labours fhould be deuoured by temporalties,
&c. Whilft the Churches are vacant, there is alwaies fome danger of a fchifme &c. If they proceed by election, ambition pro-
cureth a diuifion of the voyces : If by the Court, he that bringeth moft is beft heard, and fooneft preuaileth. And all thefe
greeuances come vpon the poore fubiects, whatfoeueris fat and
rich, the Court of Rome draweth to her felfe; and that which
the Empire as well for the worfhip of God, as for the publicke
good hath conferred vpon the Church, and ordeined to an holy end, all is vtterly peruerted through filthy couetoufneffe, and
certaine painted reafons, and new inuentions are deuifed to
colour it. And thus the Imperiall right is now made Papall, and
temporall right is made fpirituall.] Then thefe be the obferuations of the learned men of the Church of Rome long before
vs, that the Pope had intruded vpon the Emperours right: now
waht

Lib.3.cap.24.

whatsoeuer the Pope had once practised, that must be called
spirituall : Thus the Iurisdiction of the Emperor being once by
cunning or force wrested from the Emperour, being found in
the Popes hand, it was presently called spirituall Iurisdiction; as
he doth most truely obserue, *Imperiale efficitur Papale, & spirituale temporale.*

62. By all which we find the iudgement of this man to be
directly against the Popes pretensed Iurisdiction, and for the
right of temporall Magistrates : when we finde the Cardinals
of the Church of Rome, to write thus before the time of the
contention, and before M. *Luther* was borne : wee are not so
much to consider their priuate iudgements in these things, as
the receiued iudgement of the Church wherein they liued, that
is the Church of Rome : from the iudgement of that Church
they departed not ; but in these things do faithfully deliuer vnto vs the iudgement of the same Church, standing against the
iudgement of the Pope, and his Court, consisting of Friars and
flatterers. Thus we see the cause of the Reformed Churches
throughly iustified by this learned Cardinall, their separation
from the Pope and the Court of Rome warranted, because the
Pope hath first made the separation from the profession of Saint
Peter, and from the faith of holy Scriptures, and the iudgement
of auncient fathers : In which case he granteth that the Church
may depart from the Pope, and thereby doth iustifie the separation that is made.

§. VII.

Æneas Siluius.

63. AT this time wrote *Æneas Siluius*, afterward called
Pope *Pius* the second: he hath written a booke of
the actes and proceedings of the Councell of Basil : from
which I will note some things, wherein the iudgement of this
man may appeare, concurring with the iudgement of the
Church of Rome in his time, but repugnant to the Pope and his
flatterers. First handling that Text, *Tu es Petrus, & super hanc
Petram, &c.* he saith thus : *A quibus verbis ideo placuit exordiri,
quod*

Lib.1.de gesti Basil.concil.

quod aliqui verba hæc ad extollendam Rom Pontificis authoritatem solent adducere, sed vt statim patebit, alius est verborum Christi sensus. That is, [With which words I thought good to begin, becaufe fome vfe to alledge thefe words to extoll the authoritie of the Bifhop of Rome: but as it fhall foone appeare there is another fenfe of Chrifts words.] Who are they who in the iudgment of this man, do peruert the words of Chrift? Let the Iefuites aunfwere, and let them giue vs fome reafon, able to fatisfie a man of reafon, why that caufe fhould not bee helde damnable, which is condemned by their owne writers: their Bifhoppes, their Cardinals, their Popes? Let them not tell vs that this Pope *Pius* was of another mind afterward, when he was Pope: and before he was Pope he might erre; but after he was once Pope he could not erre: thefe bee plaine collufions of them who write fuch things, and illufions of fuch as beleeue them. For it is not poffible that any man fhould write, or fpeake or thinke fuch things from confcience: Shall I thinke that any learned man can thinke in confcience this to bee true, that the Pope cannot erre, when I heare the teftimonie of the Church fo full againft it? When I heare fuch as come to be Popes, refute it before they come to that place? When I heare fuch as haue beene in the place, exclaime in the extremitie of defperation, that no man in the world liueth more miferably then the Pope, that to be a Pope, is to fucceed *Romulus in Parricide*, not Peter in feeding; that no Pope can bee faued: when all this is proued by the Church of Rome, confeffed by Popes themfelues; after all this to fay the Pope cannot erre, is nothing but collufion. No man can be drawen to fuch an opinion by confcience, but by fuch worldly refpects as doe binde, and blinde, and lay wafte the confcience of them that will not loue the truth.

64. *Æneas Siluius* proceedeth, and out of S. *Hierome* expounding thofe words: *portas inferi*, the gates of hell, he proueth that they are to be vnderftood of finnes. And declareth that great finnes and malignant fpirits cannot preuaile againft the Church. *Quod de Rom. Pontifice, faith he, qui homo eft, nemo dixerit: nec illis præftemus aures qui illa verba Christi (oraui pro te*

Ibid.

Petre

Petre ne deficiat fides tua) nolunt ad Ecclesiam referri. That is, [Which thing no man can say of the B. of Rome, who is a man: neither are we to hearke to thē who will not haue those words of Christ vnderstood as spoken to the Church, when he saith, *Peter* I haue prayed for thee, that thy faith faile not.] Where he proueth out of S. *Augustine*, that those words are to be referred to the Church. And that they cannot be vnderstood of the Bi-shops of Rome, he is resolued & giueth such reasons as may re-solue any other, that will not wilfully blindfold himselfe (as ma-ny do that the blind doctrine of Iesuits may work more power-fully in them) For saith he, *Romani Episcopi aut haretici, aut infecti vitijs sunt reperti.* That is, [The Bishops of Rome haue bin found either Hereticks, or vicious men.] And concerning this Iurisdi-ction he saith: *Omnis anima potestatibus sublimioribus subdita sit: nec excipit animam Papa.* That is, [The Apostle saith, let euery soule be subiect to the higher powers: hee excepteth not the soule of a Pope.] And again, *Maxime Rom, Pontificem subiectū Ecclesia verba Christi ostendant, quum Petrū futurum Papam ad Ecclesiam remittat: dic Ecclesia.* And afterward, *Si hareticus est qui Romana Ecclesia primatum aufert &c. quanto magis hareticus erit, qui Ecclesia detrahit in qua Romana & omnes alia continentur.* In which words we find, that by the Church of Rome he vnder-standeth not the Catholicke Church dispersed ouer the world: but only a particular Church among many other, hauing only in his iudgment this priuiledge, that in respect of other Chur-ches it had a Primacy: This he saith, not for the Pope, but for the Church of Rome: which Church he holdeth but a part of the Catholick Church. For if we vnderstand the Church of Rome, that particular Church, which of old hath bin gouerned by the Romane Bishops, thisis but a particular Church: of this particu-lar, the B. of Rome is the chiefe, & head in spirituall matters. But if by the Church of Rome, we vnderstand an assembly, or vnited consent of these westerne Churches, among which the Church of Rome hath bin honored as a Mother Church: in wᶜʰ respect all these Churches, as they are vnited, are sometimes called the Romane Church. In which sense also I find that distinctiō obser-ued between the Church of Rome & the court of Rome. In this

sense

sense the particular Church of Rome is vnderstood a part and member of this, and the Pope hath alwayes beene vnderstood as subiect to this Church, and not aboue it.

65. Now that distinction which before wee haue obserued betweene the Church of Rome on the one side, and the Pope with his flatterers on the other side : is noted also by the same Author. For of the Church he saith thus : *Opinio omnium mortuorum est, si opinio vocari debet, quæ idoneis confirmatur authoritatibus, quia Rom. Pontifex vniuersali Ecclesiæ subiectus existit.* That is, [It is the opinion of all that are dead before vs, if it may be called an opinion; which is confirmed by such pregnant authorities, that the Pope is subiect to the vniuersall Church.] In which words, he declareth the iudgement of the Church which was before his time. But speaking of the Pope with his flatterers, he saith: *Sunt aliqui siue auidi gloriæ, siue quod adulando præmia exspectent, qui perigrinas quasdam & omnino nouas prædicare doctrinas cæperunt, ipsumq́ summum Pontificem ex Iurisdictione sacri concilij demere non verentur : excacauit eos ambitio.* That is, [There be some who either because they are greedy of glorie, or because by flatterie they hope for rewards, begin to preach certaine straunge and altogether new doctrines, they are not afraid to exempt the Pope out of the Iurisdiction of an holy Councell : ambition hath blinded them.] This is the religion which the Iesuites would make so auncient : heere is their high antiquitie. In the time of *Æneas Siluius* (who wrote in the yeere one thousand foure hundred and fiftie) their religion is called an absurd, a new and a straunge doctrine : herein *Siluius* is a witnesse without exception for so much of their religion, as concerneth the Papall Iurisdiction : which is in summe all the religion of the Iesuites. When thus it is marked, and marked by a Pope, their mouthes are stopped for euer. For he doth deliuer the sense, iudgement, and religion of the Church in his time, faithfully and freely, against which testimonie no exception can be taken.

66. And that these men that haue brought in this newe, straunge, monstrous religion may be throughly knowen, and no doubt or scruple left behinde ; hee describeth them thus :

Alius

Ibid.

Ibid.

Alius dicit quod primam fedem nemo iudicabit, quod neĝ, ab Augu-
fto, neĝ, ab omni clero, nec à regibus &c. iudicari valeat: Alius affer-
ere non veretur Rom. Pontificē quamuis animas caternatim fecum
ad inferos trahat, nullius reprehenfioni fore fubieĉtum. Nec confide-
rant miferi, quia quæ prædicant tantopere verba, aut ipforum fum-
morum Pontificum funt fuas fimbrias extendentium, aut eorum qui
eis adulabantur. That is, [One faith that no man may iudge the
firft fea, that he may not be iudged, either of the Emperour, nor
by all the Clergie, nor by Kings, &c. Another is not afhamed to
affirme, that though the Pope fhould draw innumerable foules
with himfelfe to hell, yet no man ought to reprooue him. Neither doe thefe wretches confider, that thefe doĉtrines which
thus they would aduance, are either the wordes of the Popes
themfelues, inlarging their fringes, or the words of their flatterers.] Then in his iudgement it is cleere, that the Church on
the one fide held the truth euen till his time, in this point of Iu-
rifdiĉton : and on the other fide, the Pope and his flatterers
maintained, as he calleth them, new and ftraunge doĉtrines of
Iurifdiĉtion : It is well to be obferued that *Æneas Siluius* before he was Pope could fo freely condemne this Papall Iurifdi-
ion : And was hee trow you, a Lutheran ? verily fo was the
Church in his time : for he doth deliuer not fo much his owne
priuate iudgement, as the iudgement of the Church in his time,
and in the times before him. For he faith it was the iudgement
of all that liued and died in the Church before him, *omnium*
mortuorum : that the Pope is to be iudged by the Church, by a
Councell ; and that therefore the Councell is aboue the Pope.
This, faith he, is the opinion of all that liued and died in the
Church. And yet hee knew well that Friars and flatterers had
before his time maintained the contrary : but thefe he regarded
not, becaufe the Church then regarded them not ; they were
but of bafe and vile accompt in refpeĉt of the Church : and fo
much the more vile, becaufe againft the iudgement of the auncient Church, againft the rules of interpretation, againft honeftie and confcience they had drawen fome textes of Scripture to maintaine this Papal Iurifdiĉtion. Thefe are they whom
thefe learned men call, *miferos,* miferable and wretched foules,

who

who will not vnderstand that all this which they bring for the Popes Iurisdiction, is nothing but the vain words of the Popes themselues, or of their flatterers.

67. Now seeing the Pope with his flatterers hath much preuailed since this time, against the expectation of these learned men : must we not conclude that they haue herein made a departure from the Church : that they are but flatterers, who now follow the Pope : that they were neuer accompted otherwise by the grauer sort of the Church of Rome : that their opinions are new and strange. Then with what countenance can the succeffours of *Æneas Siluius* put vpon vs the imputation of herefie, who follow the ingenuous, free and fincere iudgement of the same *Siluius*; leauing these opinions which are confeffed by him to be new, fond, straunge, vnreafonable deuifes of bafe flatterers, and maintaining the auncient truth, which by the testimonie of these men alwayes continued in the Church. This man with many moe, will be raifed vp in the day of iudgement, against this present generation confifting onely (euen by the confeffion of their own Bifhops, Cardinals, and Popes) of the Pope and his flatterers, forfaking the fellowfhip of the Church: here is the ground of their confcience. For let me speake onely of this part of their religion which now I handle, that is Iurifdiction : and what ground can any man finde here, whereupon he may reft his confcience ? Let them not bring vs an idle and impertinent difcourfe of their three conuerfions, which in good time by the grace of God will be reuerfed, but let them come to the point, and let them fhewe in this particular, what ground of confcience, any man may haue to reft on., for the Popes Iurifdiction : which was croffed, contradicted and inhibited by the auncient Fathers, confuted by the learned men of the Church of Rome, condemned by the Councell of the Church of Rome, maintained by none, but fuch as are thus notoriouſly branded with the ignominious titles of flatterers.

68. And becaufe the Pope and his flatterers (for fpeaking of them, I muft vfe this name and ftile which fo many writers of the Church of Rome haue vfed before me, let them not blame me, or thinke that I vilifie them : I vfe but the words of these

other

other writers whom I haue cited) Thefe men I fay, being driuen in argument from all helpes, hauing no meanes to anfwere
the learned that difputed againft them; did vfe to flie for helpe
to thefe words of the Gofpell. Thou art *Peter,* and to thee will
I giue the keyes of the kingdome of heauen : and, I haue prayed
for thee *Peter,* that thy faith faile not ; and fuch like : the fame
Author declareth that they did altogether abufe and peruert
thefe places of Scripture, againft the fenfe of the wordes, and
againft the expofitions of the auncient doctors. For thus hee
faith: *Et quia huiufmodi dicta folutionem habent, recurrunt ftatim
ad Euangelium: tu es Petrus, & tibi dabo claues regni calorum: &
rogaui pro te Petre ne deficiat fides tua,& duc in altum rete, &c.
Qua omnia hi homines miro modo fublimant, expofitionibus fancto-
rum doctorum omnino pofthabitis.* That is, [And becaufe thefe
words conteining their reafons, are all anfwered, they flie prefently to the Gofpell : thou art *Peter,* and to thee will I giue the
keyes of the kingdome of heauen : and, I haue prayed for thee
Peter that thy faith faile not, and caft thy net into the deepe, &c.
All which thefe men after a marueilous maner: raife vp to extoll
the Pope, reiecting altogether, & cafting behind the the expofitions of ancient doctors.] Then we haue one Pope full of our
fide, for he affureth vs, that this new & ftrange wrefting of thefe
textes to aduance the Popes Iurifdiction, ftandeth wholly a-
gainft the expofitions of the auncient Fathers. *Æneas Siluius*
in the fame booke, fpeaketh much in the honour of the French
Cardinall of Arles, as an efpeciall admirer of his vertues. *Lodouicus Cardinalis Arelatenfis,* faith he, *Vir omnium conftantiſsi-
mus & ad gubernationem generalium conciliorum natus.* That is,
[A man of all other, moft conftant, and one that was borne for
the gouernment of general Councels.] One teftimonie I would
produce of this Cardinall, and then wee haue three Cardinals
for vs, *Cameracenfis, Cufanus, Arelatenfis.* This Cardinall, in
the mids of the Councell of Bafil, profeffed that the doctrine of
the Popes Iurifdiction ouer generall Councels, was a new doctrine, and ftrange at that time in the Church. *Cardinalis Arelatenfis,* faith he, *ait Eugenianos nuntios impleffe Galliam, qui no-*

Ibid.

Ibid.

uam doctrinam prædicantes authoritatem Romani Pontificis fu-
pra generalia concilia magnificarent.

69. After all this, when we finde that Cardinall *Bellarmine*
and the reft of the Friars and flatterers, haue nothing to fay for
the Popes Iurifdiction, but that which is condemned by thefe
learned men , as a newe and ftraunge doctrine in the Church;
haue no other reafons to maintaine this their new doctrine,
then the peruerting of thefe texts of Scriptures, which diftor-
ting of Scriptures is exprefly cenfured by the faid learned men ,
as ftanding againft the naturall fenfe of the words, and againft
the expofitions of the ancient Fathers, writing of thofe Scriptures: when we find not one or two, or a few ; but the cry of
the whole Church againft them : who is able by any fhew of
learning to auoid our conclufion; that they who thus maintain
this Papall Iurifdiction, are the followers of their forefathers,
that is onely Friars and flatterers. And that we who denie this
Papall Iurifdiction, giuing to the Church on the one fide, and
to Soueraigne Princes on the other fide; their proper, diftinct,
auncient rights refpectiuely belonging to each of them,
are the followers and the children of our forefathers, that is the true, ancient, vnchaun-
ged Catholicke Church.

FINIS.